WILEY SERIES 7
EXAM REVIEW 2017

WILEY FINRA SERIES

This series includes the following titles:

Wiley Series 3 Exam Review 2017 + Test Bank: National Commodities Futures Examination

Wiley Series 4 Exam Review 2017 + Test Bank: The Registered Options Principal Examination

Wiley Series 6 Exam Review 2017 + Test Bank: The Investment Company and Variable Contracts Products Representative Examination

Wiley Series 7 Exam Review 2017 + Test Bank: The General Securities Representative Examination

Wiley Series 9 Exam Review 2017 + Test Bank: The General Securities Sales Supervisor Examination—Option Module

Wiley Series 10 Exam Review 2017 + Test Bank: The General Securities Sales Supervisor Examination—General Module

Wiley Series 24 Exam Review 2017 + Test Bank: The General Securities Principal Examination

Wiley Series 26 Exam Review 2017 + Test Bank: The Investment Company and Variable Contracts Products Principal Examination

Wiley Series 57 Exam Review 2017 + Test Bank: The Securities Trader Examination

Wiley Series 62 Exam Review 2017 + Test Bank: The Corporate Securities Representative Examination

Wiley Series 63 Exam Review 2017 + Test Bank: The Uniform Securities State Law Examination

Wiley Series 65 Exam Review 2017 + Test Bank: The Uniform Investment Adviser Law Examination

Wiley Series 66 Exam Review 2017 + Test Bank: The Uniform Combined State Law Examination

Wiley Series 99 Exam Review 2017 + Test Bank: The Operations Professional Examination

For more on this series, visit the website at www.efficientlearning.com/finra.

WILEY SERIES 7 EXAM REVIEW 2017

The General Securities Representative Examination

The Securities Institute of America, Inc.

WILEY

Contents

CHAPTER 3
GOVERNMENT SECURITIES   **55**

CHAPTER 4
MUNICIPAL SECURITIES 65

CHAPTER 8
MUTUAL FUNDS   199

CHAPTER 10
ISSUING CORPORATE SECURITIES

CHAPTER 14
RETIREMENT PLANS 353

CHAPTER 15
BROKERAGE OFFICE PROCEDURE

CHAPTER 16
FUNDAMENTAL AND TECHNICAL ANALYSIS

CHAPTER 19
SECURITIES INDUSTRY RULES AND REGULATIONS   457

About the Series 7 Exam

Congratulations! You are on your way to becoming a registered representative licensed to conduct business in all general securities. The Series 7 exam will be presented in a 250-question, multiple-choice format. The test will be divided into two three-hour sessions. Each candidate will have a total of six hours in which to complete the exam. A score of 72 percent or higher is required to pass. Once the first three-hour 125-question session is completed, the candidate must take at least a 30-minute break and will not have the opportunity to go back and review the questions from the first session.

The Series 7 is as much a knowledge test as it is a reading test. The writers and instructors at The Securities Institute have developed the Series 7 textbook, exam prep software, and videos to ensure that you have the knowledge required to pass the test and to make sure that you are confident in the application of the knowledge during the exam.

 IMPORTANT **EXAM NOTE**

The Series 7 exam may use the term *specialist, designated market maker* (DMM), or both to describe a member of the NYSE responsible for maintaining a fair and orderly market in a security. Test-takers are advised to be aware of this and to treat the two terms as interchangeable.

TAKING THE SERIES 7 EXAM

The Series 7 exam is presented in multiple-choice format on a touch screen computer known as the PROCTOR system. No computer skills are required, and candidates will find that the test screen works in the same way as an ordinary ATM machine. Each test is made up of 250 questions that are randomly chosen from a test bank of thousands of questions. Each Series 7 exam will have several practice questions that do not count towards the final score. The test has a time limit of six hours and is designed to provide enough time for all candidates to complete the exam. Each Series 7 exam contains questions that focus on five critical job functions performed by Series 7 registered representatives. In order to successfully complete the Series 7 exam, you will need a full understanding of the activities and knowledge required to perform these job functions as well as a complete understanding of the rules that regulate these job functions. The Series 7 exam will be made up of questions from the following areas:

Seeks business for the broker-dealer through customers and potential customers	68 questions	27%
Evaluates customers' other security holdings, financial situation and needs, financial status, tax status, and investment objectives	27 questions	11%
Opens accounts, transfers assets, and maintains appropriate account records	27 questions	11%
Provides customers with information on investments and makes suitable recommendations	70 questions	28%
Obtains and verifies customer's purchase and sales instructions, enters orders, and follows up	58 questions	23%
TOTAL	**250 Questions**	**100%**

HOW TO PREPARE FOR THE SERIES 7 EXAM

For most candidates, the combination of reading the textbook, watching the videos, and using the exam prep software is enough to successfully complete the exam. It is recommended that candidates spend at least 60 hours preparing for the exam by reading the textbook, underlining key points, watching the video class, and completing as many practice questions as possible. We recommend that candidates schedule their exam no more than one week after completing their Series 7 exam prep.

Test-Taking Tips

☐ Read the full question.

☐ Identify what the question is asking.

☐ Identify key words and phrases.

☐ Watch out for hedge clauses, for example, *except* and *not*.

☐ Eliminate wrong answers.

☐ Identify synonymous terms.

☐ Be wary of changing answers.

WHAT TYPE OF BUSINESS MAY BE CONDUCTED BY SERIES 7 REGISTERED REPRESENTATIVES?

A Series 7 registered representative may conduct business in all general securities products, including:

- Stocks, bonds, options, and rights.
- Exchange-traded funds (ETFs).
- Exchange-traded notes (ETNs).
- Warrants.
- American depositary receipts (ADRs).
- Mutual funds.
- Investment company products, direct participation programs (DPPs), real estate investment trusts (REITs), U.S. government securities, and municipal securities.
- Collateralized mortgage obligations (CMOs).

WHAT SCORE IS NEEDED TO PASS THE EXAM?

A score of 72 percent or higher is needed to pass the Series 7 exam.

ARE THERE ANY PREREQUISITES FOR THE SERIES 7?

There are no prerequisites for the Series 7 exam. A candidate is not required to have any other professional qualifications prior to taking the Series 7 exam.

HOW DO I SCHEDULE AN EXAM?

Ask your firm's principal to schedule the exam for you or to provide a list of test centers in your area. You must be sponsored by an FINRA member firm prior to making an appointment. The Series 7 exam may be taken any day that the exam center is open.

WHAT MUST I TAKE TO THE EXAM CENTER?

You should only take a picture ID with you. Everything else will be provided, including a calculator and scratch paper.

HOW LONG WILL IT TAKE TO GET THE RESULTS OF THE EXAM?

The exam will be graded as soon as you finish your final question and hit the Submit for Grading button. It will take only a few minutes to get your results. Your grade will appear on the computer screen, and you will be given a paper copy from the exam center.

If you do not pass the test, you will need to wait 30 days before taking it again. If you do not pass on the second try, you will need to wait another 30 days. If you fail the test again, you are required to wait 6 months to take the test again.

About This Book

The writers and instructors at The Securities Institute have developed the Series 7 textbook, exam prep software, and videos to ensure that you have the knowledge required to pass the test and to make sure that you are confident in the application of the knowledge during the exam. The writers and instructors at The Securities Institute are subject-matter experts as well as a Series 7 test experts. We understand how the test is written, and our proven test-taking techniques can dramatically improve your results.

Each chapter includes notes, tips, examples, and case studies with key information; hints for taking the exam; and additional insight into the topics. Each chapter ends with a practice test to ensure that you have mastered the concepts presented before moving on to the next topic.

About the Test Bank

This book is accompanied by a test bank of more than 500 questions to further reinforce the concepts and information presented here. The access card in the back of this book includes the URL and PIN code you can use to access the test bank. This test bank provides a small sample of the questions and features that are contained in the full version of the Series 7 exam prep software.

If you have not purchased the full version of the exam prep software with this book, we highly recommend it to ensure that you have mastered the knowledge required for your Series 7 exam. To purchase the exam prep software for this exam, visit The Securities Institute of America online at www.SecuritiesCE.com or call 877-218-1776.

About The Securities Institute of America

The Securities Institute of America, Inc., helps thousands of securities and insurance professionals build successful careers in the financial services industry every year.

Our securities training options include:

- Onsite training classes.
- Private tutoring.
- Classroom training.
- Interactive online video training classes.
- State-of-the-art exam preparation software.
- Printed textbooks.
- Real-time tracking and reporting for managers and training directors.

You can choose a securities training solution that matches your skill level, learning style, and schedule. Regardless of the format you choose, you can be sure that our securities training courses are relevant, tested, and designed to help you succeed. It is the experience of our instructors and the quality of our materials that make our courses requested by name at some of the largest financial services firms in the world.

To contact The Securities Institute of America, visit us on the Web at www.SecuritiesCE.com or call 877-218-1776.

CHAPTER 1

Equity Securities

INTRODUCTION

This first chapter will build the foundation upon which the rest of this text is built. A thorough understanding of equity securities will be necessary in order to successfully complete the Series 7 exam. Equity securities are divided into two types: common and preferred stock. We will examine the features of common stock and preferred stock, as well as the benefits and risks associated with their ownership. But first we must define exactly what meets the definition of a security.

WHAT IS A SECURITY?

A security is any investment product that can be exchanged for value and involves risk. In order for an investment to be considered a security, it must be readily transferable between two parties and the owner must be subject to the loss of some, or all, of the invested principal. If the product is not transferable or does not contain risk, it is not a security.

Types of Securities	Types of Nonsecurities
Common stocks	Whole life insurance
Preferred stocks	Term life insurance
Bonds	IRAs
Mutual funds	Retirement plans

(Continued)

Types of Securities	Types of Nonsecurities
Variable annuities	Fixed annuities
Variable life insurance	Prospectus
Options	Confirmations
Rights	
Warrants	
Exchange-traded funds/Exchange-traded notes	
Real estate investment trusts	
Collateralized mortgage obligations	

EQUITY = STOCK

The term *equity* is synonymous with the term *stock*. Throughout your preparation for this exam, and on the exam itself, you will find many terms that are used interchangeably. Equity or stock creates an ownership relationship with the issuing company. Once an investor has purchased stock in a corporation, he or she becomes an owner of that corporation. The corporation sells off pieces of itself to investors in the form of shares in an effort to raise working capital. Equity is perpetual, meaning that there is no maturity date for the shares and the investor may own the shares until he or she decides to sell them. Most corporations use the sale of equity as their main source of business capital.

COMMON STOCK

There are thousands of companies whose stock trades publicly and who have used the sale of equity as a source of raising business capital. All publicly traded companies must issue common stock before they may issue any other type of equity security. The two types of equity securities are common stock and preferred stock. Although all publicly traded companies must have sold or issued common stock, not all companies may want to issue or sell preferred stock. Let's take a look at the formation of a company and how common stock is created.

CORPORATE TIMELINE

The following is a representation of the steps that corporations must take in order to sell their common stock to the public, as well as what may happen to that stock once it has been sold to the public.

AUTHORIZED STOCK

Authorized stock is the maximum number of shares that a company may sell to the investing public in an effort to raise cash to meet the organization's goals. The number of authorized shares is arbitrarily determined and is set at the time of incorporation. A corporation may sell all or part of its authorized stock. If the corporation wants to sell more shares than it's authorized to sell, the shareholders must approve an increase in the number of authorized shares.

ISSUED STOCK

Issued stock is stock that has been authorized for sale and that has actually been sold to the investing public. The total number of authorized shares typically exceeds the total number of issued shares so that the corporation may sell additional shares in the future to meet its needs. Once shares have been sold to the investing public, they will always be counted as issued shares, regardless of their ownership or subsequent repurchase by the corporation. It's important to note that the total number of issued shares may never exceed the total number of authorized shares.

Additional authorized shares may be issued in the future for any of the following reasons:

- Pay a stock dividend.
- Expand current operations.
- Exchange common shares for convertible preferred or convertible bonds.
- To satisfy obligations under employee stock options or purchase plans.

OUTSTANDING STOCK

Outstanding stock is stock that has been sold or issued to the investing public and that actually remains in the hands of the investing public.

EXAMPLE   XYZ corporation has 10,000,000 shares authorized and has sold 5,000,000 shares to the public during its initial public offering. In this case, there would be 5,000,000 shares of stock issued and 5,000,000 shares outstanding.

TREASURY STOCK

Treasury stock is stock that has been sold to the investing public and then subsequently repurchased by the corporation. The corporation may elect to reissue the shares or it may retire the shares that it holds in treasury stock. Treasury stock does not receive dividends nor does it vote.

A corporation may elect to repurchase its own shares for any of the following reasons:

- To maintain control of the company.
- To increase earnings per share.
- To fund employee stock purchase plans.
- To use shares to pay for a merger or acquisition.

To determine the amount of treasury stock, use the following formula:

issued stock − outstanding stock = treasury stock

EXAMPLE If in the case of XYZ above, the company decides to repurchase 3,000,000 of its own shares, then XYZ would have 5,000,000 shares issued—2,000,000 shares and 3,000,000 shares of treasury stock.

It's important to note that once the shares have been issued, they will always be counted as issued shares. The only thing that changes is the number of outstanding shares and the number of treasury shares.

VALUES OF COMMON STOCK

A common stock's market value is determined by supply and demand and may or may not have any real relationship to what the shares are actually worth. The market value of common stock is affected by the current and future expectations for the company.

BOOK VALUE

A corporation's book value is the theoretical liquidation value of the company. The book value is found by taking all of the company's tangible assets and subtracting all of its liabilities. This will give you the total book value. To determine the book values per share, divide the total book value by the total number of outstanding common shares.

PAR VALUE

Par value, in a discussion regarding common stock, is only important if you are an accountant looking at the balance sheet. An accountant uses the par value as a way to credit the money received by the corporation from the initial sale of the stock to the balance sheet. For investors, it has no relationship to any measure of value that may otherwise be employed.

RIGHTS OF COMMON STOCKHOLDERS

As an owner of common stock, investors are owners of the corporation. As such, investors have certain rights that are granted to all common stock holders.

PREEMPTIVE RIGHTS

As a stockholder, an investor has the right to maintain a percentage interest in the company. This is known as a preemptive right. Should the company wish to sell additional shares to raise new capital, it must first offer the new shares to existing shareholders. If the existing shareholders decide not to purchase the new shares, then the shares may be offered to the general public. When a corporation decides to conduct a rights offering, the board of directors must approve the issuance of the additional shares. If the number of shares that are to be issued under the rights offering would cause the total number of outstanding shares to exceed the total number of authorized shares, then shareholder approval will be required. Existing shareholders will have to approve an increase in the number of authorized shares before the rights offering can proceed.

⬤ TEST**FOCUS!**

Number of Existing Shares	Number of New Shares	Total Shares After Offering
100,000	100,000	200,000
10,000	10,000	20,000
10% ownership	10% of offering	10% ownership

In the example above, the company has 100,000 shares of stock outstanding and an investor has purchased 10,000 of those original shares. As a result, the investor owns 10% of the corporation. The company wishing to sell 100,000 new shares to raise new capital must first offer 10% of the new shares to the current investor (10,000 shares) before the shares may be offered to the general public. So if the investor decides to purchase the additional shares, as is the case in the example, the investor will have maintained a 10% interest in the company.

A shareholder's preemptive right is ensured through a rights offering. The existing shareholders will have the right to purchase the new shares at a discount to the current market value for up to 45 days. This is known as the subscription price. Once the subscription price is set, it remains constant for the 45 days, while the price of the stock is moving up and down in the marketplace.

There are three possible outcomes for a right. They are:

1. **Exercised.** The investor decides to purchase the additional shares and sends in the money, along with the rights to receive the additional shares.
2. **Sold.** The rights have value. If the investor does not want to purchase the additional shares, they may be sold to another investor who would like to purchase the shares.
3. **Expire.** The rights will expire when no one wants to purchase the stock. This will only occur when the market price of the share has fallen below the subscription price of the right and the 45 days has elapsed.

CHARACTERISTICS OF A RIGHTS OFFERING

Once a rights offering has been declared, the company's common stock will trade with the rights attached. The stock in this situation is said to be trading "cum rights." The company's stock, which is the subject of the rights offering, will trade cum rights between the declaration date and the ex date. After the ex date, the stock will trade without the rights attached, or "ex rights." The value of the common stock will be adjusted down by the value of the right on the ex rights date. During a rights offering, each share will be issued one right. The subscription price and the number of rights required to purchase one additional share will be detailed in the terms of the offering on the rights certificate. During a rights offering, the issuer will retain an investment bank to act as a standby underwriter, and the investment bank will stand by, ready to purchase any shares that are not purchased by the rights holders.

DETERMINING THE VALUE OF A RIGHT CUM RIGHTS

In order to determine the value of one right before the ex rights date, you must use the cum rights formula. Subtract the subscription price of the right from the market price of the stock. Once the discount (if any) has been determined, divide the discount by the number of rights required to purchase one share plus one. This will determine the value of one right.

EXAMPLE   XYZ has 10,000,000 shares of common stock outstanding and is issuing 5,000,000 additional common shares through a rights offering. XYZ is trading in the marketplace at $51 per share, and the rights have a subscription price of $48 per share. Keep in mind that the stock price reflects the value of the right that is still attached to the stock.

The value of a right is determined as follows:

$$\frac{\text{(stock price} - \text{subscription price)}}{\text{(the number of rights required to purchase 1 share} + 1)}$$

$$\begin{array}{r} (\$51) \\ - \underline{(\$48)} \\ \$3 \end{array}$$

$3/3 rights = $1

Because each one of the 10,000,000 shares is entitled to receive one right and the company is offering 5,000,000 additional shares, it will require $48, plus two rights, to subscribe to one additional share. The rights agent will handle the name changes when the rights are purchased and sold in the marketplace.

DETERMINING THE VALUE OF A RIGHT EX RIGHTS

In order to determine the value of one right after the ex rights date, subtract the subscription price of the right from the market price of the stock. Once the discount (if any) has been determined, divide the discount by the number of rights required to purchase one share. This will determine the value of one right. The price of the stock on the ex rights date is adjusted down by the value of the right to reflect the fact that purchasers of the stock will no longer receive the rights.

EXAMPLE   XYZ has 10,000,000 shares of common stock outstanding and is issuing 5,000,000 additional common shares through a rights offering. XYZ is trading in the marketplace at $50 per share, and the rights have a subscription price of $48 per share. The value of a right is determined as follows:

$$\frac{\text{(stock price} - \text{subscription price)}}{\text{(the number of rights required to purchase 1 share)}}$$

$$\begin{array}{r} \$50 \\ -\ \$48 \\ \hline \$2 \end{array}$$

$2/2 rights = $1

Because each one of the 10,000,000 shares is entitled to receive one right and the company is offering 5,000,000 additional shares, it will require $48, plus two rights, to subscribe to one additional share.

STOCK SPLITS

There are times when a corporation will find it advantageous to split its stock. A corporation that has done well and seen its stock appreciate significantly may declare a forward stock split to make its shares more attractive to retail investors. Most retail investors would be more comfortable purchasing shares of a $25 stock rather than purchasing shares of a $100 stock. When a corporation declares a forward stock split the share price declines and the number of outstanding shares increase. Alternatively if a corporation has seen its share price decline significantly, it may declare a reverse stock split. A corporation would declare a reverse stock split to increase the price of its shares to make its shares more attractive to institutional investors. Many institutions have investment policies that don't allow the institution to purchase shares of low price stocks. With a reverse stock split the price of the stock increases and the number of outstanding shares decrease. With any split the overall market capitalization (the total value of all of the outstanding shares) and the value of an investor's holdings are not affected by the decision to split the stock. The following table details the effect of various types of splits on an investor's holdings, notice how the value has not changed, only the number of shares and price have changed.

Type of Split	Old	New	Value
2:1	Long 100 shares at 50	Long 200 shares at 25	$5,000
4:1	Long 100 at 100	Long 400 at 25	$10,000
3:2	Long 100 shares at 100	Long 150 shares at 66.67	$10,000
1:4	Long 1000 shares at 5	Long 250 at 20	$5,000

VOTING

Common stockholders have the right to vote on the major issues facing the corporation. Common stockholders are part owners of the company and, as a result, have a right to say how the company is run. The biggest emphasis is placed on the election of the board of directors.

Common stockholders may also vote on:

- The issuance of bonds or additional common shares.
- Stock splits.
- Mergers and acquisitions.
- Major changes in corporate policy.

Stockholders do not get to vote on executive compensation, or if the company is going to file for bankruptcy protection.

METHODS OF VOTING

There are two methods by which the voting process may be conducted: the statutory method and the cumulative method. A stockholder may cast one vote for each share of stock owned, and the method used will determine how those votes are cast. The test focuses on the election of the board of directors, so we will use that in our example.

 **TESTFOCUS!**

An investor owns 200 shares of XYZ. Two board members are to be elected, and there are four people running in the election. Under both the statutory and cumulative methods of voting, you take the number of shares owned and multiply them by the number of people to be elected to determine how many votes the shareholder has.

In this case, 200 shares × 2 = 400 votes. The method used dictates how those votes may be cast.

Candidate	Statutory	Cumulative
1	200 votes	400 votes
2		
3		
4	200 votes	

The **statutory method** requires that the votes be distributed evenly among the candidates that the investor wishes to vote for.

The **cumulative method** allows shareholders to cast all of their votes in favor of one candidate, if they so choose. The cumulative method is said to favor smaller investors for this reason. Some corporations will issue both voting and non-voting common stock. Raising additional capital through the sale of non-voting shares allows management to retain control of the company. In a two share class structure the voting shares are known as "A" shares and non-voting shares are known as "B" shares.

LIMITED LIABILITY

A stockholder's liability is limited to the amount of money that has been invested in the stock. Stockholders cannot be held liable for any amount past their invested capital.

FREELY TRANSFERABLE

Common stock and most other securities are freely transferable. That is to say that one investor may sell shares to another investor without limitation and without requiring the approval of the issuer. The transfer of a security's ownership, in most cases, is facilitated through a broker dealer. The transfer of ownership is executed in the secondary market on either an exchange or in the over-the-counter market. Ownership of common stock is evidenced by a stock certificate that identifies:

- The name of the issuing company.
- The number of shares owned.
- The name of the owner of record.
- The CUSIP number.

In order to transfer or sell the shares the owner must endorse the stock certificate or sign a power of substitution known as a stock or bond power. Signing the certificate or a stock or bond power makes the securities transferable into the new buyer's name.

THE TRANSFER AGENT

The transfer agent is the company that is in charge of transferring the record of ownership from one party to another. The transfer agent:

- Cancels old certificates registered to the seller.
- Issues new certificates to the buyer.

- Maintains and records a list of stockholders.
- Ensures that shares are issued to the correct owner.
- Locates lost or stolen certificates.
- Issues new certificates in the event of destruction.
- May authenticate a mutilated certificate.

THE REGISTRAR

The registrar is the company responsible for auditing the transfer agent to ensure that the transfer agent does not erroneously issue more shares than are authorized by the company. In the case of a bond issue, the registrar will certify that the bond is a legally binding debt of the company. The function of the transfer agent and the registrar may not be performed by a single department of any one company. A bank or a trust company usually performs the functions of the transfer agent and the registrar.

CUSIP NUMBERS

The Committee on Uniform Securities Identification Procedures issues CUSIP numbers, which are printed on the stock or bond certificates to help identify the security. CUSIP numbers must also appear on trade confirmations.

INSPECTION OF BOOKS AND RECORDS

All stockholders have the right to inspect the company's books and records. For most shareholders, this right is ensured through the company's filing of quarterly and annual reports. Stockholders also have the right to obtain a list of shareholders, but they do not have the right to review other corporate financial data that the corporation may deem confidential.

RESIDUAL CLAIM TO ASSETS

In the event of a company's bankruptcy or liquidation, common stockholders have the right to receive their proportional interest in residual assets. After all the other security holders have been paid, along with all creditors of the corporation, common stockholders may claim the residual assets. For this reason common stock is the most junior security.

WHY DO PEOPLE BUY COMMON STOCK?

The main reason people invest in common stock is for capital appreciation. They want their money to grow in value over time. An investor in common stock hopes to buy the stock at a low price and sell it at a higher price at some point in the future.

EXAMPLE	An investor purchases 100 shares of XYZ at $20 per share on March 15, 2014. On April 30th of 2015, the investor sells 100 shares of XYZ for $30 per share, realizing a profit of $10 per share, or $1,000 on the 100 shares.

INCOME

Many corporations distribute a portion of their earnings to their investors in the form of dividends. This distribution of earnings creates income for the investor, and investors in common stock generally receive dividends quarterly. The amount of income that an investor receives each year is measured relative to what the investor has paid, or will pay, for the stock and is known as the dividend yield or the current yield.

EXAMPLE	ABC pays a $.50 quarterly dividend to its shareholders. The stock is currently trading at $20 per share. What is its current yield (also known as dividend yield)?

current yield = annual income/current market price

$.50 × 4 = $ 2.00 $2/$20 = 10%

The investor in the above example is receiving 10% of the purchase price of the stock each year in the form of dividends, which, by itself, would be a nice return for the investor.

WHAT ARE THE RISKS OF OWNING COMMON STOCK?

The major risk in owning common stock is that the stock may fall in value. There are no sure things in the stock market and, even if you own stock in a great company, you may end up losing money.

DIVIDENDS MAY BE STOPPED OR REDUCED

Common stockholders are not entitled to receive dividends just because they own part of the company. It is up to the company to elect to pay a dividend. The corporation is in no way obligated to pay a dividend to common shareholders.

JUNIOR CIIILAIM ON CORPORATE ASSETS

A common stockholder is the last person to get paid if the company is liquidated. It is very possible that after all creditors and other investors are paid there will be little or nothing left for the common stockholders.

HOW DOES SOMEONE BECOME A STOCKHOLDER?

We have reviewed some of the reasons why an investor would want to become a stockholder. Now we need to review how someone becomes a stockholder. While some people purchase the shares directly from the corporation when the stock is offered to the public, most investors purchase the shares from other investors. These investor-to-investor transactions take place in the secondary market on the exchange or in the over-the-counter market. Although the transaction in many cases only takes seconds to execute, trades actually take several days to fully complete. Let's review the important dates regarding transactions, which are done for a "regular-way" settlement.

TRADE DATE

The trade date is the day when your order is actually executed. Although an order has been placed with a broker, it may not be executed on the same day. There are certain types of orders that may take several days or even longer to execute, depending on the type of order. A market order will be executed immediately, as soon as it is presented to the market, making the trade date the same day the order was entered.

SETTLEMENT DATE

The buyer of a security actually becomes the owner of record on the settlement date. When an investor buys a security from another investor, the selling investor's name is removed from the security and the buyer's name is recorded as the new owner. Settlement date is three business days after the trade date. This is known as T + 3 for all regular-way transactions in common stock, preferred stock, corporate bonds, and municipal bonds. Government bonds and options all settle the next business day following the trade date.

PAYMENT DATE

The payment date is the day when the buyer of the security has to have the money in to the brokerage firm to pay for the purchase. Under the industry rules, the payment date for common and preferred stock, and corporate and municipal bonds is five business days after the trade date or T + 5. Payment dates are regulated by the Federal Reserve Board under regulation T of the Securities Exchange Act of 1934. While many brokerage firms require their customers to have their money in to pay for their purchases sooner than the rules state, the customer has up to five business days to pay for the trade.

VIOLATION

If the customer fails to pay for the purchase within the five business days allowed, the customer is in violation of Regulation T. As a result, the brokerage firm will "sell out" and freeze the customer's account. On the sixth business day following the trade date, the brokerage firm will sell out the securities that the customer failed to pay for. The customer is responsible for any loss that may occur as a result of the sell out, and the brokerage firm may sell out shares of another security in the investor's account in order to cover the loss. The brokerage firm will then freeze the customer's account, which means that the customer must deposit money up front for any purchases for the next 90 days. After the 90 days have expired, the customer is considered to have reestablished good credit and may then conduct business in the regular way and take up to five business days to pay for the trades.

PREFERRED STOCK

Preferred stock is an equity security with a fixed-income component. Like a common stockholder, the preferred stockholder is an owner of the company. However, the preferred stockholder is investing in the stock for the fixed income that the preferred shares generate through their semiannual dividends. Preferred stock has a stated dividend rate or a fixed rate that the corporation must pay to its preferred shareholders. Growth is generally not achieved through investing in preferred shares.

FEATURES OF ALL PREFERRED STOCK

PAR VALUE

Par value on preferred stock is very important because that's what the dividend is based on. Par value for all preferred shares is $100 unless otherwise stated. Companies generally express the dividend as a percentage of par value for preferred stock.

EXAMPLE   How much would the following investor receive in annual income from the investment in the following preferred stock?

An investor buys 100 shares of TWT 9% preferred

$100 × 9% = $9 per share × 100 = $900

PAYMENT OF DIVIDENDS

The dividend on preferred shares must be paid before any dividends are paid to common shareholders. This gives the preferred shareholder a priority claim on the corporation's distribution of earnings.

DISTRIBUTION OF ASSETS

If a corporation liquidates or declares bankruptcy, the preferred shareholders are paid prior to any common shareholder, giving the preferred shareholder a higher claim on the corporation's assets.

PERPETUAL

Preferred stock, unlike bonds, is perpetual, having no maturity date. Investors may hold shares for as long as they wish or until the shares are called in by the company under a call feature.

NONVOTING

Most preferred stock is nonvoting. Occasionally the holder of a cumulative preferred stock may receive voting rights in the event the corporation misses several dividend payments.

INTEREST RATE SENSITIVE

Because of the fixed income generated by preferred shares, their price will be more sensitive to changes in interest rates than the price of their common stock counterparts. As interest rates decline, the value of preferred shares tends to increase, and when interest rates rise, the value of the preferred shares tends to fall. This is known as an inverse relationship.

TYPES OF PREFERRED STOCK

Preferred stock, unlike common stock, may have different features associated with it. Most of the features are designed to make the issue more attractive to investors and, therefore, benefit the owners of preferred stock.

STRAIGHT/NONCUMULATIVE

The straight preferred stock has no additional features. The holder is entitled to the stated dividend rate and nothing else. If the corporation is unable to pay the dividend, it is not owed to the investor.

CUMULATIVE PREFERRED

A cumulative feature protects the investor in cases when a corporation is having financial difficulties and cannot pay the dividend. Dividends on cumulative preferred stock accumulate in arrears until the corporation is able to pay them. If the dividend on a cumulative preferred stock is missed, it is still owed to the holder. Dividends in arrears on cumulative issues are always the first dividends to be paid. If the company wants to pay a dividend to common shareholders, it must first pay the dividends in arrears, as well as the stated preferred dividend, before common shareholders receive anything.

 **TESTFOCUS!**

GNR has an 8% cumulative preferred stock outstanding. It has not paid the dividend this year or for the prior three years. How much must the holders of GNR cumulative preferred be paid per share before the common stockholders are paid a dividend?

The dividend has not been paid this year nor for the previous three years, so the holders are owed four years' worth of dividends, or:

4 × $8 = $32 per share

PARTICIPATING PREFERRED

Holders of participating preferred stock are entitled to receive the stated preferred rate, as well as additional common dividends. The holder of participating preferred receives the dividend payable to the common stockholders over and above the stated preferred dividend.

CONVERTIBLE PREFERRED

A convertible feature allows the preferred stockholder to convert or exchange their preferred shares for common shares at a fixed price known as the conversion price.

EXAMPLE   TRW has issued a 4% convertible preferred stock, which may be converted into TRW common stock at $20 per share. How many shares may the preferred stockholder receive upon conversion?

number of shares = par/conversion price (CVP)

$100/$20 = 5

The investor may receive five common shares for every preferred share.

These are some additional concepts regarding convertible securities that will be addressed in the convertible bond section that follows.

CALLABLE PREFERRED

A call feature is the only feature that benefits the company and not the investor. A call feature allows the corporation to call in or redeem the preferred shares at its discretion or after some period of time has expired. Most callable preferred stock may not be called in during the first few years after their issuance. This feature, which does not allow the stock to be called in its early years, is known as call protection. Many callable preferred shares will be called at a premium price above par. For example a $100 par preferred stock may be called at $103. The main reasons a company would call in its preferred shares would be to eliminate the fixed dividend payment or to sell a new preferred stock with a lower dividend rate when interest rates decline. Preferred stock is more likely to be called by the corporation when interest rates decline.

ADJUSTABLE RATE PREFERRED

Some corporations will issue preferred shares that pay a stated dividend that adjust based on the prevailing interest rates paid in the marketplace or on a benchmark index. The rate of the dividend will be adjusted on the reset date and may be done semiannually or at longer set intervals as determined by the issuer. The adjustable rate protects the owners in times of raising interest rates and can benefit the corporation when interest rates fall. Certain adjustable rate preferred shares may have a stated floor or cap rate that set the minimum and maximum amount for the dividend rate.

 TAKENOTE!

If all other factors are the same the callable preferred stock will have the highest stated dividend rate to compensate investors for the fact that the shares may be called in by the issuer. The next highest rate will be paid to holders of straight preferred stock.

TYPES OF DIVIDENDS

CASH

A cash dividend is the most common form of dividend, and it is one that the test focuses on. A corporation will send out a cash payment in the form of a check, directly to the stockholders. For those stockholders who have their stock held in the name of the brokerage firm, a check will be sent to the brokerage firm and the money will be credited to the investor's account. Securities that are held in the name of the brokerage firm are said to be held in "street name." To determine the amount that an investor will receive, simply multiply the amount of the dividend to be paid by the number of shares.

EXAMPLE	JPF pays a $.10 dividend to shareholders. An investor who owns 1,000 shares of JPF will receive $100: 1,000 shares × $.10 = $100.

STOCK

A corporation that wants to reward its shareholders but that also wants to conserve cash for other business purposes may elect to pay a stock dividend to its shareholders. Each investor will receive an additional number of shares based on the number of shares the investor owns. The market price of the stock will decline after the stock dividend has been distributed to reflect the fact that there are now more shares outstanding; however, the total market value of the company will remain the same.

EXAMPLE	If HRT pays a 5% stock dividend to its shareholders, an investor with 500 shares will receive an additional 25 shares. This is determined by multiplying the number of shares owned by the amount of the stock dividend to be paid. **500 × 5% = 25**

PROPERTY/PRODUCT

This is the least likely way in which a corporation would pay a dividend, but it is a permissible dividend distribution. A corporation may send out to its shareholders samples of its products or portions of its property.

DIVIDEND DISTRIBUTION

If a corporation decides to pay a dividend to its common stockholders, it may not discriminate as to who receives the dividend. The dividend must be paid to all common stockholders of record. Investors who already own the stock do not need to be notified by the company that they are entitled to receive the pending dividend, because it will be sent to them automatically. However, new purchasers of the stock may or may not be entitled to receive the dividend, depending on when they purchased the stock relative to when the dividend is going to be distributed. We will now examine the dividend distribution process.

DECLARATION DATE

The declaration date is the day that the board of directors decides to pay a dividend to common stockholders of record. The declaration date is the starting point for the entire dividend process. The company must notify the regulators at the exchange or FINRA, depending on where the stock trades, at least 10 business days prior to the record date.

EX-DIVIDEND DATE

The ex-dividend date, or the ex date, is the first day when purchasers of the security are no longer entitled to receive the dividend that the company has declared for payment. Stated another way, the ex date is the first day when the stock trades without (ex) the dividend attached. The exchange or FINRA set the ex date for the stock, based on the record date determined and announced by the corporation's board of directors. Because it takes three business days for a trade to settle, the ex date is always two business days prior to the record date. If a stock is purchased prior to the ex dividend date but delivered late the buying broker dealer will send the selling broker dealer a "due bill" for the amount of the dividend owed.

RECORD DATE

This is the day when investors must have their name recorded on the stock certificate in order to be entitled to receive the dividend that was declared by the board of directors. All stockholders whose name is on the stock certificate (owners of record) will be entitled to receive the dividend. The investor would have had to have purchased the stock before the ex dividend date in order to be an owner of record on the record date. The record date is determined by the corporation's board of directors and is used to determine the shareholders who will receive the dividend.

PAYMENT DATE

This is the day when the corporation actually distributes the dividend to shareholders and it completes the dividend process. The payment date is controlled and set by the board of directors of the corporation and is usually four weeks following the record date.

STOCK PRICE AND THE EX DIVIDEND DATE

It is important to note that the value of the stock prior to the ex-dividend date reflects the value of the stock with the dividend. On the ex-dividend date, the stock is now trading without the dividend attached, and new purchasers will not receive the dividend that had been declared for payment. As a result, the stock price will be adjusted down on the ex-dividend date in an amount equal to the dividend.

 TESTFOCUS!

TRY declares a $.20 dividend payable to shareholders of record as of Thursday, August 22nd. The ex-dividend date will be two business days prior to the record date. In this case the ex date will be Tuesday, August 20th. If TRY closed on Monday, August 19th at $24 per share, the stock would open at $23.80 on Tuesday.

Sunday	Monday	Tuesday	Wednesday	Thursday	Friday	Saturday
				1	2	3
4	5	6	7	8	9	10
11	12	13	14	15	16	17
18	19	20	21	22	23	24
25	26	27	28	29	30	31

TAXATION OF DIVIDENDS

All qualified dividends received by ordinary income earners are taxed at a rate of 15% for the year the dividend is received. Investors who are classified as high income earners will have dividends taxed at a set rate of 20%. The tax rate for dividends is a hotly debated topic and may be subject to change.

SELLING DIVIDENDS

Selling dividends is a violation! A registered representative may not use the pending dividend payment as the sole basis of his or her recommendation to purchase the stock. Additionally, using the pending dividend as a means to create urgency on the part of the investor to purchase the stock is a prime example of this type of violation. If the investor were to purchase the shares just prior to the ex-dividend date simply to receive the dividend, the investor in many cases would end up worse off. The dividend in this case would actually be a return of the money that the investor used to purchase the stock and then the investor would have a tax liability when the dividend is received.

DIVIDEND DISBURSEMENT PROCESS

The corporation's dividend disbursement agent is responsible for the distribution of dividends and will send the dividends to the shareholders of record on the record date. For convenience, most investors have their securities held in the name of the broker dealer, also known as the "street name." As a result, the dividend disbursement agent will send the dividends directly to the broker dealer. The broker dealer's dividend department will collect the dividends and distribute them to the beneficial owners.

WARRANTS

A warrant is a security that gives the holder the opportunity to purchase common stock. Like a right, the warrant has a subscription price. However, the subscription price on a warrant is always above the current market value of the common stock when the warrant is originally issued. A warrant has a much longer life than a right, and the holder of a warrant may have up to 10 years to purchase the stock at the subscription price. The long life is what makes the warrant valuable, even though the subscription price is higher than the market price of the common stock when the warrant is issued.

HOW DO PEOPLE GET WARRANTS?

UNITS

Many times, companies will issue warrants to people who have purchased their common stock when it was originally sold to the public during its initial public offering (IPO). A common share that comes with a warrant attached to purchase an additional common share is known as a unit.

ATTACHED TO BONDS

Many times, companies will attach warrants to their bond offerings as a sweetener to help market the bond offering. The warrant to purchase the common stock makes the bond more attractive to the investor and may allow the company to issue the bonds with a lower coupon rate.

SECONDARY MARKET

Warrants will often trade in the secondary market just like the common stock. An investor who wishes to participate in the potential price appreciation of the common stock may elect to purchase the corporation's warrant instead of its common shares.

POSSIBLE OUTCOMES OF A WARRANT

A warrant, like a right, may be exercised or sold by the investor. A warrant may also expire if the stock price is below the warrant's subscription price at its expiration.

Rights vs. Warrants

Rights		Warrants
Up to 45 days	**Term**	Up to 10 years
Below the market	**Subscription Price**	Above the market
May trade with or without common stock	**Trading**	May trade with or without common stock or bonds
Issued to existing shareholders to ensure preemptive rights	**Who**	Offered as a sweetener to make securities more attractive

AMERICAN DEPOSITARY RECEIPTS (ADRs)/ AMERICAN DEPOSITARY SHARES (ADSs)

American depositary receipts (ADRs) facilitate the trading of foreign securities in the U.S. markets. An ADR is a receipt that represents the ownership of the foreign shares that are being held abroad in a branch of a U.S. bank. Each ADR represents ownership of between one to 10 shares of the foreign stock, and the holder of the ADR may request the delivery of the foreign shares. Holders of ADRs also have the right to vote and the right to receive dividends that the foreign corporation declares for payment to shareholders.

CURRENCY RISKS

The owner of an ADR has currency risk along with the normal risks associated with the ownership of the stock. Should the currency of the country decline relative to the U.S. dollar, the holder of the ADR will receive fewer

U.S. dollars when a dividend is paid and fewer U.S. dollars when the security is sold. It's important to note that the dividend on the ADR is paid by the corporation to the custodian bank in the foreign currency. The custodian bank will convert the dividend to U.S. dollars for distribution to the holders of the ADRs.

FUNCTIONS OF THE CUSTODIAN BANK ISSUING ADRs

ADRs are actually issued and guaranteed by the bank that holds the foreign securities on deposit. The custodian bank is the registered owner of the foreign shares and must guarantee that the foreign shares remain in the bank as long as the ADRs remain outstanding. Foreign corporations will often use ADRs as a way of generating U.S. interest in their company. The issuance of the ADR allows them to avoid the long and costly registration process for their securities.

REAL ESTATE INVESTMENT TRUSTS (REITs)

A real estate investment trust, or REIT, is a special type of equity security. REITs are organized for the specific purpose of buying, developing, or managing a portfolio of real estate. REITs may also be organized to provide mortgage financing and are known as mortgage REITs. Some hybrid REITs hold both a portfolio of real estate and mortgages. REITs are organized as a corporation or as a trust, and publicly traded REITs will trade on the exchanges or in the over-the-counter market just like other stocks. A REIT is organized as a conduit for the investment income generated by the portfolio of real estate. REITs are entitled to special tax treatment under Internal Revenue Code subchapter M. A REIT will not pay taxes at the corporate level so long as:

- It receives 75% of its income from real estate.
- It distributes at least 90% of its taxable income to shareholders.

So long as the REIT meet the above requirements, the income will be allowed to flow through to the shareholders and will be taxed at their rate. Dividends received by REIT shareholders will continue to be taxed as ordinary income. It is important to note that REITs do not pass through gains and losses only income to investors.

NON-TRADED REITs

Non-traded real estate investment trusts or REITs lack liquidity, have high fees, and can be difficult to value. The fees for investing in a non-traded REIT may be as much as 15% of the per shares price. These fees include commissions and expenses which cannot exceed 10% of the offering price. Investors are often attracted to the high yields offered by these investments. Firms who conduct business in these products must conduct ongoing suitability determination on the REITs they recommend. Firms must react to red flags in the financial statements and from the REIT's management and adjust the recommendation process accordingly or stop recommending if material changes take place that would make the REIT unsuitable. Holding periods can be eight years or more and the opportunities to liquidate the investments may be very limited. Furthermore, the distributions from the REITs themselves may be based on the use of borrowed funds and may include a return of principal which may be adversely impacted and cause the distributions to be vulnerable to being significantly reduced or stopped altogether. Distributions may exceed cash flow and the amount of the distributions, if any, are at the discretion of the Board of Directors. Non-traded REITs like exchange traded REITs must distribute 90% of the income to shareholders and must file annual reports (10-Ks) and quarterly reporrs (10-Qs) with the SEC. Broker dealers who sell non-traded REITs must provide investors with a valuation of the REIT within 18 months of the closing of the offering of shares.

Pretest

EQUITY SECURITIES

1. A company you own common stock in has just filed for bankruptcy. As a shareholder, you will have the right to receive:

    a. the par value of the common shares.

    b. new common shares in the reorganized company.

    c. a percentage of your original investment.

    d. your proportional percentage of residual assets.

2. A corporation may pay a dividend in which of the following ways?

    a. Stock

    b. Cash

    c. Stock of another company

    d. All of the above

3. ABC common stock has declined dramatically in value over the last quarter but the dividend it has declared for payment this quarter has remained the same. The dividend yield on the stock has:

    a. not changed because the board has to declare the dividend amount.

    b. gone down because the yield is a stated rate.

    c. gone up as the price of ABC has fallen.

    d. been fixed at the time of issuance.

4. The transfer agent does which of the following?

    I. Maintains and records a list of stockholders.

    II. Authorizes shares.

    III. Adjusts the number of authorized shares.

    IV. Locates lost shares.

    a. II and III
    b. I and III
    c. I and IV
    d. I and II

5. All qualified dividends for ordinary income earners are:

    a. taxed as ordinary income each year.
    b. tax-free income.
    c. taxed as special interest-free income.
    d. taxed at a set rate of 15%.

6. Which of the following is NOT a right of common stockholders?

    a. Right to elect the board of directors.
    b. Right to vote for executive compensation.
    c. Right to vote for a stock split.
    d. Right to maintain their percentage of ownership in the company.

7. Which of the following is NOT true regarding American depositary receipts (ADRs)?

    a. They are receipts of ownership of foreign shares being held abroad in a U.S. bank.
    b. Each ADR represents 100 shares of foreign stock, and the ADR holder may request delivery of the foreign shares.
    c. ADR holders have the right to vote and receive dividends that the foreign corporation declares for shareholders.
    d. The foreign country may issue restrictions on the foreign ownership of stock.

8. An investor buys a 10% preferred stock at 110, what is its current yield?

    a. 10.4%
    b. 9.1%
    c. 10%
    d. 9.5%

9. An investor buys 100 shares of XYZ 7% convertible preferred stock, which is convertible into XYZ common at $20 per share. How many common shares of XYZ common stock will the investor receive upon conversion?

   a. 5
   b. 400
   c. 500
   d. 5,000

10. An investor has purchased shares of a foreign company through an ADR. Which of the following is NOT true?

   a. The ADR may represent one or more shares of the company's common stock.
   b. The dividend will be paid in U.S. dollars.
   c. The investor may elect to exchange the ADR for the underlying common shares.
   d. The investor is subject to currency risk.

11. An investor owns 100 shares of XYZ 8% participating preferred stock. XYZ's common stock pays a quarterly dividend of $.25. How much will the investor earn each year in dividends?

   a. $825
   b. $90
   c. $180
   d. $900

12. An investor who buys a 7% cumulative preferred stock will receive semi-annual dividends of:

   a. $7 per share.
   b. 7% of the corporate profits.
   c. $3.50 per share.
   d. 3.5% of the corporate profits.

13. As the owner of a cumulative preferred stock, an investor would have all of the following rights, EXCEPT:

   a. voting if dividends are missed for a significant period of time.
   b. the right to receive past dividends not paid by the corporation.
   c. the right to exchange the preferred for the underlying common shares.
   d. the right to receive the past dividends before common holders receive a dividend.

14. Which of the following is NOT true of authorized stock?

    a. It is the maximum number of shares a company may sell.

    b. It is arbitrarily determined at the time of incorporation and may not be changed.

    c. It may be sold in total or in part when the company goes public.

    d. It may be sold to investors to raise operating capital for the company.

15. Common stockholders do not have the right to vote on which of the following issues?

    a. Election of the board of directors

    b. Stock splits

    c. Issuance of additional common shares

    d. Bankruptcy

16. Which of the following is NOT true of common dividends?

    a. They are a portion of the company's earnings.

    b. They are a source of income for the investor.

    c. They are generally paid quarterly.

    d. Their value is determined by subtracting the current yield from the current market price.

17. If a 5% stock dividend is paid to an investor who owns 800 shares of stock, the investor will receive how many shares?

    a. 4

    b. 8

    c. 40

    d. 80

18. Why might a company repurchase some of its stock to increase its treasury stock?

    a. To maintain control of the company

    b. To allow the company to pay out smaller dividends

    c. To increase the funding in the company's treasury

    d. To reassure its investors that all is well

Debt Securities

INTRODUCTION

Many different types of entities issue bonds in an effort to raise working capital. Corporations, municipalities, the U.S. government, and U.S. government agencies, all issue bonds in order to meet their capital needs. A bond represents a loan to the issuer in exchange for its promise to repay the face amount of the bond, known as the principal amount at maturity. On most bonds, the investor receives semiannual interest payments during the bond's term. These semiannual interest payments, along with any capital appreciation or depreciation at maturity, represent the investor's return. A bondholder invests primarily for the interest income that will be generated during the bond's term.

CORPORATE BONDS

Corporations will issue bonds in an effort to raise working capital to build and expand their business. Corporate bondholders are not owners of the corporation; they are creditors of the company. Corporate debt financing is known as leverage financing because the company pays interest only on the loan until maturity. Bondholders do not have voting rights so long as the company pays the interest and principal payments in a timely fashion. If the company defaults, the bondholders may be able to use their position as creditors to gain a voice in the company's management. Bondholders will always be paid before preferred and common stockholders in the event of liquidation. Interest income received by investors on corporate bonds is taxable at all levels: federal, state, and local.

TYPES OF BOND ISSUANCE

BEARER BONDS

Bonds that are issued in coupon or bearer form do not record the owner's information with the issuer and the bond certificate does not have the legal owner's name printed on it. As a result, anyone who possesses the bond is entitled to receive the interest payments by clipping the coupons attached to the bond and depositing them in a bank or trust company for payment. Additionally, the bearer is entitled to receive the principal payment at the bond's maturity. Bearer bonds are no longer issued within the United States; however, they are still issued outside the United States.

REGISTERED BONDS

Most bonds are now issued in registered form. Bonds that have been issued in registered form have the owner's name recorded on the books of the issuer, and the buyer's name will appear on the bond certificate.

PRINCIPAL-ONLY REGISTRATION

Bonds that have been registered as to principal only have the owner's name printed on the bond certificate. The issuer knows who owns the bond and who is entitled to receive the principal payment at maturity. However, the bondholder will still be required to clip the coupons to receive the semiannual interest payments.

FULLY REGISTERED

Bonds that have been issued in fully registered form have the owner's name recorded for both the interest and principal payments. The owner is not required to clip coupons, and the issuer will send out the interest payments directly to the bond holder on a semiannual basis. The issuer will also send the principal payment along with last semiannual interest payment directly to the owner at maturity. Most bonds in the United States are issued in fully registered form.

BOOK ENTRY/JOURNAL ENTRY

Bonds that have been issued in book entry or journal entry form have no physical certificate issued to the holder as evidence of ownership. The bonds are fully registered, and the issuer knows who is entitled to receive the semiannual interest payments and the principal payment at maturity. The investor's only evidence of ownership is the trade confirmation, which is generated by the brokerage firm when the purchase order is executed.

BOND CERTIFICATE

If a bond certificate is issued, it must include:

- Name of issuer
- Principal amount
- Issuing date
- Maturity date
- Interest payment dates
- Place where interest is payable (paying agent)
- Type of bond
- Interest rate
- Call feature (if any or non-callable)
- Reference to the trust indenture

BOND PRICING

Once issued, corporate bonds trade in the secondary market between investors similar to the way equity securities do. The price of bonds in the secondary market depends on all of the following:

- Rating
- Interest rates
- Term
- Coupon rate
- Type of bond
- Issuer
- Supply and demand
- Other features (i.e., callable, convertible)

Corporate bonds are always priced as a percentage of par, and the par value for all bonds is always $1,000, unless otherwise stated.

PAR VALUE

The par value of a bond is equal to the amount that the investor has loaned to the issuer. The terms *par value*, *face value*, and *principal amount* are synonymous and are always equal to $1,000. The principal amount is the amount that will be received by the investor at maturity, regardless of the price the investor paid for the bond. An investor who purchases a bond in the secondary market for $1,000 is said to have paid par for the bond.

DISCOUNT

In the secondary market, many different factors affect the price of the bond. It is not at all unusual for an investor to purchase a bond at a price that is below the bond's par value. When investors buy a bond at a price that is below the par value, they are said to be buying the bond at a discount.

PREMIUM

Often market conditions will cause the price of existing bonds to rise and make it attractive for the investors to purchase a bond at a price that is greater than its par value. Anytime an investor buys a bond at a price that exceeds its par value, the investor is said to have paid a premium.

CORPORATE BOND PRICING

All corporate bonds are priced as a percentage of par into fractions of a percent. For example, a quote for a corporate bond reading 95 actually translates into:

95% × $1,000 = $950

A quote for a corporate bond of 97-1/4 translates into:

97.25% × $1,000 = $972.50

BOND YIELDS

A bond's yield is the investor's return for holding the bond. Many factors affect the yield that an investor will receive from a bond, including:

- Current interest rates
- Term of the bond

- Credit quality of the issuer
- Type of collateral
- Convertible or callable
- Purchase price

An investor who is considering investing in a bond needs to be familiar with the bond's nominal yield, current yield, and yield to maturity.

NOMINAL YIELD

A bond's nominal yield is the interest rate that is printed, or "named," on the bond. The nominal yield is always stated as a percentage of par. It is fixed at the time of the bond's issuance and never changes. The nominal yield may also be called the coupon rate. For example, a corporate bond with a coupon rate of 8% will pay the holder $80.00 per year in interest:

8% × $1,000 = $80. The nominal yield is 8%.

CURRENT YIELD

The current yield is a relationship between the annual interest generated by the bond and the bond's current market price. To find any investment's current yield, use the following formula:

annual income/current market price

For example, let's take the same 8% corporate bond we used in the previous example on nominal yield and see what its current yield would be if we paid $1,100 for the bond:

annual income = 8% × $1,000 = $80

current market price = 110% × $1,000 = $1,100

current yield = $80/$1,100 = 7.27%

In this example, we have purchased the bond at a premium, or a price that is higher than par, and we see that the current yield on the bond is lower than the nominal yield.

Let's take a look at the current yield on the same bond if we were to purchase the bond at a discount, or a price that is lower than par. Let's see what the current yield for the bond would be if we pay $900 for the bond.

annual income = 8% × $1,000 = $80

current market price = 90% × $1,000 = $900

current yield = $80/$900 = 8.89%

In this example, we see that the current yield is higher than the nominal yield. By showing examples calculating the current yield for the same bond purchased at both a premium and a discount, we have demonstrated the inverse relationship between prices and yields. That is to say that prices and yields on income-producing investments move in the opposite direction. As the price of an investment rises, the investment's yield falls. Conversely, as the price of the investment falls, the investment's yield will rise.

YIELD TO MATURITY

A bond's yield to maturity is the investor's total annualized return for investing in the bond. A bond's yield to maturity takes into consideration the annual income received by the investor along with any difference between the price the investor paid for the bond and the par value that will be received at maturity. It also assumes that the investor is reinvesting the semiannual interest payments at the same rate. The yield to maturity is the most important yield for an investor who purchases the bond.

YIELD TO MATURITY FOR A PREMIUM BOND

The yield to maturity for a bond purchased at a premium will be the lowest of all the investor's yields. Although an investor may purchase a bond at a price that exceeds the par value of the bond, the issuer is only obligated to pay the bondholder the par value upon maturity. For example: An investor who purchases a bond at 110, or for $1,100, will receive only $1,000 at maturity, and therefore will lose the difference of $100. This loss is what causes the yield to maturity to be the lowest of the three yields for an investor who purchases a bond at a premium.

YIELD TO MATURITY FOR A DISCOUNT BOND

The yield to maturity for a bond purchased at a discount will be the highest of all of the investor's yields. In this case, the investor has purchased the bond at a price that is less than the par value of the bond. In this example, even though the investor paid less than the par value for the bond, the issuer is still obligated to pay the full par value of the bond at maturity, or the full $1,000. For example: An investor who purchases a bond at 90 or for $900 will still be entitled to receive the full par amount of $1,000 at maturity, therefore gaining $100. This gain is what causes the yield to maturity to be the highest of the three yields for an investor who purchases a bond at a discount.

CALCULATING THE YIELD TO MATURITY

When an investor purchases a bond in the secondary market at a discount, the discount must be accreted over the remaining life of the bond. The accretion of the discount will result in a higher yield to maturity. When an investor purchases a bond in the secondary market at a premium, the premium must be amortized over the remaining life of the bond. The amortization of the premium will result in a lower yield to maturity.

In order to calculate the bonds approximate yield to maturity, use the following formulas:

For a bond purchased at a discount use:

$$\frac{(\text{annual interest} + \text{annualized discount})}{\left(\dfrac{\text{price paid} + \text{par}}{2}\right)}$$

The annualized discount is found by taking the total discount and dividing it by the number of years remaining until maturity. For example, let's assume an investor purchased a 10% bond at $900 with 10 years until maturity. The bonds approximate yield to maturity would be found as follows:

$$\frac{(\$100 + \$10)}{\left(\dfrac{\$900 + \$1,000}{2}\right)}$$

In this case, the bond's approximate yield to maturity is 11.57%.

For a bond purchased at a premium, use:

$$\frac{\text{annual interest} + \text{annualized premium}}{\left(\dfrac{\text{price paid} + \text{PAR}}{2}\right)}$$

The annualized premium is found by taking the total premium and dividing it by the number of years remaining until maturity. For example, let's assume an investor purchased a 10% bond at $1,100 with 10 years until maturity.

The bond's approximate yield to maturity would be found as follows:

$$\frac{(\$100 - \$10)}{\left(\dfrac{\$1{,}100 + \$1{,}000}{2}\right)}$$

In this case, the bond's approximate yield to maturity is 8.57%.

CALCULATING THE YIELD TO CALL

In the event that the bond may be called in or redeemed by the issuer under a call feature an investor may calculate the approximate yield to call by using the approximate number of years left until the bond may be called.

 TAKENOTE!

The yield to call will always extend past the yield to maturity. The yield to call will always be the highest yield on a bond purchased at a discount, and it will always be the lowest yield for a bond purchased at a premium.

YIELD SPREADS

Investors must look at the competing yields that are offered by a wide variety of bonds. The difference in the yields offered by two bonds is known as the yield spread. Many bonds are measured by the relationship between the bond's yield and the yield offered by similar term Treasury securities. This is known as the spread over Treasuries. As perceptions about the issuer and the economy change, yield spreads will change. During times of uncertainty, investors will be less likely to hold more risky debt securities. As a result, the yield spread between Treasuries and more risky corporate debt will widen. An increase in the spread can be seen as an indication that the economy is going to go into a recession and that the issuers of lower quality debt will likely default. Alternatively, a decrease in the spread will be seen as a predictor of an improving economy.

THE REAL INTEREST RATE

Investors must calculate the effect inflation will have on the interest they receive on fixed-income securities. The interest rate received by an investor, before the effects of inflation are considered, is known as the nominal interest rate. The real interest rate is what the investor will receive after inflation is factored in. For example, if an investor is receiving an 8% interest rate on a corporate bond when inflation is running at 2%, the investor's real interest rate would be 6%. The investor's nominal interest rate consists of the real interest rate plus an inflation premium. The inflation premium factors in the expected rate of inflation during various bond maturities.

BOND MATURITIES

When a bond matures, the principal payment and the last semiannual interest payment are due. Corporations will select to issue bonds with the maturity type that best fits their needs, based on the interest rate environment and marketability.

TERM MATURITY

A term bond is the most common type of corporate bond issue. With a term bond, the entire principal amount becomes due on a specific date. For example, if XYZ corporation issued $100,000,000 worth of 8% bonds due on June 1, 2015, the entire $100,000,000 would be due to bondholders on June 1, 2015. On June 1st, bondholders would also receive their last semiannual interest payment and their principal payment.

SERIAL MATURITY

A serial bond issue is one that has a portion of the issue maturing over a series of years. Traditionally, serial bonds have larger portions of the principal maturing in later years. The portion of the bonds maturing in later years will carry a higher yield to maturity because investors who have their money at risk longer will demand a higher interest rate.

BALLOON MATURITY

A balloon issue contains a maturity schedule that repays a portion of the issue's principal over a number of years, just like a serial issue. However, with a balloon maturity the largest portion of the principal amount is due on the last date.

SERIES ISSUE

With a series issue, corporations may elect to spread the issuance of the bonds over a period of several years. This will give the corporation the flexibility to borrow money to meet its goals as its needs change.

TYPES OF CORPORATE BONDS

A corporation will issue or sell bonds as a means to borrow money to help the organization meet its goals. Corporate bonds are divided into two main categories: secured and unsecured.

SECURED BONDS

A secured bond is one that is backed by a specific pledge of assets. The assets that have been pledged become known as collateral for the bond issue or the loan. A trustee will hold the title to the collateral, and in the event of default the bondholders may claim the assets that have been pledged. The trustee will then attempt to sell off the assets in an effort to pay off the bondholders.

MORTGAGE BONDS

A mortgage bond is a bond that has been backed by a pledge of real property. The corporation will issue bonds to investors and the corporation will pledge real estate, owned by the company, as collateral. A mortgage bond works in a similar fashion to a residential mortgage. In the event of default, the bondholders take the property.

EQUIPMENT TRUST CERTIFICATES

An equipment trust certificate is backed by a pledge of large equipment that the corporation owns. Airlines, railroads, and large shipping companies will often borrow money to purchase the equipment that they need through the sale of equipment trust certificates. Airplanes, railroad cars, and ships are all good examples of the types of assets that might be pledged as collateral.

In the event of default, the equipment will be liquidated by the trustee in an effort to pay off the bondholders.

COLLATERAL TRUST CERTIFICATES

A collateral trust certificate is a bond that has been backed by a pledge of securities that the issuer has purchased for investment purposes or by shares of a wholly owned subsidiary. Both stocks and bonds are acceptable forms of collateral as long as another issuer has issued them. Securities that have been pledged as collateral are generally required to be held by the trustee for safekeeping. In the event of a default, the trustee will attempt to liquidate the securities that have been pledged as collateral and divide the proceeds among the bondholders.

It's important to note that while having a specific claim against an asset that has been pledged as collateral benefits the bondholder, bondholders do not want to take title to the collateral. Bondholders invest for the semiannual interest payments and the return of their principal at maturity.

UNSECURED BONDS

Unsecured bonds are known as debentures and have no specific asset pledged as collateral for the loan. Debentures are only backed by the good faith and credit of the issuer. In the event of a default, the holder of a debenture is treated like a general creditor.

SUBORDINATED DEBENTURES

A subordinated debenture is an unsecured loan to the issuer that has a junior claim on the issuer in the event of default relative to the straight debenture. Should the issuer default, the holders of the debentures and other general creditors will be paid before the holders of the subordinate debentures will be paid anything. Interest rates on subordinated debentures tend to be slightly higher than the interest rates on debentures as a result of the lower priority and higher risk.

INCOME/ADJUSTMENT BONDS

Corporations, usually those in severe financial difficulty, issue income or adjustment bonds. The bond is unsecured, and the investor is only promised to be paid interest if the corporation has enough income to do so. As a result of the large risk that the investor is taking, the interest rate is very high and the bonds are issued at a deep discount to par. An income bond is never an appropriate recommendation for an investor seeking income or safety of principal.

ZERO-COUPON BONDS

A zero-coupon bond is a bond that pays no semiannual interest. It is issued at a deep discount from the par value and appreciates up to par at maturity. This appreciation represents the investor's interest for purchasing the bond. Corporations, the U.S. government, and municipalities will all issue zero-coupon bonds in an effort to finance their activities. An investor might be able to purchase the $1,000 principal payment in 20 years for as little as $300 today. Because the zero-coupon bonds pay no semiannual interest and the price is so deeply discounted from par, the price of the bond will be the most sensitive to a change in the interest rates. Both corporate and U.S. government zero-coupon bonds subject the investor to federal income taxes on the annual appreciation of the bond. This is known as phantom income.

GUARANTEED BONDS

A guaranteed bond is a bond whose interest and principal payments are guaranteed by a third party, such as a parent company.

CONVERTIBLE BONDS

A convertible bond is a corporate bond that may be converted or exchanged for common shares of the corporation at a predetermined price known as the conversion price. Convertible bonds have benefits to both the issuer and the investor. Because the bond is convertible, it will usually pay a lower rate of interest than nonconvertible bonds. This lower interest rate can save the corporation an enormous amount of money in interest expense over the life of the issue. The convertible feature will also benefit the investor if the common stock does well. If the shares of the underlying common stock appreciate, the investor could realize significant capital appreciation in the price of the bond and may also elect to convert the bond into common stock in the hopes of realizing additional appreciation. As an investor in the bond, the bondholder maintains a senior position as a creditor while enjoying the potential for capital appreciation.

CONVERTING BONDS INTO COMMON STOCK

All Series 7 candidates must be able to perform the conversion calculations for both convertible bonds and preferred stock. It is essential that perspective representatives are able to determine the following:

Number of shares: To determine the number of shares that can be received upon conversion, use the following formula:

par value/conversion price

 TESTFOCUS!

XYZ has a 7% subordinated debenture trading in the market place at 120. The bonds are convertible into XYZ common stock at $25 per share. How many shares can the investor receive upon conversion?

$1,000/$25 = 40 shares

The investor is entitled to receive 40 shares of XYZ common stock for each bond owned.

Parity Price: A stock's parity price determines the value at which the stock must be priced in order for the value of the common stock to be equal to the value of the bond that the investor already owns. The value of the stock that can be received by the investor upon conversion must be equal to, or at parity with, the value of the bond. Otherwise, converting the bonds into common stock would not make economic sense. Determining parity price is a two-step process. First, one must determine the number of shares that can be received by using the formula: par value/conversion price. Then it is necessary to calculate the price of each share at the parity price. To determine parity price, use the following formula:

$$\frac{\textbf{current market value of the convertible bond}}{\textbf{number of shares to be received}}$$

In the above example, the convertible bond was quoted at 120, which equals a dollar price of $1,200. We determined that the investor could receive 40 shares of stock for each bond so the parity price equals:

$1,200/40 = $30

If the question is looking for the number of shares or the parity price for a convertible preferred stock, the formulas are the same and the only thing that changes is the par value. Par value for all preferred stocks is $100 instead of $1,000 par value for bonds.

ADVANTAGES OF ISSUING CONVERTIBLE BONDS

Only corporations may issue convertible bonds. Some of the advantages of issuing convertible bonds to the company are:

- It makes the issue more marketable.
- It can offer a lower interest rate.
- If the bonds are converted, the debt obligation is eliminated.
- The issuance of the convertible bonds does not immediately dilute ownership or earnings per share.

DISADVANTAGES OF ISSUING CONVERTIBLE BONDS

Some disadvantages to issuing convertible bonds for the company are:

- Reduced leverage upon conversion.
- Conversion causes the loss of tax-deductible interest payments.
- Conversion dilutes shareholder's equity.
- Conversion by a large holder may shift control of the company.

CONVERTIBLE BONDS AND STOCK SPLITS

If a corporation declares a stock split or a stock dividend, the conversion price of the bond will be adjusted accordingly. The trust indenture of a convertible bond will state the maximum number of shares that the corporation may issue while the bonds are outstanding, as well as the minimum price at which the additional shares may be issued.

REVERSE CONVERTIBLE SECURITIES

A corporation may issue a bond or preferred stock that allows the issuer, not the owner, to determine when and if the securities are exchanged or converted into the underlying common shares of the issuer. These reverse convertible features may be exercised at or, after a set date or, in the case of a bond, the issuer may elect to issue shares of common stock as payment in lieu of the cash principal payment due at maturity.

FORCED CONVERSION

When a bond or preferred stock contains both a call feature and a convertible feature the issuer of these securities as a strategic move to extinguish the fixed payments required by these securities may issue a call. In order to force the conversion and eliminate any cash payments certain market conditions must be in place. The key is that the value of the common stock to be received upon conversion must be worth more than the call price being offered by the company. This will traditionally occur when the underlying stock price is trading at a premium to the conversion price.

THE TRUST INDENTURE ACT OF 1939

The Trust Indenture Act of 1939 requires that corporate bond issues in excess of $5,000,000 dollars, that are to be repaid during a term in excess of one year, issue a trust indenture for the issue. The trust indenture is a contract between the issuer and the trustee. The trustee acts on behalf of all of the bondholders and ensures that the issuer is in compliance with all of the promises and covenants made to the bondholders. The trustee is appointed by the corporation and is usually a bank or a trust company. The Trust Indenture Act of 1939 only applies to corporate issuers. Both federal and municipal issuers are exempt.

BOND INDENTURE

Corporate bonds may be issued with either an open-end or closed-end indenture. Bonds issued with an open-end indenture allow the corporation to issue additional bonds secured by the same collateral and whose claim on the collateral is equal to the original issue. A closed-end indenture does not allow the corporation to issue additional bonds having an equal claim on the collateral. If the corporation wants to issue new bonds, its claim must be subordinate to the claim of the original issue or secured by other collateral.

RATINGS CONSIDERATIONS

When the rating agencies assign a rating to a debt issue, they must look at many factors concerning the issuer's financial condition, such as:

- Cash flow
- Total amount and type of debt outstanding
- Ability to meet interest and principal payments
- Collateral
- Industry and economic trends
- Management

S&P and Moody's are the two biggest ratings agencies. In order for a corporation to have its debt rated by one of these agencies, the issuer must request it and pay for the service. One of the main reasons a corporation would want to have its debt rated is because many investors will not purchase bonds that have not been rated. Additionally, if the issuer receives a higher rating, it will be able to sell the bonds with a lower interest rate. When determining the safety of a bond's interest and principal payments the rating carries more weight than the collateral. Collateral is only more important in the case of default or bankruptcy of an issuer.

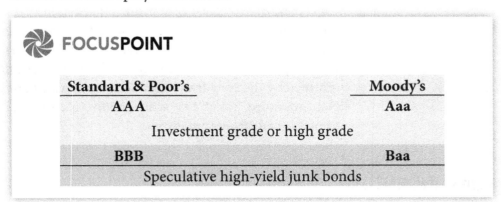

Standard & Poor's	Moody's
AAA	Aaa
Investment grade or high grade	
BBB	Baa
Speculative high-yield junk bonds	

RETIRING CORPORATE BONDS

The retirement of a corporation's debt may occur under any of the following methods:

- Redemption
- Refunding

- Prerefunding
- The exercise of a call feature by the company
- The exercise of a put feature by the investor
- A tender offering
- Open market purchases

REDEMPTION

Bonds are redeemed upon maturity, and the principal amount is repaid to investors. At maturity, investors will also receive their last semiannual interest payment.

REFUNDING

Many times corporations will use the sale of new bonds to pay off the principal of their outstanding bonds. Corporations will issue new bonds to refund their maturing bonds or call the outstanding issue in whole or in part under a call feature. This is known as refunding corporate debt. Refunding corporate debt is very similar to refinancing a home mortgage.

PREREFUNDING

A corporation may seek to take advantage of a low interest rate environment by prerefunding its outstanding bonds prior to being able to retire them under a call feature. The proceeds from the new issue of bonds are placed in an escrow account and invested in government securities. The interest generated in the escrow account is used to pay the debt service of the outstanding or prerefunded issue. The prerefunded issue will be called in by the company on the first call date. Because the prerefunded bonds are now backed by the government securities held in the escrow account, they are automatically rated AAA. Once an issue has been prerefunded, or advance refunded, the issuer's obligations under the indenture are terminated. This is known as defeasance.

CALLING IN BONDS

Many times corporations will attach a call feature to their bonds that will allow them to call in and retire the bonds, either at their discretion or on a set schedule. The call feature gives the corporation the ability to manage the amount of debt outstaying, as well as the ability to take advantage of favorable interest rate environments. Most bonds are not callable in the first several years after issuance. This is known as call protection. A call feature on a bond benefits the company, not the investor. An investor who owns bonds which have been called may sell the bonds in the market prior to the call date. The bonds must clearly be identified as being called at the time of sale and the price received will most likely be a small discount to the call price. The issuer will pay the call price plus accrued interest up to the call date. Accrued interest is the amount of interest earned on the bonds from the time the last interest payment was made by the issuer.

PUTTING BONDS TO THE COMPANY

As a way to make a bond issue more attractive to investors, a company may attach a put feature or put option on its bonds. Under a put option, the holder of the bonds may tender the bonds to the company for redemption. Some put features will allow the bondholders to put the bonds to the company for redemption if their rating falls to low or if interest rates rise significantly. A put option on a bond benefits the bondholder.

TENDER OFFERS

A company may make a tender offer in an effort to reduce its outstanding debt or as a way to take advantage of low interest rates. Tender offers may be made for both callable and noncallable bonds. Companies will usually offer a premium for the bonds in order to make the offer attractive to bondholders.

OPEN MARKET PURCHASES

Issuers, in an effort to reduce the amount of their outstanding debt, may simply repurchase the bonds in the market place.

COLLATERALIZED MORTGAGE OBLIGATION (CMO)

A collateralized mortgage obligation (CMO) is a mortgage-backed security issued by private finance companies, as well as by FHLMC and FNMA. The securities are structured much like a pass-through certificate and their term is set into different maturity schedules, known as tranches. Pools of mortgages on one- to four-family homes collateralize CMOs. Because CMOs are backed by mortgages on real estate, they are considered relatively safe investments and are often given an AAA rating. In addition to rare default risks that the owner of a CMO faces is the risk of early refinance. CMOs pay interest and principal monthly. However, they pay the principal to only one tranche at a time in $1,000 payments. The CMO pays off each tranche until the final tranche, known as a Z tranche, is paid off. The Z tranche is the most volatile CMO tranche.

CMOs AND INTEREST RATES

CMOs, like other interest-bearing investments, will be affected by a change in the interest rate environment. CMOs may experience the following if interest rates change:

- If interest rates fall, homeowners will refinance more quickly, and the investors will be paid off more quickly than they had hoped.
- The rate of principal payments may vary.
- If interest rates rise, refinancing may slow down, and the investors will be paid off more slowly than they had hoped.

Most CMOs have an active secondary market and are considered relatively liquid securities. However, the more complex CMOs may not have an active secondary market and may be considered illiquid. Interest earned by investors from CMOs is taxable at all levels: federal, state, and local.

TYPES OF CMOs

Like many other investments, there are several different types of CMOs. They are:

- Principal only (PO)
- Interest only (IO)
- Planned amortization class (PAC)
- Targeted amortization class (TAC)

PRINCIPAL-ONLY CMOs

Principal-only CMOs, as the name suggests, receive only the principal payments made on the underlying mortgage. Principal-only CMOs receive both the scheduled principal payments as well as any prepayments made by the homeowners in the pool. Because the principal-only CMO does not receive any interest payments, it is sold at a discount to its face value. The appreciation of the CMO, up to its face value represents the investor's return. The price of a principal-only CMO will be sensitive to a change in interest rates. As interest rates fall, the value of the CMO will rise as prepayments accelerate. A rise in interest rates will have the opposite effect.

INTEREST-ONLY CMOs

Interest-only CMOs receive the interest payments made by homeowners in the pool of underlying mortgages. Interest-only CMOs will also sell at a discount to their face value due to the amortization of the underlying mortgages. Interest-only CMOs will increase in value as interest rates rise and decrease in value as interest rates fall as a result of the changes in prepayments on the underlying pool of mortgages. The changes in the prepayments on the underlying mortgages will affect the number of interest payments the holder of the CMO will receive. As interest rates rise, prepayments will slow, thus increasing the number of interest payments the investor receives. The more interest payments the CMO holder receives, the more valuable the CMO becomes.

PLANNED AMORTIZATION CLASS CMO (PAC)

Planned amortization class CMOs (PACs) are paid off first and offer the investor the most protection against prepayment risk and extension risk. If prepayments come in too quickly, those principal payments will be placed into another CMO known as a support class to protect the owner of the PAC from prepayment risk. If principal payments are made more slowly, principal payments will be taken from a support class to protect the investor against extension risk.

TARGETED AMORTIZATION CLASS (TAC)

Targeted amortization class CMOs (TACs) only offer the investor protection from prepayment risk. If principal payments are made more quickly, they will be transferred to a support class. However, if principal payments come in more slowly, payments will not be taken from a support class and will be subject to extension risk.

TAKENOTE!

More complex CMOs are not suitable for all investors and investors should sign a suitability statement before investing. The secondary market for complex CMOs may also be very illiquid.

PRIVATE-LABEL CMOs

Private-label CMOs are issued by investment banks, and the payment of interest and principal payments are the responsibility of the issuing investment bank. The payments due to a holder of a private-label CMO are not guaranteed by any government agency. The credit ratings of the private-label CMOs are based on the collateral that backs the CMO and the credit rating of the issuer. If the private-label CMO uses agency issues as collateral for the CMO, those agency issues still carry the guarantee of the issuing government agency.

 TAKENOTE!

When recommending a CMO to an investor it is important that the CMO never be compared to bonds and CDs. The complex structure of CMOs have a risk and performance profile that greatly differs from these investments.

EXCHANGE-TRADED NOTES (ETNs)

Exchange-traded notes, which are sometimes known as equity-linked notes or index-linked notes, are debt securities that base a maturity payment on the performance of an underlying security or group of securities, such as an index. ETNs do not make coupon or interest payments to investors during the time the investor owns the ETN. ETNs may be purchased and sold at any time during the trading day and may be purchased on margin and sold short. One very important risk factor to consider when evaluating an ETN is the fact that ETNs are unsecured and carry the credit risk of the issuing bank or broker dealer. Similarly, principal-protected notes, or PPNs, which are structured products that guarantee the return of the investor's principal if the note is held until maturity, carry a principal guarantee that is only as good as the issuer's credit rating, and therefore are never 100% guaranteed.

EURO AND YANKEE BONDS

A Eurobond is a bond issued in domestic currency of the issuer but sold outside of the issuer's country. For example if Virgin Plc sold bonds to investors in Japan with the principal and interest payable in British pounds this would be an example of a Eurobond. A Eurobond carries significant currency risk should the value of the foreign currency fall relative to the domestic currency of the purchaser. If the foreign currency fell, the interest and principal payments to be received in the foreign currency would result in the receipt of fewer units of the domestic currency upon conversion. A Eurodollar bond is a bond issued by foreign issuer denominated in U.S. dollars and sold to investors outside of the United States and outside of the issuer's country. Eurodollar bonds are issued in barer form by foreign corporations, federal governments, and municipalities. Eurobonds trade with accrued interest and interest is paid annually. A Yankee bond is similar to a Eurodollar bond except Yankee bonds are dollar denominated bonds issued by a foreign issuer and sold to U.S. investors. If Virgin sold the same bonds to U.S. investors but the bond's interest and principal were dominated in U.S. dollars rather than in British pounds the bonds would be a Yankee bond. The advantage of a Yankee bond over a Eurobond for U.S. investors is that the Yankee bond does not have any currency risk.

VARIABLE RATE SECURITIES

The two main types of variable rate securities are Auction Rate Securities and Variable Rate Demand Obligations (VRDO). Auction Rate Securities are long-term securities that are traded as short-term securities. The interest rate paid will be reset at regularly scheduled auctions for the securities every 7, 28, or 35 days. Investors who buy or who elect to hold the securities will have the interest rate paid on the securities reset to the clearing rate until the next auction. Should the auction fail due to a lack of demand, investors who were looking to sell the securities may not have immediate access to their funds. VRDOs have the interest rate reset at set intervals daily, weekly, or monthly. The interest rate set on the VRDO is set by the dealer to a rate that will allow the instruments to be priced at par. Investors may elect to put the securities back to the issuer or a third party on the reset date. Variable rate securities may be issued as debt securities or as preferred stock offerings.

Pretest

DEBT SECURITIES

1. An investor has purchased 10 corporate bonds at a price of 135. At the end of the day, the bonds are quoted at 136.25. How much have the bonds risen in dollars?

   a. $125

   b. $12.50

   c. $1.25

   d. $.125

2. Which type of bonds require the investor to deposit coupons to receive their interest payments but have the owner's name recorded on the books of the issuer?

   a. Registered bonds

   b. Bearer bonds

   c. Book entry/journal entry bonds

   d. Principal-only bonds

3. In response to a customer's request for information on a private-label CMO, you may inform them of all of the following, EXCEPT:

   a. the securities in the portfolio are all issued by a U.S. agency and carry the same guarantees.

   b. interest payments due to investors are subject to the credit risk of the issuing broker dealer.

   c. if the interest payments in the portfolio are guaranteed by a government agency, the investor's interest payments are equally assured.

   d. private-label CMOs may carry additional risks due to the nature of the issuer's business.

4. Which of the following will be the lowest for an intermediate-term bond purchased at a premium?

   a. YTM

   b. Nominal yield

   c. YTC

   d. Current yield

5. Which bonds are issued as a physical certificate without the owner's name on them and require whoever possesses these bonds to clip the coupons to receive their interest payments and to surrender the bond at maturity in order to receive the principal payment?

   a. Registered bonds

   b. Book entry/journal entry bonds

   c. Principal-only registered bonds

   d. Bearer bonds

6. Which of the following is NOT a reason a corporation would attach a warrant to a bond?

   a. To save money

   b. To make the bond more attractive

   c. To increase the number of shares outstanding when the warrants are exercised

   d. To lower the coupon

7. Which type of bond is secured by real estate?

   a. Real estate trust certificates

   b. Mortgage bonds

   c. Equipment trust certificates

   d. Collateral trust certificates

8. Collateral trust certificates use which of the following as collateral?

   a. Real estate

   b. Mortgage

   c. Stocks and bonds issued by the same company

   d. Stocks and bonds issued by another company

9. An investor holding an 8% subordinated debenture will receive how much at maturity?

   a. $1,000

   b. $1,080

   c. $1,040

   d. Depends on the purchase price

10. An ABC corporate bond is quoted at 110 and is convertible into ABC common at 20 per share. What is the parity price for the stock?

    a. 21

    b. 22

    c. 23

    d. 24

11. An investor buys 10m of 10% corporate bonds with 5 years left to maturity. The investor pays 120 for the bonds. What is the approximate yield to maturity?

    a. 5.45%

    b. 11.1%

    c. 6%

    d. 9.2%

12. XYZ has 8% subordinated debentures trading in the market place at $120. They are convertible into XYZ common stock at $25 per share. What is the parity price of the common stock?

    a. 29

    b. 31

    c. 30

    d. 28

13. An investor would expect to realize the largest capital gain by buying bonds:

    a. that are long term when rates are high.

    b. that are short term when rates are low.

    c. that are short term when rates are high.

    d. that are long term when rates are low.

Government Securities

INTRODUCTION

The U.S. government is the largest issuer of debt. It is also the issuer with the least amount of default risk. Default risk is also known as credit risk, and it is the risk that the issuer will not be able to meet its obligations under the terms of the bond in a timely fashion. The U.S. government issues debt securities with maturities ranging from one month up to 30 years. The Treasury Department issues the securities on behalf of the federal government, and they are a legally binding obligation of the federal government. Interest earned by the investors from U.S. government securities is only taxed at the federal level. The state and local governments do not tax the interest income.

SERIES EE BONDS

The Series EE bonds are commonly known as savings bonds. They are purchased directly from the U.S. government at a discount from their face value, typically 50%. The Series EE bonds pay no semiannual interest and may be redeemed at maturity for the face value. The investor's interest is earned through the bonds appreciation towards the face value. The interest earned through this appreciation is taxable by the federal government, and the investor may pay taxes on this money each year or may wait until the bond matures. The investor may also elect to roll the matured Series EE bonds into Series HH bonds and continue to defer taxes.

SERIES HH BONDS

A Series HH bond may only be purchased by trading in matured Series EE bonds. They may not be purchased for cash. Series HH bonds, unlike EEs, pay semiannual interest and are available in denominations of $500 to $10,000 and mature in 10 years. Series HH bonds may be redeemed at their face value at any time.

TREASURY BILLS, NOTES, AND BONDS

The most widely held U.S. government securities are Treasury bills, notes, and bonds. These direct obligations of the U.S. government range from one month up to 30 years.

PURCHASING TREASURY BILLS

Treasury bills range in maturity from 4 to 52 weeks and are auctioned off by the Treasury Department through a weekly competitive auction. Large banks and broker dealers, known as primary dealers, submit competitive bids or tenders for the bills being sold. The Treasury awards the bills to the bidders who submitted the highest bid and works its way down to lower bids until all of the bills are sold. Treasury bills pay no semiannual interest and are issued at a discount from par. The bill appreciates up to par at maturity, and the appreciation represents the investor's interest. Because bills are priced at a discount from par, a higher dollar price represents a lower interest rate for the purchaser.

All noncompetitive tenders are filled before any competitive tenders are filled. A bidder who submits a noncompetitive tender agrees to accept the average of all the yields accepted by the Treasury and does not try to get the best yield. All competitive tenders are limited to a maximum amount of $500,000. All bids that are accepted and filled by the Treasury are settled in fed funds. Treasury bills range in denominations from $100 up to $1,000,000.

 TAKENOTE!

A quote for a Treasury bill has a bid that appears to be higher than the offer. But remember that the bills are quoted on a discounted yield basis. The higher bid actually represents a lower dollar price than the offer.

EXAMPLE	**Bid**	**Ask**
	2.91	2.75

TREASURY NOTES

Treasury notes are the U.S. government's intermediate-term security and range in term from one year up to 10 years. Treasury notes pay semiannual interest and are auctioned off by the Treasury every four weeks. Treasury notes are issued in denominations ranging from $100 up to $1,000,000 and may be refunded by the government. If a Treasury note is refunded, the government will offer the investor a new Treasury note with a new interest rate and maturity. The investor may always elect to receive the principal payment instead of accepting the new note.

TREASURY BONDS

Treasury bonds are the U.S. government's long-term bonds. Maturities on Treasury bonds range from 10 years up to 30 years. Treasury bonds, like Treasury notes, pay semiannual interest and are issued in denominations ranging from $100 up to $1,000,000. Some Treasury bonds may be called in at par by the Treasury. If the Treasury Department calls in a bond issue, it must give holders four months' notice before calling the bonds.

TREASURY BOND AND NOTE PRICING

Treasury notes and bonds are quoted as a percentage of par. However, unlike their corporate counterparts, Treasury notes and bonds are quoted as a percentage of par down to 32nds of 1%. For example, a Treasury bond quote of 92.02 translates into:

92-2/32% × $1,000 = $920.625

A quote of 98.04 translates into:

98.125% × $1,000 = $981.25

It is important to remember that the number after the decimal points represents 32nds of a percent.

Treasury Security	Type of Interest	Term	Priced
Bill	None	4, 13, 26, 52 weeks 1, 3, 6, 12 months	At a discount from par
Note	Semiannual	1–10 years	As a percentage of par to 32nds of 1%
Bond	Semiannual	10–30 years	As a percentage of par to 32nds of 1%

The minimum denomination for purchasing a Treasury bill, note, or bond from TreasuryDirect.gov is $100. All quotes in the secondary market are based on $1,000 par value.

 TAKENOTE!

The Treasury does not currently sell one-year bills. However, this is a policy decision; the Treasury may at anytime elect to issue one-year bills, just as it has recently decided to reissue 30-year bonds.

TREASURY STRIPS

The term Treasury "STRIPS" stands for Separate Trading of Registered Interest and Principal Securities. The Treasury securities are separated into two parts: a principal payment and semiannual interest payments. A Treasury STRIP is a zero-coupon bond that is backed by U.S. government securities. An investor may purchase the principal payment component of $1,000 due on a future date at a discount. An investor seeking some current income may wish to purchase the semiannual coupon payments due over the term of the Treasury securities. Treasury bills range in denominations from $1,000 up to $1,000,000.

TREASURY RECEIPTS

Treasury receipts are similar to Treasury STRIPS, except that broker dealers and banks create them. Broker dealers and banks will purchase large amounts of Treasury securities, place them in a trust, and sell off the interest and principal payments to different investors.

TREASURY INFLATION-PROTECTED SECURITIES (TIPS)

Treasury inflation-protected securities, or TIPS, offer the investor protection from inflation. The TIPS are sold with a fixed interest rate, and their principal is adjusted semiannually to reflect changes in the consumer price index. During times of inflation, the investor's interest payments will rise, while during times of falling prices, the principal amount of the bond will be adjusted down, and the investor will receive a lower interest payment.

AGENCY ISSUES

The federal government has authorized certain agencies and certain quasi agencies to issue debt securities that are collectively referred to as agency issues. Revenues generated through taxes, fees, and interest income back these agency securities. Investors who purchase agency securities are offered interest rates that generally fall in between the rates offered by similar-term Treasury and corporate securities. Investors who purchase agency issues in the secondary market will be quoted prices for the agency issues that are based on a percentage of par, just like corporate issue.

GOVERNMENT NATIONAL MORTGAGE ASSOCIATION (GNMA)

The Government National Mortgage Association, often referred to as Ginnie Mae, is a wholly owned government corporation and is the only agency whose securities are backed by the full faith and credit of the U.S. government. The purpose of Ginnie Mae is to provide liquidity to the mortgage markets. Ginnie Mae buys up pools of mortgages that have been insured by the Federal Housing Administration (FHA) and the Department of Veteran Affairs (VA). The ownership in these pools of mortgages is then sold off to private investors in the form of pass-through certificates. Investors in Ginnie Mae pass-through certificates receive monthly interest and principal payments based on their investment. As people pay down their mortgages, part of each payment is interest and part of each payment is principal, and both portions flow through to the investor on a monthly basis. The only real risk in owning a Ginnie Mae is the risk of early refinancing. As interest rates in the marketplace fall, people are more likely to refinance their homes and, as a result, investors will not receive the higher interest rates for as long as they had hoped. Ginnie Mae pass-through certificates are issued with a minimum denomination of $1,000, and the interest earned by investors is taxable at all levels: federal, state, and local. Yield quotes on Ginnie Mae's are based on a 12-year prepayment assumption, because most mortgages are repaid early as a result of refinancing, moving, or a homeowner simply paying off the mortgage.

FEDERAL NATIONAL MORTGAGE ASSOCIATION (FNMA)

The Federal National Mortgage Association (FNMA), also known as Fannie Mae, is a public for-profit corporation. Fannie Mae's stock trades publicly, and it is in business to realize a profit by providing mortgage capital. It's called an agency security because Fannie Mae has a credit facility with the government and receives certain favorable tax considerations. Fannie Mae purchases mortgages and, in turn, packages them to create mortgage-backed securities. These mortgage-backed notes are issued in denominations from $5,000 to $1,000,000 and pay interest semiannually. Fannie Mae also issues debentures with a minimum denomination of $10,000 that mature in 3 to 25 years. Interest is paid semiannually, and the interest earned by investors from Fannie Mae securities is taxable at all levels: federal, state, and local.

FEDERAL HOME LOAN MORTGAGE CORPORATION (FHLMC)

The Federal Home Loan Mortgage Corporation (FHLMC), also known as Freddie Mac, is also a publicly traded company in business to earn a profit on its loans. Freddie Mac purchases residential mortgages from lenders and, in turn, packages them into pools and sells off interests in those pools to investors. Interest earned by investors from FHLMC-issued securities is taxable at all levels: federal, state, and local.

FEDERAL FARM CREDIT SYSTEM (FFCS)

The Federal Farm Credit System (FFCS) is a group of privately owned lenders that provide different types of financing for farmers. The FFCS sells off Farm Credit securities in order to obtain the funds to provide to the farmers. The securities are the obligations of all the lenders in the system and are not backed by the U.S. government. The securities pay interest every six months and are only available in book-entry form. There are several lenders that you need to be aware of, and they are:

- Federal Land Bank (provides mortgage money)
- Bank of the Cooperatives (provides money for feed and grain)
- Federal Intermediate Credit Bank (provides money for tractors and equipment)

 TAKENOTE!

Both Fannie Mae and Freddie Mac have been placed in receivership by the U.S. government.

SALLIE MAE

The student loan marketing association better known as Sallie Mae provides capital for student loans for college and other higher education. Sallie Mae will issue discount notes and floating rate securities known as "floaters" with 6 month maturities. Sallie Mae, like Fannie Mae and Freddie Mac, is a publicly traded for profit corporation. Interest paid on these securities is subject to federal income taxes but generally exempt from state income taxes.

Pretest

GOVERNMENT SECURITIES

1. Your customer wants to invest in a conservative income-producing investment and is inquiring about GNMAs. She wants to know the minimum dollar amount required to purchase a pass-through certificate. You should tell her:
   a. $20,000.
   b. $10,000.
   c. there is no minimum; you can invest almost any sum.
   d. $1,000

2. Your customer buys a U.S. Treasury bond at 103.16. How much did he pay for the bond?
   a. $1,031.60
   b. $103.16
   c. $1,035.00
   d. $10,316.00

3. When is the interest on an EE savings bond paid?
   a. When redeemed
   b. Annually
   c. Quarterly
   d. Monthly

4. Which of the following is NOT true regarding Fannie Mae?

   a. It purchases mortgages and packages them to create mortgage-backed securities that pay interest semiannually.

   b. It provides an investment free of federal, state, and local taxes.

   c. It is a public for-profit corporation.

   d. Its purpose is to earn a profit by providing mortgage capital.

5. An investor purchased a Treasury bond at 95.03. How much did he pay for the bond?

   a. $9,530.00

   b. $9,500.9375

   c. $950.9375

   d. $953.00

Municipal Securities

INTRODUCTION

The Municipal Securities Rulemaking Board (MSRB) is the organization responsible for overseeing the municipal securities industry. The MSRB has no enforcement arm; its only function is to write rules and test questions. As a result, the Series 7 exam will contain a fair number of questions relating to municipal securities.

MUNICIPAL BONDS

State and local governments will issue municipal bonds in order to help local governments meet their financial needs. Most municipal bonds are considered to be almost as safe as Treasury securities issued by the federal government. However, unlike the federal government, from time to time an issuer of municipal securities does default. The degree of safety varies from state to state and from municipality to municipality. Municipal securities may be issued by:

- States.
- U.S. territorial possessions, such as Puerto Rico.
- Legally constituted taxing authorities and their agencies.
- Public authorities that supervise ports and mass transit.

TYPES OF MUNICIPAL BONDS

GENERAL OBLIGATION BONDS

General obligation bonds, also known as GOs, are full faith and credit bonds. The bonds are backed by the full faith and credit of the issuer and by its ability to raise and levy taxes. In essence, the bonds are backed by tax revenues. GOs will often be issued to fund projects that benefit the entire community, and the financed projects generally do not produce revenue of any kind. GOs would be issued, for example, to fund a local park, a new school building, or a new police station. GOs that have been issued by the state are backed by income and sales taxes, whereas those that have been issued by local governments or municipalities are backed by property taxes.

VOTER APPROVAL

General obligation bonds are a drain on the tax revenue of the state or municipality that issues them. The amount of general obligation bonds that may be issued must be within certain debt limits and requires voter approval. The maximum amount of general obligation debt that may be issued is known as the statutory debt limit. State and municipal governments may not issue general obligation debt in excess of their statutory limit.

PROPERTY TAXES

General obligation bonds issued at the local level are mostly supported by property tax revenue received from property owners. A property owner's taxes are based on the assessed value of the property, not on its actual market value. Towns will periodically send an assessor to inspect properties and determine what the properties' assessed values are.

EXAMPLE   A homeowner whose home has a market value of $100,000 will not be taxed on the entire market value of the home. If the town uses a 75% assessment rate, the home's assessed value would be $75,000.

OVERLAPPING DEBT

Taxpayers are subject to the taxing authority of various municipal authorities. Municipal debt that is issued by different municipal authorities that draw revenue from the same base of taxpayers is known as overlapping debt or coterminous debt.

EXAMPLE   The county water authority issued bonds that are supported by the property taxes levied in the county. The water authority's debt overlaps the towns' and county's other general obligation debt by drawing support from the same tax revenue. State issues are not included when determining overlapping debt because they are supported by other revenue sources, such as state sales taxes and income taxes.

REVENUE BONDS

A revenue bond is a municipal bond that has been issued to finance a revenue-producing project, such as a toll bridge. The proceeds from the issuance of the bond will construct or repair the facility, and the debt payments will be supported by revenue generated by the facility. Municipal revenue bonds are exempt from The Trust Indenture Act of 1939, but all revenue bonds must have an indenture that spells out the following:

- Rate covenant
- Maintenance covenant
- Additional bond test
- Catastrophe clause
- Call or put features
- Flow of funds
- Outside audit
- Insurance covenant
- Sinking fund

INDUSTRIAL DEVELOPMENT BONDS/ INDUSTRIAL REVENUE BONDS

An industrial revenue bond or an industrial development bond is a municipal bond issued for the benefit of a private corporation. The proceeds from the issuance of the bond will go towards building a facility or purchasing equipment for the corporation. The facility or equipment will then be leased back to the corporation, and the lease payments will support the debt service on the bonds. Interest earned by some high-income earners on industrial development bonds may be subject to the investor's alternative minimum tax. States are limited as to the amount of industrial revenue bonds that may be issued, based on the population of the state.

LEASE RENTAL BONDS

A lease-back arrangement is created when a municipality issues a municipal bond to build a facility for an authority or agency such as a school district. The proceeds of the issue would be used to build the facility that is then leased to the agency, and the lease payments will support the bond's debt service.

SPECIAL TAX BONDS

A special tax bond is issued to meet a specific goal. The bond's debt service is paid only by revenue generated from specific taxes. The debt service on special tax bonds is, in many cases, supported by "sin" taxes, such as taxes on alcohol, tobacco, gasoline, hotel and motel fees, and business licenses. Keep in mind that special tax bonds are revenue bonds, not general obligation bonds.

SPECIAL ASSESSMENT BONDS

A special assessment bond will be issued in order to finance a project that benefits a specific geographic area or portion of a municipality. Sidewalks and reservoirs are examples of projects that may be financed through issuance of special assessment bonds. The homeowners in the area that benefit from the project will be subject to a special tax assessment. The assessment will then be used to support the debt service of the bonds. Homeowners that do not benefit from the project are not subject to the tax assessment.

DOUBLE-BARRELED BONDS

Double-barreled bonds are bonds that have been issued to build or maintain a revenue-producing facility, such as a bridge or a roadway. The initial debt service is supported by the user fees generated by the facility. However, if the revenue generated by the facility is insufficient to support the bond's interest and principal payments, the payments will be supported by the general tax revenue of the state or municipality. The debt service on double-barreled bonds is backed by two sources of revenue. Because the tax revenue of the state or municipality also backs them, revenue bonds are rated and traded like general obligation bonds.

MORAL OBLIGATION BONDS

A moral obligation bond is issued to build or maintain a revenue-producing facility, such as a park or tunnel. If the revenue generated by the facility is insufficient to cover the debt service, the state legislature may vote to allocate tax revenue to cover the shortfall. A moral obligation bond does not require that the state cover any shortfall; it merely gives them the option to. Some reasons why a state may elect to cover a shortfall are:

- To keep a high credit rating on all municipal issues.
- To ensure that interest rates on their municipal issues do not rise.

NEW HOUSING AUTHORITY/ PUBLIC HOUSING AUTHORITY

New housing authority (NHA) and public housing authority (PHA) bonds are issued to build low-income housing. The initial debt service for the bonds is the rental income received from the project's tenants. Should the rental income be insufficient to cover the bond's debt service, the U.S. government will cover any shortfall. Because the payments are guaranteed by the federal government, NHA/PHA bonds are considered to be the safest type of municipal bond. NHA/PHA bonds are not considered to be double-barreled bonds because any shortfall will be covered by the federal government, not the state or municipal government.

SHORT-TERM MUNICIPAL FINANCING

States and municipalities, like other issuers, need to obtain short-term financing to manage their cash flow and will sell both short-term notes and tax-exempt commercial paper. Short-term notes are sold in anticipation of receiving other revenue and are issued an MIG rating by Moody's investor service. The MIG ratings range from 1 to 4, with a rating of MIG 1 being the highest and a rating of MIG 4 being the lowest. The types of short-term notes a state or municipality may issue are:

- Tax anticipation notes (TANs)
- Revenue anticipation notes (RANs)
- Bond anticipation notes (BANs)
- Tax and revenue anticipation notes (TRANs)

Municipal tax-exempt commercial paper matures in 270 days or less and will usually be backed by a line of credit at a bank.

ISSUING MUNICIPAL SECURITIES

Prior to issuing any bonds, a municipal issuer must authorize the issuance of the bonds through a bond resolution and obtain a preliminary legal opinion. The bond resolution authorizes the sale of the bonds and describes the issuer's obligations to the bondholders. The preliminary legal opinion helps to determine how the bonds may be offered.

SELECTING AN UNDERWRITER

Municipal officials cannot effectively tend to their duties and try to find investors to purchase the municipality's debt. As a result, municipal issuers will select an underwriter or a syndicate of underwriters to sell the bonds for them. There are two ways that the issuer may select an underwriter. An underwriter may be selected either through a negotiation with the issuer or through a competitive bidding process. Most revenue bonds are awarded to the underwriter through negotiation. In a negotiated underwriting, the issuer will select the underwriter and negotiate the best terms directly with it. Most general obligation bonds are awarded through competitive bidding. In competitive bidding, the issuer will invite underwriters to bid on the terms of the issue by publishing an official notice of sale in the *Daily Bond Buyer*. The underwriter or syndicate submitting the bid with the lowest net interest cost, or NIC, to the issuer, will be awarded the issue. The official notice of sale will include:

- Description of the issuer.
- Description of the issue.
- Dated date.
- Maturity structure.
- Date and place of sale, including the time of sale.
- Denomination of bonds.
- Call or put provisions.
- Sealed bid or other bidding provisions.
- Amount of good faith deposit required to accompany all bids.
- Name of bond council.
- Paying agent and trustee.
- Expenses allocated to issuer or purchaser.
- Terms of delivery.

- Criteria for awarding the issue.
- Right of rejection.

Interested parties will submit bids based on their ability to market the bonds on behalf of the issuer. The underwriter is trying to provide the issuer with a competitive rate on its bonds while still being able to earn a profit by selling the bonds to investors.

The official notice of sale does not include:

- The yield to maturity (YTM).
- The bond's rating.
- The name of the underwriter.
- The amount of accrued interest.

The municipal issuer prepares a bond contract for the benefit of the underwriter and issuer. The bond contract includes:

- Bond resolution.
- Trust indenture (if any).
- Applicable state and federal laws.
- Any other documentation regarding the issuer.

These documents make up the bond contract, and the issuer is required to adhere to all of the terms and conditions laid out in the various documents.

CREATING A SYNDICATE

Most municipal issues are sold to raise a substantial amount of money. In order to assist with the marketing of the issue and to spread the risk of underwriting the securities, several investment banks will form a syndicate. The syndicate is a group of underwriters responsible for selling the issue. Firms participating in a syndicate, formed to submit a bid in a competitive underwriting, must sign the syndicate letter or syndicate agreement. The syndicate letter will disclose all fees and expenses, including clearing expenses. Syndicate participants in a negotiated underwriting must sign the syndicate letter or syndicate contract. The syndicate agreement will contain:

- Each member's participation in the offering (member's commitment).
- Method of allocating bonds.

- Name of managing underwriter.
- Management fee and spread.
- Member expenses and amount of good faith deposit.
- Liability for unsold bonds.
- Type of syndicate account (eastern or western).

SYNDICATE ACCOUNTS

Each syndicate member is responsible for selling the bonds that have been allocated to it based on its participation. A syndicate member may also be responsible for selling additional bonds if another syndicate member is unable to sell its entire allocation of bonds. There are two types of syndicate accounts: eastern accounts, also known as undivided accounts, and western accounts, also known as divided accounts. In an eastern account, if any bonds remain unsold all of the underwriters must assist in selling the remaining bonds in accordance with their commitment level, regardless of which syndicate member was unable to sell them.

EXAMPLE

Let's assume that there are three investment banks participating in a syndicate to underwrite $10,000,000 worth of municipal bonds. The syndicate account is an eastern account and the investment banks' commitment levels are as follows:

Investment Bank	Commitment Percentage	Dollar Value of Bonds
A	40%	$4,000,000
B	30%	$3,000,000
C	30%	$3,000,000

If investment bank B were only able to sell $2,000,000 of its allocation, the remaining $1,000,000 of bonds would have to be sold by all syndicate members based upon their commitment levels.

The remaining bonds would be allocated as follows:

Investment Bank	Commitment Percentage	Dollar Value of Bonds
A	40%	$400,000
B	30%	$300,000
C	30%	$300,000

Even though investment bank B was responsible for the $1,000,000 of unsold bonds, it would only be required to sell 30% of the remaining bonds, or $300,000 worth, and the other syndicate members must sell the remaining bonds in line with their participation.

In a western account, or a divided account, any unsold bonds are the responsibility of the syndicate member that was unable to sell its allocation. If, in the above example, the syndicate account was a western account, syndicate member B would have to sell all $1,000,000 worth of bonds that it failed to sell originally.

SUBMITTING THE SYNDICATE BID

Syndicate members will engage in a series of meetings in order to determine the terms and conditions of their bid. The syndicate members must determine:

- The underwriter's spread.
- The reoffering yield.
- The prices and yields to be submitted to the issuer.

If all syndicate members cannot agree unanimously on one or more conditions, they must agree to accept the decision of the majority of the syndicate members. Only one bid may be submitted for each syndicate, and it will be submitted by the lead or managing underwriter.

DETERMINING THE REOFFERING YIELD

The syndicate must determine the reoffering yield that will be offered to the investing public. This is known as writing the scale. Most general obligation municipal bonds are issued with a serial maturity that matures over a period of years. The longer-term maturities carry higher yields than the bonds that mature earlier. When the syndicate has determined the prices and yields, it will submit the bid to the issuer, along with the required good faith deposit. All competitive underwritings are done on a firm commitment basis, and the winning syndicate is required to purchase all of the bonds from the issuer, even if it can't sell them to investors.

AWARDING THE ISSUE

Once all bids have been submitted, the issuer and the bond council will meet to determine which syndicate will be awarded the issue. The bid with the lowest net interest cost (NIC) will usually win the issue. The NIC takes into consideration the actual dollar amount of interest that will be paid over the life of the issue. Additionally, if the issuer received a premium for the bonds, the amount of the premium will be deducted from the net interest cost. If, however, the issuer sold the bonds at a discount, the amount of the discount will be added to the overall NIC. An alternative calculation used to award the issue would be based on the true interest cost of the issue, or the TIC. The TIC takes into consideration the time value of the money. Regardless of which method is used to award the issue, the syndicate with the best bid is awarded the issue. The issuer keeps their good faith deposit and returns the others. The manager of unsuccessful syndicates must return the good faith deposits to syndicate members within two business days. The syndicate that submits the second best bid is known as the cover bid and will be awarded the issue in the event the winning syndicate cannot meet its obligations to the issuer. The manager of the winning syndicate will open a syndicate account once the issue has been awarded, and the manager is responsible for its operation and must keep accurate books and records for all account activities.

UNDERWRITER'S COMPENSATION

The difference between the price the underwriters pay for the bonds and the price at which they resell the bonds to the public is known as the spread. The syndicate members divide up the spread according to their different roles and in accordance with their participation in the issue. The spread consist of:

- Management fee
- Underwriting fee
- Additional takedown
- Selling concession

THE MANAGEMENT FEE

The syndicate manager receives a per bond fee for its role as syndicate manager. It receives this fee on all bonds regardless of who sells them.

THE UNDERWRITING FEE

The underwriting fee is the part of the spread that is used to cover underwriting expenses. If any surplus remains after paying all expenses, the syndicate members will split the fee based on their commitment to the underwriting.

THE TOTAL TAKEDOWN

The total takedown is what syndicate members can earn on sales of the bonds to their customers. The total takedown consists of the additional takedown and the selling concession.

THE SELLING CONCESSION

The selling concession may be earned on sales of bonds made by dealers who are not syndicate members. Selling group members may purchase bonds directly from a syndicate member and earn the selling concession on sales to their customers.

$1,000 Price to Investor

Selling Concession $9.00
Additional Takedown $5.00
Underwriting Fee $4.00
Management Fee $2.00

$980 Proceeds to Issuer

 TAKENOTE!

The total takedown in this example is $14 per bond. Syndicate members will purchase the bonds from the syndicate account at $986 and may earn $14 per bond.

ORDER PERIOD

The order period is the time set by the syndicate manager during which orders will be solicited for the bonds. All orders will be filled based upon the order priority agreed to in the syndicate letter and without regard to when the order was received. The order allocation priority is very important, especially when the issue is in high demand and there are more orders than bonds available to fill the orders.

ALLOCATION MUNICIPAL BOND ORDERS

The syndicate manager must establish a method for allocating bonds based upon the priority of orders received by the syndicate. The MSRB requires that this be done in writing, and it is usually detailed in the syndicate agreement, along with the details regarding the sending of confirmations. The method under which the orders will be allocated may not be left to the syndicate manager's discretion. However, there may be circumstances under which the syndicate manager may make exceptions so long as these circumstances are detailed in the syndicate agreement. The syndicate manager must demonstrate its reasons for deviating from the agreed order, if it takes an exception to the agreed upon allocation process.

The syndicate may receive several types of orders:

- Presale orders
- Syndicate or group net orders
- Designated orders
- Member orders
- Member-related orders

PRESALE ORDERS

Presale orders are entered by institutional investors, who agree to purchase the bonds, prior to the bond's pricing and terms being finalized. Presale orders are given the highest priority when allocating bonds to customers. The total spread, less the management fee, is deposited into the syndicate account and is divided up among the syndicate members based on their participation. If any bonds remain after all presale orders are filled, they will be allocated to the syndicate orders.

SYNDICATE ORDERS/GROUP NET ORDERS

A syndicate order is one where the sales credit for the order is shared by members of the syndicate, based on their participation. A member may designate its orders as syndicate orders to give them a better chance of being filled. The entire sales credit, less the management fee, is deposited into the syndicate account. After all syndicate orders are filled, any remaining bonds will be distributed to designated orders.

DESIGNATED ORDERS

A designated order is usually submitted by a syndicate member for the account of a large institution. With a designated order, the large institution will designate which syndicate members and which syndicate member agents receive the sales credit. If any bonds remain, the next orders to be filled are the member orders.

MEMBER ORDERS

Member orders are orders submitted by syndicate members for their own customers. The syndicate member receives all of the sales credit. Member orders are traditionally smaller orders for individual accounts. If there are any bonds remaining, the last type of order to be filled is member-related orders.

MEMBER-RELATED ORDERS

The last type of order to get filled is a member-related order. A member-related order is entered for the benefit of an entity sponsored or controlled by the member, such as a proprietary mutual fund or an UIT.

All municipal securities dealers submitting an order to a syndicate, or to a member of a syndicate, must disclose the capacity in which it is acting in filling the order. The member must also disclose if the order is for the dealer's account or for an account that it controls or sponsors. Syndicate members are also required to state the name of the person for whom the order was entered, as well as the total par value of each maturity.

SALE DATE

Municipal bonds are exempt from the Securities Act of 1933 and are not subject to a cooling-off period. As a result, the bonds may be sold as soon as the issue is awarded. Sales of municipal new issues may begin on the earliest of the following:

- When the syndicate purchases the bonds from the issuer.
- Specified date of sale.
- When the syndicate receives the first order.

WHEN ISSUED CONFIRMATIONS

Because municipal bonds can be sold almost immediately once they are awarded to the syndicate, they will usually be sold before the securities are physically available for delivery. Investors who purchase municipal securities before they are physically available for delivery will receive a "when issued," or initial, confirmation. A when issued confirmation will not include the:

- Settlement date
- Accrued interest
- Total amount due

A when issued confirmation will not include the settlement date because, until the certificates are physically available for delivery, the trade cannot settle. Interest on municipal bonds starts to accrue on the "dated date." It is quite possible that the certificates will not be available for delivery until after the dated date and, as a result, the purchaser of the bonds will owe the issuer accrued interest. Because the amount of accrued interest cannot be calculated, the total amount due cannot be determined.

FINAL CONFIRMATIONS

When the certificates become available for delivery, the syndicate manager gives the syndicate members three business days' notice of the settlement date, and the syndicate members must pay for the bonds in full upon delivery. The syndicate members must send a final confirmation to the purchasers of the municipal bonds on or before completion of the transaction, which is the settlement date. All monies are due from the customer at settlement. The final confirmation shows the:

- Settlement date
- Amount of accrued interest, if any

- Total amount due
- All relevant facts relating to the trade

OTHER TYPES OF MUNICIPAL UNDERWRITINGS

Almost all municipal underwritings are done on a firm commitment basis. However, a municipal securities dealer may accept payments from customers who purchase securities that are part of an all-or-none offering, if the proceeds are escrowed. A dealer may also accept payments for an at-the-market offering, if a separate market for the securities exists outside the one maintained by the syndicate.

SYNDICATE OPERATION AND SETTLEMENT

Once the syndicate manager has settled with the issuer, the syndicate manager has two business days to return the syndicate members' good faith deposits. The syndicate manager must also:

- Send a written summary detailing how orders were allocated among members within two business days of the sale date.
- Register bonds eligible for automated comparison with a registered clearing agency.
- Provide the clearing agency with the coupon rate and settlement date.
- Make final settlement of the syndicate account and distribute all profits within 60 days of the delivery of the securities.
- Provide all syndicate members with a detailed record of the syndicate account.
- Ensure that the miscellaneous expenses detailed in the record of the syndicate account are not excessive in relation to other expenses and the size of the offering.

The syndicate manager must also maintain complete books and records relating to all syndicate business. These records include:

- A description of the securities and the total par value.
- Syndicate members and their commitment levels.
- The terms of the syndicate.

- A list of all orders received.
- A list of all securities allocated and the price at which they were sold.
- Settlement date with the issuer.
- The amount of syndicate member's good faith deposit and when received.
- The date the syndicate account was closed out.

THE OFFICIAL STATEMENT

Municipal bonds are exempt from the registration and prospectus requirements of the Securities Act of 1933. An issuer of municipal bonds is not required to provide investors with any disclosure documents whatsoever. Should the issuer decide to prepare a disclosure document, the issuer will provide investors with the official statement. The official statement will provide investors with all of the details regarding the bonds being issued. Issuers who prepare an official statement must make it available to all purchasers, as well as to any investor or broker dealer who requests one. If the final official statement is not available at the time, a request is made for information. The broker dealer may send the interested party a preliminary official statement. Alternatively, the broker dealer may prepare and forward a summary or an abstract of the official statement. If the issuer decides not to prepare an official statement, purchasers must be informed in writing that no official statement will be prepared. An official statement includes:

- The terms of the offering
- Purpose of the issue
- Summary
- Description of bonds
- Description of the issuer
- Financial data for the issuer
- Regulatory matters
- Feasibility statement
- Legal proceedings
- Type of indenture (open/closed)
- Authorization of bonds
- Security pledged, if any

- Construction plans
- Tax status

All municipal issues offered through negotiated underwritings are required to provide an official statement. The official statement must disclose:

- The underwriting spread.
- The initial offering price for each maturity.
- Any fees received from the issuer.

Prior to the completion of the transaction, the member must disclose the dealer's participation in the offering and any control or other relationship issues between the issuer and the underwriter.

BOND COUNSEL

During an offering of municipal bonds, the issuer will retain legal counsel to represent it in the transaction. The bond counsel will:

- Confirm that the issuer is legally allowed to issue the bonds.
- Confirm that the debt is a legally binding obligation of the issuer.
- Ensure that the issue has been properly announced.
- Ensure that the bond certificates have been legally printed.
- Issue a legal opinion.

THE LEGAL OPINION

The legal opinion is issued by the independent bond counsel. It states that the bonds are a legally binding obligation of the issuer and that the bonds may be legally offered for sale by the issuer. The legal opinion will also attest to the tax treatment of the interest payments received by investors who purchase the municipal bonds. An unqualified legal opinion is the most desirable for investors. An unqualified legal opinion means that the bond counsel has no reservations whatsoever regarding the issue. Should the bond counsel issue a qualified legal opinion, it indicates that there are some concerns regarding one or more of the statements in the legal opinion. The legal opinion must be attached to every municipal bond certificate. The only exception to this is if the bond has been identified as being traded ex legal. A bond could be traded ex legal if a legal opinion was never issued, as is the case with most smaller issues. A municipal bond can also be identified as being ex legal if the legal opinion was lost.

POTENTIAL CONFLICTS OF INTEREST FOR MUNICIPAL BOND UNDERWRITERS

There are many potential conflicts of interest that may come into play when engaging in the underwriting of municipal securities. Some of these require only that they be disclosed. Other more potentially serious types of conflicts require that the underwriter take certain actions to ensure that purchasers of the securities are not adversely affected.

ACTING AS A FINANCIAL ADVISER TO THE ISSUER

Broker dealers will often provide advice to state and local municipalities for a fee. Broker dealers who act as a financial adviser to issuers of municipal securities will provide guidance as to the timing and structure of potential offerings and other financial matters. Any investor who purchases a new municipal issue from a broker dealer with a financial advisory relationship with the issuer must be informed of the relationship in writing prior to the completion of the transaction. Although underwriters will advise issuers on the timing and structure of issues, as well as other financial matters, this does not create a financial advisory relationship. A financial advisory relationship is contractual in nature and must be in writing. The contract will include:

- The terms under which fees will be paid.
- Services to be provided by the broker dealer.
- Use of broker dealer's services.
- Use of services offered by a control party or by a party controlled by the broker dealer.

INFORMATION OBTAINED WHILE ACTING AS A FIDUCIARY

A broker dealer acting in a fiduciary capacity may not use the information obtained in the furtherance of its duties for its own benefit. A municipal securities dealer, acting as a financial adviser to the issuer of municipal securities, may not use the information it obtains regarding current bondholders to solicit business from them. Examples of fiduciary capacities are:

- Financial adviser
- Transfer agent
- Paying agent
- Indenture trustee
- Clearing agent
- Correspondent for another dealer
- Registrar
- Safekeeping agent

ACTING AS A FINANCIAL ADVISER AND AN UNDERWRITER

When a firm acts as both the financial adviser and underwriter to an issuer, potential conflicts of interest arise. The MSRB has set strict rules regarding these situations. The MSRB requires:

- The nature of the financial advisory relationship to be disclosed.
- The amount of the compensation received by the member to be disclosed.
- That prior to entering into a negotiated underwriting, the firm must receive the issuer's consent and must inform the issuer of the potential conflicts and must terminate the advisory relationship.
- The issuer must acknowledge the receipt of the information relating to the conflicts, in writing.
- That prior to submitting a bid for a competitive underwriting the broker dealer must receive the issuer's approval.
- That in the event the broker dealer acts as an underwriter, that all purchasers be informed of the financial advisory relationship.

POLITICAL CONTRIBUTIONS

FINRA enforces the rules enacted by the MSRB for its members that engage in municipal securities business. MSRB Rule G-38 puts strict limits on the amount of political contributions that may be made by a municipal finance professional (MFP). An MFP is an agent who is primarily engaged in any of the following:

- Soliciting municipal underwriting.
- Acting as a financial adviser or consultant.
- Trading or selling municipal securities.
- Providing investment advice or issuing research reports relating to municipal securities to the public.
- Directing supervisors of any agent acting in the above capacity.
- Acting as an executive who oversees municipal dealers or departments.

MFPs may only make political contributions to candidates in an election in which they are eligible to vote. The maximum amount of their contribution is limited to $250 per candidate per election. If an MFP donates more than $250 or makes a contribution to a candidate in an election in which he or she is not able to vote, a violation has occurred, and the employing firm will be banned from engaging in municipal securities business with the issuer for two years. The two-year ban will follow the MFP should the MFP change firms. Both the new firm and the previous employer will be subject to the amount of time that remains on the two-year ban. Should an MFP make a political contribution to an incumbent that would subject the employing firm to a ban, that ban will expire if the incumbent loses the election. This political contribution does not apply to federal elections such as for Senators.

EXAMPLE   If an MFP donated $200 to a mayoral candidate in a district where the MFP does not live and, as a result, could not vote in the election, the employing firm could not underwrite that municipality's debt for two years.

If an MFP contributes more than $250 or contributes to a candidate that he or she is not entitled to vote for, the employing firm must notify the issuer by filing forms G37 and G38 by the last day of the month following the end of each calendar quarter. These forms will tell the issuer:

- The amount of the contribution and the contributor category.
- The name and title of the political official and his or her political party.
- A list of the municipal issuers the firm engages in business with.

If the contribution is in line with MSRB Rule 37, the employing firm is not required to file forms G37 and G38. If an executive officer gives more than $250, the donation must be reported, but the firm would not be banned from engaging in municipal securities business with the issuer. Additionally, if the firm employs consultants to help the firm obtain municipal securities business from issuers, the firm must send forms G37 and G38 to the MSRB at the end of each calendar quarter listing:

- The name of the consultant or company.
- The role in which the consultant is acting and the amount of compensation.
- A list of municipal securities business obtained by using the consultant.
- A copy of all consulting agreements.
- Termination dates for consulting agreements.

The dealer also must disclose information relating to the use of consultants to the issuers. The dealer may disclose the information on an issue-specific basis or on an issuer-specific basis. If the dealer notifies issuers on an issuer basis, the dealer must send issuers updated information annually even if there have been no changes.

MUNICIPAL BOND TRADING

Municipal bonds trade over the counter in the secondary market much like OTC stocks. Municipal bond dealers provide quotes on the bonds that they deal in to other broker dealers. A two-sided market or quote consists of: (1) a bid, which is the price at which the dealer is willing to purchase the securities, and (2) an offer, which is the price at which the dealer is willing to sell the securities. However, unlike most stocks, many municipal bonds are not actively traded in the secondary market. It is not unusual to see a dealer posting a request for a quote on an issue such as "bids wanted" or "offers wanted" for an inactive municipal bond. Most municipal bonds are quoted and traded on a yield to maturity basis. This type of quote is known as a basis quote. Some municipal revenue term bonds are quoted and traded as a percentage of par and are known as dollar bonds.

BONA FIDE QUOTES

All quotations published by a municipal securities dealer must be bona fide, or firm, quotes. That is, the dealer publishing the quote must be willing to buy or sell the bonds at those prices. Firm quotes are based on the dealer's judgment as to the value of the securities and must be reasonably related to the prevailing market. The dealer may also consider their inventory position in the securities and overall market conditions when determining its quote.

INFORMATIONAL QUOTES

A dealer may provide an interested party with a quote that is only offered to inform the inquiring party as to the approximate market conditions for the security. A workable indication would give the inquiring party an idea of where the dealer may be willing to buy or sell the security but it does not obligate the dealer to trade at those prices. A nominal quote is for informational purposes only and does not require that the dealer trade at those prices. Examples of qualifiers that indicate that the dealer is not providing firm quotes are:

- "It looks like"
- "It's around"
- "Last I saw"
- "Subject"
- "Work it out"
- "Nominal"

OUT FIRM QUOTES

Because municipal bonds do not trade as actively as stocks, time is not as crucial as it is when executing an equity transaction. Municipal dealers will often hold firm quotes for a dealer who expresses interest in the bonds. Holding a firm quote is known as an out firm quote.

EXAMPLE   A municipal securities dealer gives a quote to a dealer interested in purchasing the bonds of "6.12% firm for 45 minutes with a 5-minute recall." The municipal dealer is willing to sell the bonds to the purchasing dealer at a yield to maturity of 6.12% and will be willing to do so for 45 minutes. However, if during that 45 minutes another interested party wishes to purchase the same bonds, the second interested buyer will receive a subject quote based upon the fact that the selling dealer is still obligated to sell the securities to the first buyer. The selling dealer will then contact the first buyer and give them 5 minutes' notice to buy the bonds or lose the right to do so at the quoted price. If the first dealer fails to purchase the bonds within the time allowed by the 5-minute recall, the selling dealer may then trade the bonds with the second interested party at 6.12%. Municipal securities dealers may only report trades that actually occur.

EXECUTING A CUSTOMER'S MUNICIPAL BOND ORDERS

A municipal bond dealer may elect to execute a customer's order on either an agency basis and charge a commission or on a principal basis and charge a markup or markdown. A municipal dealer may not act as both an agent and as a principal when executing an order. When a dealer executes a customer's order on an agency basis, some of the factors used to determine a fair and reasonable commission are:

- The availability of the security
- The expense of execution
- The value of the security
- The services offered by the member
- Other fees or consideration received

When executing a customer's order on an agency basis the dealer must make a reasonable effort to get the customer the best price available.

If the member elects to execute the customer's order on a principal basis, some of the factors used to determine the amount of the markup or markdown are:

- The dealer's opinion as to the value of the security.
- The expense of execution.
- The total dollar amount involved.
- The fact that the dealer is entitled to a profit.

Dealers who execute orders on a principal basis do not need to show the amount of the markup on the confirmation.

CUSTOMER CONFIRMATIONS

All customers must receive a written confirmation of each transaction at or before the completion of the transaction. Completion of the transaction is considered to be the settlement date. All confirmations must show:

- Whether the customer bought or sold.
- Trade date.
- Settlement date.
- Extended principal.
- Accrued interest.
- Total amount due or owed.
- Name and phone number of the broker dealer.
- Whether the firm acted as agent or principal.
- The type of securities registration (full or principal only).
- Whether the securities have been called or prerefunded and call date and price.
- Principal denominations other than $1,000 or $5,000 par.
- A statement that the contra party's name will be provided on request for agency transactions.
- The dated date if it affects accrued interest.
- The CUSIP number.
- Whether the bond interest is taxable or subject to AMT.
- Whether the bonds are ex legal.
- Any qualifier that may affect the payment of interest or principal.

CONFIRMATIONS FOR ZERO-COUPON MUNICIPAL BONDS

The confirmation for a zero-coupon municipal bond must reflect an interest rate of zero. The confirmation must also contain a statement that the annual accretion of interest is not reflected.

CONFIRMATIONS FOR MUNICIPAL CMOs

All confirmations for municipal CMOs must contain a statement that the yield to maturity will vary based upon the speed at which payments are received.

The confirmation must also contain a statement that information describing the conditions will be made available upon request.

CONFIRMATIONS FOR VARIABLE RATE MUNICIPAL BONDS

Confirmations for a municipal security issued with a varying interest rate must state that the coupon and yield to maturity will vary.

YIELD DISCLOSURE

An investor purchasing a municipal bond must be informed of the lowest possible yield that may be realized as a result of purchasing the bond. This is sometimes known as the "yield to worst." The lowest possible yield must appear on the confirmation. An investor who purchases a municipal bond at a discount must be shown the yield to maturity, as this will be the lowest possible yield. An investor who purchases a callable bond at a premium must be shown the yield to call, as this will be the lowest possible yield. The yield to call on a bond always extends past its yield to maturity. On a bond purchased at a premium, this will be lower than the yield to maturity because the investor will have fewer years to amortize the premium that has been paid for the bond. Conversely, for a callable bond purchased at a discount, the yield to call will be the highest yield because it will allow the investor to earn the entire discount in a shorter period of time. Municipal bonds purchased as a percentage of par, also known as dollar bonds, must show the price as well as the lowest possible yield.

SOURCES OF MUNICIPAL BOND MARKET INFORMATION

Investors have a number of sources that they may refer to in order to obtain information relating to the municipal bond market. They are:

- The *Daily Bond Buyer*: The *Daily Bond Buyer* is published daily and provides information on new issues of municipal bonds, including official notices of sale; the 30-day visible supply, which is the total par value of municipal bonds being offered for sale in the next 30 days; and the placement ratio, which is the amount of the previous week's offerings that were actually purchased.
- Thomson Muni Market Monitor: Formerly Munifacts, Muni Market Monitor provides secondary market quotes for municipal securities.

- The REVDEX 25: A yield-based index that tracks the health of the revenue bond market. A weekly index of 25 revenue bonds with 30 years to maturity rated A or better. As the index rises, bond prices are falling and yields are rising.
- 40-Bond Index: A daily price-based index composed of 40 GO and revenue bonds. As the index rises, bond prices are rising and yields are falling.
- 20-Bond Index: A weekly index made up of 20 GO bonds with 20 years to maturity rated A or better.
- 11-Bond Index: A weekly index composed of 11 of the 20 bonds from the 20-Bond Index rated AA or better. These yields will always be lower than the yields on the 20-Bond index, because the average quality of the bonds is better.
- *The Blue List:* An industry publication that provides a list of dealers interested in trading particular issues. *The Blue List* will also contain information relating to new public housing authority issues.

RECOMMENDING MUNICIPAL BONDS

MSRB members as well as non-MSRB member broker dealers who recommend municipal bonds to investors are required to ensure that all recommendations are suitable. A suitability determination should be made based upon a review of the investor's:

- Investment objectives
- Tax status
- Finances
- Risk tolerance

Traditionally, municipal bonds will be the most appropriate for higher income earners who are seeking to minimize their tax liabilities. Investors in a low tax bracket will many times be better off in a corporate bond of equal quality.

TAXATION OF MUNICIPAL BONDS

The interest earned by investors from municipal bonds is free from federal income taxes. The doctrine of reciprocal immunity, established by the

Supreme Court in 1895, sets forth that the federal government will not tax the interest earned by investors from municipal securities and that the states will not tax interest earned by investors on federal securities. The decision that established this doctrine was repealed in 1986 and allows for the federal taxation of municipal bond interest. This, however, is highly unlikely.

TAX EQUIVALENT YIELD

It's important for investors to consider the tax implications of investing in municipal bonds. Because the interest earned from municipal bonds is federally tax free, municipal bonds will offer a lower rate than other bonds of similar quality. Even though the rate is oftentimes much lower, the investor may still be better off with the lower rate municipal than with a higher rate corporate bond. Investors in a higher tax bracket will realize a greater benefit from the tax exemption than investors in a lower tax bracket. To determine where an investor would be better off after taxes, you must look to the tax equivalent yield, which is found by using the following formula:

$$\frac{\textbf{tax-free yield}}{\textbf{(100\% − investor's tax bracket)}}$$

For example, let's take an investor considering purchasing a municipal bond with a coupon rate of 7%. The investor is also considering investing in a corporate bond instead. The investor is in the 30% federal tax bracket and wants to determine which bond is going to offer the greatest return after taxes:

tax equivalent yield = 7%/(100% − 30%) = 7%/.7 = 10%

In this example, if the corporate bond of similar quality does not yield more than 10%, then the investor will be better off with the municipal bond. However, if the corporate bond yields more than 10%, the investor will be better off with the corporate bond.

PURCHASING A MUNICIPAL BOND ISSUED IN THE STATE IN WHICH THE INVESTOR RESIDES

If an investor purchases a municipal bond issued within the state in which he or she resides, then the interest earned on the bond will be free from federal, state, and local income taxes.

TRIPLE TAX FREE

Municipal bonds that have been issued by a territory such as Puerto Rico or Guam are given tax-free status for the interest payments from federal, state, and local income taxes.

ORIGINAL ISSUE DISCOUNT (OID) AND SECONDARY MARKET DISCOUNTS

Purchasers of original issue discount (OID) bonds, as well as those that have been purchased in the secondary market, are required to accrete the discount over the number of years remaining to maturity. That is to say, the investors must "step up" their cost base by the annualized discount each year.

EXAMPLE   If an investor purchases a municipal bond in the secondary market at $900 with 10 years remaining to maturity, the investor would be required to step up the cost base each year by the annualized discount. The annualized discount is found by:

total discount
_____
# of years to maturity

$100/10 years = $10 per year

The investor in the above example would have to step up the cost base $10 per year. So in the third year, if the investor sold the bond at $925, the investor would have a $5 loss because the cost base would be $930.

If an investor purchases a municipal bond and sells it at a profit at some time in the future, the capital gain is taxable as ordinary income.

AMORTIZATION OF A MUNICIPAL BOND'S PREMIUM

Investors who purchase municipal bonds at a premium are required to amortize the premium over the number of years remaining to maturity. That is to say, the investor must "step down" the cost base by the annualized premium each year.

EXAMPLE   If an investor purchases a municipal bond in the secondary market at $1,100 with 10 years remaining to maturity, the investor would be required to step down the cost base each year by the annualized premium. The annualized premium is found by:

total premium
_____
# of years to maturity

$100/10 years = $10 per year

The investor in the above example would have to step down the cost base $10 per year. So in the third year, if the investor sold the bond at $1,075, the investor would have a $5 gain because the cost base would be $1,070.

BOND SWAPS

An investor from time to time may wish to sell a bond at a loss for tax purposes. The loss will be realized when the investor sells the bond. The investor may not repurchase the bond, or a bond that is substantially the same, for 30 days after the sale is made. The investor may purchase bonds that differ as to the issuer, the coupon, or maturity, thus creating a bond swap and not a wash sale. A wash sale would result in the loss being disallowed by the IRS, because a bond swap does not affect the investor's ability to claim the loss.

ANALYZING MUNICIPAL BONDS

The quality and safety of municipal bonds vary from issuer to issuer. Investors who purchase municipal securities need to be able to determine the risk that may be associated with a particular issuer or with a particular bond.

ANALYZING GENERAL OBLIGATION BONDS

The quality of a general obligation bond is largely determined by the financial health of the issuing state or municipality. General obligation bonds are supported through the tax revenue that has been received by the issuer. The ability of the issuer to levy and collect tax revenue varies from state to state and from municipality to municipality. It is important that the fundamental health of the issuer be examined before investing in municipal bonds. Just as investors would read a company's financial reports before purchasing its stock or bonds, investors should read a state or municipality's reports before purchasing its bonds.

THE DEBT STATEMENT

Evaluating an issuer's debt statement is an important part of analyzing general obligation bonds. A review of the debt statement will allow the investor to determine the type and amount of debt that the issuer has outstanding. The following can be determined when reviewing the debt statement:

- The total amount of debt
- All types of debt issued
- Estimated full valuation of property
- Assessed value of property
- Assessment percentage
- Estimated population

SELF-SUPPORTING DEBT

Municipal bonds whose debt service is supported through revenue generated by user fees are known as self-supporting debt. For example, a revenue bond that was issued to build a toll bridge would be considered self-supporting debt. Self-supporting debt is not considered a drain on the tax revenue of the issuer because its debt service comes from user fees.

NET DIRECT DEBT

The amount of an issuer's net direct debt is determined by subtracting the self-supporting debt from the issuer's total amount of outstanding debt, including all general obligation issues and short-term notes. Also, the amount of any sinking fund debt is subtracted from the total debt. Sinking fund debt is backed by the cash in the sinking fund. An issuer's net direct debt is determined as follows:

> **total debt issued**
> **− self-supporting debt**
> **− sinking fund debt**
> **net direct debt**

NET TOTAL DEBT

When determining the ability of the issuer to meet its financial obligations an investor must look at all of the issuer's obligations. In many cases, the issuer will be responsible for a portion of overlapping debt. The issuer will be required to pay a portion of the debt service for a bond offering that was issued by another authority based on benefits it receives from the project. By adding the issuer's overlapping debt to their net direct debt, we can determine the issuer's net total debt. To determine the issuer's net total debt, use the following formula:

> **total debt issued**
> **− self-supporting debt**
> **− sinking fund debt**
> **net direct debt**
> **+ overlapping debt**
> **net total debt**

COMMUNITY FACTORS

Certain community factors must be looked at in order to determine the quality of the issuer's financial health. Factors to be considered are:

- Per capita income
- Population trends
- Economic diversity
- Property values
- Fair market values relative to assessed values
- Statutory debt limits
- Retail sales and banking information

SOURCES OF TAX REVENUE

General obligation bonds are backed by the tax revenue of the state or municipality. Sources of tax revenue at the state level are:

- Income taxes
- Sales taxes

Sources of tax revenue at the municipal level are:

- Property taxes/ad valorem taxes
- Fines
- License fees
- Hotel/motel taxes
- Business and franchise taxes
- Personal property taxes
- City income taxes

Property taxes are based on the assessed value of the property, not on its actual market value.

EXAMPLE   A homeowner, whose home has a market value of $200,000, will not be taxed on the entire market value of the home. If the town uses a 75% assessment rate, the home's assessed value would be $150,000.

DETERMINING PROPERTY TAXES

To determine a homeowner's tax liability for the year, you must multiply the assessed value by the millage rate. One mill equals 1/10 of 1%. If the above homeowner lived in a town with a millage rate of 10 mills, the homeowner's tax liability would be determined as follows:

$150,000 assessed value $\times$ 10 mills (millage rate) = $1,500 tax liability

IMPORTANT FINANCIAL RATIOS FOR GENERAL OBLIGATION BONDS

There are certain financial ratios that will help investors determine the ability of the issuer to meet its debt service obligations for general obligation bonds. They are:

- Taxes per capita = total tax revenue/total population
- Debt per capita = net total debt/total population

- Net debt: assessed value = net total debt/total assessed value
- Net debt: estimated value = net total debt/total estimated value
- Collection ratio = tax revenue collected/taxes assessed
- Coverage ratio or times interest earned = debt service/total revenues

The debt service ratio will show how much of a burden debt service is placing on the tax revenue of the issuer, while the debt trend will show whether the issuer's overall debt is increasing or decreasing. It is unlikely that you will be asked to calculate these ratios. It is more likely that you will be asked to recognize what ratios are used to evaluate a general obligation bond.

ANALYZING REVENUE BONDS

The quality of a revenue bond is determined by the ability of the financed facility to generate enough revenue to maintain the facility and to support the bond's debt service. An investor should look at the following when evaluating a revenue bond:

- The economic feasibility of the project
- Competing facilities
- Source of revenue
- Revenue pledge
- Call or put provisions

TYPES OF REVENUE PLEDGE

A revenue bond must spell out exactly how it will allocate the revenue it receives from the facility. A revenue bond may be issued with either a net revenue pledge or with a gross revenue pledge. With a net revenue pledge, the flow of funds is as follows:

- Operation and maintenance
- Debt service account
- Maintenance reserve account
- Renewal and replacement fund
- Surplus account

With a gross revenue pledge, the flow of funds is as follows:

- Debt service account
- Operation and maintenance
- Maintenance reserve account
- Renewal and replacement fund
- Surplus account

A net revenue pledge is actually preferable for the bondholders even though they get paid after the operation and maintenance expenses. If revenue is not sufficient after paying the debt service on a gross revenue pledge, the facility will not be able to be maintained properly and will deteriorate. As the facility deteriorates, fewer people will use it and the revenues will fall further. A bondholder wants the facility to be maintained properly.

MUNICIPAL FUND SECURITIES

State and local governments may create investment trusts or investment pools known as municipal fund securities that are marketed through broker dealers. The most common type of municipal fund securities are educational savings plans, or 529 plans, which are detailed in Chapter 14, and local government investment pools (LGIPs). LGIPs allow state and local governments to manage their cash reserves and to receive money market rates on the funds. LGIPs may also be created to invest the proceeds of a bond offering if the proceeds of the offering are intended to be used to call in an existing bond issue. If the LGIP was created to prerefund an existing issue, additional restrictions will apply as to the type of investments that may be purchased by the pool. LGIPs that are created to manage cash reserves must only invest in securities on the state's legal or approved list. The legal list usually includes investments such as:

- Commercial paper rated in the two highest categories.
- U.S. government and agency debt.
- Bankers' acceptances.
- Repurchase agreements.

- Municipal debt issues within the state.
- Investment company securities.
- Certificates of deposit.
- Savings accounts.

Each state has an investment advisory board that works with the state treasury office to administer the pools. The main objective of these pools is safety of principal, with liquidity and interest income as secondary objectives. The pools require that the following be detailed in writing:

- Delegation of authority to make investments.
- Annual investment activity reports.
- Statement of safekeeping of securities.

Municipal fund securities are not considered to be investment companies and are not required to register under the Investment Company Act of 1940. Additionally, prepaid tuition plans are not considered to be municipal fund securities. LGIP employees who market the plans directly to investors are exempt from MSRB rules; however, if the LGIP is marketed to investors by employees of a broker dealer, the broker dealer and all of its employees are subject to MSRB rules.

MUNICIPAL SECURITIES RULEMAKING BOARD (MSRB)

The Municipal Securities Rulemaking Board, or MSRB, was established by the Securities Acts Amendments of 1975. This established the MSRB as the self-regulatory organization for municipal securities dealers. The MSRB oversees the issuance and trading of municipal securities and requires underwriters and dealers to act ethically in all of their dealings. The MSRB has no enforcement functions; it only writes rules and test questions.

The MSRB's rules are enforced by other agencies, such as:

- FINRA & SEC for non-MSRB member broker dealers
- FDIC for non-national banks that are not FRB members
- FRB for non-national banks that are FRB members
- Office of the Comptroller of the Currency for national banks

The MSRB has laid out general rules that must be adhered to. The general rules are:

G-1 A bank that has a separately identifiable department or division dealing in municipal securities must adhere to MSRB rules and is classified as an MSRB member.

G-2 Sets standards of professional qualification for all firms and agents engaged in municipal securities business. No firm may engage in municipal securities business unless the firm and all associated persons have qualified under MSRB rules.

G-3 Both agents and principals must qualify by exam by passing the Series 7, prior to November 7, 2011, or Series 52 in the case of an agent, or the Series 53 in the case of an MSRB principal, and both must comply with the continuing education requirements. MSRB rules require a 90-day apprenticeship period before agents may engage in transactions with the public.

G-4 Sets rules relating to statutory disqualifications. Both dealers and agents are disqualified from becoming a member of the MSRB if they have been suspended or expelled by any other industry regulator or have been convicted of a securities crime.

G-5 Disciplinary actions by other regulatory agencies such as FINRA or SEC may constitute a violation of MSRB rules as well and may be a cause for action.

G-6 All municipal securities dealers must post a fidelity bond, as required by their SRO, to protect the public from employee dishonesty.

G-7 All municipal securities dealers must maintain information concerning associated persons, including disciplinary actions, and forms U4 and U5.

G-8 Municipal securities dealers must maintain books and records and designate qualified persons to prepare and maintain such records.

G-9 Municipal securities dealers must preserve records for three years total, two years readily accessible. Customer complaints relating to municipal securities must be maintained for six years.

G-10 A municipal securities dealer who receives a written customer complaint must deliver a copy of the investor brochure to that customer and must file the complaint in the complaint file, indicating what action was taken, if any.

G-11 A municipal securities dealer must establish order priority for sales of new issue municipal securities during the underwriting period.

G-12 Establishes uniform practice among dealers for municipal securities transactions.

G-13 Municipal securities dealers who publish quotes relating to municipal securities must only publish bona fide quotes, unless they are clearly indicated as being nominal.

G-14 Municipal securities dealers may only report sales that actually occurred and must report the sale in a timely manner.

G-15 Sets rules relating to confirmation, clearance, and settlement of transactions with customers.

G-16 All municipal securities dealers must have a periodic compliance examination at least every 24 months.

G-17 All municipal securities dealers must deal fairly in the conduct of municipal securities business.

G-18 Municipal securities dealers must make a reasonable effort to obtain the best price when executing customer transactions.

G-19 Municipal securities dealers must ensure the suitability of all recommendations and transactions.

G-20 Municipal securities dealers are limited to gifts and gratuities of $100 per person per year for the employee of another member.

G-21 Municipal securities dealers must be truthful in all advertising.

G-22 Municipal securities dealers must inform clients of any control relationship that exists between the dealer and an issuer of municipal securities.

G-23 Municipal securities dealers must inform customers if they act as a financial adviser to the issuer. If they act as underwriter and financial adviser, they must inform the client in writing and disclose the amount of the compensation received.

G-24 Municipal securities dealers may not use information obtained in fiduciary or agency capacity to solicit business.

G-25 Municipal securities dealers may not improperly use customer assets.

G-26 Municipal securities dealers must cooperate to effect customer account transfers.

G-27 Municipal securities dealers must designate a principal to supervise the activities of the firm and its agents.

G-28 Municipal securities dealers opening an account for the employee of another member must promptly notify the employing member in writing and send duplicate confirmations and statements.

G-29 Every municipal securities dealer must keep a copy of the MSRB Rule Book in each office and must make it available to customers upon request.

G-32 Every purchaser of a new issue of municipal securities must get a copy of the official statement upon delivery of the securities, if one was prepared.

G-33 All municipal securities dealers must calculate accrued interest for municipal bonds that trade "and interest" and must use a 360-day year in the calculation of accrued interest.

G-34 A municipal securities dealer that is the managing underwriter of a new issue of municipal securities must apply for a CUSIP number for the new issue.

G-35 MSRB arbitration rules provide guideline for the settling of disputes between members.

G-36 A municipal securities dealer who is underwriting a new issue of municipal securities must deliver two copies of the official statement to the MSRB.

G-37 A municipal securities dealer may not conduct municipal securities business with an issuer for two years after having made political contributions in excess of $250.

G-38 Municipal securities dealers that engage the services of consultants must have a written contract with the consultant and must disclose the relationship to the MSRB and the issuer.

G-39 All municipal securities dealers conducting telemarketing may only contact noncustomers between the hours of 8 a.m. and 9 p.m. in their time zone.

G-40 All municipal securities dealers shall appoint a principal as a primary electronic mail contact to serve as the official contact person for purposes of electronic mail between the dealer and the MSRB.

G-41 No dealer shall be qualified as an MSRB member unless he or she has complied with the anti-money-laundering compliance program of another agency.

Pretest

MUNICIPAL SECURITIES

1. An MSRB member executes an order for an institutional customer in the marketplace. The customer purchases municipal bonds issued 10 years ago, maturing in 5 years. According to rule G-15, all of the following must be on the customer's confirmation, EXCEPT:

    a. the CUSIP number.

    b. the extended principal.

    c. the type of securities registration.

    d. the legal opinion.

2. A customer in the 30% tax bracket is considering investing in a municipal bond with a current yield of 6%. If the customer were to consider a corporate bond of equal quality, the corporate bond must yield at least:

    a. 8.57%

    b. 7.8%

    c. 9%

    d. 4.2%

3. Trades between two MSRB members must be reported to which of the following?

    a. NSCC

    b. NYSE

    c. FINRA

    d. MSRB

4. A customer of an MSRB member firm must be allowed to review which of the following

   a. Trading records

   b. Commission runs

   c. MSRB Rule Book

   d. Compliance manual

5. A new employee of an MSRB member firm must wait how long before dealing with the public.

   a. 45 days

   b. 30 days

   c. 60 days

   d. 90 days

6. You have purchased municipal bonds whose proceeds have been used to build a new school in your town. The bonds are trading ex legal. What is the most likely reason for this?

   a. The bonds are illegal.

   b. The legal opinion is in doubt.

   c. No legal opinion was obtained.

   d. The legal opinion was lost.

7. A round lot for municipal bonds is:

   a. $10,000 of par value.

   b. $1,000 of par value.

   c. $50,000 of par value.

   d. $100,000 of par value.

8. Why is it important for the investor to consider the tax implications of investing in municipal bonds?

   a. The rate of interest from municipal bonds is higher than other types of bonds.

   b. Investors in higher tax brackets may realize a greater benefit from investing in municipal bonds than investors in a lower tax bracket, because interest is federally tax-free.

   c. The rate of interest is lower in corporate bonds than in municipal bonds.

   d. The investor may earn less interest in other types of securities.

9. When considering investing in a municipal bond, the opinion stating it's a binding obligation of the issuer is issued by the:

    a. MSRB.

    b. bond counsel.

    c. SEC.

    d. governor.

10. Which of the following is the safest type of municipal bond?

    a. GO

    b. Revenue bonds

    c. PHA/NHA

    d. Double-barreled bonds

11. As a municipal bond trader, you call a market maker asking for a quote on a specific municipal bond. The trader responds, "I have them 6.1 bid offered 5.9 out firm." What does this mean?

    a. That is a firm quote, and you may trade at those prices with the market maker immediately.

    b. The dealer is obligated to another party at those prices.

    c. The quote is for informational purposes only.

    d. The trader would have to "go out" to another dealer to get the bonds at those prices.

12. An investor buys 100m of NY 4% GOs due February 1, 2020. The bond is an OID bond. Any capital appreciation at maturity will be:

    a. ordinary income.

    b. a capital gain.

    c. a short swing profit.

    d. subject to the investor's AMT.

13. An investor who purchases a municipal bond at a premium must:

    a. accrete the premium.

    b. amortize the premium.

    c. add it to their cost base over time.

    d. reduce the amount of his or her income by the amount of the premium over time.

14. Which of the following is NOT true of municipal bonds?

    a. If an investor buys a municipal bond issued within the state where he or she resides, the interest is free from federal, state, and local taxes.

    b. If an investor buys a municipal bond and sells it at a profit, the capital gain is taxed as ordinary income.

    c. If an investor buys a municipal bond and sells it at a profit, the capital gain is not taxed federally, but it is taxed by the state and local governments.

    d. If an investor buys a municipal bond issued by a territory such as Guam or the U.S. Virgin Islands, the interest is tax-free on all levels.

15. A syndicate member participating in the underwriting of a municipal issue filling a customer's order will receive:

    a. additional takedown.

    b. syndicate fees only.

    c. total takedown.

    d. the selling concession.

16. Your state is selling municipal bonds to raise money to improve existing toll roads. The underwriting will most likely be awarded to a syndicate:

    a. with the lowest TIC.

    b. through competitive bid.

    c. through negotiation.

    d. with the lowest NIC.

17. An investor is in the 30% tax bracket and invests in a municipal bond that yields 5%. The tax equivalent yield would be:

    a. 7.14%.

    b. 3.84%.

    c. 5.26%.

    d. 9.56%.

18. Of the following, which can issue a municipal bond?

    I. Counties

    II. States

    III. Cities

    IV. Turnpike authorities

    a. I, II, and III

    b. II and III

    c. I only

    d. I, II, III, and IV

19. Regarding a municipal bond underwriting, which of the following is a violation?

    a. An MSRB member that acts as a financial adviser for the issuer submits a competitive bid with the issuer's approval.

    b. An MSRB member that acts as the adviser to the issuer offers the new bonds to a list of current bondholders obtained from the issuer.

    c. An MSRB member who is a financial adviser to an issuer terminates the relationship to submit a negotiated bid.

    d. An MSRB member that had a financial advisory relationship with the issuer discloses its total compensation for a negotiated underwriting.

20. The portion of a county's debt that a city is responsible for is known as:

    a. double-barreled debt.

    b. overlapping debt.

    c. prorated debt.

    d. shared debt.

The Money Market

INTRODUCTION

The money market is a place where issuers go to obtain short-term financing. An issuer who needs funds for a short term, typically under one year, will sell short-term instruments known as money market instruments to obtain the necessary funds. Corporations, municipalities, and the U.S. government will all use the money market to obtain short-term financing.

MONEY MARKET INSTRUMENTS

Money market instruments are highly liquid fixed-income securities issued by governments and corporations with high credit ratings. Because of the high quality of the issuers and because of the short-term maturities, money market instruments are considered very safe.

CORPORATE MONEY MARKET INSTRUMENTS

Both corporations and banks sell money market instruments to obtain short-term financing. These money market instruments issued will include:

- Bankers' acceptances
- Negotiable certificates of deposit
- Commercial paper
- Federal funds loans

- Repurchase agreements
- Reverse repurchase agreements

BANKERS' ACCEPTANCES

In order to facilitate foreign trade (import/export), corporations use bankers' acceptances (BAs). The BA acts like a line of credit or a postdated check. The BA is a time draft that will be cleared by the issuing bank on the day it comes due to whomever presents it for payment. The maturity dates on BAs range from as little as one day to a maximum of 270 days (nine months).

NEGOTIABLE CERTIFICATES OF DEPOSIT

A negotiable certificate of deposit (CD) is a time deposit with a fixed interest rate and a set maturity ranging from 30 days to 10 years or more. A negotiable CD, unlike the traditional CD, may be exchanged or traded between investors. The minimum denomination for a negotiable CD is $100,000. Many negotiable CDs are issued in denominations exceeding $1,000,000, but the FDIC only insures the first $250,000.

COMMERCIAL PAPER

The largest and most creditworthy corporations use commercial paper as a way to obtain short-term funds. Commercial paper is an unsecured promissory note or an IOU issued by the corporation. Corporations will sell commercial paper to finance such things as short-term working capital or to meet their cash needs due to seasonal business cycles. Commercial paper maturities range from one day to a maximum of 270 days. It is issued at a discount to its face value and has an interest rate that is below what a commercial bank would typically charge for the funds. Commercial paper is typically issued in book entry form. There are two types of commercial paper: direct paper and dealer paper. With direct paper, the issuer sells the paper directly to the public without the use of a dealer. Dealer paper is sold to dealers who then resell the paper to investors.

FEDERAL FUND LOANS

Federal fund loans are loans between two large banks that are typically made for short periods of time in amounts of $1,000,000 or more. These loans may be exchanged in the money market between investors.

REPURCHASE AGREEMENTS

A repurchase agreement is a fully collateralized loan made between a dealer and a large institutional investor. These loans are usually collateralized with U.S. government securities that have been sold to the lender. The borrower (seller) agrees to repurchase the securities from the lender at a slightly higher price. The slightly higher price represents the lender's interest.

REVERSE REPURCHASE AGREEMENT

In a reverse repurchase agreement, the institutional investor initiates the transaction by selling the securities to the dealer and agrees to repurchase them at a later time. In a reverse repurchase agreement, the borrower (seller) is the institution, not the dealer.

FIXED VS. OPEN REPURCHASE AGREEMENTS

With a fixed repurchase agreement, the borrower (seller) agrees to repurchase the securities at a fixed price on a specified date. With an open repurchase agreement, the date of the repurchase is not fixed, and the open repurchase agreement becomes a demand note for the lender and may be called in.

 TAKENOTE!

Corporate issues with less than one year remaining to maturity, regardless of the original maturity, may be traded in the money market.

GOVERNMENT MONEY MARKET INSTRUMENTS

The federal government and many of its agencies will go to the money market to obtain short-term funds. Government money market instruments include:

- Treasury bills.
- Treasury and agency securities with less than one year remaining.
- Short-term discount notes issued by government agencies.

MUNICIPAL MONEY MARKET INSTRUMENTS

State and local government will sell securities in the municipal money market to obtain short-term financing. The municipal money market instruments are:

- Bond anticipation notes.
- Tax anticipation notes.
- Revenue anticipation note.
- Tax and revenue anticipation notes.
- Tax-exempt commercial paper.

Government and municipal issues with less than one year to maturity, regardless of the original maturity, may be traded in the money market.

INTERNATIONAL MONEY MARKET INSTRUMENTS

Often large institutions will place U.S. dollars in foreign accounts to earn a higher rate of interest. These dollars being held outside of the United States are known as Eurodollars. A U.S. dollar–denominated account outside of the United States is known as a Eurodollar deposit. These deposits typically have maturities of up to 180 days, and they are traded between large European banks and institutions, much like federal fund loans in the United States.

INTEREST RATES

Interest rates, put simply, are the cost of money. Overall interest rates are determined by the supply and demand for money, along with any upward price movement in the cost of goods and services, known as inflation. There are several key interest rates upon which all other rates depend:

- Discount rate
- Federal funds rate
- Broker call loan rate
- Prime rate

THE DISCOUNT RATE

The discount rate is the interest rate that the Federal Reserve Bank charges on loans to member banks. A bank may borrow money directly from the Federal Reserve by going to the discount window, and the bank will be charged the discount rate. The bank is then free to lend out this money at a higher rate and earn a profit, or it may use these funds to meet a reserve requirement shortfall. Although a bank may borrow money directly from the Federal Reserve, this is discouraged, and the discount rate has become largely symbolic.

FEDERAL FUNDS RATE

The federal funds rate is the rate that member banks charge each other for overnight loans. The federal funds rate is widely watched as an indicator for the direction of short-term interest rates.

BROKER CALL LOAN RATE

The broker call loan rate is the interest rate that banks charge on loans to broker dealers to finance their customers' margin purchases. Many broker dealers will extend credit to their customers to purchase securities on margin. The broker dealers will obtain the money to lend to their customers from the bank, and the loan is callable or payable on demand by the broker dealer.

PRIME RATE

The prime rate is the rate that banks charge their largest and most creditworthy corporate customers on loans. The prime rate has lost a lot of its significance in recent years because mortgage lenders are now basing their rates on other rates, such as the 10-year Treasury note. The prime rate is, however, very important for consumer spending, because most credit card interest rates are based on prime plus a margin.

LONDON INTERBANK OFFERED RATE/LIBOR

LIBOR is the most widely used measure of short term interested rates around the world. The LIBOR rate is the market-driven interest rate charged by and between financial institutions similar to the fed funds rate in the United States. LIBOR loans range from one day to one year and the rate is calculated by the British Banker's Association in a variety of currencies including euros, U.S. dollars and yen.

Pretest

THE MONEY MARKET

1. Which of the following is NOT a corporate money market instrument?
   a. Negotiable certificates of deposit
   b. Treasury bills
   c. Federal funds
   d. Commercial paper

2. Which of the following is NOT true of money market instruments?
   a. They are highly liquid fixed-income securities.
   b. They are issued by corporations with high credit ratings, and are thus considered safe.
   c. They are considered risky because of the short-term maturities.
   d. They are a method used to obtain short-term financing.

3. The money market is a place where issuers go to:
   a. obtain long-term financing.
   b. obtain short-term financing.
   c. offer higher interest rates for a higher yield.
   d. exchange money market instruments to their mutual benefit.

4. Which of the following could trade in the money market?
   a. Short-term equity
   b. Newly issued corporate bonds
   c. Newly issued options contracts
   d. A Treasury note issued nine years ago

5. Which of the following may always trade in the money market?
   a. T bond
   b. T note
   c. ADR
   d. Bankers' acceptance

6. The maximum duration for a piece of commercial paper is:
   a. 45 days.
   b. 10 years.
   c. 1 year.
   d. 9 months.

Economic Fundamentals

INTRODUCTION

Economics, put simply, is the study of shortages—supply versus demand. As the demand for a product or service rises, the price of those products or services will also tend to rise. Alternatively, if the provider of those goods or services tries to flood the market with those goods or services, the price will tend to decline as the supply outpaces the demand. The supply and demand model works for all goods and services, including stocks, bonds, real estate, and money. Series 7 candidates will see a fair number of questions on economics.

GROSS DOMESTIC PRODUCT (GDP)

A country's gross domestic product, or GDP, measures the overall health of a nation's economy. The GDP is defined as the value of all goods and services produced in a country, including consumption, investments, government spending, and exports minus imports during a given year.

Economists chart the health of the economy by measuring the country's GDP and by monitoring supply and demand models, along with the nation's business cycle. A country's economy is always in flux. Periods of increasing output are always followed by periods of falling output. The business cycle has four distinct stages:

1. Expansion
2. Peak

3. Contraction

4. Trough

EXPANSION

During an expansionary phase, an economy will see an increase in overall business activity and output. Corporate sales, manufacturing output, wages, and savings will all increase while the economy is expanding or growing. An economy cannot continue to grow indefinitely, and GDP will top out at the peak in the business cycle. An economic expansion is characterized by:

- Increasing GDP
- Rising consumer demand
- Rising stock market
- Rising production
- Rising real estate prices

PEAK

As the economy tops out, the GDP reaches its maximum output for this cycle as wages, manufacturing, and savings all peak.

CONTRACTION

During a contraction, GDP falls, along with productivity, wages, and savings. Unemployment begins to rise, the stock market begins to fall, and corporate profits decline as inventories rise.

TROUGH

The economy bottoms out in the trough as GDP hits its lowest level for the cycle. As GDP bottoms out, unemployment reaches its highest level, wages bottom out, and savings bottom out. The economy is now poised to enter a new expansionary phase and start the cycle all over again.

RECESSION

A recession is defined as a period of declining GDP that lasts at least six months or two quarters. Recessions may vary in degree of severity and in duration. Extended recessions may last up to 18 months and may be accompanied by steep down turns in economic output. In the most severe recessions falling prices erode businesses' pricing power, margins, and profits as deflation takes hold. Recessions are generally triggered by an overall decrease in spending by businesses and consumers. As businesses and consumers pull back spending overall demand falls. Businesses and consumers will often reduce spending as a cautionary measure in response to an economic event or shock such as a financial crises or the busting of a bubble in an inflated asset class such as real estate or the stock market.

DEPRESSION

A depression is characterized by a decline in GDP that lasts at least 18 months or six consecutive quarters. GDP often falls by 10% or more during a depression. A depression is the most severe type of recession and is accompanied by extremely high levels of unemployment and frozen credit markets. The steep fall in demand is more likely to lead to deflation during a depression.

ECONOMIC INDICATORS

There are various economic activities that one can look at to try to identify where the economy is in the business cycle. An individual can also use these economic indicators as a way to try and predict the direction of the economy in the future. The three types of economic indicators are:

1. Leading indicators
2. Coincident indicators
3. Lagging indicators

LEADING INDICATORS

Leading indicators are business conditions that change prior to a change in the overall economy. These indicators can be used as a gauge for the future direction of the economy. Leading indicators include:

- Building permits.
- Stock market prices.
- Money supply (M2).
- New orders for consumer goods.
- Average weekly initial claims in unemployment.
- Changes in raw material prices.
- Changes in consumer or business borrowing.
- Average work week for manufacturing.
- Changes in inventories of durable goods.

COINCIDENT INDICATORS

Changes in the economy cause an immediate change in the activity level of coincident indicators. As the business cycle changes, the level of activity in coincident indicators can confirm where the economy is. Coincident indicators include:

- GDP
- Industrial production
- Personal income
- Employment
- Average number of hours worked
- Manufacturing and trade sales
- Nonagricultural employment

LAGGING INDICATORS

Lagging indicators will only change after the state of the economy has changed direction. Lagging indicators can be used to confirm the new direction of the economy. Lagging indicators include:

- Average duration of unemployment
- Corporate profits

- Labor costs
- Consumer debt levels
- Commercial and industrial loans
- Business loans

SCHOOLS OF ECONOMIC THOUGHT

The study of economics is a social science with many different schools of thought. Economics has been referred to as the dismal science as it is largely focused on the study of shortages. Economists all generally believe that low inflation and low unemployment are signs of a healthy economy. However, the different schools of economic thought believe that economic prosperity can be restored or maintained through very different approaches.

CLASSICAL ECONOMICS

The classical economic theory also known as supply side economics believes that lower taxes, and less government regulation will stimulate growth and increase demand through higher employment. Less regulation of business creates lower barriers to entry for employers and allows employers to produce goods at lower prices and to create more jobs. As a result of the lower prices, lower taxes, and higher employment, aggregate demand in the economy will increase positively impacting the nation's gross domestic product.

KEYNESIAN ECONOMICS

John Maynard Keynes first published his theories on economics in 1936 during the great deprecation. The Keynesian Economic model believes that a mixed economy based on private and public sector efforts would produce desired economic conditions. Keynesians believe that the decisions made in the private sector can lead to supply and demand imbalances and also that an active policy response from the public sector in the form of government spending (fiscal policy) and adjustments to the money supply (monetary policy) is required.

THE MONETARISTS

Economists who subscribe to monetary economics believe that the supply of money in the economy can influence the direction of the economy and prices as a whole. During times of low demand and high unemployment the economy can be stimulated by increasing the money supply. As more money enters the system interest rates fall increasing demand. As more money enters the system the value of the currency tends to decline and during times of expansionary monetary policy inflation may increase. Milton Friedman the founder of the monetarist movement believed that the main focus of central banks should be on price stability.

ECONOMIC POLICY

The government has two tools that it can use to try to influence the direction of the economy. Monetary policy, which is controlled by the Federal Reserve Board, determines the nation's money supply, whereas fiscal policy is controlled by the President and Congress and determines government spending and taxation.

TOOLS OF THE FEDERAL RESERVE BOARD

The Federal Reserve Board will try to steer the economy through the business cycle by adjusting the level of money supply and interest rates. The Fed may:

- Change the reserve requirement for member banks.
- Change the discount rate charged to member banks.
- Set target rates for federal fund loans.
- Buy and sell U.S. government securities through open market operations.
- Change the amount of money in circulation.
- Use moral suasion.

RESERVE REQUIREMENT

Member banks must keep a percentage of their depositors' assets in an account with the Federal Reserve. This is known as the reserve requirement. The reserve requirement is intended to ensure that all banks maintain a certain level of liquidity. Banks are in business to earn a profit by lending money. As the bank accepts accounts from depositors, it pays them interest on their money. The bank, in turn, takes the depositors' money and loans it out at higher rates, earning the difference. If the Fed wanted to stimulate the economy, it might reduce the reserve requirement for the banks, which would allow the banks to lend more. By making more money available to borrowers, interest rates will fall, and, therefore, demand will increase, helping to stimulate the economy. If the Fed wanted to slow down the economy, it might increase the reserve requirement. The increased requirement would make less money available to borrowers. Interest rates would rise as a result, and the demand for goods and services would slow down. Changing the reserve requirement is the least used Fed tool.

CHANGING THE DISCOUNT RATE

The Federal Reserve Board may change the discount rate in an effort to guide the economy through the business cycle. Remember that the discount rate is the rate that the Fed charges member banks on loans. This rate is highly symbolic, but as the Fed changes the discount rate all other interest rates change with it. If the Fed wanted to stimulate the economy, it would reduce the discount rate. As the discount rate falls, all other interest rates fall with it, decreasing the cost of money. The lower interest rate should encourage borrowing and demand to help stimulate the economy. If the Fed wanted to slow the economy down, it would increase the discount rate. As the discount rate increases, all other rates go up with it, raising the cost of borrowing. As the cost of borrowing increases, demand and the economy slow down.

FEDERAL OPEN MARKET COMMITTEE

The Federal Open Market Committee (FOMC) is the Fed's most flexible tool. The FOMC will buy and sell U.S. government securities in the secondary market through open market operations in order to control the money supply. If the Fed wants to stimulate the economy and reduce rates, it will buy government securities. When the Fed buys the securities, money is instantly sent into the banking system. As the money flows into the banks, more money is available to lend. Because there is more money available, interest rates will go down, and borrowing and demand should increase to stimulate the economy. If the Fed wants to slow the economy down, it will sell U.S.

government securities. When the Fed sells the securities, money flows from the banks and into the Fed, thus reducing the money supply. Because there is less money available to be loaned out, interest rates will increase, slowing borrowing and demand. This will have a cooling effect on the economy. The FOMC also issues statements that can "jawbone" investors to take certain actions and sets a benchmark for what it believes the Fed funds rate should be. However, the marketplace is the ultimate factor in setting the Fed funds rate.

MONEY SUPPLY

Prior to determining an appropriate economic policy, economists must have an idea of the amount of money that is in circulation, along with the amount of other types of assets that will provide access to cash. Economists gauge the money supply using three measures. They are:

- M1
- M2
- M3

M1
M1 is the largest and most liquid measure of the nation's money supply. It includes:

- Cash
- Demand deposits (checking accounts)

M2
M2 includes all the measures in M1 plus:

- Money market instruments.
- Time deposits of less than $100,000.
- Negotiable CDs exceeding $100,000.
- Overnight repurchase agreements.

M3
M3 includes all of the measures in M1 and M2 plus:

- Time deposits greater than $100,000.
- Repurchase agreements with maturities greater than one day.

DISINTERMEDIATION

Disintermediation occurs when people take their money out of low-yielding accounts offered by financial intermediaries or banks and invest money in higher yielding investments.

MORAL SUASION

The Federal Reserve Board will often use moral suasion as a way to influence the economy. The Fed is very powerful and very closely watched. By simply implying or expressing its views on the economy it can slightly influence the economy.

Monetarists believe that a well-managed money supply, with an increasing bias, will produce price stability and will promote the overall economic health of the economy. Milton Friedman is believed to be the founder of the monetarist movement.

FISCAL POLICY

Fiscal policy is controlled by the President and Congress and determines how they manage the budget and government expenditures to help steer the economy through the business cycle. Fiscal policy may change the levels of:

- Federal spending.
- Federal taxation.
- Creation or use of federal budget deficits or surpluses.

Fiscal policy assumes that the government can influence the economy by adjusting its level of spending and taxation. If the government wanted to stimulate the economy, it could increase spending. The assumption here is that as the government spends more it will increase aggregate demand and, therefore, productivity. Additionally, if the government wanted to stimulate the economy, it could reduce the level of taxation. As the government reduces taxes, it leaves a larger portion of earnings for the consumers and businesses to spend. This should also have a positive impact on aggregate demand. Alternatively, if the government wanted to slow down the economy, it could reduce spending to lower the level of aggregate demand or raise taxes to reduce demand by taking money out of the hands of the consumers. John Maynard Keynes believed that it was the duty of the government to be involved with controlling the direction of the economy and the nation's overall economic health.

Both the Federal Reserve Board and the federal government monitor the overall health of the U.S. economy. In doing so, they look at various indicators, including the:

- Consumer price index
- Inflation/deflation
- Real GDP

CONSUMER PRICE INDEX (CPI)

The consumer price index (CPI) is made up of a basket of goods and services that consumers most often use in their daily lives. The CPI is used to measure the rate of change in overall prices. A CPI that is rising would indicate that prices are going up and that inflation is present. A falling CPI would indicate that prices are falling and that deflation is present.

INFLATION/DEFLATION

Inflation is the persistent increase in prices, while deflation is the persistent decrease in prices. Both economic conditions can harm a county's economy. Inflation will eat away at the purchasing power of the dollar and results in higher prices for goods and services. Deflation will erode corporate profits as weak demand in the market place drives prices for goods and services lower.

REAL GDP

Real GDP is adjusted for the effects of inflation or deflation over time. GDP is measured in constant dollars so that the gain or loss of the dollar's purchasing power will not show up as a change in the overall productivity of the economy.

Both monetary policy and fiscal policy have a major effect on the stock market as a whole.

The following are bullish for the stock market:

- Falling interest rates
- Increasing money supply
- Increasing government spending
- Falling taxes

The following are bearish for the stock market:

- Increasing taxes
- Increasing interest rates
- Falling government spending
- Falling money supply

INTERNATIONAL MONETARY CONSIDERATIONS

The world has become a global marketplace. Each country's economy is affected to some degree by the economies of other countries. Currency values relative to other currencies will impact a country's international trade and the balance of payments. The amount of another country's currency that may be received for a country's domestic currency is known as the exchange rate. The balance of payments measures the net inflow (surplus) or outflow (deficit) of money. The largest component of the balance of payments is the balance of trade. When a country sells its goods abroad it creates a credit to the country's balance of trade account when a country imports goods from abroad that creates a debit in the country's balance of trade account. As exchange rates fluctuate, one country's goods may become more expensive, while another county's goods become less expensive. A weak currency benefits exporters, while a strong currency benefits importers. Foreign investment also impacts a country's balance of payments. When a corporation in one country invests in a foreign country to build a plant the country where that plaint is built would realize a credit to its balance of payments account. The country where the corporation is domiciled would realize a debit to its balance of payments account.

YIELD CURVE ANALYSIS

Economists and investors may analyze both the cost of borrowed funds given various maturities and the general health of the economy by looking at the shape of the yield curve. With a normal, ascending, positive or upward slopping yield curve the level of interest rates increase as the term of the maturity increases. Simply put lenders are going to demand higher interest rates on longer term loans. The longer the lenders have to wait to be repaid and the longer their money is at risk the higher the level of compensation (interest) required to make the loan. Higher interest rates also compensate the lenders for the time value of money. The dollars received in 10, 20, or 30 years will be worth less than the value of the dollars loaned to borrowers today. An upward slopping curve is present during time of economic prosperity and depicts the expectation of increased interest rates in the future. The yield curve will also graphically demonstrate investor's expectations about inflation. The higher the expectations are for inflation the higher the level of corresponding interest rates for the period of high inflation. Occasionally the yield curve may become inverted, negative, or downward slopping during times when demand for short term funds are running much higher than the demand for longer term loans or in times where the federal reserve board has increased short term rates to combat an economy that is growing too quickly and threatening long term price stability. With an inverted yield curve interest rates on short term loans far exceed the interest rates on longer term loans. An inverted yield curve tends to normalize quickly and is often a precursor to a recession. The yield curve may also flatten out when the interest rates for both short term and long term loans are approximately equal to one another.

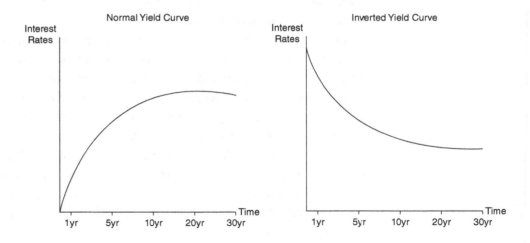

Pretest

ECONOMIC FUNDAMENTALS

1. During an inflationary period, the price of which of the following will fall the most?

   a. Preferred stock

   b. Treasury bills

   c. Treasury bonds

   d. Common stock

2. All of the following are bullish for the stock market, EXCEPT:

   a. falling taxes.

   b. increasing government spending.

   c. increasing the money supply.

   d. increasing interest rates.

3. According to economic theory, which of the following is NOT true?

   a. As supply rises, price tends to fall.

   b. As supply rises, price tends to rise.

   c. A moderately increasing money supply promotes price stability.

   d. As demand rises, price tends to rise.

4. Which one of the following interest rates is controlled by the Federal Reserve Board?

    a. Prime rate

    b. Federal funds rate

    c. Broker call loan rate

    d. Discount rate

5. Which of the following does NOT indicate a downturn in the business cycle?

    a. Rising inventories

    b. High consumer debt

    c. Falling inventories

    d. Falling stock prices

6. A bank that is unable to meet its reserve requirement could borrow money from another bank and pay the:

    a. federal funds rate.

    b. broker call loan rate.

    c. prime rate.

    d. discount rate.

7. What two tools does the U.S. government use to try to influence the direction of the economy?

    a. Monetary policy and fiscal policy

    b. Prime rate policy and fiscal policy

    c. Monetary policy and prime rate policy

    d. Fiscal policy and money market policy

8. Fiscal policy is controlled by which of the following?

    I. President

    II. FOMC

    III. Congress

    IV. FRB

    a. I and IV

    b. I and II

    c. II and IV

    d. I and III

9. The Federal Reserve board sets all of the following, EXCEPT:

    a. monetary policy.

    b. the reserve requirement.

    c. government spending.

    d. the discount rate.

10. A decline in the GDP must last at least how long to be considered a recession?

    a. Two quarters

    b. One quarter

    c. Six quarters

    d. Four quarters

Options

INTRODUCTION

An option is a contract between two parties that determines the time and price at which a stock may be bought or sold. The two parties to the contract are the buyer and the seller. The buyer of the option pays money, known as the option's premium, to the seller. For this premium, the buyer obtains a right to buy or sell the stock, depending on what type of option is involved in the transaction. Because the seller received the premium from the buyer, it now has an obligation to perform under that contract. Depending on the option involved, the seller may have an obligation to buy or sell the stock. Series 7 candidates can expect to see a large number of questions on options. Most of these questions will be on equity options. The remaining questions will cover nonequity options. We will begin with equity options.

OPTION CLASSIFICATION

Options are classified as to their type, class, and series. There are two types of options: calls and puts.

CALL OPTIONS

A call option gives the buyer the right to buy, or to "call," the stock from the option seller at a specific price for a certain period of time. The sale of a call option obligates the seller to deliver or sell that stock to the buyer at that specific price for a certain period of time.

PUT OPTIONS

A put option gives the buyer the right to sell, or to "put," the stock to the seller at a specific price for a certain period of time. The sale of a put option obligates the seller to buy the stock from the buyer at that specific price for a certain period of time.

OPTION CLASSES

An option class consists of all options of the same type for the same underlying stock. For example, all XYZ calls would be one class of options and all XYZ puts would be another class of option.

Class 1	Class 2
XYZ June 50 Calls	XYZ June 50 Puts
XYZ June 55 Calls	XYZ June 55 Puts
XYZ July 50 Calls	XYZ July 50 Puts
XYZ July 55 Calls	XYZ July 55 Puts
XYZ August 50 Calls	XYZ August 50 Puts

OPTION SERIES

An option series is the most specific classification of options and consists of only options of the same class with the same exercise price and expiration month. For example, all XYZ June 50 calls would be one series of options, and all XYZ June 55 calls would be another series of options.

BULLISH VS. BEARISH

BULLISH

Investors who believe that a stock price will increase over time are said to be bullish. Investors who buy calls are bullish on the underlying stock. That is, they believe that the stock price will rise and they have paid for the right to purchase the stock at a specific price, known as the exercise price or strike price. An investor who has sold puts is also considered to be bullish on the stock. The seller of a put has an obligation to buy the stock and, therefore, believes that the stock price will rise.

BEARISH

Investors who believe that a stock price will decline are said to be bearish. The seller of a call has an obligation to sell the stock to the purchaser at a specified price and believes that the stock price will fall and is therefore bearish. The buyer of a put wants the price to drop so that the stock can be sold at a higher price to the seller of the put contract. These investors are also considered to be bearish on the stock.

	Calls	Puts
Buyers	Bullish Have right to buy stock, want stock price to rise	Bearish Have right to sell stock, want stock price to fall
Sellers	Bearish Have obligation to sell stock, want stock price to fall	Bullish Have obligation to buy stock, want stock price to rise

Buyer vs. Seller

Buyer		Seller
Owner Long	**Known as**	Writer Short
Rights	**Has**	Obligations
Maximum speculative profit	**Objective**	Premium income
With an opening purchase	**Enters the contract**	With an opening sale
Exercise	**Wants the option to**	Expire

POSSIBLE OUTCOMES FOR AN OPTION

EXERCISED

If the option is exercised, the buyer has elected to exercise the right to buy or sell the stock, depending on the type of option involved. Exercising an option obligates the seller to perform under the contract.

SOLD

Most individual investors will elect to sell their rights to another investor rather than exercise their rights. The investor who buys the option from them will acquire all the rights of the original purchaser.

EXPIRE

If the option expires, the buyer has elected not to exercise the right, and the seller of the option is relieved of the obligation to perform.

EXERCISE PRICE

The exercise price is the price at which an option buyer may buy or sell the underlying stock, depending on the type of option involved in the transaction. The exercise price is also known as the strike price.

CHARACTERISTICS OF ALL OPTIONS

All standardized option contracts are issued and their performance is guaranteed by the Options Clearing Corporation (OCC). Standardized options trade on the exchanges, such as the Chicago Board Options Exchange and the American Stock Exchange.

All option contracts are for one round lot of the underlying stock or 100 shares. To determine the amount that an investor either paid or received for the contract take the premium and multiply it by 100. If an investor paid $4 for 1 KLM August 70 call, the investor paid $400 for the right to buy 100 shares of KLM at $70 per share until August. If another investor paid $2 for 1 JTJ May 50 put, the investor paid $200 for the right to sell 100 shares of JTJ at $50 until May.

MANAGING AN OPTION POSITION

In an option trade, both the buyer and seller establish the position with an opening transaction. The buyer has an opening purchase, and the seller has an opening sale. To exit the option position, an investor must "close out" the position. The buyer of the option may exit a position through:

- A closing sale.
- Exercising the option.
- Allowing the option to expire.

The seller of an option may exit or close out a position through:

- A closing purchase.
- Having the option exercised or assigned to the seller.
- Allowing the option to expire.

Most individual investors do not exercise their options and will simply buy and sell options in much the same way as they would buy or sell other securities.

BUYING CALLS

Investors who purchase a call believe that the underlying stock price will rise and that they will be able to profit from the price appreciation. Investors who purchase calls can control the underlying stock and profit from its appreciation while limiting their loss to the amount of the premium paid for the calls. Buying calls allows investors to maximize their leverage, and they may realize a more significant percentage return based on their investment. When looking to establish a position, buyers must determine:

- Their maximum gain
- Their maximum loss
- Their breakeven

MAXIMUM GAIN LONG CALLS

When an investor has a long call position, the maximum gain is always unlimited. The investor profits from a rise in the stock price. Because there is no limit to how high a stock price may rise, the maximum gain is unlimited, just as with a stock.

MAXIMUM LOSS LONG CALLS

Whenever an investor is long or owns a stock, the maximum loss is always limited to the amount invested. When investors purchase a call option, the amount they pay for the option, or their premium, is always going to be their maximum loss.

DETERMINING THE BREAKEVEN FOR LONG CALLS

An investor who has purchased calls must determine where the stock price must be at expiration in order for the investor to breakeven on the transaction. An investor who has purchased calls has paid the premium to the seller in the hopes that the stock price will rise. The stock must appreciate by enough to cover the cost of the investor's option premium in order to breakeven at expiration. To determine an investor's breakeven point on a long call use the following formula:

$$breakeven = strike\ price + premium$$

EXAMPLE An investor has established the following option position:

Long 1 XYZ May 30 call at 3

The investor's maximum gain, maximum loss, and breakeven will be:

Maximum gain: Unlimited
Maximum loss: $300 (the amount of the premium paid)
Breakeven: $33 = 30 + 3 (strike price + premium)

If at expiration XYZ is at exactly $33 per share and the investor sells or exercises the option, the investor will breakeven, excluding transactions costs.

SELLING CALLS

Investors who sell calls believe that the underlying stock price will fall and that they will be able to profit from a decline in the stock price. An investor who sells a call is obligated to deliver the underlying stock if the buyer decides to exercise the option. When looking to establish a position, sellers must determine:

- Their maximum gain
- Their maximum loss
- Their breakeven

MAXIMUM GAIN SHORT CALLS

For an investor who has sold uncovered or naked calls, the maximum gain is always limited to the amount of the premium the investor received when the calls were sold.

MAXIMUM LOSS SHORT CALLS

An investor who has sold uncovered or naked calls does not own the underlying stock and, as a result, has unlimited risk and the potential for an unlimited loss. The seller of the calls is subject to a loss if the stock price increases. Because there is no limit to how high a stock price may rise, there is no limit to the amount of the investor's loss.

DETERMINING THE BREAKEVEN FOR SHORT CALLS

An investor who has sold calls must determine where the stock price must be at expiration in order to breakeven on the transaction. An investor who has sold calls has received the premium from the buyer in the hopes that the stock price will fall. If the stock appreciates, the investor may begin to lose money. The stock price may appreciate by the amount of the option premium received, and the investor will still breakeven at expiration. To determine an investor's breakeven point on a short call use the following formula:

breakeven = strike price + premium

EXAMPLE   An investor has established the following option position:

Short 1 XYZ May 30 call at 3

The investor's maximum gain, maximum loss, and breakeven will be:

Maximum gain: $300 (the amount of the premium received)
Maximum loss: Unlimited
Breakeven: $33 = 30 + 3 (strike price + premium)

If at expiration XYZ is at exactly $33 per share and the investor closes out the transaction with a closing purchase or has the option exercised against him or her, the investor will breakeven, excluding transactions costs.

Notice the relationship between the buyer and the seller:

	Call Buyer	Call Seller
Maximum gain	Unlimited	Premium received
Maximum loss	Premium paid	Unlimited
Breakeven	Strike price + premium	Strike price + premium
Wants option to	Exercise	Expire

Because an option is a two-party contract, the buyer's maximum gain is the seller's maximum loss, and the buyer's maximum loss is the seller's maximum gain. Both the buyer and the seller will breakeven at the same point.

BUYING PUTS

Investors who purchase puts believe that the underlying stock price will fall and that they will be able to profit from a decline in the stock price. Investors who purchase puts can control the underlying stock and profit from its price decline while limiting their loss to the amount of the premium paid for the puts. Buying puts allows investors to maximize their leverage while limiting their losses. Thus, they may realize a more significant percentage return based on their investment. When looking to establish a position, buyers must determine:

- Their maximum gain
- Their maximum loss
- Their breakeven

MAXIMUM GAIN LONG PUTS

An investor who has purchased a put believes that the stock price will fall. There is, however, a limit to how far a stock price may decline. A stock price may never fall below zero. As a result, the investor who believes that the stock price will fall has a limited maximum gain. To determine the maximum gain for the buyer of a put, use the following formula:

maximum gain = strike price − premium

MAXIMUM LOSS LONG PUTS

Whenever an investor is long or owns a stock, the maximum loss is always limited to the amount invested. When an investor purchases a put option, the amount the investor paid for the option or the premium is always going to be the maximum loss.

DETERMINING THE BREAKEVEN FOR LONG PUTS

An investor who has purchased a put believes that the stock price will decline. In order for the investor to breakeven on the transaction, the stock price must fall by enough to offset the amount of the premium paid for the option. At expiration the investor will breakeven at the following point:

breakeven = strike price − premium

EXAMPLE

An investor has established the following option position:

Long 1 XYZ May 30 put at 4

The investor's maximum gain, maximum loss, and breakeven will be:

Maximum gain: $26, or $2,600 for the whole position (strike price − premium)
Maximum loss: $400 (the amount of the premium paid)
Breakeven: $26 = 30 − 4 (strike price − premium)

If at expiration XYZ is at exactly $26 per share and the investor sells or exercises the option, the investor will breakeven, excluding transactions costs.

SELLING PUTS

Investors who sell puts believe that the underlying stock price will rise and that they will be able to profit from a rise in the stock price. An investor who sells a put is obligated to purchase the underlying stock if the buyer decides to exercise the option. When looking to establish a position, sellers must determine:

- Their maximum gain
- Their maximum loss
- Their breakeven

MAXIMUM GAIN SHORT PUTS

For an investor who has sold uncovered or naked puts, the maximum gain is always limited to the amount of the premium received when the puts were sold.

MAXIMUM LOSS SHORT PUTS

An investor who has sold a put believes that the stock price will rise. There is, however, a limit to how far a stock price may decline. A stock price may never fall below zero. As a result, the investor who believes that the stock price will rise has a limited maximum loss. The worst thing that can happen for investors who are short a put is that the stock goes to zero and they are forced to purchase it at the strike price from the owner of the put. To determine the maximum loss for the seller of a put, use the following formula:

maximum loss = strike price − premium

DETERMINING THE BREAKEVEN FOR SHORT PUTS

Whenever investors have sold a put, they believe that the stock price will rise. If the stock price begins to fall, the investor becomes subject to loss. In order for the investor to breakeven on the transaction, the stock price must fall by the amount of the premium that was received for the option. At expiration, the investor will breakeven at the following point:

breakeven = strike price − premium

EXAMPLE

An investor has established the following option position:

Short 1 XYZ May 30 put at 4

The investor's maximum gain, maximum loss, and breakeven will be:

Maximum gain: $400 (the amount of the premium received)
Maximum loss: $26, or $2,600 for the whole position (strike price − premium)
Breakeven: $26 = 30 − 4 (strike price − premium)

If at expiration XYZ is at exactly $26 per share and the investor closes out the position with a closing purchase or has the option exercised against him or her, the investor will breakeven, excluding transactions costs.

Notice the relationship between the buyer and the seller:

	Put Buyer	Put Seller
Maximum gain	Strike price − premium	Premium received
Maximum loss	Premium paid	Strike price − premium
Breakeven	Strike price − premium	Strike price − premium
Wants option to	Exercise	Expire

Because an option is a two-party contract, the buyer's maximum gain is the seller's maximum loss and the buyer's maximum loss is the seller's maximum gain. Both the buyer and the seller will breakeven at the same point.

OPTION PREMIUMS

The price of an option is known as its premium. Factors that determine the value of an option and, as a result, its premium, are:

- The relationship of the underlying stock price to the option's strike price.
- The amount of time to expiration.
- The volatility of the underlying stock.
- Supply and demand.
- Interest rates.

    An option can be:

- In the money
- At the money
- Out of the money

These terms describe the relationship of the underlying stock to the option's strike price. These terms do not describe how profitable the position is.

IN THE MONEY OPTIONS

A call is in the money when the underlying stock price is greater than the call's strike price.

EXAMPLE	An XYZ June 40 call is $2 in the money when XYZ is at $42 per share.
	A put is in the money when the underlying stock price is lower than the put's strike price.

EXAMPLE	An ABC October 70 put is $4 in the money when ABC is at $66 per share. It would only make sense to exercise an option if it was in the money.

AT THE MONEY OPTIONS

Both puts and calls are at the money when the underlying stock price equals the option's exercise price.

EXAMPLE	If FDR is trading at $60 per share, all of the FDR 60 calls and all of the FDR 60 puts will be at the money.

OUT OF THE MONEY OPTIONS

A call is out of the money when the underlying stock price is lower than the option's strike price.

EXAMPLE An ABC November 25 call is out of the money when ABC is trading at $22 per share.

A put option is out of the money when the underlying stock price is above the option's strike price.

EXAMPLE A KDC December 50 put is out of the money when KDC is trading at $54 per share.

It would not make sense to exercise an out of the money option.

	Calls	Puts
In the money	Stock price > strike price	Stock price < strike price
At the money	Stock price = strike price	Stock price = strike price
Out of the money	Stock price < strike price	Stock price > strike price

INTRINSIC VALUE AND TIME VALUE

An option's total premium is composed of intrinsic value and time value. An option's intrinsic value is equal to the amount the option is in the money. Time value is the amount by which an option's premium exceeds its intrinsic value. In effect, the time value is the price an investor pays for the opportunity to exercise the option. An option that is out of the money has no intrinsic value; therefore, the entire premium consists of time value.

EXAMPLE An XYZ June 40 call is trading at $2 when XYZ is trading at $37 per share. The June 40 call is out of the money and has no intrinsic value; therefore, the entire $2 premium consists of time value. If an XYZ June 40 put is trading at $3 when XYZ is at $44 dollars per share, then the entire $3 is time value.

If in the above example the options were in the money and the premium exceeded the intrinsic value of the option, the remaining premium would be time value.

EXAMPLE An XYZ June 40 call is trading at $5 when XYZ is trading at $42 per share. The June 40 call is in the money and has $2 in intrinsic value; therefore, the rest of the premium consists of the time value of $3. If an XYZ June 40 put is trading at $4 when XYZ is at $39 the put is in the money by $1 and the rest of the premium or $3 is time value.

USING OPTIONS AS A HEDGE

Many investors will use options to hedge a position that they have established in the underlying stock. Options can be used to guard against a loss or to protect a profit the investor has in a position. Options in this case will operate like an insurance policy for the investor.

LONG STOCK LONG PUTS/MARRIED PUTS

An investor who is long stock and wishes to protect the position from downside risk will receive the most protection by purchasing a protective put. By purchasing the put, the investor has locked in or set a minimum sale price that the investor will receive in the event of the stock's decline for the life of the put. The minimum sale price in this case is equal to the strike price of the put. Long puts can be used with long stock to guard against a loss or to protect an unrealized profit. However by purchasing the put, the investor has increased the breakeven point by the amount of the premium paid to purchase the put. When looking to establish a long stock long put position, investors must determine:

- Their maximum gain
- Their breakeven
- Their maximum loss

MAXIMUM GAIN LONG STOCK LONG PUTS

Investors who are long stock and long puts have a maximum gain that is unlimited because they own the stock.

BREAKEVEN LONG STOCK LONG PUTS

To determine an investor's breakeven with a long stock, long put position you must add the option premium to the cost of the stock.

breakeven = stock price + premium

EXAMPLE   An investor establishes the following position:

Long 100 XYZ at 55
Long 1 XYZ June 55 put at 3

The investor will breakeven if the stock goes to $58. The stock price has to appreciate by enough to offset the amount of the premium that the investor paid for the option. If at expiration, the stock is at $58 per share and the put expires, the investor will have broken even, excluding transaction costs.

MAXIMUM LOSS LONG STOCK LONG PUTS

In order to determine an investor's maximum loss with a long stock long put position, you must first determine the breakeven, as outlined above. Once you have determined the breakeven, use the following formula:

maximum loss = breakeven − strike price

Let's take another look at the previous example, only this time let's use it to determine the investor's maximum loss.

EXAMPLE

An investor establishes the following position:

Long 100 XYZ at 55
Long 1 XYZ June 55 put at 3

We have already determined that the investor will breakeven if the stock goes to $58. To determine the maximum loss, we subtract the put's strike price from the investor's breakeven as follows:

58 − 55 = 3

The investor's maximum loss is $3 per share or $300 for the entire position. Notice that the option's premium is the investor's maximum loss. When the purchase price of the stock and the strike price of the put are the same, the investor's maximum loss is equal to the premium paid for the option.

Let's take a look at another example where the investor's purchase price is different from the strike price of the put.

EXAMPLE

An investor establishes the following position:

Long 100 XYZ at 58
Long 1 XYZ June 55 put at 2

In order to find the investor's maximum loss, we first need to determine the breakeven. This investor will breakeven if the stock goes to $60, which is found by adding the stock price to the premium the investor paid for the put. To find their maximum loss, we subtract the put's strike price from the breakeven.

$$60 - 55 = 5$$

The investor's maximum loss on this position is $5 per share, or $500 for the entire position.

An investor who is long stock and long puts has limited the potential losses and has received the maximum possible protection while retaining all of the appreciation potential.

LONG STOCK SHORT CALLS/COVERED CALLS

Investors who are long stock can receive some partial downside protection and generate some additional income by selling calls against the stock they own. Investors will receive downside protection or will hedge their position by the amount of the premium received from the sale of the call. While the investors will receive partial downside protection, they will also give up any appreciation potential above the call's strike price. Investors who are going to establish a covered call position must determine:

- Their breakeven
- Their maximum gain
- Their maximum loss

BREAKEVEN LONG STOCK SHORT CALLS

By selling the calls, the investor has lowered the breakeven on the stock by the amount of the premium received from the sale of the call. To determine the investor's breakeven in this case, the price to which the stock can fall, use the following formula:

purchase price of the stock − premium received

EXAMPLE   An investor establishes the following position:

Long 100 ABC at 65
Short 1 ABC June 65 call at 4

Using the formula above we get:

$$65 - 4 = 61$$

The stock price in this case can fall to $61 and the investor will still breakeven.

MAXIMUM GAIN LONG STOCK SHORT CALLS

Investors who have sold call options on the stock that they own have limited the amount of their gain. Any appreciation of the stock beyond the call's strike price belongs to the investor who purchased the call. To determine an investor's maximum gain on a long stock short call position use the following formula:

maximum gain = strike price − breakeven

Let's use the same example to determine the investor's maximum gain.

EXAMPLE   An investor establishes the following position:

Long 100 ABC at 65
Short 1 ABC June 65 call at 4

Using the formula above we get:

65 − 61 = 4

The investor's maximum gain is $4 per share, or $400 for the entire position. Notice that because the purchase price of the stock and the strike price of the call are the same, the investor's maximum gain is equal to the amount of the premium received on the sale of the call.

Let's look at an example where the strike price and the purchase price for the stock are different.

EXAMPLE   An investor establishes the following position:

Long 100 ABC at 65
Short 1 ABC June 70 call at 2

The investor will breakeven at $63, which is found by subtracting the premium received from the investor's purchase price for the stock. To determine their maximum gain, we subtract the breakeven from the strike price and we get:

70 − 63 = 7

The investor's maximum gain is $7 per share, or $700 for the entire position.

MAXIMUM LOSS LONG STOCK SHORT CALLS

An investor who has sold cover calls has only received partial downside protection in the amount of the premium received. As a result, the investor is still subject to a significant loss in the event of an extreme downside move in the stock price. To determine an investor's maximum loss when they are long stock and short calls use the following formula:

maximum loss = breakeven − 0

Said another way, an investor is subject to a loss equal to their breakeven price per share.

EXAMPLE

An investor establishes the following position:

Long 100 ABC at 65
Short 1 ABC June 70 call at 2

The investor will breakeven at $63, which is found by subtracting the premium received from the investor's purchase price for the stock. To determine the investor's maximum loss, we only need to look at the breakeven, and we get a maximum loss of $63 per share, or $6,300 for the entire position. The investor will realize the maximum loss if the stock goes to zero.

SHORT STOCK LONG CALLS

Investors who sell stock short believe that they can profit from a fall in the stock price by selling it high and repurchasing it cheaper. An investor who has sold stock short is subject to an unlimited loss if the stock price should begin to rise. Once again, there is no limit to how high a stock price may rise. An investor who has sold stock short would receive the most protection by purchasing a call. A long call could be used to guard against a loss or to protect a profit on a short stock position. By purchasing the call, the investor has set the maximum price that he or she will have to pay to repurchase the stock for the life of the option. Before establishing a short stock long call position, investors will have to determine:

• Their breakeven
• Their maximum gain
• Their maximum loss

DETERMINING THE BREAKEVEN FOR SHORT STOCK LONG CALLS

An investor who has sold stock short will profit from a fall in the stock price. When investors purchase a call to protect their position, the stock price must fall by enough to offset the premium they paid for the call. To determine the breakeven for a short stock long call position, use the following formula:

breakeven = stock price − premium

EXAMPLE	An investor establishes the following position:

Short 100 ABC at 60
Long 1 ABC October 60 call at 2

Using the above formula we get:

60 − 2 = 58

The stock would have to fall to $58 by expiration in order for the investor to breakeven.

MAXIMUM GAIN SHORT STOCK LONG CALLS

The maximum gain on the short sale of stock is always limited because a stock cannot fall below zero. When an investor has a short stock long call position, the maximum gain is found by using the following formula:

maximum gain = breakeven − 0

Said another way, the investor's maximum gain per share would be equal to the breakeven price per share.

EXAMPLE	An investor establishes the following position:

Short 100 ABC at 60
Long 1 ABC October 60 call at 2

Using the above formula we get:

58 − 0 = 58

If the stock fell to $0 by expiration, the investor would realize a maximum gain of $58 per share, or $5,800 for the entire position.

MAXIMUM LOSS SHORT STOCK LONG CALL

Investors who have sold stock short and have purchased a call to protect their position are only subject to a loss up to the strike price of the call. In order to determine the investor's maximum loss, use the following formula:

maximum loss = strike price − breakeven

| EXAMPLE | An investor establishes the following position: |

Short 100 ABC at 60
Long 1 ABC October 60 call at 2

60 − 58 = 2

The investor is subject to a loss of $2 per share, or $200 for the entire position. Notice that the price at which the investor sold the stock short at and the strike price of the call are the same. As a result, the investor has set a maximum repurchase price equal to the price at which the investor sold the stock short. The investor's maximum loss when the sale price and strike price are the same is the amount of the premium that the investor paid for the call. Let's take a look at a position where the sale price of the stock and strike price of the option are different.

| EXAMPLE | An investor establishes the following position: |

Short 100 ABC at 56
Long 1 ABC October 60 call at 2

This investor will breakeven at $54 per share. To determine the maximum loss, subtract the breakeven from the strike price of the option.

60 − 54 = 6

The investor is subject to a loss of $6 per share, or $600 for the entire position.

SHORT STOCK SHORT PUTS

Investors who have sold stock short can receive some protection and generate premium income by selling puts against their short stock position. Selling puts against a short stock position will only partially hedge the unlimited upside risk associated with any short sale of stock. Additionally, the investor, in exchange for the premium received for the sale of the put, has further limited the maximum gain. Before entering a short stock short put position, investors must determine:

- Their breakeven
- Their maximum gain
- Their maximum loss

BREAKEVEN SHORT STOCK SHORT PUTS

Investors who have sold stock short and have sold puts against their position are subject to a loss if the stock price begins to rise. To determine how high a stock price could rise after establishing a short stock short put position and still allow the investor to breakeven, use the following formula:

EXAMPLE   breakeven = stock price + premium

An investor establishes the following position:

> Short 100 ABC at 55
> Short 1 ABC November 55 put at 4

Using the above formula we get:

> 55 + 4 = 59

In this case, the stock could rise to $59 by expiration and still allow the investor to breakeven, excluding transaction costs.

MAXIMUM GAIN SHORT STOCK SHORT PUTS

An investor who has established a short stock short put position has limited the amount of gain even further by selling puts, because the investor will be required to purchase the shares at the put's strike price if the stock declines. To determine the investor's maximum gain, use the following formula:

maximum gain = breakeven − strike price

EXAMPLE   An investor establishes the following position:

> Short 100 ABC at 55
> Short 1 ABC November 55 put at 4

The investor will breakeven at 59 found by adding the stock price of 55 and the option premium of 4 together.

Using the above formula we get:

$$59 - 55 = 4$$

The investor's maximum gain in this case is $4 per share, or $400 for the entire position. The investor received a total of $59 per share by establishing the position. If the stock fell to zero, the investor would still be required to repurchase the shares at 55 under the terms of the put contract. Notice that the sale price and the put's exercise price are the same and that the amount of the investor's maximum gain is equal to the amount of the premium received.

Let's look at a position where the sale price of the stock and the strike price of the put are different.

EXAMPLE

An investor establishes the following position:

Short 100 XYZ at 60
Short 1 XYZ November 55 put at 4

The investor will breakeven at 64. The investor received $64 dollars per share in total proceeds for establishing the position. To determine the investor's maximum gain using the formula above we get:

$$64 - 55 = 9$$

The investor's maximum gain is $9 per share, or $900 for the total position.

MAXIMUM LOSS SHORT STOCK SHORT PUTS

Investors who have sold puts against their short stock position have only limited their loss by the amount of the premium received from the sale of the put. As a result, the investor's loss in a short stock short put position is still unlimited.

Underlying Position	Most Protection	Some Protection and Income
Long stock	Long puts	Short calls
Short stock	Long calls	Short puts

 **TESTFOCUS!**

It's important to note that when investors want the most protection, they will buy the hedge. When investors want some protection and income, they will sell the hedge.

MULTIPLE OPTION POSITIONS AND STRATEGIES

Option strategies that contain positions in more than one option can be used effectively by investors to meet their objective and to profit from movement in the underlying stock price. The Series 7 exam focuses on straddles and spreads.

LONG STRADDLES

A long straddle is the simultaneous purchase of a call and a put on the same stock with the same strike price and expiration month. An option investor would purchase a straddle when he or she expects the stock price to be extremely volatile and to make a significant move in either direction. An investor who owns a straddle is neither bullish nor bearish. Such investors are not concerned with whether the stock moves up or down in price, so long as it moves significantly. An investor may purchase a straddle just prior to a company announcing earnings, with the belief that if the company beats its earnings estimate the stock price will appreciate dramatically. Or, if the company's earnings fall short of expectations, the stock price will decline dramatically. Before establishing a long straddle, investors must determine the following:

- Their maximum gain
- Their maximum loss
- Their breakeven

Let's look at an example.

EXAMPLE   XYZ is trading at $50 per share and is set to report earnings at the end of the week. An investor with the above opinion establishes the following position:

Long 1 XYZ April 50 call at 4
Long 1 XYZ April 50 put at 3

MAXIMUM GAIN LONG STRADDLE

Because the investor in a long straddle owns the calls, the investor's maximum gain is always going to be unlimited.

MAXIMUM LOSS LONG STRADDLE

An investor's maximum loss on a long straddle is going to be limited to the total premium paid for the straddle. The total premium is found using the following formula:

$$total\ premium = call\ premium + put\ premium$$

Let's look at an example.

EXAMPLE

Long 1 XYZ April 50 call at 4
Long 1 XYZ April 50 put at 3

To determine the investor's maximum loss, simply add the premiums together:

$$4 + 3 = 7$$

The investor's maximum loss is $7 per share, or $700 for the entire position. The investor will only realize the maximum loss on a long straddle if the stock price at expiration is exactly equal to the strike price of both the call and put and both options expire worthless. If, at expiration, XYZ closes at exactly $50, the investor in this case will suffer the maximum possible loss.

BREAKEVEN LONG STRADDLE

Because the position contains both a put and a call, the investor is going to have two breakeven points, one breakeven for the call side of the straddle and one for the put side of the straddle.

To determine the breakeven point for the call side of the straddle, use the following formula:

$$breakeven = call\ strike\ price + total\ premium$$

EXAMPLE

Long 1 XYZ April 50 call at 4
Long 1 XYZ April 50 put at 3

Total premium = 7

$$50 + 7 = 57$$

The investor will breakeven if XYZ appreciates to $57 per share at expiration. The stock has to appreciate by enough to offset the total premium cost.

Alternatively, to determine the breakeven point for the put side of the straddle use the following formula:

breakeven = put strike price − total premium

$$50 - 7 = 43$$

If XYZ was to fall to $43 per share at expiration, the investor would breakeven. The stock would have to fall by enough to offset the total premium cost. If the stock appreciated past $57 per share or was to fall below $43 per share, the position would become profitable for the investor.

 FOCUSPOINT

An investor who is long a straddle wants the stock price outside of the breakeven points. In the above case, that would be either above $57 per share or below $43 per share.

SHORT STRADDLES

A short straddle is the simultaneous sale of a call and a put on the same stock with the same strike price and expiration month. Options investors would sell a straddle when they expect the stock price to trade within a narrow range or to become less volatile and not to make a significant move in either direction. An investor who is short a straddle is neither bullish nor bearish. Such investors are not concerned with whether the stock moves up or down in price, so long as it does not move significantly. An investor may sell a straddle just after a period of high volatility, with the belief that the stock will now move sideways for a period of time. Investors must determine the following before establishing a short straddle:

- Their maximum gain
- Their maximum loss
- Their breakeven

MAXIMUM GAIN SHORT STRADDLE

An investor's maximum gain with a short straddle is always going to be limited to the amount of the premium received. Let's look at the same position from before; only this time let's look at it from the seller's point of view.

EXAMPLE

XYZ is trading at $50 and an option investor establishes the following position:

Short 1 XYZ April 50 call at 4
Short 1 XYZ April 50 put at 3

To determine the investor's maximum gain, simply add the premiums together.

$$4 + 3 = 7$$

The investor's maximum gain is $7 per share, or $700 for the entire position. An investor who is short a straddle will only realize the maximum gain if the stock closes at the strike price at expiration and both options expire worthless. In this case, if XYZ closes at exactly $50 the investor will have a $700 profit on the entire position.

MAXIMUM LOSS SHORT STRADDLE

Because the investor in a short straddle is short the calls, the investor's maximum loss is always going to be unlimited.

BREAKEVEN SHORT STRADDLE

Just like with a long straddle, the investor is going to have two breakeven points, one breakeven for the call side of the straddle and one for the put side.

To determine the breakeven point for the call side of the straddle, use the following formula:

breakeven = call strike price + total premium

EXAMPLE

Short 1 XYZ April 50 call at 4
Short 1 XYZ April 50 put at 3

Total premium = 7

$$50 + 7 = 57$$

The investor will breakeven if XYZ appreciates to $57 per share at expiration. Alternatively, to determine the breakeven point for the put side of the straddle use the following formula:

breakeven = put strike price − total premium

50 − 7 = 43

If XYZ was to fall to $43 per share at expiration, the investor would breakeven. If the stock appreciated past $57 per share or was to fall below $43 per share, the investor would begin to lose money.

 FOCUSPOINT

An investor who is short a straddle wants the stock price inside of the breakeven points. In the above case, that would be either below $57 per share or above $43 per share.

Position	Max Gain	Max Loss	Breakeven	At Expiration
Long straddle	Unlimited	Total premium	Strike price + or − total premium	Profitable if outside breakeven
Short straddle	Total premium	Unlimited	Strike price + or − total premium	Profitable if inside breakeven

 TESTFOCUS!

To help you remember where an investor wants the stock to be at expiration, use the mnemonic device for straddles, SILO: Short Inside Long Outside.

SPREADS

A spread is created through the simultaneous purchase and sale of two options of the same class with different exercise prices, expiration months, or both. There are several different types of spreads that may be created using either calls or puts:

- Price spread/vertical spread/money spread
- Calendar spread/time spread/horizontal spread
- Diagonal spread

PRICE SPREAD/VERTICAL SPREAD

A price spread or vertical spread consists of one long option and one short option of the same class with different strike prices. The position is normally called a price spread because of the difference in strike prices between the long and short options. It may also be called a vertical spread because of the way the options are listed in the option chain or in the newspaper. A price spread could be established in either calls or puts as follows:

EXAMPLE Long 1 TRY May 40 call
Short 1 TRY May 50 call

A price spread could also be established using puts:

Long 1 TRY April 60 put
Short 1 TRY April 50 put

CALENDAR SPREAD/TIME SPREAD

A calendar spread or time spread contains one long option and one short option of the same class with different expiration months. It may also be called a horizontal spread because of how the options are listed in the option chain or in the newspaper.

EXAMPLE Short 1 TRY June 40 call
Long 1 TRY August 40 call

A time spread could also be established using puts:

Short 1 TRY January 60 put
Long 1 TRY April 60 put

DIAGONAL SPREAD

A diagonal spread consists of one long option and one short option of the same class that have different strike prices and expiration months. The position is called a diagonal spread because of the way the options are listed in the option chain or in the newspaper.

EXAMPLE   Short 1 TRY June 50 call
                     Long 1 TRY August 40 call

A diagonal spread could also be established using puts:

>   Short 1 TRY March 40 put
>   Long 1 TRY August 50 put

ANALYZING SPREADS/PRICE SPREADS

Investors who are bullish or bearish can use spreads to profit from their opinion about prices in the marketplace. We will use price spreads to determine:

- If the investor is bullish or bearish.
- If the position has resulted in a net debit or credit.
- The maximum gain.
- The maximum loss.
- The breakeven point.
- If the investor wants the options to be exercised or to expire.
- If the investor wants the difference in the premiums to widen or narrow.

BULL CALL SPREADS/DEBIT CALL SPREADS

To establish a bull call spread, the investor purchases the call with the lower strike price and simultaneously sells the call with the higher strike price. An investor who believes that the stock price will rise may purchase the call with the lower strike price and sell the call with the higher strike price to offset the risk of losing all of the premium paid for the long call. A bull call spread will always be debit spread because the right to purchase a stock at a lower price for the same amount of time will always be worth more than the right to purchase the same stock at a higher price.

A bull call spread could be established as follows:

>   Long 1 XYZ April 40 call at 3
>   Short 1 XYZ April 50 call at 1

By selling the April 50 call, the investor has reduced the maximum loss from $300 to $200 for the entire position. By selling the April 50 call, the investor has also limited the upside potential on the position.

Before entering into a bull call spread, investors must determine:

- Their maximum gain
- Their maximum loss
- Their breakeven

MAXIMUM GAIN BULL CALL SPREAD

The investor's maximum gain on a bull call spread has been limited because the investor sold the call with the higher strike price. Any appreciation past the strike price of the short call will belong to the investor who purchased the call. To determine the maximum gain on a bull call spread, use the following formula:

difference in the strike prices − net premium paid

Using the same example we get:

Long 1 XYZ April 40 call at 3

Short 1 XYZ April 50 call at 1

$10 − 2 = 8$

The investor's maximum gain is $8 per share, or $800 for the entire position. The investor will realize the maximum gain if both options are exercised.

MAXIMUM LOSS BULL CALL SPREAD

An investor who is long a bull call spread has a maximum loss equal to the amount of the net premium paid for the spread. An investor will realize the maximum loss if both options expire worthless at expiration.

BREAKEVEN BULL CALL SPREAD

To determine where the stock has to be at expiration for the investor to breakeven, use the following formula:

lower strike price + net premium

Using the same example we get:

Long 1 XYZ April 40 call at 3

Short 1 XYZ April 50 call at 1

$**40 + 2 = 42**$

If, at expiration, XYZ is at $42 per share, the investor will breakeven on the position, excluding transaction costs. If the stock is higher than $42 per share, the investor will make money. If it is lower than $42, the investor will lose money.

SPREAD PREMIUMS BULL CALL SPREAD

An investor who has established a bull call spread has bought the spread and paid a net premium to establish the position. The investor will realize a profit on the spread if the difference in the premiums increase or widens. Let's look at our example again:

Long 1 XYZ April 40 call at 3

Short 1 XYZ April 50 call at 1

The difference between the premium on the long April 40 call and the short April 50 call is 2. If the difference in the value of the premiums increases or widens, the investor will make money.

Let's look at the value of the same spread at expiration given different closing prices for XYZ.

	Opened at	XYZ at 45	XYZ at 50	XYZ at 30
Long 1 XYZ April 40 Call	3	5	10	0
Short 1 XYZ April 50 Call	1	0	0	0
Difference	2	5	10	0
Profit/Loss	N/A	$300	$800	($200)

Notice that the difference between the premiums can never widen past the amount of the spread. This is a 10-point spread; therefore, the difference between the value of the premiums may never widen past 10.

BEAR CALL SPREADS/CREDIT CALL SPREADS

To establish a bear call spread, the investor sells the call with the lower strike price and simultaneously buys the call with the higher strike price. Investors who believe that the stock price will fall may sell the call with the lower strike price and purchase the call with the higher strike price to ensure that their maximum loss is not unlimited. A bear call spread or credit call spread could be established as follows:

Short 1 XYZ April 40 call at 3

Long 1 XYZ April 50 call at 1

Before entering into a bear call spread, investors must determine:

- Their maximum gain
- Their maximum loss
- Their breakeven

MAXIMUM GAIN BEAR CALL SPREAD/CREDIT CALL SPREAD

The maximum gain for a bear call spread is equal to the net premium or credit received by the investor when the spread was sold. Using the same example we get:

Short 1 XYZ April 40 call at 3

Long 1 XYZ April 50 call at 1

The net premium received by the investor is $2 per share, or $200 for the entire position. This amount represents the investor's maximum gain. The investor will realize the maximum gain if both options expire.

MAXIMUM LOSS BEAR CALL SPREAD

The investor's maximum loss on a bear call spread has been limited because the investor bought the call with the higher strike price. If the investor was only short a naked call, the maximum loss would be unlimited. To determine the maximum loss on a bear call spread, use the following formula:

difference in the strike prices – net premium received

Using the same example we get:

Short 1 XYZ April 40 call at 3

Long 1 XYZ April 50 call at 1

10 – 2 = 8

The investor's maximum loss is $8 per share, or $800 for the entire position. The investor will realize the maximum loss if both options are exercised.

BREAKEVEN BEAR CALL SPREAD

To determine where the stock has to be at expiration for the investor to breakeven, use the following formula:

lower strike price + net premium

Using the same example we get:

> Short 1 XYZ April 40 call at 3
>
> Long 1 XYZ April 50 call at 1
>
> **40 + 2 = 42**

If at expiration XYZ is at $42 per share, the investor will breakeven on the position, excluding transaction costs. If the stock is higher than $42 per share, the investor will lose money. If it is lower than $42, the investor will make money.

SPREAD PREMIUMS BEAR CALL SPREAD

An investor who has established a bear call spread has sold the spread and received a net premium or credit to establish the position. The investor will realize a profit on the spread if the difference in the premiums decreases or narrows. Let's look at our example again:

> Short 1 XYZ April 40 call at 3
>
> Long 1 XYZ April 50 call at 1

The difference between the premium on the short April 40 call and the long April 50 call is 2. If the difference in the value of the premiums decreases or narrows, the investor will make money.

Let's look at the value of the same spread at expiration, given different closing prices for XYZ.

	Opened at	XYZ at 45	XYZ at 50	XYZ at 30
Short 1 XYZ April 40 Call	3	5	10	0
Long 1 XYZ April 50 Call	1	0	0	0
Difference	2	5	10	0
Profit/Loss	N/A	($300)	($800)	$200

Let's compare a bull call spread with a bear call spread.

Position	Max Gain	Max Loss	Breakeven	At Expiration
Bull call spread	Difference in strike prices – premium paid	Net premium paid	Lower strike price + premium	Profitable if spread widens
Bear call spread	Net premium received	Difference in strike prices – premium received	Lower strike price + premium	Profitable if spread narrows

BEAR PUT SPREADS/DEBIT PUT SPREADS

An investor wishing to profit from a decline in a stock price may establish a bear put spread, also known as a debit put spread. A bear put spread will always be a debit put spread because the right to sell a stock at a higher price is always going to be worth more than the right to sell the same stock at a lower price for the same amount of time. To establish a debit put spread, the investor will purchase the put with the higher strike price and sell the put with the lower strike price. By selling the put with the lower strike price, the investor has reduced the maximum loss by the amount of the premium received.

The investor has also limited the maximum gain, and any profit from the decline of the stock past the lower put's strike price will belong to the investor who purchased the put. Investors must determine the following before establishing a bear put spread:

- Their maximum gain
- Their maximum loss
- Their breakeven

MAXIMUM GAIN BEAR PUT SPREAD/ DEBIT PUT SPREAD

The maximum gain for an investor who has established a bear put spread is found by using the following formula:

difference in the strike prices – net premium paid

Long 1 XYZ April 50 put at 4

Short 1 XYZ April 40 put at 1

Using the same example we get:

10 − 3 = 7

The investor's maximum gain is $7 per share, or $700 for the entire position. The investor will realize the maximum gain if both options are exercised.

MAXIMUM LOSS BEAR PUT SPREAD

An investor who is long a bear put spread has a maximum loss equal to the amount of the net premium paid for the spread. An investor will realize the maximum loss if both options expire worthless at expiration.

BREAKEVEN BEAR PUT SPREAD

To determine an investor's breakeven point on a bear put spread, use the following formula:

higher strike price − net premium paid

Using the same example we get:

> Long 1 XYZ April 50 put at 4
>
> Short 1 XYZ April 40 put at 1

50 − 3 = 47

XYZ would have to fall to $47 per share by expiration for the investor to breakeven. If at expiration XYZ has fallen below $47, the investor will make money. At any point above $47, the investor will lose money.

SPREAD PREMIUMS BEAR PUT SPREAD

An investor who has established a bear put spread has bought the spread and paid a net premium to establish the position. The investor will realize a profit on the spread if the difference in the premiums increase or widens. Let's look at our example again:

> Long 1 XYZ April 50 put at 4
>
> Short 1 XYZ April 40 put at 1

The difference between the premiums on the long April 50 put and the short April 40 put is 3. If the difference in the value of the premiums increases or widens, the investor will make money.

Let's look at the value of the same spread at expiration, given different closing prices for XYZ.

	Opened at	XYZ at 45	XYZ at 50	XYZ at 30
Long 1 XYZ April 50 put	4	5	0	20
Short 1 XYZ April 40 Put	1	0	0	10
Difference	3	5	0	10
Profit/Loss	N/A	$200	($300)	$700

BULL PUT SPREADS/CREDIT PUT SPREADS

An investor wishing to profit from a rise in a stock price may establish a bull put spread, also known as a credit put spread. A bull put spread will always be a credit put spread because the right to sell a stock at a higher price is always going to be worth more than the right to sell the same stock at a lower price for the same amount of time. To establish a bull put spread or credit put spread, the investor would sell the put with the higher strike price and purchase the put with the lower strike price. An investor could profit from a rise in the stock price by establishing a bull put spread as follows:

Short 1 XYZ April 50 put at 4

Long 1 XYZ April 40 put at 1

Before establishing a bull put spread, investors need to determine:

- Their maximum gain
- Their maximum loss
- Their breakeven

MAXIMUM GAIN BULL PUT SPREAD

The maximum gain for a bull put spread is equal to the credit received by the investor when the spread was sold. Using the same example we get:

Short 1 XYZ April 50 put at 4

Long 1 XYZ April 40 put at 1

The investor received a net credit of $3 per share, or $300 for the entire position. The investor will realize the maximum gain if both options expire.

MAXIMUM LOSS BULL PUT SPREAD

The maximum loss on a bull put spread is found by using the following formula:

difference in the strike prices – net premium received

Short 1 XYZ April 50 put at 4

Long 1 XYZ April 40 put at 1

Using the same example we get:

10 – 3 = 7

The investor's maximum loss is $7 per share, or $700 for the entire position. The investor will realize their maximum loss if both options are exercised.

BREAKEVEN BULL PUT SPREAD

To determine an investor's breakeven point on a bull put spread, use the following formula:

higher strike price – net premium received

Short 1 XYZ April 50 put at 4

Long 1 XYZ April 40 put at 1

Using the same example we get:

50 – 3 = 47

XYZ could to fall to $47 per share by expiration and the investor would still breakeven. If at expiration XYZ is above $47, the investor will make money. At any point below $47, the investor will lose money.

SPREAD PREMIUMS BULL PUT SPREAD

An investor who has established a bull put spread has sold the spread and received a net premium to establish the position. The investor will realize a profit on the spread if the difference in the premiums decreases or narrows. Let's look at our example again:

Short 1 XYZ April 50 put at 4

Long 1 XYZ April 40 put at 1

The difference between the premiums on the short April 50 put and the long April 40 put is 3. If the difference in the value of the premiums decreases or narrows, the investor will make money.

Let's look at the value of the same spread at expiration, given different closing prices for XYZ.

	Opened at	XYZ at 45	XYZ at 50	XYZ at 30
Short 1 XYZ April 50 put	4	5	0	20
Long 1 XYZ April 40 Put	1	0	0	10
Difference	3	5	0	10
Profit/Loss	N/A	($200)	$300	($700)

Let's compare a bear put spread with a bull put spread.

	Max Gain	Max Loss	Breakeven	At Expiration
Bear put spread	Difference in strike prices – premium paid	Net premium paid	Higher strike price – premium	Profitable if spread widens
Bull put spread	Net premium received	Difference in strike prices – premium received	Higher strike price – premium	Profitable if spread narrows

COMBINATIONS

A combination like a straddle is the simultaneous purchase or sale of a call and a put on the same underlying stock with the same expiration date but with different strike prices.

Investors may establish a long combination when they feel that the stock will make a significant move. A long combination may be established as follows:

Long 1 XYZ May 70 call at 2

Long 1 XYZ May 60 put at 1

An investor may elect to purchase a combination instead of a straddle, because the overall premium paid for the position will be less than the premium for a straddle. An investor may also establish a short combination as follows:

Short 1 XYZ May 70 call at 2

Short 1 XYZ May 60 put at 1

USING A T CHART TO EVALUATE OPTION POSITIONS

Many option positions can be evaluated by simply analyzing the flow of funds into or out of the investor's account. To analyze option positions, use the following T chart:

Debit	Credit

A debit in the customer's account results in an outflow of funds, whereas a credit results in an inflow of funds.

Let's analyze several option positions using the T chart. An investor buys 1 XYZ June 50 call at 5

Debit	Credit
5	

The purchase of the call results in a net debit equal to the amount of the premium paid by the investor. To determine the investor's breakeven, add the price that the investor would have to pay for the stock if the investor exercised the call option. This will always be equal to the call's strike price. If the investor exercised the option, the flow of funds would look as follows:

Debit	Credit
5	
50	

55

This investor would breakeven at expiration if XYZ was at 55.
Let's look at the flow of funds for an investor who buys a put.

An investor purchases 1 ABC June 70 put at 4

Debit	Credit
4	

The purchase of the put results in a net debit equal to the amount of the premium that the investor paid for the option. To determine the investor's breakeven, enter the price that the investor would receive from exercising the put as a credit. This will always be equal to the put's strike price. Remember that the owner of the put will sell the stock if the option is exercised and the sale of stock will always result in a credit into the account. If the investor exercised the option, the flow of funds will look as follows:

Debit	Credit
4	70

66

The difference between the debit and credit will equal the investor's breakeven. Let's look at the flow of funds for an investor who is long stock and short a call. An investor is long 100 TRY at 50 and short 1 TRY May 55 call at 3.

Debit	Credit
50	3

47

The investor has paid 50 for the stock and received 3 from the sale of the call; therefore, the investor's net outlay of cash is 47, and this will be the breakeven. That is to say that the stock could fall to 47 and the investor would still breakeven. To determine the investor's maximum gain, enter the sales proceeds from the sale of the stock in the credit column. This will be equal to the strike price of the option if the option was exercised against the investor and the stock was called away.

Debit	Credit
50	3
	55

8

Let's look at the flow of funds for an investor who is long stock and long a put.

An investor is long 100 shares of ABC at 42 and long 1 ABC November 40 put at 2.

Debit	Credit
42	
2	

44

Because the investor has purchased both the stock and the protective put, ABC must rise to 44 in order for the investor to breakeven. The investor's maximum loss will be realized if ABC falls and the put has to be exercised. To determine the maximum loss, enter the sales proceeds from the exercise of the put in the credit column.

Debit	Credit
42	40
2	

4

The investor's maximum loss will be $4 per share.

Let's look at the flow of funds for an investor who is short stock and long a call.

An investor is short 100 shares of DOG at 43 and is long 1 DOG May 45 call at 3. The flow of funds will look as follows:

Debit	Credit
3	43

40

DOG would have to fall to 40 in order for the investor to break even. The investor will realize the maximum possible loss if DOG rises and has to exercise the call to close out the position. The flow of funds in that case will look as follows:

Debit	Credit
3	43
45	

5

If the investor has to repurchase DOG at 45, the investor would realize the maximum loss of $5 per share.

Let's look at the flow of funds for an investor who is short stock and short a put.

An investor is short 100 shares of DOG at 43 and short 1 DOG June 40 put at 2. The flow of funds will look as follows:

Debit	Credit
	43
	2

45

DOG could rise to 45 and the investor would still breakeven.

If DOG falls and the stock is put to the investor at the strike price of the short put, the flow of fund will be as follows:

Debit	Credit
40	43
	2

5

If the stock is put to the investor at 40, the investor will realize the maximum profit of $5 per share.

The T chart is also effective in analyzing positions created from multiple-option positions, such as straddles and spreads. Let's look at the flow of funds for a long straddle.

An investor is long 1 XYZ October 70 call at 4 and long 1 XYZ October 70 put at 2:

Debit	Credit
4	
2	

6

The investor's maximum loss is the net debit, or $6 per share. Remember that a straddle has two breakevens: one for the call side and one for the put side. The investor in this case will breakeven at 76 on the call side and 64 on the put side. If the investor was short the straddle, the premiums would have been entered on the credit side of the chart, and that would represent the investor's maximum gain.

Spreads are created by the simultaneous purchase and sale of two options of the same type on the same underlying security that differ in strike price, expiration month, or both. Because the investor is purchasing and selling options, the T chart will have entries in both the debit and credit columns. Let's look at the flow of funds for a bull call spread.

An investor establishes the following position:

Long 1 TRY May 30 call at 2

Short 1 TRY May 40 call at 1

Debit	Credit
2	1

1

The investor's maximum loss is $1 per share because that was the net debit in the account. If the investor established a bear call spread by being short this spread, the position would have resulted in a net credit in the account of $1 per share, and that would be the investor's maximum gain.

The T chart can be used to help determine:

- Maximum gain
- Maximum loss
- Breakeven

for all option positions.

INDEX OPTIONS

In an effort to gauge the market's overall performance, industry participants developed indexes. Two of the most widely followed indexes are the Dow Jones Industrial Average (DJIA) and the Standard and Poor's 500 (S&P 500). There are two types of indexes: broad-based indexes, such as the S&P 500 (SPX) or S&P 100 (OEX), that track a large number of stocks, and narrow indexes, such as the semiconductor index (SOX), that track only a particular industry.

INDEX OPTION SETTLEMENT

Investors who want to take a position in index options will purchase calls and puts just like investors in stock options. However, an index is not a security, and it cannot be physically delivered if the option is exercised. An investor cannot call the index away from someone who is short a call and cannot put an index to an investor who is short a put. As a result, the exercise of index options will be settled in cash. Option holders who elect to exercise the option will have their account credited the in-the-money amount, in cash. The amount that will be credited to their account will be the in-the-money amount at the close of the market on the day of exercise. To determine the option's premium and the amount of money to be delivered upon the exercise index options, use 100 as a multiplier.

EXAMPLE

An investor establishes the following position:

Long 1 OEX March 550 call at $4

The investor has purchased an S&P 100 (OEX) 550 call for $4. The contract value is 55,000, and the total premium paid by the investor is $400. The investor is bullish on the overall market and believes the market will rise and the OEX will be higher than 550 by expiration. If at expiration the index is at 556.20, the investor's account will be credited the in-the-money amount, as follows:

$$
\begin{array}{r}
556.20 \\
-550.00 \\
\hline
6.20 \\
\times\,100 \\
\hline
\$620.00
\end{array}
$$

The investor's account will be credited $620. Because the investor paid $400 for the option, the investor's profit is $220.

EXERCISING AN INDEX OPTION

It is usually not wise to exercise an index option prior to its expiration because the investor would lose any amount of time value contained in the option's premium. Additionally, if the investor exercises an option at 10:00 a.m., the investor will receive the in-the-money amount as of the close of the market that day. It is quite possible for an investor to exercise an in-the-money option at 10:00 a.m. and have the option be out of the money at the close of business because the market moved against the investor. In both scenarios, it is better to sell the option.

INDEX OPTION POSITIONS

An investor may establish all of the following positions using index options:

- Long calls and puts
- Short calls and puts
- Long spreads and straddles
- Short spreads and straddles
- Long and short combinations

    Index options may also be used to:

- Speculate on the direction of the market.
- Protect a long portfolio by purchasing puts or selling calls.
- Protect a short portfolio by purchasing calls or selling puts.

CAPPED INDEX OPTIONS

A capped index option trades like a spread and will automatically be exercised if the option goes 30 points in the money.

INTEREST RATE OPTIONS

Investors can use interest rate options to speculate on the direction of interest rates or to hedge a portfolio of Treasury securities. Investors can establish a position in either price-based options or rate-based options to achieve their objective.

PRICE-BASED OPTIONS

Price-based options are used by investors to speculate on or to hedge against a change in the price of Treasury securities. As interest rates change, the prices of Treasury securities will move in the opposite direction. Interest rates and bond prices are inversely related to each other. An investor who believes that interest rates are likely to rise would purchase price-based puts or sell price-based calls. Alternatively, an investor who believes that rates are likely to fall will purchase price-based calls or sell price-based puts. Price-based options on Treasury notes and bonds are based on a $100,000 par amount of a specific Treasury note or bond. Price-based options for Treasury bills are based on $1,000,000 par value. Price-based options, when exercised, will result in the delivery of the specific security.

PREMIUMS FOR PRICE-BASED OPTIONS TREASURY NOTES AND BONDS

Treasury notes and bonds are priced as a percentage of par down to 32nds of 1%. Price-based options are also quoted as a percentage of par down to 32nds of 1%.

EXAMPLE

A May Treasury bond 103 call on a 7% Treasury maturing in October 2015 is quoted at 1.16. The premium is calculated as follows:

1.16 = 1 16/32% × $100,000
1.5% × $100,000 = $1,500

The investor will pay $1,500 for the right to purchase this 7% Treasury bond maturing on October 2015 at 103.

To determine the investor's potential profit and loss on price-based options, use the same rules that were applied to equity options. This investor will breakeven if this bond is trading at 104.16 at expiration. Price-based options settle with the delivery of the underlying security two business days after the option has been exercised. The buyer must pay the exercise price plus accrued interest on the underlying security.

PREMIUMS FOR PRICE-BASED OPTIONS TREASURY BILLS

Price-based options for Treasury bills are based on $1,000,000 par value of a 13-week Treasury bill that has yet to be issued. The option's premium is quoted as an annualized percentage of the $1,000,000 par value. Because there are four 13-week quarters in a year, the premium would have to be divided by four to determine the amount owed or due.

EXAMPLE

A price-based Treasury bill option is quoted at 1%.

1% × $1,000,000 = $10,000
$10,000/4 = $2,500

Because the Treasury bill covered by the option has not yet been issued, an investor may not write a covered Treasury bill call. If a Treasury bill option is exercised, the Treasury bills will be delivered the following Thursday. Because Treasury bills are issued at a discount, the buyer does not owe accrued interest.

RATE-BASED OPTIONS

An investor may speculate on interest rates or hedge a portfolio by using rate-based options. Rate-based options are open for trading based on the most recently issued Treasury bill, note, or bond. Because an investor cannot deliver a "rate," rate-based options settle in cash and use a contract multiplier of 100. Rate-based options have a direct correlation to a change in interest rates. An investor who believes that rates will rise would purchase rate-based calls or sell rate-based puts. An investor who believes that rates are going to fall would purchase rate-based puts or sell rate-based calls.

EXAMPLE

An investor believes that rates are going to rise and purchases 1 March 70 call at 5.

The strike price of 70 = an interest rate of 7%.
The premium of 5 = 5 × 100 = $500.

If rates were to go to 8% by expiration, the investor would have a $500 profit:

$$\begin{array}{r} 80 \\ -70 \\ \hline 10 \end{array}$$

The 7% call option would be 10 points in the money at expiration, and the investor's account would be credited $1,000. This is found by multiplying the in-the-money amount by the contract multiplier of 100. Because the investor paid $500 for the option, the investor's profit would be $500.

	Rates Up	Rates Down	Settlement
Price-based options	Buy puts or sell calls	Buy calls or sell puts	Underlying security is delivered
Rate-based options	Buy calls or sell puts	Buy puts or sell calls	In cash

FOREIGN CURRENCY OPTIONS

The value of one currency relative to another constantly fluctuates. The U.S. dollar is the benchmark against which the value of all other currencies is measured. At any given point, one U.S. dollar may buy more or less of another country's currency. Businesses engaged in international trade can hedge their currency risks through the use of foreign currency options. Foreign currency options may also be used by investors to speculate on the direction of a currency's value relative to the U.S. dollar.

FOREIGN CURRENCY OPTION BASICS

As the value of another country's currency rises, the value of the U.S. dollar falls. As a result, it would now take more U.S. dollars to purchase one unit of that foreign currency. Conversely, if the value of the foreign currency falls, the value of the U.S. dollar will rise, and it would now take fewer U.S. dollars to purchase one unit of the foreign currency. The value of foreign currencies is inversely related to each other. U.S. investors can only trade options on the foreign currency. No options trade domestically on the U.S. dollar. Foreign currency options trade on the Nasdaq/OMX/PHLX stock exchange. The exchange sets the strike prices and the amount of the foreign currency covered under each contract. Foreign currency options that are exercised settle in the delivery of U.S. dollars.

To calculate the total premium for a foreign currency option use the following table:

Currency	Australian Dollar	British Pound	Canadian Dollar	Euro	Japanese Yen	Swiss Franc
Contract size	10,000	10,000	10,000	10,000	1,000,000	10,000
Premium quote	Cents per unit	Cents per unit	Cents per unit	Cents per unit	Hundredth of cents per unit	Cents per unit
Quote	$.01	$.01	$.01	$.01	$.0001	$.01

To calculate the total premium, multiply the quoted premium by .01. If the option is for the Japanese yen, multiply the quoted premium by .0001. Once you have determined the quoted premium, multiply it by the number of foreign currency units covered by the contract.

 TAKENOTE!

You will not be required to remember the amount of the foreign currency covered under the contract. If you receive a question relating to foreign currency, the question will contain the amount of the foreign currency covered under the contract.

BUYING FOREIGN CURRENCY CALLS AND PUTS

Businesses and investors will trade foreign currency options for very different reasons. A business will trade foreign currency options to manage its foreign currency risk. An importer will purchase calls on the foreign currency of the country where it purchases products to reduce the risk of that country's currency rising in value in relation to the U.S. dollar. If the country's currency becomes stronger, it will take more U.S. dollars to purchase the same amount of the foreign currency. As a result, the cost to the importer will rise. Alternatively, in the case of an exporter, a fall in the value of a foreign currency will make its products more expensive to the foreign customer and will make its products less attractive. As a result, the exporter, to manage its foreign currency risk, will purchase puts on the foreign currency.

 TESTTIP!

Remember the mnemonic EPIC: exporters buy puts, importers buy calls.

An investor in foreign currency options would take the following positions given the following circumstances:

An investor would buy calls or sell puts if:

- There is good economic news from that country.
- The stock market in that country rises.
- There is a large discovery of oil or gold in that country.
- Government instability subsides.

An investor would buy puts and sell calls if:

- There is bad economic news from that country.
- The stock market in that country falls.
- There is an increase in political instability.

THE OPTION CLEARING CORPORATION

The Option Clearing Corporation (OCC) was created and is owned by the exchanges that trade options. The OCC issues all standardized options and guarantees their performance. The OCC does not guarantee a customer against a loss; it only guarantees the option's performance. The OCC guarantees that if an investor who is short an option is unable to perform the obligation under the contract, the investor who is exercising the contract will still be able to do so without any delay. Without this performance guarantee, the trading of standardized options would be impossible. The OCC issues option contracts the day after the trade date, and all standardized options will settle on the next business day or trade date plus one. When an investor closes out its position through either a closing purchase or sale, the OCC will eliminate the closing investor's obligations or rights from its books. All standardized options of the same series are interchangeable or fungible. For example, all XYZ April 50 calls are the same. In order to meet the prospectus requirements of the Securities Act of 1933, the OCC publishes a disclosure document known as the Characteristics and Risks of Standardized Options. All option investors must be given this document prior to or at the time their account is approved for options trading. Should the OCC update the options disclosure document, the updated risk disclosure document must be sent to all investors who transact business in the type of options subject to the update.

THE OPTIONS MARKETS

Standardized options trade on exchanges through a dual-auction process similar to that for listed stocks. All standardized options are known as listed options. However, large institutions may trade specialized options OTC. The terms and conditions of the contract may be negotiated with the OTC options dealer. Listed options trade on the following exchanges:

- CBOE
- NYSE/AMEX
- NYSE/ARCA
- Nasdaq/OMX/PHLX
- PSE

While the NYSE is the premier exchange for listed stocks, the Chicago Board Option Exchange (CBOE) is the premier exchange for listed options.

THE CHICAGO BOARD OPTION EXCHANGE

The CBOE functions in many ways exactly like other exchanges, except that it has one major difference. The CBOE does not use a specialist system like the one used on all other exchanges. The specialist system requires that the specialist member maintain a fair and orderly market in the security in which it specializes and that it buys and sells for its own account. However, on the CBOE, the duty of maintaining a fair and orderly market is given to an exchange employee known as an order book official or board broker. The personnel trading on the options floors are:

- Order book official or specialist
- Market maker/registered option trader/local
- Spread broker
- Commission house broker
- Two-dollar broker

ORDER BOOK OFFICIAL

An order book officials on the CBOE is an employee of the exchange who maintains a fair and orderly market for the options he or she has been assigned. Order book officials also maintain a book of limit and stop orders left with them and will execute an order when the order's conditions are met. Order book officials may not trade for their own accounts.

SPECIALIST

A specialist is a member of any other option exchange that is required to maintain a fair and orderly market for the options in which he or she specializes. Specialists are required to buy and sell from their own accounts in the absence of public orders and must execute stop and limit orders left with them.

OPTIONS MARKET MAKERS

An option market maker is an individual member of the exchange who is required to maintain a two-sided market in the options he or she trades. A two-sided market consists of both a bid and an offer. An options market maker must display a two-sided market at all times. An options marker maker may also be called a registered options trader or a local. These members trade for their own profit and loss.

COMMISSION HOUSE BROKER

A commission house broker is an employee of a member organization and will execute orders for the member's customers and for the member's own account.

TWO-DOLLAR BROKER

A two-dollar broker is an independent member who will execute orders for commission house brokers when they are too busy managing other orders.

SPREAD BROKER

A spread broker is an independent member who specializes in executing multiple-option orders, such as spreads and straddles, for a fee.

OPENING AND CLOSING OPTION PRICES

Options begin trading as soon as an opening price for the underlying security may be determined. Options are opened for trading through a rotation that accepts orders and quotes for the series of calls that expire the soonest and have the lowest strike price. The rotation continues through all the near-term series of call options and continues to the call options that expire further out. Once all of the calls are open, the rotation continues with the puts, starting with the puts with the highest strike price and the nearest expiration.

Listed options also close on a rotation as soon as a closing price can be determined for the underlying security. A rotation can also be imposed during fast market conditions if the specialist or the order book official determines that the market is not operating in an orderly fashion. If a stock is halted, all option trading on that stock is also halted until the stock reopens.

ORDER EXECUTION

Most customer orders, which are market orders or executable limit orders, will be routed electronically to the trading post for execution. The electronic order routing system bypasses the firm's commission house broker and the order is executed automatically and an execution report is sent back to the brokerage firm. If the customer's order cannot be executed immediately the order will become part of the book. The more complex orders will be handled by the firm's commission house broker.

EXPIRATION AND EXERCISE

The OCC has set the following rules for stock and narrow-based index options expiration and exercise:

- Options cease trading at 4:00 p.m. EST (3:00 p.m. CST) on the third Friday of each month prior to expiration.
- Option holders who wish to exercise their options must do so by 5:30 p.m. EST (4:30 p.m. CST) on the third Friday of each month.
- All options expire at 11:59 p.m. EST (10:59 p.m. CST) on the third Friday of each month.
- All options held by public customers will automatically be exercised if they are 1 cent in the money.
- All options held by broker dealers will automatically be exercised if they are 1 cent in the money.

The OCC has set the following rules for broad based option expiration and exercise:

- Options cease trading at 4:15 p.m. EST (3:15 p.m. CST) on the third Friday of each month prior to expiration.
- Option holders who wish to exercise their options must do so by 5:30 p.m. EST (4:30 p.m. CST) on the third Friday of each month.
- All options expire at 11:59 p.m. EST (10:59 p.m. CST) on the third Friday of each month.

The following rules have been set for foreign currency options expiration and exercise:

- Foreign currency options trade on the Nasdaq/PHLX from 9:30 a.m. to 4:00 p.m. EST.
- Options expire at 11:59 p.m. EST on the third Friday of each month.
- Position limits are 600,000 contracts on the same side of the market.

AMERICAN VS. EUROPEAN EXERCISE

There are two styles of options that trade in the United States: American and European. An American-style option may be exercised at any time by the holder during the life of the contract. A European-style option may only be exercised by the holder at expiration. If an investor who is long an option decides to exercise the option, the OCC will randomly assign the exercise notice to a broker dealer who is short that option. The broker dealer must then assign the exercise notice to a customer who is short that option. The broker dealer may use any fair method for randomly assigning exercise notices.

MARKET VOLATILITY OPTIONS/VIX

The rate of change in prices is known as volatility. Active traders, in many cases, need both volatility in prices and changes in the volatility of prices to realize profits. Investors also can speculate on market volatility by trading VIX options. VIX options measure the market volatility of the S&P 500 (SPX) by calculating the spread between the bid and ask of S&P 500 index options. The VIX calculation uses the spread from the two closest option expiration cycles with at least eight days remaining to expiration to calculate a 30-day volatility for the index. VIX options trade from 8:30 a.m. to 3:15 p.m. CST in 1 to 2.5 point intervals and differ from other options in several ways.

VIX options:

- Are European style exercise.
- Expire Wednesday 30 days prior to the third Friday of the following month.
- Settlement values are quoted under the symbol VRO.

FLEX OPTIONS

Large and sophisticated investors often need to set up trades based on their specific needs. For these investors, the terms and conditions of standardized options often do not meet their requirements. Flex options allow investors to set the:

- Expiration.
- Strike price (can be set as a dollar amount or as a percentage of the price of the underlying security, rounded to the nearest $.01).
- Expiration style (American or European).
- Value of the contract.

The expiration for flex options can be set from one day up to 15 years. However, a flex option may not expire on any day that is on or within two business days of a nonflex option expiration date. Flex options are not subject to positions limits, but are subject to reporting requirements. A trader must present the specifics of the desired flex option contract in the trading crowd to receive a market or quote for the flex option by either stepping into the crowd or electronically via the CBOE's CFLEX system. The exchanges may set minimum values for flex options contracts and there is a limited secondary market for the flex option after the position has been established. Flex options can trade on the following instruments:

- Equities
- ETFs
- Indexes
- Currencies

The exercise of the flex option for equities and ETFs will result in the delivery of the underlying security the next business day following the receipt of an exercise notice. Each flex option for equities and ETFs is for 100 shares of the underlying instrument.

WEEKLY OPTIONS

The CBOE has introduced weekly options designed to provide investors with the ability to speculate on the direction of a stock or index based on the release of pending news such as an earnings release or an announcement from the Federal Reserve board relating to an interest rate decision. Weekly options also will allow investors who are long or short to hedge their positions for only the period of time that includes the pending news release. As such, the investor will be able to buy the hedge at a much lower premium due to the extremely short time frame of the option. Weekly options are listed on Thursday and expire the following Friday. New weeklies are listed each week, however, no new weekly options will be listed that expire in the same week as standard options.

MINI OPTIONS

The options exchanges have begun offering option contracts that allow an investor to speculate or to hedge a position in a high priced security that is less than 100 shares. With many stocks trading well into the triple digits, individual investors often can only afford to purchase a small number of shares (also known as an odd lot). These investors who wish to hedge a small position would not be able to effectively do so with a standard option contract covering 100 shares. Mini options cover 10 shares of the underlying security. To determine the total premium an investor would pay or receive, you must multiply the premium by the 10 shares covered under the contract rather than 100 shares for a standard option contract. Mini stock options are American style exercise and the exercise of mini stock options will result in the delivery of the underlying shares. Options also trade on the mini S & P 500. The mini S & P 500 contract has a value equal to 1/10 of the value of the S & P 500 contract. For example, if the S & P 500 was trading at 1,950 the mini contract would be trading at 195. Options on the mini S & P use a multiplier of 100. Options on the mini S & P are European exercise and can only be exercised at expiration. The exercise of options on the mini S & P result in the delivery of cash.

POSITION AND EXERCISE LIMITS

In order to prevent large investors from manipulating the price of a stock or the value of an index, the exchanges have set maximum limits for the size of a position that may be established on the same side of the market. The current maximum limit is 250,000 contracts on the same side of the market. The bullish side of the market is:

- Long calls and short puts

The bearish side:

- Long puts and short calls

EXAMPLE   If an investor is long 40,000 calls, the maximum number of puts the investor could sell is 35,000 if the maximum position limit was 75,000 contracts.

STOCK SPLITS AND STOCK DIVIDENDS

Whenever an underlying security declares a stock split or a substantial stock dividend, the terms of the option contract must be adjusted. The exam will focus on forward stock splits. When a company declares a forward stock split, such as a 2 for 1 or 3 for 1, the number of contracts will increase and the option's strike price will be adjusted down. Each contract will still be for 100 shares, and the investor's aggregate exercise price will always remain the same. If the split that was declared by the company is not an even split, the number of shares covered by the contract will increase, and the strike price will be adjusted down. If a contract is for more than 100 shares an * (asterisk) will appear next to the quote.

EXAMPLE

Type of Split	Old Contract	New Contract
2:1	1 XYZ Oct 70 call	2 XYZ Oct 35 calls
4:1	5 ABC April 60 puts	20 ABC April 15 puts
3:2	1 XYZ April 60 call	1 (150 sh) April 40 call

Options are not adjusted for cash dividends but are adjusted for stock dividends.

EXAMPLE   If an investor owns 1 XYZ May 40 call and XYZ declares a 10% stock dividend, the investor will now own 1 XYZ (110) May 36 call.

The number of shares covered by the contract will increase, and the strike price will be adjusted down. The number of shares is rounded down to the next whole share.

TAXATION OF OPTIONS

An investor who purchases a call or put that expires worthless will have a short-term capital loss. An investor who purchases long-term LEAPS (long-term equity anticipation securities), which have a term of up to 39 months and that eventually expire, will have a long-term capital loss. The writer of both LEAPS and traditional options that expire worthless will have a short-term capital gain.

CLOSING AN OPTION POSITION

Executing an order to close an option position will result in a capital gain or capital loss if the closing price differs from the opening price.

EXERCISING A CALL

If an investor exercises a call option, the option's premium is added to the investor's cost base for the stock to determine any capital gain or capital loss. If an investor wrote a call, the call options premium must be added to the option's strike price to determine the investor's proceeds on the sale of the stock.

EXERCISING A PUT

An investor who exercises a put must subtract the put's premium from the option's strike price to determine the proceeds from the sale. A put writer who is exercising a put must subtract the premium from the strike price to determine the cost base for the stock.

PROTECTIVE PUTS

An investor who has purchased a protective put on a stock held less than 12 months will cap the holding period for that stock at 12 months and will have a short-term gain or loss on the sale of the stock. If the stock was held for more than 12 months before purchasing the put, any gain or loss will be long term.

COVERED CALLS

An investor who sells out of the money calls will not change the holding period for the stock if the calls expire. An investor who sells deep in the money calls on a stock held less than 12 months will have a short-term gain or loss.

OPTION COMPLIANCE

All advertising and sales literature relating to options must be approved by the designated registered options and security futures principal (SROSFP) before it is first used. Educational material relating to options is not advertising or sales literature, but must inform the readers how they may obtain information about the risks of option investing.

OPTION AGREEMENT

All new option accounts must be approved by the registered options principal prior to the first option trade. An option investor must sign and return the option agreement within 15 days of the account's approval to trade options. If the investor fails to return the option agreement within 15 days, no new option positions may be opened and the investor will be limited to closing transactions only until the options agreement is signed and returned.

Pretest

OPTIONS

1. You sold 10 IBM May 95 puts at 5.70. Your maximum gain is:
   a. $570.
   b. $5,700.
   c. unlimited.
   d. $95,000.

2. An investor who is short 1 U.S. T bond 103 call receives an exercise notice. The investor will receive:
   I. $10,300.
   II. $103,000.
   III. Accrued interest.
   IV. A full semiannual interest payment.
   a. I and IV
   b. II and IV
   c. II and III
   d. I and III

3. The exercise of a call option results in the delivery of the stock:
   a. the same day.
   b. the next business day.
   c. in two business days.
   d. in three business days.

4. Your customer sells 10 IBM Nov 95 puts to open at 3.15. The customer's maximum gain is:

   a. unlimited.

   b. $95,000.

   c. $3,150.

   d. $91,850.

5. You are long 10,000 shares of XYZ at 42 and are concerned about a market decline and you would like to take in some additional income. You should:

   a. sell 10 XYZ Oct 45 puts.

   b. sell 100 XYZ Oct 45 calls.

   c. sell 100 XYZ Oct 45 puts.

   d. sell 10 XYZ Oct 45 calls.

6. Which of the following are true about an option?

   I. It is a contract between two parties that determines the time and place at which a security may be bought or sold.

   II. The two parties are known as the buyer and the seller. The money paid by the buyer of the option is known as the option's premium.

   III. The buyer has bought the right to buy or sell the security depending on the type of option.

   IV. The seller has an obligation to perform under the contract, possibly to buy or sell the stock depending on the option involved.

   a. I, III, and IV

   b. I, II, III, and IV

   c. I, II, and III

   d. II, III, and IV

7. You bought the following:

   10 XYZ April 75 calls at 3.40
   10 XYZ April 75 puts at 4.10

   Your maximum gain is:

   a. unlimited.

   b. $67,500.

   c. $7,500.

   d. $82,500.

8. You think that bond prices are going to decline, and you want to profit from the move. You would most likely buy:

    I. Rate-based puts.

    II. Rate-based calls.

    III. Price-based puts.

    IV. Price-based calls.

    a. II and III

    b. I and IV

    c. I and III

    d. III and IV

9. A bullish investor would establish which of the following?

    I. Credit put spread

    II. Long straddle

    III. Debit call spread

    IV. Short straddle

    a. I and II

    b. I and III

    c. II and III

    d. II and IV

10. Your customer sold 15 XYZ Aug 70 calls and bought 15 XYZ Aug 90 calls. What does your customer want to happen?

    I. The options to be exercised

    II. The options to expire

    III. The spread to widen

    IV. The spread to narrow

    a. I and IV

    b. II and IV

    c. II and III

    d. I only

11. Which of the following are bearish?

    I. Call seller

    II. Put seller

    III. Call buyer

    IV. Put buyer

    a. II and III

    b. II and IV

    c. I and IV

    d. I and II

12. A U.S. importer is buying $10,000,000 worth of goods from a Japanese manufacturer. The payment will be made six months from now in Japanese Yen. To provide a hedge, the U.S. importer would do which of the following?

    a. Buy calls on the U.S. dollar

    b. Buy puts on the U.S. dollar

    c. Buy calls on the Japanese yen

    d. Buy puts on the Japanese yen

13. Capped index options automatically exercise if they go how far in the money?

    a. 60 points

    b. 30 points

    c. 50 points

    d. 100 points

14. An investor buys 10 XYZ Nov 75 calls at 4.10 on Monday May 11th. The trade will settle on:

    a. Thursday, May 14.

    b. Tuesday, May 12.

    c. Monday, May 11.

    d. Monday, May 18.

15. Which of the following issues standardized options?

    a. The exchanges

    b. The OCC

    c. The company

    d. Nasdaq

16. A customer establishes the following position:
    Sold 10 ABC Oct 50 puts at 4
    Bought 10 ABC Oct 40 puts at 1
    The customer's maximum gain is:

    a. $1,000.

    b. $7,000.

    c. $4,000.

    d. $3,000.

17. An aggressive investor sells short 1,000 shares of OnNet.com at $30 per share. To gain the maximum protection, he should:

    a. sell 10 OnNet June 30 puts.

    b. sell 10 OnNet June 30 calls.

    c. buy 10 OnNet June 30 puts.

    d. buy 10 OnNet June 30 calls.

18. An investor opening an options account would least likely be approved to do which of the following?

    a. Naked calls

    b. Naked puts

    c. Long straddles

    d. Short straddles

19. An investor buys 10 XYZ May 70 calls at 3.10 when XYZ is at 68. At expiration, the stock is at 77 and the investor closes out the position at its intrinsic value. What is the profit or loss?

    a. $7,000 profit

    b. $7,000 loss

    c. $3,100 loss

    d. $3,900 profit

20. The OCC is the:

    a. Options Clearing Corporation.

    b. Options Counseling Committee.

    c. Options and Claims Corporation.

    d. Options Clearing Committee.

21. Which of the following will create a diagonal spread?

    I. Short 10 XYZ Oct 50 puts

    II. Long 10 XYZ Oct 60 puts

    III. Long 10 XYZ Nov 50 puts

    IV. Long 10 XYZ Nov 40 puts

    a. I and IV

    b. II and IV

    c. I and II

    d. I and III

22. An option customer establishes the following position:

Bought 15 XYZ March 50 calls at 5
Bought 15 XYZ March 50 puts at 4.10
The maximum possible gain on this position is:

    a. $45,000.

    b. $41,900.

    c. unlimited.

    d. $13,600.

23. A fixed-income investor may not write a:

    a. price-based cover call.

    b. rate-based covered call.

    c. price-based put spread.

    d. rate-based put spread.

24. Your existing customer has just been approved by your firm's ROP to trade options. How long does the customer have to return the signed option agreement?

   a. 5 days

   b. 45 days

   c. 15 days

   d. 30 days

25. The OCC is:

   a. wholly owned by the exchanges.

   b. wholly owned by the NYSE and FINRA.

   c. the self-regulatory body for the options industry.

   d. a division of the SEC.

Mutual Funds

INTRODUCTION

We examined many of the different types of securities that an investment company may purchase in order to achieve its objectives. In this chapter, we will look at how an investment company pools investors' funds in order to purchase a diversified portfolio of securities. It is imperative that all candidates have a complete understanding of how an investment company operates. Some of the test focus points will be on:

- Types of investment companies
- Investment company structure
- Investment company registration
- Investment company taxation
- Investment strategies and recommendations
- Investor benefits

INVESTMENT COMPANY PHILOSOPHY

An investment company is organized as either a corporation or as a trust. Money from individual investors is then pooled together into a single account and used to purchase securities that will have the greatest chance of helping the investment company reach its objectives. All investors jointly own the portfolio that is created through these pooled funds, and each investor has an undivided interest in the securities. No single shareholder has any right or claim that exceeds the rights or claims of any other shareholder, regardless of the size of the investment. Investment companies offer individual investors the opportunity to have their money managed by professionals who may otherwise only offer their services to large institutions. Through diversification, the investor may participate in the future growth or income generated from the large number of different securities contained in the portfolio. Both diversification and professional management should contribute significantly to the attainment of the objectives set forth by the investment company. There are many other features and benefits that may be offered to investors that will be examined later in this chapter.

TYPES OF INVESTMENT COMPANIES

All investment company offerings are subject to the Securities Act of 1933, which requires the investment company to register with the Securities and Exchange Commission (SEC) and to give all purchasers a prospectus. Investment companies are also all subject to the Investment Company Act of 1940, which sets forth guidelines on how investment companies operate. The Investment Company Act of 1940 breaks down investment companies into three different types:

1. Face-amount company (FAC)
2. Unit investment trust (UIT)
3. Management investment company (mutual fund)

FACE-AMOUNT COMPANY/FACE-AMOUNT CERTIFICATES

An investor may enter into a contract with an issuer of a face-amount certificate to contract to receive a stated or fixed amount of money (the face amount) at a stated date in the future. In exchange for this future sum, the investor must deposit an agreed upon lump sum or make scheduled installment payments over time. Face-amount certificates are rarely issued these days, because most of the tax advantages that the investment once offered have been lost through changes in the tax laws.

UNIT INVESTMENT TRUST (UIT)

A unit investment trust (UIT) will invest either in a fixed portfolio of securities or in a nonfixed portfolio of securities. A fixed UIT will traditionally invest in a large block of government or municipal debt. The bonds will be held until maturity, and the proceeds will be distributed to investors in the UIT. Once the proceeds have been distributed to the investors, the UIT will have achieved its objective and will cease to exist. A nonfixed UIT will purchase mutual fund shares in order to reach a stated objective. A nonfixed UIT is also known as a contractual plan. Both types of UITs are organized as trusts and operate as a holding company for the portfolio. UITs are not actively managed, and they do not have a board of directors or investment advisers. Both types of UITs issue units or shares of beneficial interest to investors that represent as undivided interest in the underlying portfolio of securities. UITs must maintain a secondary market in the units or shares to offer some liquidity to investors.

MANAGEMENT INVESTMENT COMPANY (MUTUAL FUND)

A management investment company employs an investment adviser to manage a diversified portfolio of securities designed to obtain its stated investment objective. The management company may be organized as either an open-end company or as a closed-end company. The main difference between an open-end company and a closed-end company is how the shares are purchased and sold. An open-end company offers new shares to any investor who wants to invest. This is known as a continuous primary offering. Because the offering of new shares is continuous, the capitalization of the open-end fund is unlimited. Stated another way, an open-end mutual fund may raise as much money as investors are willing to put in. An open-end fund must repurchase its own shares from investors who want to redeem them. There is no secondary market for open-end mutual fund shares. The shares must be purchased from the fund company and redeemed to the fund company. A closed-end fund offers common shares to investors through an initial public offering (IPO), just like a stock. Its capitalization is limited to the number of authorized shares that have been approved for sale. Shares of the closed-end fund will trade in the secondary market in investor-to-investor transactions on an exchange or in the over-the-counter market (OTC), just like common shares.

OPEN-END VS. CLOSED-END FUNDS

Although both open-end and closed-end funds are designed to achieve their stated investment objective, the manner in which they operate is different. The following is a side-by-side comparison of the important features of both open-end and closed-end funds and shows how those features differ between the fund types.

Feature	Open End	Closed End
Capitalization	Unlimited continuous primary offering	Single fixed offering through IPO
Investor may purchase	Full and fractional shares	Full shares only
Securities offered	Common shares only	Common and preferred shares and debt securities
Shares are purchased and sold	Shares are purchased from the fund company and redeemed to the fund company	Shares may be purchased only from the fund company during IPO then secondary market transactions between investors
Share pricing	Shares are priced by formula $NAV + SC = POP$	Shares are priced by supply and demand
Shareholder rights	Dividends and voting	Dividends, voting, and preemptive

DIVERSIFIED VS. NONDIVERSIFIED

Investors in a mutual fund will achieve diversification through their investment in the fund. However, in order to determine if the fund itself is a diversified fund the fund must meet certain requirements. The Investment Company Act of 1940 has laid out an asset allocation model that must be followed in order for the fund to call itself a diversified mutual fund. It is known as the 75-5-10 test, and the requirements are as follows:

75%—75% of the fund's assets must be invested in securities of other issuers. Cash and cash equivalents are countered as part of the 75%. A cash equivalent may be a T-bill or a money market instrument.

5%—The investment company may not invest more than 5% of its assets in any one company.

10%—The investment company may not own more than 10% of any company's outstanding voting stock.

EXAMPLE   The XYZ fund markets itself as a diversified mutual fund. It has $10,000,000,000 in net assets, and the investment adviser thinks that the ABC Company would be a great company to acquire for $300,000,000. Because XYZ markets itself as a diversified mutual fund, it would not be allowed to purchase the company even though the price of $300,000,000 would be less than 5% of the fund's assets. The investment company must meet both the diversification requirements of 5% of assets and 10% of ownership in order to continue to market itself as a diversified mutual fund.

INVESTMENT COMPANY REGISTRATION

Investment companies are regulated by both the Securities Act of 1933 and by the Investment Company Act of 1940. An investment company must register with the SEC if the company operates to own, invest, reinvest, or trade in securities. A company must also register with the SEC as an investment company if the company has 40% or more of its assets invested in securities other than those issued by the U.S. government or one of the company's subsidiaries.

REGISTRATION REQUIREMENTS

Before an investment company may register with the SEC, it must meet certain minimum requirements. An investment company may not register with the SEC unless it has the following:

- Minimum net worth of $100,000.
- At least 100 shareholders.
- Clearly defined investment objectives.

An investment company may be allowed to register without having 100 shareholders and without a net worth of $100,000 if it can meet these requirements within 90 days.

Investment companies must file a full registration with the SEC before the offering becomes effective. The investment company is considered to have registered when the SEC receives its notice of registration. The investment company's registration statement must contain:

- The type of investment company (open-end, closed-end, etc.).
- Biographical information on the officers and directors of the company.
- Name and address of each affiliated person.

- Plans to concentrate investments in any one area (i.e., sector fund).
- Plans to invest in real estate or commodities.
- Borrowing plans.
- Conditions under which investment objective may be changed through a vote of shareholders.

Once registered the investment company may:

- Raise money through the sale of shares.
- Lend money to earn interest.
- Borrow money on a limited basis.

An investment company obtains its investment capital from shareholders through the sale of shares. Once it's operating, it may lend money to earn interest, such as by purchasing bonds or notes. An investment company, however, may not lend money to employees. An investment company may borrow money for such business purposes as to redeem shares. If the investment company borrows money it must have $3 in equity for every dollar that it wants to borrow. Another way of saying that is that the investment company must maintain an asset-to-debt ratio of at least 3:1 or of at least 300%.

An investment company is prohibited from:

- Taking over or controlling other companies.
- Acting as a bank or a savings and loan.
- Receiving commission for executing orders or for acting as a broker.
- Continuing to operate with less than 100 shareholders or less than $100,000 net worth.

Unless the investment company meets strict capital and disclosure requirements, it may not engage in any of the following:

- Selling securities short.
- Buying securities on margin.
- Maintaining joint accounts.
- Distributing its own shares.

Regardless of the makeup of its investment holdings, all of the following are exempt from the registration requirements of an investment company:

- Broker dealers
- Underwriters
- Banks and savings and loans
- Mortgage companies
- Real estate investment trusts (REITs)
- Security holder protection committees

INVESTMENT COMPANY COMPONENTS

Investment companies have several different groups that serve specialized functions. Each of these groups plays a key role in the investment company's operation. They are:

- The board of directors
- The investment adviser
- The custodian bank
- The transfer agent

BOARD OF DIRECTORS

Management companies have an organizational structure that is similar to that of other companies. The board of directors oversees the company's president and other officers who run the day-to-day operations of the company. The board and the corporate officers concern themselves with the business and administrative functions of the company. They do not manage the investment portfolio. The board of directors:

- Defines investment objectives.
- Hires the investment adviser, custodian bank, and transfer agent.
- Determines what type of funds to offer (i.e., growth, income, etc.).

The board of directors is elected by a vote of the shareholders. The Investment Company Act of 1940 governs the makeup of the board. The Investment

Company Act of 1940 requires that at majority or at least 51% of the board be noninterested persons. A noninterested person is a person whose only affiliation with the fund is as a member of the board. Therefore, a maximum of 49% of the board may hold another position within the fund company or may otherwise be interested in the fund. An affiliated person is anyone who could exercise control over the company, such as an accountant. An affiliated person may also include:

- Broker dealer
- Attorney
- Immediate family of an affiliated person
- Anyone else the SEC designates

Both affiliated and interested parties are prohibited from selling securities or property to the investment company or any of its subsidiaries. Anyone who has been convicted of any felony or securities-related misdemeanor or who has been barred from the securities business may not serve on the board of directors.

INVESTMENT ADVISER

The investment company's board of directors hires the investment adviser to manage the fund's portfolio. The investment adviser is a company, not a person, that must also determine the tax consequences of distributions to shareholders and ensure that the investment strategies are in line with the fund's stated investment objectives. The investment adviser's compensation is a percentage of the net assets of the fund, not a percentage of the profits, although performance bonuses are allowed. The investment adviser's fee is typically the largest expense of the fund, and the more aggressive the objective, the higher the fee. The investment adviser may not borrow from the fund and may not have any securities-related convictions.

CUSTODIAN BANK

The custodian bank or the exchange member broker dealer that has been hired by the investment company physically holds all of the fund's cash and securities. The custodian holds all of the fund's assets for safekeeping and provides other bookkeeping and clerical functions for the investment company, such as maintaining books and records for accumulation plans for investors. All fund assets must be kept segregated from other assets. The custodian must ensure that only approved persons have access to the account and that all distributions are done in line with SEC guidelines.

TRANSFER AGENT

The transfer agent for the investment company handles the issuance, cancellation, and redemption of fund shares. The transfer agent also handles name changes and may be part of the fund's custodian or a separate company. The transfer agent receives an agreed upon fee for its services.

MUTUAL FUND DISTRIBUTION

Most mutual funds do not sell their own shares directly to investors. The distribution of the shares is the responsibility of the underwriter. The underwriter for a mutual fund is also known as the sponsor or distributor. The underwriter is selected by the fund's board of directors and receives a fee in the form of a sales charge for the shares it distributes. As the underwriter receives orders for the mutual fund shares, it purchases the shares directly from the fund at the net asset value (NAV). The sales charge is then added to the NAV as the underwriter's compensation. This process of adding the sales charge to the NAV is responsible for the mutual fund pricing formula, which is NAV + SC = POP.

The underwriter may purchase shares from the mutual fund only to fill customer orders. It may not hold mutual fund shares in inventory in anticipation of receiving future customer orders.

SELLING GROUP MEMBER

Most brokerage firms maintain selling agreements with mutual fund distributors, which allows them to purchase mutual fund shares at a discount from the public offering price (POP). Selling group members may then sell the mutual fund shares to investors at the POP and earn part of the sales charge. In order to purchase mutual fund shares at a discount from the POP, the selling group member must be a member of FINRA. All non-FINRA members and suspended members must be treated as members of the general public and pay the public offering price.

 **TAKENOTE!**

As a professional courtesy registered representatives are allowed to purchase mutual fund shares for their own investment account at or near the NAV.

DISTRIBUTION OF NO-LOAD MUTUAL FUND SHARES

No-load mutual funds do not charge a sales charge to the investors who invest in the mutual fund. Because there is no sales charge, the mutual fund may sell the shares directly to investors at the NAV.

DISTRIBUTION OF MUTUAL FUND SHARES

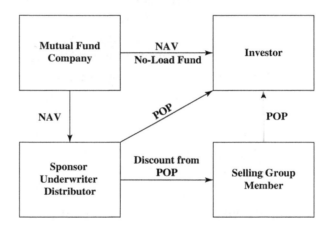

MUTUAL FUND PROSPECTUS

The prospectus is the official offering document for open-end mutual fund shares. The prospectus, or information on where to obtain a prospectus, must be presented to all purchasers of the fund either before or during the sales presentation. The prospectus is the fund's full disclosure document and provides details regarding:

- Fund's investment objectives
- Sales charges
- Management expenses
- Fund services

- Performance data for the past one, five, and 10 years, or for the life of the fund

The prospectus, which is given to most investors, is the summary prospectus. Investors who want additional information regarding the mutual fund may request a statement of additional information. The statement of additional information will include details regarding the following as of the date it was published:

- Fund's securities holdings
- Balance sheet
- Income statement
- Portfolio turnover data
- Compensation paid to the board of directors and investment advisory board

A summary prospectus that contains past performance data is known as an advertising prospectus. Requirements regarding updating and using a mutual fund prospectus are as follows.

A MUTUAL FUND PROSPECTUS

The mutual fund prospectus:

- Should be updated by the fund every 12 months.
- Must be updated by the fund every 13 months.
- May be used by a representative for up to 16 months.
- Should be discarded after 16 months from publication.

Mutual funds are also required to disclose either in the prospectus or in its annual report to shareholders:

- A performance comparison graph showing the performance of the fund.
- Names of the officers and directors who are responsible for the portfolio's day-to-day management.
- Disclosure of any factors that materially affected performance over the latest fiscal year.

Mutual funds are required to include summary information at the front of its statutory prospectus. The purpose of this summary information is to clearly convey all of the most pertinent information an investor would require to make an informed decision about the fund. The terms to be detailed in the summary information include the fund's investment objectives, past performance, costs, and the biographical information for the management of the fund. Also covered in the summary information will be the principal investment strategies, compensation, purchase and redemptions, and tax implications. Mutual funds may use this information to create a "mutual fund profile" for investors. Investors may use the profile to purchase the mutual fund shares but the investor must be given information on where to obtain a statutory prospectus and the statement of additional information for the fund.

CHARACTERISTICS OF OPEN-END MUTUAL FUND SHARES

All open-end mutual fund shares are sold through a continuous primary offering, and each new investor receives new shares from the fund company. The new shares are created for investors as their orders are received by the fund. Investors purchase shares from the fund company at the POP and redeem them to the fund company at the NAV. The mutual fund has seven calendar days to forward the proceeds to an investor after receiving a redemption request. If the investor has possession of the mutual fund certificates, the fund then has seven calendar days from the receipt of the certificate by the custodian to forward the proceeds. Suspension of the seven-day rule may be allowed only if:

- The NYSE is closed for an extraordinary reason.
- The NYSE's trading is restricted or limited.
- The liquidation of the securities would not be practical.
- An SEC order has been issued.

ADDITIONAL CHARACTERISTICS OF OPEN-END MUTUAL FUNDS

Open-end mutual funds also have the following characteristics:

- Diversification.
- Professional management.
- Low minimum investment.
- Easy tax reporting (form 1099).
- Reduction of sales charges through breakpoint schedule, letter of intent, and rights accumulation.
- Automatic reinvestment of dividends and capital gains distributions.
- Structured withdrawal plans.

MUTUAL FUND INVESTMENT OBJECTIVES

EQUITY FUNDS

The only investment that will meet a growth objective is common stock. Growth funds seeking capital appreciation will invest in the common stock of corporations whose business is growing more rapidly than other companies and more rapidly than the economy as a whole. Growth funds seek capital gains and do not produce significant dividend income.

EQUITY INCOME FUND

An equity income fund will purchase both common and preferred shares that have a long track record of paying consistent dividends. Preferred shares are purchased by the fund for their stated dividend. Utility stocks are also purchased, because utilities traditionally pay out the highest percentage of their earnings to shareholders in the form of dividends. Other common shares of blue chip companies may also be purchased.

SECTOR FUNDS

Mutual funds that concentrate 25% or more of their assets in one business area or region are known as sector funds. Technology, biotech, and gold funds would all be examples of sector funds that concentrate their investments in one business area. A Northeast growth fund would be an example of a sector fund that concentrates its assets geographically. Sector funds traditionally carry higher risk-reward ratios. If the sector does well, the investor may enjoy a higher rate of return. If, however, the sector performs poorly, the investor may suffer larger losses. The high risk-reward ratio is due to the fund's concentration in one area.

INDEX FUNDS

An index fund is designed to mirror the performance of a large market index such as the S&P 500 or the Dow Jones Industrial Average. An index fund's portfolio is composed of the stocks that are included in the index that the fund is designed to track. The fund manager does not actively seek out stocks to buy or sell, making an index fund an example of a fund that is passively managed. If the stock is in the index it will usually be in the portfolio. Portfolio turnover for an index fund is generally low, which helps keep the fund's expenses down.

GROWTH AND INCOME (COMBINATION FUND)

A growth and income fund, as the name suggests, invests to achieve both capital appreciation and current income. The fund will invest a portion of its assets in shares of common stock that offer the greatest appreciation potential and will invest a portion of its assets in preferred and common shares that pay high dividends in order to produce income for investors.

BALANCED FUNDS

A balanced fund invests in both stocks and bonds, according to a predetermined formula. For example, the fund may invest 70% of its assets in equities and 30% of its assets in bonds.

ASSET ALLOCATION FUNDS

Asset allocation funds invest in stocks, bonds, and money market instruments, according to the expected performance for each market. For example, if the portfolio manager feels that equities will do well, the manager may invest more money in equities. Alternatively, if the manager feels that the bond market will outperform equities, the manager may shift more money into the debt markets.

OTHER TYPES OF FUNDS

There are other types of equity funds, such as foreign stock funds that invest outside the United States, and special situation funds that invest in takeover candidates and restructuring companies. A final type of fund is an option income fund, which purchases shares of common stock and sells call options against the portfolio in order to generate premium income for investors. Because the fund has sold call options on the shares it owns, it will limit the capital appreciation of the portfolio.

ALTERNATIVE FUNDS

Alternative funds also known as alt funds or liquid alts invest in nontraditional assets or illiquid assets and may employ alternative investment strategies. There is no standard definition for what constitutes an alt fund, but alt funds are often marketed as a way for retail investors to gain access to hedge funds and actively managed programs that will perform well in a variety of market conditions. These funds claim to reduce volatility, increase diversification, and produce higher returns when compared to long only equity funds and income funds, while providing liquidity. Recommendations for alt funds must be based on the specific strategies employed by the fund, not merely as one overall investment. Retail communication must accurately and fairly detail each fund's operations and objectives in line with the information in the prospectuses. FINRA is concerned that registered representatives and retail investors will not understand how fund will react in certain market conditions or how the fund manager will approach those market conditions. These funds must be reviewed during the new product review process even if the firm has a selling agreement with the fund.

FLOATING RATE BANK LOAN FUNDS

These funds invest in bank loans that are traditionally designed for institutional investors. More and more funds and ETFs available to retail investors are investing in these products. The loans are designed to hedge interest rate risk. However, the floating rate loans contain increased liquidity, credit, and call risks to the funds who invest in these products. Floating rate bank loans are also difficult to value and have long settlement times. Funds that invest in these products may have liquidity issues if faced with large redemptions.

BOND FUNDS

Investors who invest in bond funds are actually purchasing an equity security that represents their undivided interest in a portfolio of debt. Corporations, the U.S. government, states, and local municipalities may have issued the debt in the portfolio. Bond funds invest mainly to generate current income for investors through interest payments generated by the bonds in the portfolio.

CORPORATE BOND FUNDS

Corporate bond funds invest in debt securities that have been issued by corporations. The debt in the portfolio could be investment grade, or it could be speculative such as in a high yield or junk bond fund. Dividend income that is generated by the portfolio's interest payments is subject to all taxes.

GOVERNMENT BOND FUNDS

Government bond funds invest in debt securities issued by the U.S. government, such as Treasury bills, notes, and bonds. Many funds also invest in the debt of government agencies such as those issued by the Government National Mortgage Association, also known as Ginnie Mae. Government bond funds provide current income to investors, along with a high degree of safety of principal. Dividends based upon the interest payments received from direct Treasury obligations are only subject to federal taxation.

MUNICIPAL BOND FUNDS

Municipal bond funds invest in portfolios of municipal debt. Investors in municipal bond funds receive dividend income, which is free from federal taxes because the dividends are based on the interest payments received from the municipal bonds in the portfolio. Investors are still subject to taxes for any capital gains distributions or for any capital gains realized through the sale of the mutual fund shares.

MONEY MARKET FUNDS

Money market funds invest in short-term money market instruments such as bankers' acceptances, commercial paper, and other debt securities with less than one year remaining to maturity. Money market funds are no-load funds that offer the investor the highest degree of safety of principal along with current income. The NAV for money market funds is always equal to $1; however, this is not guaranteed. Investors use money market funds as a place to hold idle funds and to earn current income. Interest is earned by investors daily and is credited to their accounts monthly. Most money market funds offer check-writing privileges, and investors must receive a prospectus prior to investing or opening an account.

MONEY MARKET GUIDELINES

Money market funds must adhere to certain guidelines in order to qualify as a money market fund, such as:

- The prospectus must clearly state on its cover that the fund is not insured or guaranteed by the U.S. government and that the fund's net asset value may fall below $1.
- Securities in the portfolio may have a maximum maturity of 13 months.
- The average maturity for securities in the portfolio may not exceed 90 days.
- No more than 5% of the fund's assets may be invested in any one issuer's debt securities.
- Investments are limited to the top two ratings awarded by a nationally recognized ratings agency (i.e., S&P or Moody's).

- 95% of the portfolio must be in the top ratings category, with no more than 5% being invested in the second tier.

VALUING MUTUAL FUND SHARES

Mutual funds must determine the NAV of the fund's shares at least once per business day. Most mutual funds will price their shares at the close of business of the NYSE (4:00 p.m. EST). The mutual fund prospectus will provide the best answer as to when the fund calculates the price of its shares. The calculation is required to determine both the redemption price (NAV) and the purchase price (POP) of the fund's shares. The price, which is received by an investor who is redeeming shares, and the price that is paid by an investor who is purchasing shares, will be based upon the price, which is next calculated after the fund has received the investor's order. This is known as forward pricing. To calculate the fund's NAV, use the following formula:

assets – liabilities = NAV

To determine the NAV per share, simply divide the total net asset value by the total number of outstanding shares:

$$\frac{\textbf{total NAV}}{\textbf{total \# of shares}}$$

 TESTFOCUS!

If XYZ mutual fund has $10,000,000 in assets and $500,000 in liabilities, what is the fund's NAV?

assets – liabilities = NAV
$10,000,000 – $500,000 = $9,500,000

If XYZ has 1,000,000 shares outstanding, its NAV per share would be:

$$\frac{\textbf{total NAV}}{\textbf{total \# of shares}} \qquad \frac{\textbf{\$9,500,000}}{\textbf{1,000,000}}$$

NAV per share = $9.50

CHANGES IN THE NAV

The net asset value of a mutual fund is constantly changing as security prices fluctuate and as the mutual fund conducts its business. The following illustrates how the NAV per share will be affected given certain events.

INCREASES IN THE NAV

The net asset value of the mutual fund will increase if:

- The value of the securities in the portfolio increase.
- The portfolio receives investment income, such as interest payments from bonds.

DECREASES IN THE NAV

The net asset value will decrease if:

- The value of the securities in the portfolio fall in value.
- The fund distributes dividends or capital gains.

NO EFFECT ON THE NAV

The following will have no effect on the net asset value of the mutual fund share:

- Investor purchases and redemptions.
- Portfolio purchases and sales of securities.
- Sales charges.

SALES CHARGES

The maximum allowable sales charge that an open-end fund may charge is 8.5% of the POP. The sales charge that may be assessed by a particular fund will be detailed in the fund's prospectus. It is important to note that the sales charge is not an expense of the fund; it is a cost of distribution, which is born by the investor. If the fund charges a sales charge to invest and a redemption fee at the time an investor liquidates his or her shares the combination of the sales charge and redemption fee may not be greater than 8.5%. The sales charges pay for all of the following:

- Underwriter's commission.
- Commission to brokerage firms and registered representatives.

CLOSED-END FUNDS

Closed-end funds do not charge a sales charge to invest. An investor who wants to purchase a closed-end fund will pay the current market price plus whatever the brokerage firm charges to execute the order.

EXCHANGE-TRADED FUNDS (ETFs)

In recent years exchange-traded funds, or ETFs, have gained a lot of popularity. ETFs are created through the purchase of a basket of securities that are designed to track the performance of an index or sector. ETFs are not actively managed and provide investors with lower costs and the ability buy, sell, and sell short the ETF at any point during the trading day and may be purchased on margin. Certain types of ETFs are designed to provide returns and performance characteristics of positions that take on the leverage. Such ETFs are often known as ultra, or double, ETFs. These ETFs may provide returns that are double or more of the return of an index, or double or more the inverse return of an index.

ETFs THAT TRACK ALTERNATIVELY WEIGHTED INDICES

Investing in ETFs that track Indexes has become popular investment strategy. As a result new products have come to market that track the performance of alternative indexes. Equal weight, alternatively weighted, fundamentally weighted, and volatility weighted ETFs offer exposure to other investment styles and may provide enhanced performance. These ETFs present additional risk factors that both registered representatives and investors need to understand. These funds are sometimes marketed as having better performance than other indices which could be cause for a concern as the ETFs that track these indices may be complex, thinly traded, and hard to understand for both representatives and retail investors. The lack of liquidity can lead to wider spreads causing the product to be expensive to buy and sell for investors. The portfolios often have high turnover which can lead to increased transaction costs for the ETF.

FRONT-END LOADS

A front-end load is a sales charge that investors pay when they purchase shares. The sales charge is added to the NAV of the fund, and the investor purchases the shares at the POP. The sales charge, in essence, is deducted from the gross amount invested, and the remaining amount is invested in the portfolio at the NAV. Shares that charge a front-end load are known as A shares.

EXAMPLE

XYZ mutual fund has a NAV of $9.50 and a POP of $10 and a sales charge percentage of 5%. How much in sales charges would an investor pay if he were to invest $10,000 in the fund?

$$
\begin{array}{cc}
\$10,000 & \$10,000 \\
\underline{\times\, 5\%} & \underline{-\, \$500} \\
\$500 = \text{sales charge} & \$9{,}500 \text{ invested in the portfolio at NAV}
\end{array}
$$

BACK-END LOADS

A back-end load is also known as a contingent differed sales charge (CDSC). An investor in a fund that charges a back-end load will pay the sales charge at the time of redemption of the fund's shares. The sales charge will be assessed on the value of the shares that have been redeemed, and the amount of the sales charge will decline as the holding period for the investor increases. The following is a hypothetical back-end load schedule:

Years Money Left in Portfolio	Sales Charge
1	8.5%
2	7%
3	5%
4	3%
5	1.5%
5 years or more	0%

The mutual fund prospectus will detail the particular schedule for back-end load sales charges. Mutual fund shares that charge a back-end load are also known as B shares.

OTHER TYPES OF SALES CHARGES

There are other ways in which a mutual fund assesses a sales charge. Shares that charge a level load based on the NAV are known as level-load funds, or C shares. Shares that charge an asset-based fee and a back-end load are known as D shares.

12B-1 FEES

Most mutual funds charge an asset-based distribution fee to cover expenses related to the promotion and distribution of the fund's shares. The amount of the fee will be determined annually as a percentage of the NAV or as a flat fee. The 12B-1 fee will be charged to the shares quarterly, reducing the investor's overall return on the fund. Because a 12B-1 fee reduces the return, it is a type of sales load. 12B-1 fees cover such things as the printing of prospectuses and certain sales commissions to agents. To start and continue a 12B-1 fee, three votes must initially approve the fee and annually reapprove it. The three votes that are required are:

- A majority vote of the board of directors.
- A majority vote of the noninterested board of directors.
- A majority vote of the outstanding shares.

    To terminate a 12B-1 fee, only two votes are required. They are:

- A majority vote of the noninterested board of directors.
- A majority vote of the outstanding shares.

LIMITS OF A 12B-1 FEE

A mutual fund that distributes its own shares and markets itself as a no-load fund may charge a 12B-1 fee that is no more than .25 percent. If the fund charges a 12B-1 fee that is greater than .25 percent, it may not be called a no-load fund. Other funds that do not call themselves a no-load fund are limited to .75 percent of assets, and the amount of the 12B-1 fee must be reasonably related to the anticipated level of expenses incurred for promotion and distribution. All 12B-1 fees are reviewed quarterly.

CALCULATING A MUTUAL FUND'S SALES CHARGE PERCENTAGE

Many times an investor may know only the NAV and the POP for a given mutual fund and not the sales charge percentage that is charged by the fund.

To determine the sales charge percentage given the NAV and the POP, use the following formula.

$$SC\% = \frac{POP - NAV}{POP}$$

 FOCUS**POINT**

$$SC\% = \frac{POP - NAV}{POP} = \frac{10 - 9.50}{10} = .50 = 5\% \quad POP = \$10$$

FINDING THE PUBLIC OFFERING PRICE

There will also be times when an investor knows the NAV of a fund and the sales charge percentage but does not know the POP that must be paid to invest in the fund. To calculate the POP given the sales charge percentage and the NAV, use the following formula:

$$POP = \frac{NAV}{100\% - SC\%}$$

 FOCUS**POINT**

Let's use the same fund as above. XYZ has an NAV of $9.50 and a sales charge percentage of 5%. to determine the POP, simply plug the numbers into the formula as follows:

$$POP = \frac{9.50}{100\% - SC\%} = \frac{9.50}{100\% - 5\%} = \frac{9.50}{.95} = \$10.00$$

SALES CHARGE REDUCTIONS

The maximum allowable sales charge that may be assessed by an open-end mutual fund is 8.5% of the public offering price. If a mutual fund charges 8.5%, it must offer the following three privileges to investors:

1. Breakpoint sales charge reductions that reduce the amount of the sales charge based on the dollar amount invested.

2. Rights of accumulation that will reduce the sales charge on subsequent investments based on the value of the investor's account.

3. Automatic reinvestment of dividends and capital gains at the NAV.

If a mutual fund does not offer all three of these benefits to investors, the maximum allowable sales charge that may be charged drops to 6.25%. Although a mutual fund that charges 8.5% must offer these features, most mutual funds that charge less than 8.5% also offer them.

BREAKPOINT SCHEDULE

As an incentive for investors to invest larger sums of money into a mutual fund, the mutual fund will reduce the sales charge based upon the dollar amount of the purchase. Breakpoint sales charge reductions are available to any "person," including corporations, trusts, couples, and accounts for minors. Breakpoint sales charge reductions are not available to investment clubs or to parents and their adult children investing in separate accounts. The following is an example of a breakpoint schedule that a family of funds might use:

Dollar Amount Invested	Sales Charge
$1–24,999	8.5%
$25,000–74,999	7%
$75,000–149,999	5%
$150,000–499,999	3%
$500,000 or Greater	1%

A breakpoint schedule benefits all parties: the fund company, the investor, and the representative. It is important to note that the fund's distributor will keep track of the investor's contributions to determine if the investor qualifies for a breakpoint. If the same investor holds the fund at different broker dealers the value of both accounts will be combined to determine breakpoint eligibility.

LETTER OF INTENT

An investor who might not be able to reach a breakpoint with a single purchase may qualify for a breakpoint sales charge reduction by signing a letter of intent. A letter of intent will give the investor up to 13 months to reach the dollar amount subscribed to. The letter of intent is binding only on the fund company, not on the investor. The additional shares that will be purchased as a result of the lower sales charge will be held by the fund company in an escrow account. If the investor fulfills the letter of intent, the shares are released to the investor. Should the investor fail to reach the agreed-upon breakpoint, the sales charge will be adjusted. The investor may choose to pay the adjusted sales charge by either sending a check or by allowing some of the escrowed shares to be liquidated.

BACKDATING A LETTER OF INTENT

An investor may backdate a letter of intent up to 90 days to include a prior purchase, and the 13-month window starts from the backdate. For example, if an investor backdates a letter of intent by the maximum of 90 days allowed, then the investor has only 10 months to complete the letter of intent.

BREAKPOINT SALES

A breakpoint sale is a violation committed by a registered representative who is trying to earn larger commissions by recommending the purchase of mutual fund shares in a dollar amount that is just below the breakpoint that would allow the investor to qualify for a reduced sales charge. A breakpoint violation may also be considered to have been committed if a representative spreads out a large sum of money over different families of funds. A registered representative must always notify an investor of the availability of a sales charge reduction, especially when the investor is depositing a sum of money that is close to the breakpoint.

RIGHTS OF ACCUMULATION

Rights of accumulation allow the investor to qualify for reduced sales charges on subsequent investments by taking into consideration the value of the investor's account, including the growth. Unlike a letter of intent, there is no time limit and, as the account grows over time, the investor can qualify for lower sales charges on future investments. The sales charge reduction is not retroactive and does not reduce the sales charges on prior purchases. To qualify for the breakpoint, the dollar amount of the current purchase is calculated into the total value of the investor's account.

 **TESTFOCUS!**

Using the breakpoint schedule presented earlier, let's look at an investor's account over the last three years:

	Deposit	Sales Charge
Year 1	$5,000	8.5%
Year 2	$5,000	8.5%
Year 3	$5,000	8.5%

Let's assume that the investor's account has increased in value by $6,000, making the total current value of the account $21,000. The investor has another $5,000 to invest this year and, because there is a sales charge reduction available at the $25,000 level, the investor will pay a sales charge of 7% on the new $5,000.

AUTOMATIC REINVESTMENT OF DISTRIBUTIONS

Investors may elect to have their distributions automatically reinvested in the fund and use the distributions to purchase more shares. Most mutual funds will allow investors to purchase the shares at the NAV when they reinvest distributions. This feature has to be offered by mutual funds charging a sales charge of 8.5%. However, it is offered by most other mutual funds as well.

OTHER MUTUAL FUND FEATURES

COMBINATION PRIVILEGES

Most mutual fund companies offer a variety of portfolios to meet different investment objectives. The different portfolios become known as a family of funds. Combination privileges allow an investor to combine the simultaneous purchases of two different portfolios to reach a breakpoint sales charge reduction.

EXAMPLE   An investor purchases $15,000 worth of an income fund and, at the same time, invests $40,000 into a growth portfolio offered by the same fund company. If the fund company offers a breakpoint sales charge reduction at $50,000, the investor would qualify for the lower sales charge under combination privileges.

CONVERSION OR EXCHANGE PRIVILEGES

Most mutual fund families will offer their investors conversion or exchange privileges that allow investors to move money from one portfolio to another offered by the same fund company without paying another sales charge. Another way of looking at this is that the fund company allows the investor to redeem the shares of one portfolio at the NAV and use the proceeds to purchase shares of another portfolio at the NAV. The IRS sees this as a purchase and a sale, and the investor will have to pay taxes on any gain on the sale of portfolio shares. Other exchange conditions are as follows:

- Dollar value of purchase may not exceed sales proceeds.
- Purchase of new portfolio must occur within 30 days.
- The sale may not include a sales charge refund.
- No commission may be paid to a registered representative of broker dealer.

An investor who moves money between portfolios which carry back-end loads under the exchange privilege will not pay the sales charge on the shares of the portfolio redeemed. The investor's holding period used to determine the ultimate amount of the backend sales charge will be the date of the original purchase. That is to say the investor's holding period carries over to the subsequent portfolio.

 FOCUSPOINT

An aggressive investor has $20,000 invested in ABC high growth fund that has an NAV of $12 and a POP of $12.60. The investor wants to move the money into the ABC biotech fund that has an NAV of $17.20 and a POP of $17.90. ABC offers conversion privileges, so the investor will redeem the shares of the growth portfolio at $12 and will purchase 1162.79 shares of the biotech portfolio at $17.20.

30-DAY EMERGENCY WITHDRAWAL

Many mutual funds will provide investors with access to their money in a time of unexpected financial need. If the investor needs to liquidate mutual fund shares for emergency purposes, the investor will be able to reinvest an equal sum of money at the portfolio's NAV if the money is reinvested within 30 days. This is usually a one-time privilege, and the NAV used to purchase the shares is the NAV on the day of the reinvestment.

TAXATION OF MUTUAL FUNDS

Mutual funds are classified under the Internal Revenue Code subchapter M as a conduit for investment income. This classification allows the mutual fund to avoid paying taxes on the income it distributes to investors, as long as the mutual fund distributes at least 90% of its net investment income. If a mutual fund pays out at least 90% of the net investment income, it pays taxes only on what it retains. If the mutual fund pays out less than 90% of the net investment income, such as 89%, then the mutual fund will pay taxes on 100% of the investment income, including the amount it distributed.

net investment income = dividend income + interest income − expenses

The following are not considered when determining net investment income:

- Average net assets
- Long-term capital gains
- Short-term capital gains

A mutual fund must pay out dividends based on net investment income at least once every 12 months. Many mutual funds pay out dividends as often as monthly and send out 100% of the net investment income. Dividends are paid to mutual fund investors in a manner similar to the way that dividends are paid to investors in common or preferred stock. The main difference is the ex-dividend date. Because all new investors purchase new mutual fund shares directly from the fund company, when the fund receives their order there is no three-day settlement required to transfer ownership from one investor to another. The mutual fund investor is considered an owner of record on the day the order is received by the fund company, if it is before the calculation of the NAV. Because of this, the ex-dividend date for an open-end mutual fund is the day after the record date. The order of dates for an open-end fund dividend distribution is as follows:

- Declaration date
- Record date
- Ex-dividend date
- Payment date

Just like stock and closed-end mutual funds, the value of the open-end mutual fund share will be reduced by the amount of the dividend on the ex-dividend date, and selling dividends is a violation.

DISTRIBUTION OF CAPITAL GAINS

If the mutual fund holds a security and it increases or decreases in value, then the mutual fund has an unrealized capital gain or loss. Unrealized gains and losses in the mutual fund portfolio affect the NAV of the fund but have no tax consequences for the investor. When the fund liquidates securities, the gain or loss is realized and creates tax consequences for the investor. If the fund has held the securities that were sold at a gain and are the basis for the distribution for more than one year, then the investor has a long-term capital gain and is taxed at the ordinary income rate of the recipient. Securities that were held for less than one year create a short-term capital gain and are treated as an income distribution. A mutual fund may make long-term capital gains distributions no more than once per year.

RECEIVING AND REINVESTING DISTRIBUTIONS

All distributions made by a mutual fund are paid in cash. The investor has the option of either receiving the cash in the form of a check from the fund or reinvesting the distribution and using it to purchase more shares. Many mutual funds allow investors to reinvest both capital gain and dividend distributions at the NAV or at a discount to the POP. The mutual fund, in order to allow reinvestment of distributions below the POP, must:

- Offer reinvestment to investors, who are nonparticipants in the plan, the opportunity to reinvest each distribution.
- Detail the reinvestment plan to all shareholders at least once per year.

- Detail the plan in the prospectus.
- The fund company must not incur any additional charges for offering the plan.

A small service charge may be applied to the reinvestment of each distribution.

Some mutual funds may elect to treat the reinvestment of dividends and capital gains differently. If the fund company only allows shareholders to reinvest their capital gains distributions at the NAV or at a discount to the POP, the mutual fund must:

- Offer each investor an opportunity to reinvest each capital gain distribution.
- Detail the plan in the prospectus.
- Notify shareholders of the availability of the plan at least once per year.

The IRS taxes all distributions, regardless of whether they are reinvested or received by the investor, as if the investor actually received the check. Mutual funds will send form 1099 to investors detailing their tax liability for the previous year.

CALCULATING GAINS AND LOSSES

When mutual fund investors sell their shares, in most cases they will have a capital gain or loss. In order to determine if there is a gain or loss, the investor must first calculate the cost basis, or cost base. An investor's cost base, simply put, is equal to the price the investor paid for the shares, in most cases. Once an investor knows the cost base, calculating any gain or loss becomes easy. A capital gain is realized when the investor sells the shares at a price that is greater than the cost base.

EXAMPLE   An investor who purchased a mutual fund at $10 per share three years ago and receives $14 per share upon redeeming the fund shares has a $4 capital gain, which is found by subtracting the cost base from the sales proceeds: $14 − $10 = $4. If the investor had 1,000 shares, the capital gain would be $4,000.

An investor's cost base is always returned tax-free. A capital loss is realized when investors sell the shares at a price that is less than their cost base. If the investor in the previous example were to have sold the mutual fund shares at

$8 instead of $14, the investor would have a $2 capital loss, or a total capital loss of $2,000 for the entire position. Again, this is found by subtracting the cost base from the sales proceeds: $8 – $10 = –$2.

COST BASE OF MULTIPLE PURCHASES

Mutual fund investors who have been accumulating shares through multiple purchases must determine their cost base through one of the following methods.

FIFO (FIRST IN, FIRST OUT)

If the investor does not identify which shares are being sold at the time of sale, the IRS will assume that the first shares that were purchased are the first shares that are sold under the FIFO method. In many cases, this will result in the largest capital gain, and, as a result, the investor will have the largest tax liability.

SHARE IDENTIFICATION

An investor may, at the time of the sale, specify which shares are being sold. By keeping a record of the purchase prices and the dates that the shares were purchased, the investor may elect to sell the shares that create the most favorable tax consequences.

AVERAGE COST

Investors may decide to sell shares based on their average cost. An investor must determine the average cost by using the following formula:

$$\text{average cost} = \frac{\text{total dollars invested}}{\text{total \# of shares purchased}}$$

Once an investor has elected to use the average-cost method to calculate gains and losses, the method may not be changed without IRS approval.

PURCHASING MUTUAL FUND SHARES

Mutual fund investors must receive a prospectus and open an account prior to investing any money with the fund. At the time the investor opens the account, the investor must determine what to do with any distributions from the fund. The investor may elect to receive the distributions or to reinvest them into the fund and use the distribution to purchase additional shares. Once the account is set up an investor may purchase shares through any of the following methods:

- Lump sum investment
- Dollar-cost averaging
- Contractual plan

LUMP SUM DEPOSIT

Investors may simply purchase mutual fund shares by depositing a fixed sum of money and leaving it there for the fund to invest. The investors may reinvest or receive distributions and may make additional investments into the account as they choose.

STRUCTURED ACCUMULATION PLANS
Investors may accumulate mutual fund shares by making regular investments into either a voluntary or contractual accumulation plan.

VOLUNTARY ACCUMULATION PLANS
Mutual fund investors may set up a schedule to invest regularly into a specific mutual fund. Investors may simply send the money to the fund or they may allow the fund to debit their checking account. Some funds require a minimum initial investment. An investor should check the fund prospectus for particulars. If the investor skips a scheduled investment, there is no penalty.

DOLLAR-COST AVERAGING

One of the more popular methods to accumulate mutual fund shares is through a process known as dollar-cost averaging. An investor purchases mutual fund shares through regularly scheduled investments of a fixed dollar amount. An investor may elect to invest $100 per month into a mutual fund by having the fund company debit the money from a checking account. As the share price of the mutual fund fluctuates, the investor's $100 investment will purchase fewer shares when the market price of the mutual fund share is high and it will purchase more shares when the market price is low. As the market price of the mutual fund share continues to fluctuate over time, the investor's average cost per share should always be lower than the average price per share, allowing the investor to liquidate the shares at a profit. Dollar-cost averaging does not, however, guarantee a profit, because a mutual fund share could continue to decline until the share price hits zero. All Series 7 candidates should be able to determine an investor's average cost and average price per share.

FOCUSPOINT

Let's look at the dollar-cost averaging results for an investor who is depositing $100 per month into a mutual fund whose share price has been fluctuating widely over that time.

The 12 should be 12.5 and the 67 should be 67.5

Investment	Share Price	Number of Shares Purchased
$100	$20	5
$100	$12.5	8
$100	$10	10
$100	$25	4
$400	$67.5	27 totals

In order to calculate the investor's average cost per share, use the following formula:

$$\text{average cost} = \frac{\text{total dollars invested}}{\text{total \# of shares invested}}$$

Using the numbers from the example, we get:

$$\text{average cost} = \frac{\$400}{27} = \$14.81$$

In order to determine the average price that the investor paid per share, use the following formula:

$$\text{average price} = \frac{\text{total of purchase prices}}{\text{number of purchases}}$$

Using the numbers from the example, we get:

$$\text{average price} = \frac{67.5}{4} = \$16.875$$

The example illustrates the effects of dollar-cost averaging into a mutual fund with a fluctuating market price. The result is an average cost per share that is significantly lower than the investor's average price per share. The change in the mutual fund share price is more dramatic than will usually be experienced in real life, and the investor will normally have to invest into the fund for a longer period of time before achieving similar results.

CONTRACTUAL ACCUMULATION PLANS

With a contractual accumulation plan, the investor enters into a contract and agrees to invest a fixed dollar amount into the plan over a specific period of time. With a contractual plan, the contract is only binding on the fund company, not on the investor. However, the investor may face penalties for failing to complete the contract. Some contractual plans will allow the investor to begin a plan with as little as a $20 monthly investment; this is often lower than the fund's minimum investment. Most contractual plans are organized as UITs. The investor is actually investing into the UIT that issues units of beneficial interest and, in turn, the UIT invests the money by purchasing mutual fund shares. Because the investor is purchasing units from the UIT, which is investing in mutual fund shares, the investor must get two prospectuses, one for the UIT and one for the mutual fund.

SALES CHARGES

A contractual plan company may be organized as a front-end load plan under the Investment Company Act of 1940 or as a spread-load plan under the Investment Company Act Amendments of 1970. Under both plans, the maximum sales charge over the life of the plan is 9% of the total payments. However, the plans assess the sales charges differently. The front-end load plan may charge up to 50% of the first year's payments as sales charges, while the spread-load plan seeks to spread the sales charge over a longer period of time and may only deduct 20% of the first year's payments as sales charges. The following illustrates the key characteristics of both plans:

Characteristic	Front End Load	Spread Load
Maximum sales charge over life of the plan	9%	9%
Maximum sales charge in the first year	50%	20%
Maximum sales charge in the first 48 months	No limit	Maximum average of 16% per year
45-day free look	Refund of NAV + SC	Refund of NAV + SC
Termination of plan in the first 18 months	Refund of NAV + sales charges exceeding 15% of total payments	Refund of NAV only

45-DAY FREE LOOK

Each investor will have the right to terminate the contractual plan within 45 days from receiving the notice of the plan's sales charges from the custodian. An investor terminating a plan within the free-look period is entitled to receive the current NAV of the fund plus a refund of 100% of the sales charges.

WITHDRAWAL PLANS

Investors seeking to obtain access to their money in a mutual fund may redeem all or a portion of their shares or may enter into any of the following systematic withdrawal plans:

- Fixed dollar amount
- Fixed share amount
- Fixed percentage
- Fixed time

FIXED DOLLAR AMOUNT

An investor may need a specific dollar amount from the fund on a regular basis to meet current needs. Under a fixed-dollar withdrawal plan, the mutual fund will sell enough of the investor's shares in order to send them the fixed dollar amount required on a periodic basis, such as monthly.

FIXED SHARE

An investor may wish to regularly redeem a fixed number of shares and have the proceeds forwarded. The mutual fund will follow the investor's instructions and redeem the fixed number of shares and forward the proceeds to the investor on a systematic basis.

FIXED PERCENTAGE

An investor may wish to have a certain percentage of the account forwarded on a regular basis, such as 3% monthly. The mutual fund will liquidate 3% of the investor's account and forward the proceeds.

Most mutual funds require a minimum account balance before an investor may enter into a systematic withdrawal plan and may not allow the investor to make additional investments into the account while the withdrawal plan is in effect. A withdrawal plan is not guaranteed, and the plan may fall short in either the dollar amount or the length of time.

FIXED TIME

An investor may also elect to have the value of the account paid out over a fixed period of time, such as five years. The fund will send out checks equal to 1/60 of the account value on a monthly basis, and the account will be depleted by the end of the 60th month.

RECOMMENDING MUTUAL FUNDS

Mutual funds are designed to be longer term investments and are generally not used to time the market. When determining suitability for investors the registered representative must first make sure that the investment objective of the mutual fund matches the investor's objective. Once several funds have been selected that meet the client's objective the representative must then compare costs, fees, and expenses among the funds. Priority should be given to any fund company with whom the investor maintains an investment. If the client's objective has changed the fund most likely offers conversions privileges which will allow the investor to move into another portfolio without paying any sales charge. If the investor is committing new capital the fund company most likely offers combination privileges and rights of accumulation which will help the investor reach a sale charge reduction. Switching fund companies and/or spreading out investment dollars among different fund companies are red flags for breakpoint sale violation and abusive sales practices. The amount of time the investor is seeking to hold the investment will be a determining factor as to which share class is the most appropriate. Investors who have longer holding periods may be better off in B shares that assess a sales charge upon redemption based on their holding period. Investors who have shorter time horizons will be better of choosing A shares over B shares as the expenses associated with B shares tend to be higher. Important to note is that making a large investment in class B shares is a red flag for a break point sale violation as the large dollar amount would have most likely resulted in a reduced sales charge for the investor. Investors with relatively short holding periods or who want to actively move money between funds to try to time the market would be best off with C shares which charge a level load each year.

STRUCTURED RETAIL PRODUCTS/SRPs

Members firms have been creating their own proprietary products for distribution and sale to retail investors. These SRPs include complex products such as structured notes with complicated payout structures. These SRPs may use proprietary indexes as reverence assets that are hard to track making the products difficult to understand for retail investors. The payout structure may also be based on longer terms and other conditions adding to the complexity of the products. Firms must ensure that its representatives understand the performance characteristics and operational risks prior to recommending these products to investors. All members who create retail communications relating to SRPs must file the communications with FINRA within 10 business days of first use. FINRA is concerned that member firms in an effort to increase revenue will offer complex SRPs through distributors who do not have the knowledge or expertise to properly understand or recommend the products. If the member engages a wholesaler to sell its SRPs the member must have written supervisory procedures in place to "know your distributor" to ensure that the distribution channels have controls in place regarding the proper training of representatives who sell the products to customers. Additional concerns are created when there are potential conflicts of interest between the creator of the SRP and the wholesale distributor such as when the two companies are affiliated.

Pretest

MUTUAL FUNDS

1. Why does a mutual fund make breakpoint sale charge reductions available to investors?

    a. To encourage investors to invest larger sums of money into a mutual fund

    b. To guarantee parents and their adult children greater returns when they invest in separate accounts

    c. To encourage investors to invest in more than one mutual fund

    d. To encourage personal investors only, by excluding corporations and trusts, to invest greater sums for greater returns

2. Your customer invested $7,000 in a mutual fund two months ago. She now wants to invest a significant amount of her savings in this fund. She will need some time to reach the breakpoint for a sales charge reduction and would like to include her original purchase of $7,000. Which of the following is true regarding her letter of intent?

    a. Your client should make a lump sum investment to gain the maximum appreciation on her portfolio.

    b. The letter of intent may not be backdated to include the original purchase.

    c. The letter of intent may be backdated to include the original amount and to realize a reduced sales charge.

    d. The letter of intent may be backdated to include the original purchase, and there will be a sales charge reduction made for the original investment only.

3. All of the following investors qualify for breakpoint sales charge reductions, EXCEPT:

   a. an adult and a minor child.

   b. an investment club.

   c. a trust.

   d. a corporation.

4. Once registered, an investment company may do all of the following, EXCEPT:

   a. lend money to earn interest.

   b. borrow money on a limited basis.

   c. act as a bank or savings and loan.

   d. raise money through the sale of shares.

5. A mutual fund may sell its own shares to investors if it is a:

   a. front-end load fund.

   b. nondiversified fund.

   c. back-end load fund.

   d. no-load fund.

6. The investment adviser of an investment company does all but which of the following?

   a. Manages the fund's portfolio and may not borrow from it.

   b. Is a person hired by the board of directors and may not have any securities-related convictions.

   c. Determines the tax consequences of distributions and strategies.

   d. Is the highest paid member of the investment company's team.

7. In order to start and continue an investment company, it must have at least:

   a. 1,000 shareholders.

   b. 100 shareholders.

   c. 10 shareholders.

   d. 90 shareholders.

8. A unit investment trust may do all of the following, EXCEPT:
   a. cease to exist after the objective has been met.
   b. maintain a secondary market in the units to offer some liquidity to investors.
   c. be actively managed by its board of directors.
   d. invest in a large block of government or municipal debt.

9. An aggressive growth fund has realized substantial appreciation in its portfolio and would like to send out the gains to the shareholders. How often may the fund do this type of distribution?
   a. Monthly
   b. As declared by the board of directors
   c. Annually
   d. Quarterly

10. What is the maximum amount that a diversified fund may invest in any one target company?
    a. 5%
    b. 10%
    c. 8.5%
    d. 7%

11. Which of the following is the pricing formula for an open-end mutual fund?
    a. $POP - SC = NAV$
    b. $NAV = assets - liabilities$
    c. $Supply + demand = POP$
    d. $NAV + SC = POP$

12. An investor has $70,000 to invest in a mutual fund with a POP of 20 and a sales charge of 8.5%. A breakpoint sales charge reduction is available to investors who invest $50,000 or more and they are charged 6% as a sales charge to invest. How many shares will this investor be able to purchase?
    a. 3,500
    b. 3,595
    c. 3,723
    d. 3,291

13. An open-end mutual fund has the following:

Average net assets	$ 500,345,000
Dividends received	$ 22,450,000
Interest received	$ 21,670,000
Operating expenses	$ 5,250,000
Capital gains	$ 7,150,000

If the fund wants to retain its status as a regulated investment company under subchapter M, it must send out to its shareholders at least which of the following amounts?

a. $34,983,000

b. $42,133,000

c. $51,270,000

d. $38,870,000

14. Which of the following is true regarding the ex dividend date for an open-end mutual fund?

I.   It is set by FINRA.

II. It is the day before the record date.

III. It is set by the board of directors.

IV. It is the day after the record date.

a. II and III

b. III and IV

c. I and IV

d. I and II

15. A mutual fund prospectus must be updated every:

a. 13 months.

b. 12 months.

c. 16 months.

d. 270 days.

16. In order to charge the maximum allowable sales charge of 8.5%, the mutual fund company must offer all of the following, EXCEPT:

a. rights of accumulation.

b. reinvestment of distributions at NAV.

c. breakpoint sales charge reductions.

d. conversion privileges.

17. During a broad-based market advance, which of the following would most likely realize the least amount of capital gains?

   a. A large cap growth fund

   b. A small cap growth fund

   c. An option income fund

   d. A technology fund

18. A mutual fund prospectus is important in all of the following, EXCEPT:

   a. it is the fund's full disclosure document.

   b. it is usually a summary prospectus, but investors can request additional information.

   c. it must be presented to all purchasers after the sales presentation.

   d. it is the official offering document for all open-end mutual fund shares.

19. Which of the following is NOT a way to accumulate mutual fund shares?

   a. Contractual plan

   b. Deferred investment

   c. Lump sum

   d. Dollar-cost averaging

Variable Annuities

INTRODUCTION

This chapter will cover a variety of important topics relating to annuity products. Many investors choose to purchase annuities to help plan for retirement. Over the years a wide range of annuity products have been developed to meet different investment objectives and risk profiles. This section will cover both variable and fixed annuities. Candidates will need a complete understanding of how annuities function in order to successfully complete the exam.

ANNUITIES

An annuity is a contract between an individual and an insurance company. Once the contract is entered into, the individual becomes known as the annuitant. There are three basic types of annuities that are deigned to meet different objectives. They are:

1. Fixed annuity
2. Variable annuity
3. Combination annuity

Although all three types allow the investor's money to grow tax deferred, the type of investments made and how the money is invested varies according to the type of annuity.

FIXED ANNUITY

A fixed annuity offers investors a guaranteed rate of return regardless of whether the investment portfolio can produce the guaranteed rate. If the performance of the portfolio falls below the rate that was guaranteed, the insurance company owes investors the difference. Because the purchaser of a fixed annuity does not have any investment risk, a fixed annuity is considered to be an insurance product, not a security. Representatives who sell fixed annuity contracts must have an insurance license. Because fixed annuities offer investors a guaranteed return, the money invested by the insurance company will be used to purchase conservative investments such as mortgages and real estate. These are investments whose historical performance is predictable enough so that a guaranteed rate can be offered to investors. All of the money invested into fixed annuity contracts is held in the insurance company's general account. Because the rate that the insurance company guarantees is not very high, the annuitant may suffer a loss of purchasing power due to inflation risk.

VARIABLE ANNUITY

An investor seeking to achieve a higher rate of return may elect to purchase a variable annuity. Variable annuities seek to obtain a higher rate of return by investing in stocks, bonds, or mutual fund shares. These securities traditionally offer higher rates of return than more conservative investments. A variable annuity does not offer the investor a guaranteed rate of return, and the investor may lose all or part of their principal. Because the annuitant bears the investment risk associated with a variable annuity, the contract is considered to be both a security and an insurance product. Representatives who sell variable annuities must have both their securities license and their insurance license. The money and securities contained in a variable annuity contract are held in the insurance company's separate account. The separate account is named such because the variable annuity's portfolio must be kept "separate" from the insurance company's general funds. The insurance company must have a net worth of $1,000,000, or the separate account must have a net worth of $1,000,000, in order for the separate account to begin operating. Once the separate account begins operations, it may invest in one of two ways:

1. Directly
2. Indirectly

DIRECT INVESTMENT

If the money in the separate account is invested directly into individual stocks and bonds, the separate account must have an investment adviser to actively manage the portfolio. If the money in the separate account is actively managed and invested directly, then the separate account is considered to be an open-end investment company under the Investment Company Act of 1940 and must register as such.

INDIRECT INVESTMENT

If the separate account uses the money in the portfolio to purchase mutual fund shares, it is investing in the equity and debt markets indirectly and no investment adviser is required to actively manage the portfolio. If the separate account purchases mutual fund shares, then the separate account is considered to be a unit investment trust under the Investment Company Act of 1940 and must register as such.

COMBINATION ANNUITY

For investors who feel that a fixed annuity is too conservative and that a variable annuity is too risky, a combination annuity offers the annuitant features of both a fixed and variable contract. A combination annuity has a fixed portion that offers a guaranteed rate and a variable portion that tries to achieve a higher rate of return. Most combination annuities will allow the investor to move money between the fixed and variable portions of the contract. The money invested in the fixed portion of the contract is invested in the insurance company's general account and used to purchase conservative investments such as mortgages and real estate. The money invested in the variable side of the contract is invested in the insurance company's separate account and used to purchase stocks, bonds, or mutual fund shares. Representatives who sell combination annuities must have both their securities license and their insurance license.

BONUS ANNUITY

An insurance company that issues annuity contracts may offer incentives to investors who purchase their variable annuities. Such incentives are often referred to as bonuses. One type of bonus is known as premium enhancement. Under a premium enhancement option the insurance company will make an additional contribution to the annuitant's account based on the premium paid by the annuitant. For example, if the annuitant is contributing $1,000 per month, the insurance company may offer to contribute an additional 5%, or $50, per month to the account. Another type of bonus offered to annuitants is the ability to withdraw the greater of the account's earnings or up to 15% of the total premiums paid without a penalty. Although the annuitant will not have to pay a penalty to the insurance company, there may be income taxes and a 10% penalty tax owed to the IRS. Bonus annuities often have higher expenses and longer surrender periods than other annuities, and these additional costs and surrender periods need to be clearly disclosed to perspective purchasers. In order to offer bonus annuities the bonus received must outweigh the increased costs and fees associated with the contract. Fixed annuity contracts may not offer bonuses to purchasers.

EQUITY INDEXED ANNUITY

Equity indexed annuities offer investors a return that varies according to the performance of a set index, such as the S&P 500. Equity indexed annuities will credit additional interest to the investor's account based on the contract's participation rate. If a contract sets the participation rate at 70% of the return for the S&P 500 index, and the index returns 5%, the investor's account will be credited for 70% of the return, or 3.5%. The participation rate may also be shown as a spread rate. If the contract had a spread rate of 3% and the index returned 10% the investor's contract would be credited 7%. Equity index annuities may also set a floor rate and a cap rate for the contract. The floor rate is the minimum interest rate that will be credited to the investor's account. The floor rate may be zero or it may be a positive number, depending on the specific contract. The contract's cap rate is the maximum rate that will be credited to the contract. If the return of the index exceeds the cap rate, the investor's account will only be credited up to the cap rate. If the S&P 500 index returns 11% and the cap rate set in the contract is 9%, the investor's account will only be credited 9%.

Feature	Fixed Annuity	Variable Annuity
Payment received	Guaranteed/fixed	May vary in amount
Return	Guaranteed minimum	No guarantee/return may vary in amount
Investment risk	Assumed by insurance company	Assumed by investor
Portfolio	Real estate, mortgages, and fixed-income securities	Stocks, bonds, or mutual fund shares

(Continued)

Portfolio held in	General account	Separate account
Inflation	Subject to inflation risk	Resistant to inflation
Representative registration	Insurance license	Insurance and securities license

RECOMMENDING VARIABLE ANNUITIES

There are a number of factors that will determine if a variable annuity is a suitable recommendation for an investor. Variable annuities are meant to be used as supplements to other retirement accounts such as IRAs and corporate retirement plans. Variable annuities should not be recommended to investors who are trying to save for a large purchase or expense such as college tuition or a second home. Variable annuity products are more appropriate for an investor who is looking to create an income stream. A deferred annuity contract would be appropriate for someone seeking retirement income at some point in the future. An immediate annuity contract would be more appropriate for someone seeking to generate current income and who is perhaps already retired. Many annuity contracts have complex features and cost structures which may be difficult for both the representative and investor to understand. The benefits of the contract should outweigh the additional costs of the contract to ensure the contract is suitable for the investor. Illustrations regarding performance of the contract may use a maximum growth rate of 12% and all annuity applications must be approved or denied by a principal based on suitability within 7 business days of receipt. A Series 24 or Series 26 principal may approve or deny a variable annuity application presented by either a Series 6 or Series 7 registered representative. 1035 exchanges allow investors to move from one annuity contract to another without incurring tax consequences. 1035 exchanges can be a red flag and a cause for concern over abusive sales practices. Because most annuity contracts have surrender charges that may be substantial, 1035 exchanges may result in the investor being worse off and may constitute churning. FINRA is concerned about firms who employ compensation structures for representatives which may incentivize the sale of annuities over other investment products with lower costs and which may be more appropriate for investors. Firms should guard against incentivizing agents to sell annuity products over other investments. Members should ensure proper product training for registered representatives and principals for annuities and must have adequate supervision to monitor sales practices and to test their product knowledge. The focus should be to detect problematic and abusive sales practices. L share annuity contracts are designed with shorter surrender periods but have higher costs to investors. The sales of L share annuity contracts can be a red flag for compliance personnel and may constitute abusive sales practices.

ANNUITY PURCHASE OPTIONS

An investor may purchase an annuity contract in one of three ways. They are:

1. Single-payment deferred annuity
2. Single-payment immediate annuity
3. Periodic-payment deferred annuity

SINGLE-PAYMENT DEFERRED ANNUITY

With a single-payment deferred annuity, the investor funds the contract completely with one payment and defers receiving payments from the contract until some point in the future, usually after retirement. Money being invested in a single-payment deferred annuity is used to purchase accumulation units. The number and value of the accumulation units varies as the distributions are reinvested and the value of the separate account's portfolio changes.

SINGLE-PAYMENT IMMEDIATE ANNUITY

With a single-payment immediate annuity, the investor funds the contract completely with one payment and begins receiving payments from the contract immediately, normally within 60 days. The money that is invested in a single-payment immediate annuity is used to purchase annuity units. The number of annuity units remains fixed and the value changes as the value of the securities in the separate accounts portfolio fluctuate.

PERIODIC-PAYMENT DEFERRED ANNUITY

With a periodic-payment annuity the investor purchases the annuity by making regularly scheduled payments into the contract. This is known as the accumulation stage. During the accumulation stage, the terms are flexible and, if the investor misses a payment, there is no penalty. The money invested in a periodic-payment deferred annuity is used to purchase accumulation units. The number and value of the accumulation units fluctuate with the securities in the separate account's portfolio.

ACCUMULATION UNITS

An accumulation unit represents the investor's proportionate ownership in the separate account's portfolio during the accumulation or differed stage of the contract. The value of the accumulation unit will fluctuate as the value of the securities in the separate account's portfolio changes. As the investor makes contributions to the account or as distributions are reinvested, the number of accumulation units will vary. An investor will only own accumulation units during the accumulation stage when money is being paid into the contract or when receipt of payments is being deferred by the investor, such as with a single-payment deferred annuity.

ANNUITY UNITS

When an investor changes from the pay-in or deferred stage of the contract to the payout phase, the investor is said to have annuitized the contract. At this point, the investor trades in their accumulation units for annuity units. The number of annuity units is fixed and represents the investor's proportional ownership of the separate account's portfolio during the payout phase. The number of annuity units that the investor receives when the contract is annuitized is based on the payout option selected, the annuitant's age and sex, the value of the account, and the assumed interest rate.

 TAKENOTE!

Most annuities allow the investor to designate a beneficiary who will receive the greater of the value of the account or the total premiums paid if the investor dies during the accumulation stage.

ANNUITY PAYOUT OPTIONS

Annuity contracts are not subject to the contribution limits or the required minimum distributions of qualified plans. An investor in an annuity has the choice of taking a lump sum distribution or receiving scheduled payments from the contract. If the investor decides to annuitize the contract and receive scheduled payments, once the payout option is selected it may not be changed.

The following is a list of typical payout options, in order from the largest monthly payment to the smallest. They are:

- Life only/straight life
- Life with period certain
- Joint with last survivor

LIFE ONLY/STRAIGHT LIFE

This payout option will give the annuitant the largest periodic payment from the contract, and the investor will receive payments from the contract for his or her entire life. However, when the investor dies, no additional benefits are paid to the estate. If an investor has accumulated a large sum of money in the contract and dies unexpectedly shortly after annuitizing the contract, the insurance company keeps the money in the investor's account.

LIFE WITH PERIOD CERTAIN

A life with period certain payout option will pay out from the contract to the investor or to his or her estate for the life of the annuitant or for the period certain, whichever is longer. If an investor selects a 10-year period certain when the contract is annuitized and the investor lives for 20 years, payments will cease upon the death of the annuitant. However, if the same investor died only two years after annuitizing the contract, payments would go to the estate for another eight years.

JOINT WITH LAST SURVIVOR

When an investor selects a joint with last survivor option, the annuity is jointly owned by more than one party and payments will continue until the last owner of the contract dies. For example, if a husband and wife are receiving payments from an annuity under a joint with last survivor option and the husband dies, payments will continue to the wife for the rest of her life. The payments received by the wife could be at the same rate as when the husband was alive or at a reduced rate, depending on the contract. The monthly payments will initially be based on the life expectancy of the youngest annuitant.

FACTORS AFFECTING THE SIZE OF THE ANNUITY PAYMENT

All of the following determine the size of the annuity payments:

- Account value
- Payout option selected
- Age
- Sex
- Account performance vs. the assumed interest rate (AIR)

THE ASSUMED INTEREST RATE (AIR)

When an investor annuitizes a contract, the investor trades the accumulation units in for annuity units. Once the contract has been annuitized, the insurance company sets a benchmark for the separate account's performance, known as the assumed interest rate (AIR). The AIR is not a guaranteed rate of return; it is only used to adjust the value of the annuity units up or down, based upon the actual performance of the separate account. The assumed interest rate is an earnings target that the insurance company sets for the separate account. The separate account must meet this earnings target in order to keep the annuitant's payments at the same level. As the value of the annuity unit changes, so does the amount of the payment that is received by the investor. If the separate account outperforms the AIR, an investor would expect his or her payments to increase. If the separate account's performance fell below the AIR, the investor could expect his or her payments to decrease. The separate account's performance is always measured against the AIR, never against the previous month's performance. An investor's annuity payment is based on the number of annuity units owned by the investor multiplied by the value of the annuity unit. When the performance of the separate account equals the AIR, the value of the annuity unit will remain unchanged, and so will the investor's payment. Selecting an AIR that is realistic is important. If the AIR is too high and the separate account's return cannot equal the assumed rate, the value of the annuity unit will continue to fall, and so will the investor's payment. The opposite is true if the AIR is set too low. As the separate account outperforms the AIR, the value of the annuity unit will continue to rise, and so will the investor's payment. The AIR is only relevant during the payout phase of the contract when the investor is receiving payments and owns annuity units. The AIR does not concern itself with accumulation units during the accumulation stage or when benefits are being deferred.

TAXATION

Contributions made to an annuity are made with after tax dollars. The money the investor deposits becomes the investor's cost base and is allowed to grow tax deferred. When the investor withdraws money from the contract, only the growth is taxed. The cost base is returned to the investor tax-free. All money in excess of the investor's cost base is taxed as ordinary income.

TYPES OF WITHDRAWALS

An investor may begin withdrawing money from an annuity contract through any of the following options:

- Lump sum
- Random
- Annuitizing

Both lump sum and random withdrawals are done on a LIFO basis, last in first out. The growth portion of the contract is always considered to be the last money that was deposited and is taxed at the ordinary income rate of the annuitant. If the annuitant is under age 59-1/2 and takes a lump sum or random withdrawal, the withdrawal will be subject to a 10% tax penalty, as well as ordinary income taxes. An investor who needs to access the money in a variable annuity contract may be allowed to borrow from the contract so long as interest is charged on the loan and the loan is repaid by the investor, the investor will not be subject to taxes.

ANNUITIZING THE CONTRACT

When an investor annuitizes the contract and begins to receive monthly payments, part of each payment is the return of the investor's cost base and a portion of each payment is the distribution of the account's growth. To determine how much of each payment is taxable and how much is the return of principal, the investor would look at the exclusion ratio.

Contracts that are annuitized prior to age 59-1/2 under a life income option are not subject to the 10% tax penalty, nor are withdrawals due to disability or death.

EXPENSES AND GUARANTEES

An insurance company faces several risks with issuing annuity contracts. As a result of these risks, the insurance company deducts fees from the separate account to help it absorb these risks. These fees are:

- Mortality expense risk fee
- Operating expense risk fee

MORTALITY EXPENSE RISK FEE

An annuity guarantees to pay the investor for as long as the investor lives. Annuity payments are based in large part on the individual's life expectancy. Should the individual live beyond what the insurance company had projected, it may begin to lose money. As protection, the insurance company will deduct a mortality expense fee from the separate account.

OPERATING EXPENSE RISK FEE

The insurance company must have an understanding of how much it costs it to be in the business of issuing annuity contracts before it can offer to make payments to investors. The insurance company will deduct an operating expense risk fee from the separate account to help absorb the costs of issuing annuity contracts and to protect itself against costs unexpectedly rising. Costs such as salaries, rent, and general operating expenses are all examples of costs that could unexpectedly rise.

OTHER CHARGES

SALES CHARGES

There is no maximum sales charge for an annuity contract. The sales charge that is assessed must be reasonable in relation to the total payments over the life of the contract. Most annuity contracts have back-end sales charges or surrender charges similar to a contingent deferred sales charge.

INVESTMENT MANAGEMENT FEES

The individuals running the separate account are professionals and are compensated for their management of the account through a fee-based agreement. A fee is deducted from the separate account to cover this management expense. The more aggressive the portfolio, the larger the management fee.

VARIABLE ANNUITY VS. MUTUAL FUND

Feature	Variable Annuity	Mutual Fund
Maximum sales charge	No Max	8.5%
Investment adviser	Yes	Yes
Custodian bank	Yes	Yes
Transfer agent	Yes	Yes
Voting	Yes	Yes
Management	Board of managers	Board of directors
Taxation of growth and reinvestments	Tax-deferred	Currently taxed
Lifetime income	Yes	No
Costs and fees	Higher	Lower

Pretest

VARIABLE ANNUITIES

1. A variable annuity contract holder is seeking to receive the maximum monthly payment when she annuitizes her contract. Which payout option would be the most suitable for her?

    a. Total unit payout

    b. Life with period certain

    c. Life only

    d. Joint with last survivor

2. An investor who owns a fixed annuity is subject to:

    a. expense risk.

    b. investment risk.

    c. purchasing power risk.

    d. mortality risk.

3. The assumed interest rate will affect which of the following?

    I. The amount of the annuity payment

    II. The value of the accumulation unit

    III. The amount of the payment into the plan

    IV. The value of the annuity unit

    a. I and III

    b. II and III

    c. III and IV

    d. I and IV

4. An investor in a variable annuity may change his payout option:

   a. upon the death of a spouse for joint with last survivor.

   b. to convert to a lump sum withdrawal.

   c. if his financial needs change significantly.

   d. under no circumstances.

5. Which of the following is NOT a way an investor may purchase a variable annuity?

   a. Single-payment deferred annuity

   b. Single-payment immediate annuity

   c. Periodic-payment immediate annuity

   d. Periodic-payment deferred annuity

6. An investor has deposited $14,500 into a variable annuity over a three-year period. The money has grown to $17,800. The investor is 61 years old and must make a random withdrawal of $3,000. On what amount must he pay taxes?

   a. $0

   b. $3,000

   c. $700

   d. $2,300

7. Which of the following is NOT guaranteed by a fixed annuity?

   a. Income for life

   b. Protection from inflation

   c. Rate of return

   d. Protection from investment risk

8. You have been investing in a variable annuity that invests indirectly in the stock market. The separate account would have to be registered as a(n):

   a. closed-end investment company.

   b. UIT.

   c. investment fund.

   d. open-end investment company.

9. Which of the following is NOT true of annuity units?

   a. When an investor annuitizes a contract, he trades in his accumulation units for annuity units.

   b. The number of annuity units is variable depending on the fluctuation of the investments.

   c. The number of annuity units an investor receives depends partially upon the annuitant's age and sex.

   d. The number of annuity units an investor receives depends partially upon the payout option selected, the value of the account, and the assumed interest rate.

10. An investor has deposited $22,000 into a variable annuity over the last year. The value has fallen to $19,800. The investor is 41 years old and must make a random withdrawal of $1,500. On what amount must he pay taxes?

    a. $1,500

    b. $0

    c. $700

    d. $2,300

Issuing Corporate Securities

INTRODUCTION

The Securities Act of 1933 was the first major piece of securities industry regulation that was brought about largely as a result of the stock market crash of 1929. Other major laws were also enacted to help prevent another meltdown of the nation's financial system, such as the Securities Exchange Act of 1934, but we will start our review with the Securities Act of 1933, as it regulates the issuance of corporate securities.

THE SECURITIES ACT OF 1933

The Securities Act of 1933 was the first major piece of securities industry legislation and it regulates the primary market. The primary market consists exclusively of transactions between issuers of securities and investors. In a primary market transaction, the issuer of the securities receives the proceeds from the sale of the securities. The Securities Act of 1933 requires nonexempt issuers (typically corporate issuers) to file a registration statement with the Securities and Exchange Commission (SEC). The registration statement will be under review by the SEC for a minimum of 20 days. During this time, known as the cooling-off period, no sales of securities may take place. If the SEC requires additional information regarding the offering, the SEC may issue a deficiency letter or a stop order that will extend the cooling-off period beyond the original 20 days. The cooling-off period will continue until the SEC has received all of the information it had requested. The registration statement that is formally known as an S1 is the issuer's full disclosure document for the registration of the securities with the SEC.

THE PROSPECTUS

While the SEC is reviewing the security's registration statement, a registered representative is very limited as to what he or she may do with regard to the new issue. During the cooling-off period, the only thing that a registered representative may do is obtain indications of interest from clients by providing them with a preliminary prospectus, also known as a red herring. The term *red herring* originated from the fact that all preliminary prospectuses must have a statement printed in red ink on the front cover stating: "that these securities have not yet become registered with the SEC and therefore may not be sold." An indication of interest is an investor's or broker dealer's statement of interest in purchasing the securities being offered. The preliminary prospectus contains most of the same information that will be contained in the final prospectus, except for the offering price and the proceeds to the issuer. The preliminary prospectus will usually contain a price range for the security to be offered. All information contained in a preliminary prospectus is subject to change or revision.

THE FINAL PROSPECTUS

All purchasers of new issues must be given a final prospectus before any sales may be allowed. The final prospectus serves as the issuer's full disclosure document for the purchaser of the securities. If the issuer has filed a prospectus with the SEC and the prospectus can be viewed on the SEC's website, the prospectus will be deemed to have been provided to the investor through the access equals delivery rule. Once the issuer's registration statement becomes effective, the final prospectus must include:

- Type and description of the securities
- Price of the security
- Use of the proceeds
- Underwriter's discount
- Date of offering
- Type and description of underwriting
- Business history of issuer

TAKENOTE!

Only the final prospectus may be delivered electronically. The preliminary prospectus must be delivered in hard copy.

- Biographical data for company officers and directors
- Information regarding large stockholders
- Company financial data
- Risks to purchaser
- Legal matters concerning the company
- SEC disclaimer

PROSPECTUS TO BE PROVIDED TO AFTERMARKET PURCHASERS

Certain investors who purchase securities in the secondary market just after a distribution must also be provided with the final prospectus. The term for which a prospectus must be provided depends largely on the type of offering and where the issue will be traded in the aftermarket. If the security has an aftermarket delivery requirement, a prospectus must be provided by all firms that execute a purchase order for the security during the term. The aftermarket prospectus delivery requirements may be met electronically and are as follows:

- For IPOs: 90 days after being issued for securities quoted on the OTCBB or in the pink sheets, 25 days for listed or Nasdaq securities.
- Additional offerings: 40 days for securities quoted on the OTCBB or in the pink sheets. No aftermarket requirement for listed or Nasdaq securities.

SEC DISCLAIMER

The SEC reviews the issuer's registration statement and the prospectus but does not guarantee the accuracy or adequacy of the information contained within them. The SEC disclaimer must appear on the cover of all prospectuses and states: "These securities have not been approved or disapproved by the SEC nor have any representations been made about the accuracy of the adequacy of the information."

MISREPRESENTATIONS

Financial relief for misrepresentations made under the Securities Act of 1933 is available for purchasers of any security that is sold under a prospectus that is found to contain false or misleading statements. Purchasers of the security may be entitled to seek financial relief from any or all of the following:

- The issuer
- The underwriters
- Officers and directors
- All parties who signed the registration statement
- Accountants and attorneys who helped prepare the registration statement

TOMBSTONE ADS

Tombstone ads are the only form of advertising that is allowed during the cooling-off period. A tombstone ad is an announcement and description of the securities to be offered. A tombstone ad lists the names of the underwriters, where a prospectus may be obtained, and a statement that the tombstone ad does not constitute an offer to sell the securities and that the offer may only be made by a prospectus. Tombstone ads are traditionally run to announce the new issue, but they are not required and do not need to be filed with the SEC.

FREE RIDING AND WITHHOLDING/FINRA RULE 5130

FINRA Rule 5130 has replaced the free-riding and withholding rule. FINRA Rule 5130 requires that a broker dealer obtain an eligibility statement from all account owners who purchase a new issue of stock within 12 months prior to the purchase. A broker dealer underwriting a new issue must make a complete and bona fide offering of all securities being issued to the public and may not withhold any of the securities for:

- The account of underwriters.
- The account of another broker dealer.
- The account of a firm employee or the account of those who are financially dependent upon the employee.
- The account of employees of other FINRA members.

An exception to FINRA Rule 5130 applies to employees of limited broker dealers who engage solely in the purchase and sale of investment company products or direct participation programs (DPPs). Employees of limited broker dealers may purchase new issues. This exemption applies only to the employees of the limited broker dealer, not to the firm itself. These rules are in effect for all initial public offerings, but are especially prevalent when dealing with a hot issue. A hot issue is one that trades at an immediate premium to its offering price in the secondary market. A broker dealer may not free ride by withholding securities for its own account or for the accounts of those listed above. There are some people who may purchase hot issues so long as the amount is not substantial and they have a history of purchasing new issues. These conditionally approved people are:

- Officers and employees of financial institutions
- Nonsupported family members
- Accountants, attorneys, and finders associated with the underwriting
- Accounts where the restricted persons interest is limited to 10% or less or where a maximum of 10% of the allocation of new is for the benefit of such persons. This is known as the carve out procedure.

If the demand for the new issue is great, the syndicate may purchase additional shares from the issuer under a greenshoe provision. This will increase the offering by up to 15%. Alternatively, if the demand for the issue is not great, the syndicate may have to support the issue in the aftermarket to ensure that the shares are distributed without a great deal of volatility. The syndicate may enter a single stabilizing bid to support the issue and may only enter the stabilizing bid at or below the offering price. FINRA Rule 5130 covers initial offerings of common stock only. Exempt from the rule are offerings of additional issues, bonds, and preferred shares. These offerings may be purchased by registered persons.

UNDERWRITING CORPORATE SECURITIES

Once a business has decided that it needs to raise capital to meet its organizational objectives, it must determine how to raise the needed capital. Most corporations at this point will hire an investment banker, also known as an underwriter, to advise them. The underwriter works for the issuer, and it is the underwriter's job to advise the client about what type of securities to offer. The issuer and the underwriter together determine whether stocks or bonds should be issued and what the terms will be. The underwriter is responsible for trying to obtain the financing at the best possible terms for the issuer. The underwriter will:

- Market the issue to investors.
- Assist in the determination of the terms of the offering.
- Purchase the securities directly from the issuer to resell to investors.

The issuer is responsible for:

- Filing a registration statement with the SEC.
- Registering the securities in the states in which it will be sold, also known as blue-skying the issue.
- Negotiating the underwriter's compensation and obligations to the issuer.

TYPES OF UNDERWRITING COMMITMENTS

FIRM COMMITMENT

In a firm commitment underwriting, the underwriter guarantees to purchase all of the securities being offered for sale by the issuer regardless of whether they can sell them to investors. A firm commitment underwriting agreement is the most desirable for the issuer because it guarantees all of the money right away. The more in demand the offering is, the more likely it is that it will be done on a firm commitment basis. In a firm commitment, the underwriter puts its own money at risk if it can't sell the securities to investors.

MARKET OUT CLAUSE

An underwriter offering securities for an issuer on a firm commitment basis is assuming a substantial amount of risk. As a result, the underwriter will insist on having a market out clause in the underwriting agreement. A market out clause would free the underwriter from its obligation to purchase all of the securities in the event of a development that impairs the quality of the securities or that adversely affects the issuer. Poor market conditions are not a reason to invoke the market out clause.

BEST EFFORTS

In a best efforts underwriting, the underwriter will do its best to sell all of the securities that are being offered by the issuer, but in no way is the underwriter obligated to purchase the securities for its own account. The lower the demand for an issue, the greater the likelihood that it will be done on a best efforts basis. Any shares or bonds in a best efforts underwriting that have not been sold will be returned to the issuer.

MINI-MAXI

A mini-maxi is a type of best efforts underwriting that does not become effective until a minimum amount of the securities have been sold. Once the minimum has been met, the underwriter may then sell the securities up to the maximum amount specified under the terms of the offering. All funds collected from investors will be held in escrow until the underwriting is completed. If the minimum amount of securities specified by the offering cannot be reached, the offering will be canceled and the investors' funds that were collected will be returned to them.

ALL OR NONE (AON)

With an all-or-none (AON) underwriting, the issuer has determined that it must receive the proceeds from the sale of all of the securities. Investors' funds are held in escrow until all of the securities are sold. If all of the securities are sold, the proceeds will be released to the issuer. If all of the securities are not sold, the issue is canceled, and the investors' funds will be returned. Contingent offerings must have a qualified financial institution QFI to act as an escrow agent for the offering. A general securities broker dealer, bank, or trust company may act as an escrow agent.

STANDBY

A standby underwriting agreement will be used in conjunction with a preemptive rights offering. All standby underwritings are done on a firm commitment basis. The standby underwriter agrees to purchase any shares that current shareholders do not purchase. The standby underwriter will purchase the shares at the right's discounted subscription price.

TYPES OF OFFERINGS

INITIAL PUBLIC OFFERING (IPO)/NEW ISSUE

An initial public offering (IPO) is the first time that a company has sold its stock to the public. The issuing company receives the proceeds from the sale minus the underwriter's compensation.

SUBSEQUENT PRIMARY/ADDITIONAL ISSUES

In a subsequent primary offering, the corporation is already publicly owned and the company is selling additional shares to raise new financing.

PRIMARY OFFERING VS. SECONDARY OFFERING

In a primary offering, the issuing company receives the proceeds from the sale minus the underwriter's compensation. In a secondary offering, a group of selling shareholders receives the proceeds from the sale minus the underwriter's compensation. A combined offering has elements of both the primary offering and the secondary offering. Part of the proceeds goes to the company and part of the proceeds goes to a group of selling shareholders.

AWARDING THE ISSUE

There are two ways in which the corporation may select an underwriter. A corporation may elect to have multiple underwriters submit bids and choose the underwriter with the best bid. This is known as a competitive bid underwriting. A company may elect to select one firm to sell the issue and negotiate the terms of the offering with it. This is known as a negotiated underwriting. Most corporate offerings are awarded on a negotiated basis, while municipal bonds offerings are usually awarded through competitive bidding.

THE UNDERWRITING SYNDICATE

Because most corporate offerings involve a large number of shares and a very large dollar amount, they will be offered through several underwriters known as the underwriting syndicate. The syndicate is a group of investment banks that have agreed to share the responsibility of marketing the issue. The managing underwriter, also known as the lead underwriter or book running manager, leads the syndicate.

SELLING GROUP

The syndicate may form a selling group in an effort to help market the issue. Members of the selling group have no underwriting responsibility and may only sell the shares to investors for a fee known as the selling concession.

UNDERWRITER'S COMPENSATION

The group of broker dealers that make up the underwriting syndicate will be compensated based upon their role as a syndicate member. The only syndicate member that may earn the entire spread is the lead or managing underwriter.

MANAGEMENT FEE

The lead or managing underwriter will receive a fee known as a management fee for every share that is sold. In most cases, the managing underwriter is the firm that negotiated the terms of the offering with the issuer and formed the syndicate.

UNDERWRITER'S FEE

The underwriter's fee is the cost of bringing the issue to market, and is a fee assessed for each share that is sold by the syndicate. If there is any money remaining after all expenses are paid, the syndicate members will split it based upon their commitment level in the underwriting.

SELLING CONCESSION

The selling concession will be paid to any syndicate member or selling group member who sells the shares to the investors. The selling concession is the only fee that the selling group members may earn.

UNDERWRITING SPREAD

The total amount of the management fee, the underwriting fee, and the selling concession make up the total underwriting spread. This is the difference between the gross proceeds of the offering and the net proceeds to the issuer.

PUBLIC OFFERING PRICE: $12
SELLING CONCESSION $1.50
UNDERWRITING FEE $.75
MANAGEMENT FEE $.25
PROCEEDS TO ISSUER $9.50 PER SHARE

In this example, the underwriting spread is $2.50 per share.

FACTORS THAT DETERMINE THE SIZE OF THE UNDERWRITING SPREAD

There are many factors that determine the amount of the underwriter's compensation for offering the securities on behalf of the issuer. Some of the factors are:

- The type of securities to be offered.
- The size of the issue.
- The quality of the securities to be issued.
- The perceived demand for the securities.
- The type of underwriting agreement.
- The quality of the issuer's business.

EXEMPT SECURITIES

Certain securities are exempt from the registration provisions of the Securities Act of 1933 because of the issuer or the nature of the security. Although the securities may be exempt from the registration and prospectus requirements of the act, none are exempt from the antifraud provisions of the act. Examples of exempt securities are:

- Debt securities with maturities of less than 270 days and sold in denominations of $50,000 or more.
- Employee benefit plans.
- Option contracts, both puts and calls, on stocks and indexes.

Examples of exempt issuers are:

- U.S. government
- State and municipal governments
- Foreign national governments
- Canadian federal and municipal governments
- Insurance companies
- Banks and trusts
- Religious and charitable organizations

EXEMPT TRANSACTIONS

Sometimes a security that would otherwise have to register is exempt from the registration requirements of the Securities Act of 1933 because of the type of transaction that is involved. The following are all exempt transactions:

- Private placements/Regulation D offerings
- Rule 144
- Regulation A offerings
- Rule 145
- Rule 147 intrastate offerings

PRIVATE PLACEMENTS/REGULATION D OFFERINGS

A private placement is a sale of securities that is made to a group of accredited investors and the securities are not offered to the general public. Accredited investors include institutional investors and individuals who:

- Earn at least $200,000 per year if single.

Or

- Earn at least $300,000 jointly with a spouse.

Or

- Have a net worth of at least $1,000,000 without the primary residence.

Sales to nonaccredited investors are limited to 35 in any 12-month period. No commission may be paid to representatives who sell a private placement to a nonaccredited investor. All investors in private placements must hold the securities fully paid for at least six months and sign a letter stating that they are purchasing the securities for investment purposes. Stock purchased through a private placement is known as lettered stock, legend stock, or restricted stock, because there is a legend on the stock certificate that limits the ability of the owner to transfer or sell the securities. There is no limit as to how many accredited investors may purchase the securities. The limits on the amount of money that may be raised under the various regulation D offerings are as follows:

Rule 504 D allows issuers to raise up to $1 million

Rule 505 D allows issuers to raise between $1 million and $5 million

Rule 506 D allows issuers to raise an unlimited amount of capital

The JOBS Act now allows investors to view private placement documents online so long as the website requires an investor to submit a questionnaire documenting assets, income, and investment experience. This questionnaire must be reviewed and if qualified for participation the issuer or broker dealer may assign the investor a username and password granting them access to view the details of the offerings.

RULE 144

This rule regulates how control or restricted securities may be sold. Rule 144 designates:

- The holding period for the security.
- The amount of the security that may be sold.
- Filing procedures.
- The method of sale.

Control securities are owned by officers, directors, and owners of 10% or more of the company's outstanding stock. Control stock may be obtained by insiders through open-market purchases or through the exercise of company stock options. There is no holding period for control securities. However, insiders are not allowed to earn a short swing profit through the purchase and sale of control stock in the open market. If the securities were held less than six months, the insider must return any profit to the company.

Restricted securities may be purchased by both insiders and investors though a private placement or be obtained through an offering other than a public sale. Securities obtained through a private placement or other nonpublic means need to be sold under Rule 144 in order to allow the transfer of ownership. Restricted stock must be held fully paid for six months. After six months, the securities may be sold freely by noninsiders so long as the seller has not been affiliated with the issuer in the last three months. Rule 144 sets the following volume limits for both restricted and control stock during any 90-day period. The seller must file Form 144 at the time the order is entered and is limited to the greater of:

- The average weekly trading volume for the preceding four weeks.

Or

- 1% of the issuer's total outstanding stock.

For orders for 5,000 shares or less and that do not exceed $50,000, Form 144 does not need to be filed. If the owner of restricted stock dies, their estate may sell the shares freely without regard to the holding period or volume limitations of Rule 144.

 TAKENOTE!

Securities may be sold under Rule 144 four times per year. The securities sold under Rule 144 become part of the public float and the seller, not the issuer, receives the proceeds of the sale.

PRIVATE INVESTMENT IN A PUBLIC EQUITY (PIPE)

Public companies that wish to obtain additional financing without selling securities to the general public may sell securities to a group of accredited investors through a private placement. The accredited investors in most cases will be institutional investors who wish to invest a large amount of capital. Common stock, convertible or nonconvertible debt, and rights and warrants may all be sold to investors through a PIPE transaction. Obtaining capital through a PIPE transaction benefits the public company in a number of ways:

- Reduced transaction cost.
- Term disclosure only upon completion of the transaction.
- Increased institutional ownership.
- Quick closing.

Securities sold through a PIPE transaction are subject to Rule 144. If the issuer files a registration statement after the closing of the offering, sales may begin immediately upon the effective date.

REGULATION A OFFERINGS

A Regulation A offering allows the issuer to raise up to $5,000,000 in any 12-month period. Of that $5 million, no more than $1.5 million may be offered or sold by selling shareholders. The JOBS Act of 2012 increased the amount that may be raised under a Regulation A offering to $50 million. This exemption from full registration allows smaller companies access to the capital markets without having to go through the expense of filing a full registration statement with the SEC. The issuer will instead file an abbreviated notice of sale or offering circular known as a 1-A with the SEC and purchasers of the issue will be given a copy of the offering circular rather than a final prospectus. Purchasers of the issue must have the preliminary or final offering circular mailed to them 48 hours before mailing the confirmation. The same 20-day cooling-off period also applies to Regulation A offerings

The JOBS Act further refined Regulation A into two tiers, with Regulation A now sometimes being referred to as Regulation A plus. Tier 1 allows issuers to raise up to $20 million. Of this $20 million no more than $6 million may be offered by selling shareholders Tier 2 allows issuers to raise up to $50 million of which no more than $15 million may be offered by selling shareholders.

RULE 145

Rule 145 requires that shareholders approve any merger or reorganization of the company's ownership. Any merger or acquisition will be reported to the SEC on Form S-4. Stockholders must be given full disclosure of the proposed transaction or reclassification and must be sent proxies to vote on the proposal. Rule 145 covers:

- Mergers involving a stock swap or offer of another company's securities in exchange for their current stock.
- Reclassification involving the exchange of one class of the company's securities for another.

- Asset transfers involving the dissolution of the company or the distribution or sale of a major portion of the company's assets.

RULE 147 INTRASTATE OFFERING

Rule 147 pertains to offerings of securities that are limited to one state. Because the offering is being made only in one state, it is exempt from registration with the SEC and is subject to the jurisdiction of the state securities administrator. In order to qualify for an exemption from SEC registration the issue must meet the following criteria:

- The issuer must have its headquarters in that state.
- 80% of the issuer's income must be received in that state.
- 80% of the offering's proceeds must be used in that state.
- 80% of the issuer's assets must be located in that state.
- 100% of purchasers must be located in that state.
- Purchasers must agree not to resell the securities to an out-of-state resident for nine months.
- If the issuer is using an underwriter, the broker dealer must have an office in that state.

CROWDFUNDING

Crowdfunding has become a popular way for issuers to raise capital from small investors. Issuers may offer securities to investors for purchase through a broker dealer or through a registered crowdfunding portal. The portal must be registered with the SEC and must also be a FINRA member firm. Issuers who raise capital through crowdfunding may not engage directly in crowdfunding as a way to sell shares to investors. Issuers who sell shares through crowdfunding must register the securities with the SEC by filing form C. Because most of the securities are speculative in nature, broker dealers and crowdfunding portals must offer educational material to investors who are considering purchasing securities offered through crowdfunding. The material must detail the risks involved in making investments in companies through the crowdfunding process as well as the fact that the securities have a limited amount of liquidity. Investors who purchase shares through crowdfunding may not sell the shares for 12 months. Shares however may be transferred earlier to a relative or to a trust controlled by the investor or as a result of death or divorce. Early transfer will also be allowed if the purchaser is an accredited investor or if the securities are part of an SEC registered offering. Investors who purchase shares are limited to the amount of securities they may purchase through the crowdfunding process in any 12 month period. Investors who have annual income or a net worth of less than $100,000 are limited to purchasing the greater of $2,000 worth of securities or 5% of their annual income or net worth. If the investor uses the 5% calculation to determine their purchase limit the amount the person may purchase will be the lesser of the two amounts. Investors who have an annual income or a net worth greater than $100,000 may invest the lesser of 10% of their annual income or net worth up to a maximum of $100,000.

Pretest

ISSUING CORPORATE SECURITIES

1. A syndicate has published a tombstone ad prior to the issue becoming effective. Which of the following must appear in the tombstone?

    I. A statement that the registration has not yet become effective.

    II. A statement that the ad is not an offer to sell the securities.

    III. Contact information.

    IV. No commitment statement.

    a. III and IV

    b. II and III

    c. I and II

    d. I, II, III, and IV

2. During a new issue registration, false information is included in the prospectus to buyers. Which of the following may be held liable to investors?

    I. Officers of the issuer

    II. Accountants

    III. Syndicate members

    IV. People who signed the registration statement

    a. I and III

    b. I, II, and IV

    c. I, II, and III

    d. I, II, III, and IV

3. A syndicate may enter a stabilizing bid:

   a. whenever the price begins to decline.

   b. at or below the offering price.

   c. to ensure an increase from the offering price.

   d. to cover over allotments only.

4. Corporations may do all of the following, EXCEPT:

   a. issue preferred stock only.

   b. issue nonvoting common stock.

   c. sell stock out of the treasury.

   d. repurchase its own shares.

5. Issuance of which of the following would require the approval of existing shareholders?

   a. Mortgage bonds

   b. Collateral trust bonds

   c. Prior lien bonds

   d. Equipment trust certificates

6. During an underwriting of a hot issue, the syndicate exercises its green-shoe provision. This will allow them to buy an additional:

   a. 20% of the offering.

   b. 25% of the offering.

   c. 15% of the offering.

   d. 10% of the offering.

7. Which of the following is NOT a type of offering?

   a. Rule 149 offering

   b. Subsequent primary offering

   c. Secondary offering

   d. Combined offering

8. Once a company decides to raise long-term capital to meet its needs, it will:

    a. approach the money market to determine how much capital can be raised.

    b. hire an underwriter to advise the issuer about the type of securities to issue.

    c. hire a dealer to issue stock for public purchase.

    d. hire a broker to issue stock for public purchase.

9. A firm participating in the offering of a private placement may sell the private placement to:

    a. no more than 12 nonaccredited investors in any 12-month period.

    b. no more than 6 nonaccredited investors in any 12-month period.

    c. no more than 35 nonaccredited investors in any 12-month period.

    d. no more than 15 nonaccredited investors in any 12-month period.

10. A company doing a preemptive right offering would most likely use what type of underwriting agreement?

    a. Best efforts

    b. Firm commitment

    c. All or none

    d. Standby

11. A syndicate distributing a new issue of common stock contains 9 syndicate members and 12 selling group members. The stock will be listed on the Nasdaq. How many bids may be entered for the syndicate?

    a. 9

    b. 1

    c. 21

    d. 0

12. The subscription price of a right is:

    a. the price offered to current stockholders during a subsequent primary offering.

    b. the price of buying shares from a broker.

    c. the price a market maker pays to buy shares.

    d. the price at which the new shareholders can purchase new shares.

13. The SEC has been reviewing a company's registration statement and would like clarification on a few items. It would most likely:

    a. call the company.

    b. issue a stop order.

    c. issue a deficiency letter.

    d. call the lead underwriter.

14. Which of the following is NOT a type of underwriting commitment?

    a. Primary commitment

    b. Standby commitment

    c. Best efforts commitment

    d. Firm commitment

15. XYZ has just gone public and is quoted on the Nasdaq Capital Market. Any investor who buys XYZ must get a prospectus for how long?

    a. 30 days

    b. 90 days

    c. 60 days

    d. 45 days

16. A red herring given to a client during the cooling-off period will contain all of the following, EXCEPT:

    a. proceeds to the company.

    b. use of proceeds.

    c. biographies of officers and directors.

    d. a notice that all the information is subject to change.

17. A member of the selling group assisting in the distribution of securities in an undivided syndicate is:

    a. not liable for a percentage of the unsold securities.

    b. liable for a percentage of the unsold securities.

    c. required to purchase unsold shares for its own account.

    d. responsible for a percentage of the total offering.

Trading Securities

INTRODUCTION

Investors who do not purchase their stocks and bonds directly from the issuer must purchase them from another investor. Investor-to-investor transactions are known as secondary market transactions. In a secondary market transaction, the selling security owner receives the proceeds from the sale. Secondary market transactions may take place on an exchange or in the over-the-counter market known as Nasdaq. Although both facilitate the trading of securities, they operate in a very different manner. We will begin by looking at the types of orders that an investor may enter and the reasons for entering the various types of orders. Series 7 candidates can expect a number of questions on trading securities.

TYPES OF ORDERS

Investors can enter various types of orders to buy or sell securities. Some orders guarantee that the investor's order will be executed immediately. Other types of orders may state a specific price or condition under which the investor wants the order to be executed. All orders are canceled day orders unless otherwise specified. All day orders will be canceled at the end of the trading day if they are not executed. An investor may also specify that the order remain active until canceled. This type of order is known as good till cancel, or GTC.

MARKET ORDERS

A market order will guarantee that the investor's order is executed as soon as the order is presented to the market. A market order to either buy or sell guarantees the execution but not the price at which the order will be executed. When a market order is presented for execution, the market for the security may be very different from the market that was displayed when the order was entered. As a result, the investor does not know the exact price that the order will be executed at. A market order takes priority over an immediately executable limit order.

BUY LIMIT ORDERS

A buy limit order sets the maximum price that the investor will pay for the security. The order may never be executed at a price higher than the investor's limit price. Although a buy limit order guarantees that the investor will not pay over a certain price, it does not guarantee an execution. If the stock continues to trade higher away from the investor's limit price, the investor will not purchase the stock and may miss a chance to realize a profit.

SELL LIMIT ORDERS

A sell limit order sets the minimum price that the investor will accept for the security. The order may never be executed at a price lower than the investor's limit price. Although a sell limit order guarantees that the investor will not receive less than a certain price, it does not guarantee an execution. If the stock continues to trade lower away from the investor's limit price, the investor will not sell the stock and may miss a chance to realize a profit or may realize a loss as a result.

 FOCUSPOINT

It's important to remember that even if an investor sees stock trading at the limit price it does not mean that the order was executed because there could have been stock ahead of the investor at that limit price.

STOP ORDERS/STOP-LOSS ORDERS

A stop order or stop-loss order can be used by investors to limit or guard against a loss or to protect a profit. A stop order will be placed away from the market in case the stock starts to move against the investor. A stop order is not a live order; it has to be elected. A stop order is elected and becomes a live order when the stock trades at or through the stop price. The stop price is also known as the trigger price. Once the stock has traded at or through the stop price, the order becomes a market order to either buy or sell the stock, depending on the type of order that was placed.

BUY STOP ORDERS

A buy stop order is placed above the market and is used to protect against a loss or to protect a profit on a short sale of stock. A buy stop order could also be used by a technical analyst to get long the stock after the stock breaks through resistance.

EXAMPLE   An investor has sold 100 shares of ABC short at $40 per share. ABC has declined to $30 per share. The investor is concerned that if ABC goes past $32 it may return to $40. To protect his profit he enters an order to buy 100 ABC at 32 stop. If ABC trades at or through $32, the order will become a market order to buy 100 shares, and the investor will cover the short at the next available price.

SELL STOP ORDERS

A sell stop order is placed below the market and is used to protect against a loss or to protect a profit on the purchase of a stock. A sell stop order could also be used by a technical analyst to get short the stock after the stock breaks through support.

EXAMPLE   An investor has purchased 100 shares of ABC at $30 per share. ABC has risen to $40 per share. The investor is concerned that if ABC falls past $38 it may return to $30. To protect her profit she enters an order to sell 100 ABC at 38 stop. If ABC trades at or through $38, the order will become a market order to sell 100 shares, and the investor will sell her short at the next available price.

If in the same example the order to sell 100 ABC at 38 stop was entered GTC, we could have a situation such as this:

ABC closes at 39.40. The following morning ABC announces that it lost a major contract, and ABC opens at 35.30. The opening print of 35.30 elected the order, and the stock would be sold on the opening or as close to the opening as practical.

STOP-LIMIT ORDERS

An investor would enter a stop-limit order for the same reasons as he or she would enter a stop order. The only difference is that once the order has been elected the order becomes a limit order instead of a market order. The same risks that apply to traditional limit orders apply to stop-limit orders. If the stock continues to trade away from the investor's limit, the investor could give back all of the profits or suffer large losses.

OTHER TYPES OF ORDERS

There are several other types of orders that an investor may enter. They are:

- All or none (AON)
- Immediate or cancel (IOC)
- Fill or kill (FOK)
- Not held (NH)
- Market on open (MOO)/market on close (MOC)

All-or-none orders: AON orders may be entered as day orders or GTC. All-or-none orders, as the name implies, indicate that the investor wants to buy or sell all of the securities or none of them. AON orders are not displayed in the market because of the required special handling, and the investor will not accept a partial execution.

Immediate-or-cancel orders: The investor wants to buy or sell whatever can be sold immediately; whatever is not filled is canceled.

Fill-or-kill orders: The investor wants the entire order executed immediately or the entire order canceled.

Not-held orders: The investor gives discretion to the floor broker as to the time and price of execution. All retail NH orders given to a representative are considered day orders unless the order is received in writing from the customer and entered GTC.

Market-on-open/market-on-close orders: The investor wants the order executed on the opening or closing of the market or as reasonably close to the opening or closing as practical. If the order is not executed, it is canceled. Partial executions are allowed.

> **TAKENOTE!**
>
> The SEC has granted permission to the NYSE to stop using FOK and IOC orders.

THE EXCHANGES

The most recognized stock exchange in the world is the New York Stock Exchange (NYSE). There are, however, many exchanges throughout the United States that all operate in a similar manner. Exchanges are dual-auction markets. They provide a central marketplace where buyers and sellers come together in one centralized location to compete with one another. Buyers compete with other buyers to be the highest price anyone is willing to pay for the security, and sellers compete with other sellers to be the lowest price at which anyone is willing to sell a security. All transactions in an exchange-listed security that are executed on the exchange have to take place in front of the specialist, or designated market maker (DMM), for that security. The specialist/DMM is an exchange member who is responsible for maintaining a fair and orderly market for the stock in which he or she specializes. The specialist/DMM stands at the trading post where all the buyers and sellers must go to conduct business in the security. This is responsible for the crowd that you see on the news and financial reports when they show the floor of the exchange. All securities that trade on an exchange are known as listed securities.

PRIORITY OF EXCHANGE ORDERS

Orders that are routed to the trading post for execution are prioritized according to price and time. If the price of more than one order is the same, orders will be filled as follows:

- **Priority:** The order that was received first gets filled first.
- **Precedence:** If the time and price are the same, the larger order gets filled.
- **Parity:** If all conditions are the same, the orders are matched in the crowd and the shares are split among the orders.

THE ROLE OF THE DESIGNATED MARKET MAKER/DMM

The DMM (formerly known as a specialist) is an independent exchange member who has been assigned a stock or group of stocks for which he or she is the designated market maker. Designated market makers are responsible for:

- Maintaining a fair and orderly market for the securities.
- Buying for their own account in the absence of public buy orders.
- Selling from their own account in the absence of public sell orders.
- Acting as an agent by executing public orders left with them.

A large amount of capital is required to fulfill the requirements of a DMM. As a result, most specialists/DMMs are employees of member firms. Although the specialist is not required to participate in every transaction, every transaction for that security that is executed on the exchange must take place in front of the designated market maker. The specialist may act as either an agent or as a principal if he or she plays a role in the transaction.

THE DMM ACTING AS A PRINCIPAL

In the absence of public orders the DMM is required to provide liquidity and price improvement for the stocks in which they are the designated market maker. DMMs are required to trade against the market and may now trade for their own account at prices that would compete with public orders.

EXAMPLE   If the public market for XYZ is quoted as follows:

	Bid	**Offer**
10 × 10	**20.45**	**20.55**

There is a 20.45 bid for 1000 shares and 1000 shares offered at 20.55.

If a public sell order came in to sell the stock, the DMM could purchase the stock for their own account at 20.45 because they are on parity with the public. The DMM could also purchase the stock for their own account at 20.50 and would be improving the price that the seller would be receiving. This is known as price improvement. Alternatively, if a public buy order came in, the DMM could sell the stock from their own account at 20.55, because they are now allowed to compete with the public. They could also sell the stock to the customer at 20.50 because, once again, that would be providing price improvement for the order.

THE DESIGNATED MARKET MAKER/ DMM ACTING AS AN AGENT

The DMM is also required to execute orders that have been left with her. Orders that have been left with the DMM for execution are said to have been "left or dropped on the DMM's book." The DMM is required to maintain a book of public orders and to execute them when market conditions permit. The types of orders that may be left with the DMM are:

- Buy and sell limit orders
- Stop orders
- Stop-limit orders
- Both day and GTC orders
- AON orders

The DMM will execute the orders if and when she is able to and will send a commission bill to the member who left the order with her for execution. This is known as a specialist bill and is usually only a cent or two per share. The DMM is also required to quote the best market for the security to any party that asks. The best or inside market is composed of the highest bid and lowest offer. This is made up from bids and offers contained in the DMM's book and in the trading crowd. The inside market is also the market that is displayed to broker dealers and agents on their quote system.

When quoting the inside market, the DMM will add all of the shares bid for at the highest price and all of the shares offered at the lowest price to determine the size of the market. There are certain types of orders that are not included when determining the inside market, they are:

- Stop orders
- AON orders

A DMM may not accept the following types of orders:

- Market orders
- Immediately executable limit orders
- NH orders
- IOC orders
- FOK orders

Market orders and immediately executable limit orders are filled as soon as they reach the crowd, so there is nothing to leave with the specialist. In the case of an NH order, once a floor broker is given discretion as to time and price, it may not give it to another party.

A DMM's book may look something like the following example:

Buy	XYZ	Sell
5 Goldman 10 JPM	20	
	20.05	
	20.10	1 Prudential 5 Fidelity
	20.15	2 Morgan
5 Merrill Stp	20.20	

The inside market for XYZ based on the DMM's book would be:

	Bid	Ask
15 × 6	20.00	20.10

Buyers are bidding for 1,500 shares, and sellers are offering 600 shares of XYZ.

 **TAKENOTE!**

The buy stop entered over the market by Merrill is not contained in the quote, because the order has not been elected.

CROSSING STOCK

A floor broker from time to time may get an order from both a buyer and a seller in the same security. The floor broker may be allowed to pair off, or cross, the orders and execute both orders simultaneously. In order for the floor broker to cross the stock, the DMM must allow it and the floor broker must announce the orders in an effort to obtain price improvement for the orders. The floor broker must offer the stock for sale at a price above the current best bid and may purchase the stock using the buy order if no price improvement has been offered. This will then complete the cross, and both orders will be filled.

DO NOT REDUCE (DNR)

GTC orders that are placed underneath the market and left with the DMM for execution will be reduced for the distribution of dividends. Orders that will be reduced are:

- Buy limits
- Sell stops

These orders are reduced because when a stock goes ex dividend its price is adjusted down. To ensure that customer orders placed below the market are only executed as a result of market activity, the order will be adjusted down by the value of the dividend.

| EXAMPLE | A customer has placed an order to buy 500 XYZ at 35 GTC. XYZ closed yesterday at 36.10. XYZ goes ex dividend for 20 cents and opens the next day at 35.90. The customer's order will now be an order to purchase 500 XYZ at 34.80 GTC.

If the customer had entered the order and specified that the order was not to be reduced for the distribution of ordinary dividends, it would have remained an order to purchase 500 shares at 35. The order in this case would have been entered as:

Buy 500 XYZ 35 GTC DNR

Orders placed above the market are not reduced for distributions.

ADJUSTMENTS FOR STOCK SPLITS

GTC orders that are left with the specialist must be adjusted for stock splits. Orders that are placed above and below the market will be adjusted so that the aggregate dollar value of the order remains the same.

| EXAMPLE | A customer has placed a GTC order. Let's look at what happens to the order if the company declares a stock split:

Type of Split	Old Order	New Order
2:1	Buy 100 at 50	Buy 200 at 25
2:1	Sell 100 at 100	Sell 200 at 50
3:2	Buy 100 at 100	Buy 150 at 66.67
3:2	Sell 100 at 60	Sell 150 at 40

Notice that in all of the examples the value of the customer's order remained the same. To calculate the adjustment to an open order for a forward stock split, multiply the number of shares by the fraction and the share price by the reciprocal of the fraction. Such as:

Buy 100 at 50 after a 2:1 stock split

$100 \times 2/1 = 200$

$50 \times 1/2 = 25$

The value of the order was $5,000 both before and after the order.

STOPPING STOCK

A DMM, as a courtesy to a public customer, may guarantee an execution price while trying to find an improved or better price for the public customer. This is known as stopping stock if an order comes into the crowd to purchase 500 ABC at the market when ABC is quoted as follows:

	Bid	**Ask**
15 × 20	40	40.20

If the DMM stopped the customer, he would guarantee that the customer would pay no more than 40.20 for the 500 shares. The specialist would then try to obtain a better price for the customer and would then try to attract a seller by displaying a higher bid for that customer's order. ABC may now be quoted after the DMM stopped the stock as:

	Bid	**Ask**
5 × 20	40.10	40.20

In this case, the DMM is trying to buy the stock for the customer 10 cents cheaper than the current best offer. If, however, a buyer comes into the crowd and purchases the stock that is offered at 40.20, the specialist must sell the customer 500 shares from his own account no higher than 40.20.

COMMISSION HOUSE BROKER

A commission house broker is an employee of a member organization and will execute orders for the member's customers and for the member's own account.

TWO-DOLLAR BROKER

A two-dollar broker is an independent member who will execute orders for commission house brokers when he or she is too busy managing other orders.

REGISTERED TRADERS

A registered trader is an exchange member who trades for his or her own account and for his or her own profit and loss. Orders may not originate on the floor of the NYSE; however, registered traders are active on other exchanges, such as the AMEX (now part of NYSE). A supplemental liquidity provider/ SLP is an off-the-floor market maker that directs orders to the floor of the NYSE for its own account. The SLP may compete with the DMM for order execution and must display a bid or offer at least 10% of the time. The SLP will receive a rebate from the NYSE when an order is executed against the SLP's quote that added liquidity to the market.

SUPER DISPLAY BOOK (SDBK)

Most customer orders will never be handled by a floor broker. Floor brokers usually only handle the large complex institutional orders. Customer orders will be electronically routed directly to the trading post for execution via the Super Display Book (SDBK) system. The SDBK bypasses the floor broker and sends the order right to the DMM for execution. If the order can be immediately executed, the system will send an electronic confirmation of the execution to the submitting broker dealer. All listed securities are eligible to be traded over the SDBK system. All preopening orders that can be matched up are automatically paired off by the system and executed at the opening price. Any preopening orders that cannot be paired off are routed to the trading post for inclusion on the display book.

SHORT SALES

An investor who believes that a stock price has appreciated too far and is likely to decline may profit from this belief by selling the stock short. In a short sale, the customer borrows the security in order to complete delivery to the buying party. The investor sells the stock high hoping that it can be bought back at a cheaper price. It is a perfectly legitimate investment strategy. The investor's first transaction is a sell and the investor exits the position by repurchasing the stock. The short sale of stock has unlimited risk because there is no limit as to how high the stock price may go. The investor will lose money if the stock appreciates past the sales price.

REGULATION OF SHORT SALES/ REGULATION SHO

The SEC continues to adopt new rules relating to the short sale of securities. Regulation SHO has been adopted to update prior short sale regulations and covers:

- Definitions and order marking.
- Suspension of uptick and plus bid requirements.
- Borrowing and delivery requirements for securities.

Under Regulation SHO, the SEC has prohibited any SRO from adopting any price criteria as a requirement of executing a short sale.

RULE 200 DEFINITIONS AND ORDER MARKING

Rule 200 updates the definition of who is determined to be long a security. As new derivatives and trading systems and strategies have been introduced, amendments to the short sale rules under the Securities Exchange Act of

1934 needed to be updated. Most of the prior rules and definitions remain unchanged. The new updates under Rule 200 are:

- A person is considered long the security if he or she holds a security future contract and has been notified that he or she will receive the underlying security.
- A broker dealer must aggregate its net positions in securities unless it qualifies to allow each independent trading unit to aggregate its positions independently.

A broker dealer may qualify to have its various trading departments determine their net long or short positions independently if:

- Traders are only assigned to one independent trading unit at any one time.
- Traders in each independent trading unit employ their own trading strategies and do not coordinate their trading with other independent trading units.
- The firm has documented each aggregation unit and the independent trading objectives of each unit.
- The firm supports the independent nature of each trading unit.
- At the time a sell order is entered each independent aggregation unit determines its net position for the security.

The order marking requirements of Rule 200 require the broker dealer to mark all orders long, short, or short exempt. The definition of long and short include the definitions in the affirmative determination rule and have been expanded to include the following:

- An order may be marked long if the investor or broker dealer has possession of the security and can reasonably be expected to deliver the security by the settlement date.
- An order must be marked short if the investor or broker dealer has possession of the security but cannot reasonably be expected to deliver the security by the settlement date.
- An order does not need to be marked short exempt if the seller is only relying on a price test exemption under the tick test or bid test rule.

RULE 203 SECURITY BORROWING AND DELIVERY REQUIREMENTS

A broker dealer may not accept an order to sell short an equity security for the account of a customer or for its own account without having borrowed the security, having arranged to borrow the security, or without having a reasonable belief that the security can be borrowed. A broker dealer can rely on an easy-to-borrow list of securities so long as the list is less than 24 hours old. For sell orders that were marked long, the broker dealer must deliver the securities by settlement date and may not borrow the securities to complete delivery. However, a broker dealer may borrow securities to complete delivery under the following exceptions:

- To complete delivery to the buyer when a customer fails to deliver.
- The security is being loaned to another broker dealer.
- A fail to deliver resulting from a good faith mistake and a buy in would create an undue hardship.

A broker dealer must close out all customer fails to deliver within 35 days of the trade date. The broker dealer must borrow the securities or buy in the securities of a like kind and quantity.

A broker dealer is exempt from the locating requirements for short sales if:

- The broker dealer has accepted an order to sell short an equity security short from another broker dealer. The broker dealer entering the order is required to locate the securities unless the broker dealer accepting the order has a contractual obligation to comply.
- Transactions in securities futures.
- Transactions that are executed in accordance with bona fide market making.
- Transactions executed by a specialist, block positioner, or dealer.
- An order where the customer has been determined to be long and will deliver the security when restrictions have been removed or expired. The seller must deliver the securities within 35 calendar days. If the broker dealer does not receive the securities, it must buy in the customer or borrow the securities.

THRESHOLD SECURITIES

The self-regulatory organizations (SROs) are responsible for the inclusion of securities on the threshold securities list. The SROs monitor reports from the National Securities Clearing Corporation (NSCC) to determine which securities meet the definition of a threshold security. A threshold security is an equity security that meets the following criteria:

- The security is registered under Section 12 of the Securities Exchange Act of 1934.
- There is an aggregate fail-to-deliver position at a clearing firm of 10,000 shares or more for five consecutive settlement days and such position represents 0.5% or more of the issuer's outstanding securities.
- The security has been included on the threshold securities list by an SRO and the list has been distributed by the SRO to its members.

A broker dealer who has a fail to deliver in a threshold security at a clearing firm for 13 consecutive settlement days must immediately close out the position by buying securities of a like kind and quantity. A broker dealer with a fail to deliver in a threshold security for 13 consecutive settlement dates may not accept an order to sell the security short from another person and may not sell the security short for its own account without having located the security until the fail to deliver has been closed out. Clearing firms that provide clearing services to other broker dealers may allocate or distribute a fail-to-deliver position in threshold securities to its broker dealer customers who are responsible for the fail to deliver. By allocating the fail-to-deliver position to its broker dealer customers who established the position, the obligation to close out the position is transferred from the clearing firm to the broker dealer customers who established the position. The 13-day requirement does not apply to any fail-to-deliver position that was established prior to a security becoming a threshold security. If a market maker cannot borrow a threshold security to execute transactions in connection with bona fide market-making activities, the market maker is entitled to an excused withdrawal from that security. A security will cease to be considered a threshold security if it does not exceed the specific fails to deliver criteria for five consecutive settlement days. Firms must maintain a record of customer and firm short positions. The firm must file a short-interest report twice per month for short positions that have settled by the 15th and as of the last trading day of each month, using FINRA's Regulation Filing Application (RFA). All reports are required to be filed with the firm's designated examining authority (FINRA or NYSE) by the end of the second business day following the settlement date.

LISTING REQUIREMENTS FOR THE NYSE

Only corporations that meet the strict listing requirements may have their stock traded on the NYSE. In order to become listed, a company must have:

- At least 400 shareholders owning at least 100 shares.
- At least 1,100,000 publicly held shares.

If the issuer ever wants to have its stock delisted from the NYSE, the following conditions must be met:

- The board of directors must approve the action.
- The 35 largest shareholders must be notified.
- The board's audit committee must approve the action.

OVER THE COUNTER/NASDAQ

Securities that are not listed on any of the centralized exchanges trade over the counter or on the Nasdaq. Nasdaq stands for National Association of Securities Dealers Automated Quotation System. It is the interdealer network of computers and phone lines that allows securities to be traded between broker dealers. Nasdaq is not an auction market but has been granted exchange status by the SEC. It is a negotiated market. One broker dealer negotiates a price directly with another broker dealer. None of the other interested parties for that particular security have any idea of what terms are being proposed. The broker dealers may communicate over their Nasdaq workstations or can speak directly to one another over the phone.

MARKET MAKERS

Because there are no specialists for the OTC markets, bids and offers are displayed by broker dealers known as market makers. A market maker is a firm that is required to display a two-sided market. A two-sided market consists of a simultaneous bid and offer for the security quoted through the Nasdaq workstation. The market maker must be willing to buy the security and the bid price, which it has displayed, as well as be willing to sell the security at the offering price, which it has displayed. These are known as firm quotes. There is no centralized location for the Nasdaq market; it is simply a network of computers that connects broker dealers throughout the world. Market makers purchase the security at the bid price and sell the security at the offering price. Their profit is the difference between the bid and the offer, which is known as the spread. Rule changes and new trading systems known as ECNs, or electronic communication networks, have narrowed the spreads on stocks significantly in recent years.

NASDAQ SUBSCRIPTION LEVELS

Broker dealers will subscribe to the Nasdaq workstation services that meet their firm's requirements. The levels of service are:

Level I: Nasdaq Level I subscription service only provides information relating to the inside market and provides quotes for registered representatives.

Level II: Nasdaq Level II subscription service is for broker dealers that are order-entry firms. Level II allows the broker dealer to see the inside market, as well as the quotes of all market makers and to execute orders over the Nasdaq workstation.

Level III: Nasdaq Level III is the highest level of service offered over the Nasdaq workstation. Level III contains all of the features of Level II and allows the firms to enter and update their own markets. Level III is only for approved market makers.

Nasdaq TotalView: Nasdaq TotalView quotation service allows professionals and nonprofessionals to view the entire Nasdaq book for securities traded over Nasdaq. TotalView displays the price and size quoted by all market makers, exchanges, and ECNs. TotalView also displays the total size of the market for the five best-priced quotes as well as order imbalance information for all Nasdaq crossing sessions.

NASDAQ QUOTES

Most actively traded Nasdaq stocks are quoted by a large number of market makers. As market makers enter their quotes, some will be above or below the inside market. A market maker whose quote is above or below the inside market is said to be away from the market. As the market makers adjust their quotes, the market maker who is publishing the highest bid for the security has its bid displayed at the top of the list and its bid is published as the best bid to anyone with a Nasdaq Level I subscription. The market maker publishing the lowest offer will have its offer listed at the top of the list and published as the lowest offer to anyone with a Nasdaq Level I subscription. As a result, the best bid and offer from any two market makers will make up the inside market.

EXAMPLE

XYAD

	Bid	Ask
	15.00	**15.05**
MM 1	14.90	15.10
MM 2	15.00	15.20
MM 3	14.85	15.05
MM 4	14.95	15.15
MM 5	14.98	15.18

Note: Notice how the inside market for XYAD consists of the bid from market maker 2 and the offer from market maker 3. All of the other market makers are away from the market.

NOMINAL NASDAQ QUOTES

All quotes published over the Nasdaq workstation are firm quotes. Dealers who fail to honor their quotes have committed a violation known as backing away. Dealers who provide quotes over the phone that are clearly indicated as being subject or nominal cannot be held to trade at those prices. Nasdaq qualifiers are:

- "It looks like"
- "It's around"
- "Subject"
- "Nominal"
- "Work it out"
- "Last I saw"

A response of "it is" would indicate a firm quote. A firm quote is always good for at least one round lot or 100 shares.

AUTOMATED CONFIRMATION SYSTEM (ACT)/
TRADE REPORTING FACILITY (TRF)

The ACT/TRF systems facilitate the reporting and clearing of trades executed through Nasdaq and other OTC environments. ACT/TRF transactions include:

- Nasdaq Global and Capital market securities
- Non-Nasdaq OTC securities
- Third-market trades
- Nasdaq Convertible bonds

All ACT/TRF eligible transactions must be reported to ACT/TRF within 10 seconds of the transaction.

NASDAQ EXECUTION SYSTEMS

Most Nasdaq trades are executed over the Nasdaq workstation using one of its automated execution systems. These systems allow dealers to execute orders without having to speak with one another on the phone.

THE NASDAQ MARKET CENTER
EXECUTION SYSTEM (NMCES)

The Nasdaq Market Center Execution System, also known as NMCES, accepts market orders and immediately executable limit orders for both customer and firm accounts. Orders may be entered for up to 999,999 shares per order. The orders will immediately be routed to dealers on the inside market for automatic execution. Larger orders may be split up to meet the maximum order volume. However, a broker dealer may not split orders that would otherwise be able to be entered into the Nasdaq system in an effort to increase fees or rebates. This would be considered order shredding, which is a violation. Orders executed through the Nasdaq execution system are automatically reported to ACT.

THE NASDAQ OPENING CROSS

The Nasdaq opening cross begins at 9:28 a.m. At this time, the Nasdaq execution system automatically executes orders. Orders placed after 9:28 a.m. may not be canceled. Orders placed after 9:28 a.m. may only be changed if the change to the order makes the order more aggressive. A change that increases the size of the order or improves the price would make the order more aggressive. For a buy order an improved price would be a higher limit price, for a sell order an improved price would be a lower limit price. All orders that are executed during the opening cross will be reported to ACT with a modifier. The opening cross creates the Nasdaq official opening price (NOOP). Like the opening cross, Nasdaq has developed the closing cross to determine the Nasdaq official closing price.

NON-NASDAQ OTCBB

The OTC Bulletin Board (OTCBB) provides two-sided electronic quotes for OTC securities that cannot meet the listing standard of an exchange or Nasdaq. Direct participation programs (DPPs) and American depositary receipts (ADRs) will often be quoted on the OTCBB. The OTCBB is operational from 7:30 a.m. to 6:30 p.m. The OTCBB displays:

- Real-time quotes
- Volume
- Last sale price

  Quotes that may be entered over the OTCBB by a market maker include:

- Bid wanted
- Offer wanted
- Bid only
- Offer only
- Two-sided quotes
- Quote modifications

Quotes displayed over the OTCBB are firm quotes unless they are quoting DPP programs. Quotes entered on the OTCBB must be for the minimum size for that security. The minimum quote size for the security depends on the price of the security being quoted. Quotes for DPP are subject quotes and may only be updated twice per day, once between 8:30 and 9:30 a.m. and at 12:30 p.m.

PINK OTC MARKET

Securities that do not qualify for listing on the Nasdaq or that have been delisted from Nasdaq or one of the exchanges may be quoted on the pink OTC market. The Pink OTC market is an electronic marketplace. Pink OTC Market facilitate trading for securities that are quoted on the pink sheets that do not meet the listing standards of any exchange or marketplace. All two-sided quotes displayed in the Pink OTC Market are firm quotes. The pink OTC Market also provides a list of phone numbers for market makers who display subject quotes. Stocks quoted on the pink OTC Market trading at under $5 per share are known as penny stocks. A firm that executes a customer's order for a pink OTC Market security is required to make a reasonable effort to obtain the best price for the customer. The firm is required to obtain quotes from at least three market makers for the security prior to executing the customer's order. If the security has less than three market makers, the firm is required to obtain a quote from all market makers.

THIRD MARKET

The third market consists of transactions in exchange-listed securities executed over the counter through the Nasdaq workstation. A broker dealer may wish to simply purchase or sell an exchange-listed security directly with another brokerage firm instead of executing the order on the floor of the exchange. These transactions are known as third-market transactions. All third-market transactions are reported through TRF to the consolidated tape for display.

FOURTH MARKET

A fourth-market transaction is a transaction between two large institutions without the use of a broker dealer. The computer network that facilitates these transactions is known as INSTINET. Large blocks of stock, both listed and unlisted, trade between large institutional investors in the fourth market.

Although many trades in the fourth market are executed through the INSTINET system, many large portfolio managers execute internal crosses, which go unreported. Proprietary trading systems are not considered part of the fourth market, because these systems are either registered as broker dealers or are operated by broker dealers. Trades executed by large institutions via proprietary networks are sometimes referred to as dark pools, because the supply or demand for a security is unseen by market participants.

READING THE CONSOLIDATED TAPE

The consolidated tape system reports trades as they occur in the various markets. Securities that are primarily listed on the NYSE will be reported to consolidated tape A regardless of the market where the trade was executed. Securities primarily listed on the NYSE may trade on regional exchanges such as the Pacific Stock Exchange or over Nasdaq in the third market. Consolidated tape B reports trade for securities primarily listed on the AMEX and regional exchanges. All transactions must be reported to the consolidated tape within 30 seconds of execution.

The consolidated tape reports trades for round lots as they occur. Remember that one round lot is always 100 shares unless otherwise indicated.

EXAMPLE   Let's look at the tape as it displays trades for various securities just after the market opens:

Open......KO44.05...10s.T24.02....99s.C.46.04...12,000s ABC.34.20...

The above tape has reported the following:

- 100 shares of Coca Cola traded at 44.05.
- 1,000 shares of AT&T traded at 24.02.
- 9,900 shares of Citi Group traded at 46.04.
- 12,000 shares of ABC traded at 34.20.

Note: For trades in excess of 10,000 shares, the entire volume will be reported on the tape.

Let's look at another tape:

X 15s24 .24...MCD27 .05....XYZ prC 5s/s.24.04...

The above trade has reported the following:

- 1,500 shares of USX traded at 24 followed by 100 shares of USX at 24.
- 100 shares of McDonalds traded at 27 followed by 100 shares at 27.05.
- 50 shares of XYZ preferred C traded at 24.04.

Note: The s/s indicates that a round lot for XYZ prC is 10 shares.

The tape can display other information and qualifiers relating to the trades reported, such as:

- SLD: A trade reported late or out of sequence.
- Halt: A security that has been halted from trading.
- OPD: The print is the opening print for the security after a delayed opening or after a halt.
- Pr: Preferred stock.
- R/T: Rights.
- W/S: Warrants.

During active or fast market conditions the tape may enact one or more of the following conditions:

- Digits and volume deleted
- Repeat prices omitted
- Minimum prices omitted

During fast market conditions when digits and volume have been deleted, a trade for 500 shares of XYZ at 46.50 would appear as: XYZ6.50. When repeat prices have been omitted, only trades that differ in price from the last transaction will be displayed. When minimum price variations have been omitted, only trades that differ by the minimum increment will be displayed.

EXCHANGE QUALIFIERS

The following table will help identify the exchange symbols for trades and quotes:

NYSE N	Boston B	OTCBB U
Nasdaq Q	Pacific P	Philadelphia X
ADF D	Chicago M	Cincinnati C

BROKER VS. DEALER

The term *broker dealer* actually refers to the two capacities in which a firm may act when executing a transaction. When a firm is acting as a broker, it is acting as the customer's agent and is merely executing the customer's order for a fee known as a commission. The role of the broker is simply to find someone willing to buy the investor's securities if the customer is selling or to find someone willing to sell the securities if the customer is seeking to buy. The firm acts as a dealer when it participates in the transaction by taking the opposite side of the trade. For example, the firm may fill a customer's buy order by selling the securities to the customer from the firm's own account or the dealer may fill the customer's sell order by buying the securities for its own account. A brokerage firm is always acting as a dealer or in a principal capacity when it is making markets over the counter.

Broker	Dealer
Executes customer's orders	Participates in the trade as a principal
Charges a commission	Charges a markup or markdown
Must disclose the amount of the commission	Makes a market in the security
	Must disclose the fact that it is a market maker, but not the amount of the markup of markdown

FINRA 5% MARKUP POLICY

FINRA has set a guideline to ensure that the prices investors pay and receive for securities are reasonably related to the market for the securities. As a general rule, FINRA considers a charge of 5% to be reasonable. The 5% policy is a guideline, not a rule. Factors that go towards what is considered reasonable are:

- The price of the security.
- The value of the transaction.
- The type of security.
- The value of the member's services.
- Execution expenses.

When a customer is executing an order for a low priced or low total dollar amount, a firm's minimum commission may be greater than 5% of the transaction.

EXAMPLE   A customer wants to purchase 1,000 shares of XYZ at $1. If the firm's minimum commission is $100, that would be 10% of the trade. But in this case it would be okay.

Stocks generally carry a higher degree of risk than bonds and, as a result, stocks justify a higher commission or profit to the dealer. Full-service firms may be able to justify a larger commission simply based on the value of the services they provide.

MARKUPS/MARKDOWNS WHEN ACTING AS A PRINCIPAL

A firm that executes customer orders on a principal basis is entitled to a profit on those transactions. If the firm is selling the security to the customer, it will charge the customer a markup. In the case of the firm buying the securities from the customer, it will charge the customer a markdown. The amount of the markup or markdown that a firm charges the customer is based on the inside market for the security.

EXAMPLE

Let's assume that the brokerage firm is a market maker in ABCD. In the morning, the firm purchased shares of ABCD for its own account at 9.50. The stock has been trading higher all day and is now quoted as follows:

Bid	Ask
10.00	10.05

If a customer wants to purchase 100 shares ABCD from the dealer in the above example, the customer's markup would be based on the current offering price of 10.05. As a result, the maximum amount the firm could charge the customer for the stock would be 10.552 per share, or $1,055.20 for the entire order, which would include a 5% markup. Notice that the markup to the customer did not take into consideration the firm's actual cost.

If a customer wanted to sell 100 shares of ABCD using the above quote, the minimum proceeds to the customer would be 9.50 per share, or $950 for entire order, which would include a 5% markdown.

To determine the maximum or minimum prices for a customer, use the following:

- 105% of the offer price for customers who are purchasing the security.
- 95% of the bid price for customers who are selling the security.

When determining the amount of the markup or markdown, the following are excluded:

- The firm's actual cost.
- The firm's quote if it is a market maker in the security.

RISKLESS PRINCIPAL TRANSACTIONS

If a brokerage firm receives a customer order to buy or sell a security and the firm does not have an inventory position in the security, the firm may still elect to execute the order on a principal basis. If the firm elects to execute the order on a principal basis, this is known as a riskless principal transaction. Because the dealer is only taking a position in the security to fill the customer's order, the dealer is not taking on any risk. As a result, the markup or markdown on riskless transactions will be based on the dealer's actual cost, not on the inside market. Let's look at an example:

EXAMPLE	**Bid**	**Ask**
	10.00	**10.05**

A customer wants to purchase 100 shares of ABCD from the dealer, and the dealer executes the order on a principal basis by purchasing the shares for its own account at 10.02 only to immediately resell the stock to the customer. The markup in this case must be based on the dealer's actual cost of 10.02, and the maximum the dealer could charge the customer would be 10.521 per share, or $1,052.10 for the entire order.

PROCEEDS TRANSACTIONS

In a proceeds transaction, the customer sells a security and uses the proceeds from that sale to purchase another security on the same day. FINRA's 5% policy states that a firm may only charge the customer a combined commission or markup and markdown of 5% for both transactions, not 5% on each.

THE ORDER AUDIT TRAIL SYSTEM (OATS)

In order to ensure that customer orders are transmitted to the marketplace in a timely manner, FINRA developed the Order Audit Trail System (OATS). OATS tracks an order through each stage of its life, from receipt to execution or cancellation. Each firm is required to synchronize clocks used for reporting to within one second of the National Institute of Standardized Time's atomic clock and must display time in hours, minutes, and seconds. Firms are only requested to collect and submit data in milliseconds if the firm collects the data. Firms are required to submit daily electronic OATS reports to FINRA. OATS reports must be made by 8 a.m. on the day after the trade date. For trades executed on Friday, OATS reports are due by 8 a.m. Saturday morning. Daily OATS reports must be made for each order, and each order must have a unique identifier.

TRADE REPORTING AND COMPLIANCE ENGINE (TRACE)

Most transactions in fixed-income securities take place in the OTC market. FINRA members must use the TRACE system to report transactions in eligible fixed-income securities within 15 minutes of execution. Eligible fixed-income securities include:

- Domestic and foreign corporate debt registered with the SEC.
- Dollar-denominated debt that is depository eligible.
- Investment grade and noninvestment grade issues.
- Securities issued under the Securities Act of 1933 that are part of a 144A transaction.

Securities that are exempt from the TRACE reporting requirements include:

- Government (sovereign) debt
- Municipal debt
- Convertible corporate debt
- CMOs
- Repurchase agreements
- Money market instruments
- Mortgage-backed securities
- Asset-backed securities
- Development bank debt

CIRCUIT BREAKERS

The NYSE, Nasdaq, and SEC continue to develop and test circuit breakers that will act as a safety net during times of exorbitant price changes in the market as a whole or in the price of individual securities. The NYSE has enacted rules to help restore orderly market conditions during periods of heightened volatility. Rule 80B halts all trading if the S&P 500 falls by 7%, 13%, or 20% in any given day. A level 1 (7%) or level 2 (13%) decline occurring between 9:30 p.m. and 3:25 p.m. EST will result in a trading halt in all stocks for 15 minutes. In the case of a level 1 or level 2 decline on a day when the market closes early, trading will be halted for 15 minutes if the decline occurs between 9:30 a.m. and 12:25 p.m. EST. Once trading resumes after a level 1 halt, trading will not be halted again unless the S&P 500 decline reaches a level 2, or 13% decline. Similarly in the case of a level 2 decline, trading would not be halted again once resumed until the S&P 500 reached a level 3, or 20% decline. A level 3 (20%) decline occurring at any time during the day will halt all trading for the rest of the day.

The base level that regulates Rule 80B is based on the daily closing value of the S&P 500. All orders that are in hand or on the DMMs book prior to a market halt will be treated as GTC orders except market on close and limit on close orders, which will be canceled.

LIMIT UP LIMIT DOWN (LULD)

The SEC approved the use of a Limit Up Limit Down (LULD) rule. This rule is designed to ensure that prices of individual securities reflect fundamental prices based on supply and demand and do not move outside of established parameters based on errors or manipulative actions. Upper and lower trading bands will be established based on the average reference price of the security over the preceding 5 minute period. The reference price is the algorithmic mean of all eligible transactions reported during the 5 minute period and does not include transactions reported at a volume weighted average price (VWAP). If the stock price moves outside of the established bands trading will be paused for 5 minutes if the stock cannot return to the limit price within 15 seconds. During this 15 second period the stock will be subject to a limit state of limit up or limit down. If no trades take place at or inside the limit price the 5 minute trading pause will occur. Once fully implemented the LULD is intended to replace the single stock circuit breaker rule. Tier 1 and tier 2 securities will have trading bands of 5 and 10% respectively from 9:45 a.m.–3:35 p.m. EST. To accommodate additional price discovery during the opening and closing of the market those bands will be expanded to 10 and 20% respectively from 9:30 a.m.–9:45 a.m. and from 3:35 p.m.–4:00 p.m. Any aggressive orders placed outside of the price band will be re priced by the Nasdaq system to the price band limit price.

ARBITRAGE

Arbitrage is an investment strategy used to take advantage of market inefficiencies and to profit from the price discrepancies that result from those inefficiencies. There are three types of arbitrage. They are:

1. Market arbitrage
2. Security arbitrage
3. Risk arbitrage

Market arbitrage: Securities that trade in more than one market will sometimes be quoted and traded at different prices. Market arbitrage consists of the simultaneous purchase and sale of the same security in two different markets to take advantage of the price discrepancy.

Security arbitrage: Securities that give the holder the right to convert or exercise the security into the underlying stock may be purchased or sold to take advantage of price discrepancies between that security and the underlying common stock. Securities arbitrage consists of the purchase or sale of one security and the simultaneous purchase or sale of the underlying security.

Risk arbitrage: Risk arbitrage tries to take advantage of the price discrepancies that come about as a result of a takeover. A risk arbitrageur will short the stock of the acquiring company and purchase the stock of the company being acquired.

Pretest

TRADING SECURITIES

1. When making markets over the counter, the firm is acting in what capacity?

   a. Dealer

   b. Both

   c. Neither

   d. Broker

2. A bearish investor would have the hardest time establishing a short position in a:

   a. preferred stock.

   b. listed put option.

   c. nonconvertible corporate bond.

   d. GO municipal bond.

3. Which of the following may NOT trade on the floor of the NYSE?

   a. Two-dollar broker

   b. Regular member

   c. Commission house broker

   d. Allied member

4. Your brokerage firm acts as a market maker for several high-volume stocks that are quoted on the Nasdaq. What is the firm's consideration for being a market maker?

   a. Commission

   b. Fees

   c. Spread

   d. 5%

5. Which of the following is NOT a type of order?

   I. All or none

   II. Fill or kill

   III. Mini/maxi

   IV. Best efforts

   a. I and II

   b. II and IV

   c. I and IV

   d. III and IV

6. INTC has been hitting a lot of resistance at $30. A technical analyst who wants to buy the stock would most likely place what type of order?

   a. Limit order to buy at $30

   b. Market order

   c. Buy stop at $31

   d. Buy limit at $29

7. Which of the following subjects the investor to unlimited risk?

   a. Selling stock short

   b. Converting a bond into the underlying common stock

   c. Purchasing a call

   d. Selling a naked put

8. The inside market is:

 I. Highest offer

 II. Lowest offer

 III. Highest bid

 IV. Lowest bid

 a. II and III

 b. I and II

 c. I and IV

 d. I and III

9. Which of the following is true of the DMMs on the NYSE?

 a. They work for themselves.

 b. They are appointed by a vote of the company's board.

 c. They work for the exchange.

 d. They work for the company whose stock they trade.

10. Which of the following is most likely to trade in a round lot of 10 shares?

 a. Municipal bonds

 b. Corporate bonds

 c. Listed equity

 d. Preferred stock

11. The consolidated tape reads 30s/s XYZ Pr C 84.15. What does this mean?

 a. 30,000 shares of XYZ Pr C sold at 84.15.

 b. 30 shares of XYZ Pr C sold at 84.15.

 c. 3,000 shares of XYZ Pr C sold at 84.15.

 d. 300 shares of XYZ Pr C sold at 84.15.

12. A bullish investor would enter which of the following orders?

 a. A sell limit thinking that the stock price will rise.

 b. A sell stop below the market.

 c. A buy stop above the market.

 d. DNR GTC.

13. ABC Technologies, a very volatile stock, closes at $180 per share. Your customer has placed an order to sell 500 ABC at 165 stop limit 160 GTC. After the close, the company announces bad earnings and the stock opens at 145. What happened to your customer's order?

   a. It has been canceled because the stock price is below the limit price.

   b. It has been elected and has become a limit order.

   c. It has been elected and executed.

   d. It has been canceled because the stock price is below the stop price.

Customer Accounts

INTRODUCTION

Prior to executing a customer's order, the firm must open an account for the customer. NYSE rules require that representatives obtain all vital information relating to the customer. Series 7 candidates will see many types of questions dealing with customer accounts on their exam.

Prior to opening an account for any new customer, a registered representative must complete and sign a new account form. Account ownership is divided into five main types:

1. Individual
2. Joint
3. Corporate
4. Trust
5. Partnership

The registered representative should try to obtain as much information about the customer as possible. The representative should obtain the following information about the customer:

- Full name and address
- Home and work phone numbers
- Social security or tax ID number
- Employer, occupation, and employer's address
- Net worth

- Investment objectives
- Estimated annual income
- Bank/brokerage firm reference
- Whether the client is employed by a bank or broker dealer
- Any third-party trading authority
- Citizenship
- Legal age
- How account was obtained
- Whether client is an officer, a director, or a 10% stockholder of a publicly traded company

All new accounts must be accepted and signed by a principal of the firm. The principal must accept the account in writing for the firm either before or promptly after the first trade is executed. The principal accepts the account by signing the new account card. The representative who introduced the account and the name of the representative who will manage the account should be noted on the new account card as evidence that he or she introduced the account to the firm. Once the account is opened, the firm must send the customer a copy of the new account form within 30 days of the opening of the account and within 30 days of any material change in the customer's information. Firms are also required to verify the account information at least once every 36 months. The customer never has to sign anything to open a new cash account. However, some firms have the customer sign a customer agreement upon opening a new account, but this is not required. The customer agreement will state the policies of the firm and will usually contain a predispute arbitration clause. The predispute clause requires that any potential dispute arising out of the relationship be settled in binding arbitration. The predispute arbitration clause must be presented in a certain format and include:

- A disclosure that arbitration is final and binding.
- A disclosure that the findings of the arbitrators are not based on legal reasoning.
- A statement that the discovery process is generally more limited than the discovery process in a legal proceeding.
- A statement that the parties are waiving their right to a jury trial.

- A statement that the customer must be provided with a copy of the pre-dispute clause and must verify its receipt with a signature.
- A disclosure that a minority of the arbitration panel will be affiliated with the securities industry.

If the predispute clause is contained in the customer agreement, there must be a highlighted disclosure just above the signature line.

If the customer requests a copy of the predispute arbitration agreement the firm must send it to the customer within 10 days. A firm may also have the customer sign a signature card. A signature card will allow the firm to verify the customer's written instructions that are sent in to the firm.

Customers who do not wish to disclose financial information may still open an account if there is reason to believe that the customer can afford to maintain the account. All registered representatives should update the customer's information regularly and note any changes in the following:

- Address
- Phone number
- Employer
- Investment objectives
- Marital status

Registered representatives are also required to maintain an accurate and up-to-date listing of all of their customers' transactions and investment holdings.

Customers are not required to provide their educational background when opening an account.

HOLDING SECURITIES

Upon opening an account, the investor must decide where the securities are to be held. The following methods are available:

- Transfer and ship
- Transfer and hold in safekeeping
- Hold in street name
- Receipt versus payment (RVP)/delivery versus payment (DVP)

TRANSFER AND SHIP

Securities that are to be transferred and shipped will be registered in the customer's name and will be sent to the customer's address of record.

TRANSFER AND HOLD IN SAFEKEEPING

Securities that are to be transferred and held in safekeeping will be registered in the customer's name and will be held by the brokerage firm. The broker dealer may charge a fee for the safekeeping of the securities. Customers may now elect to hold securities registered in their name electronically in the book entry form through the Direct Registration System (DRS). The DRS offered through the depository trust corporation will allow investors to hold their securities on the books of the issuer or the transfer agent. Investors who hold securities with the DRS will receive a statement from the issuer or transfer agent.

HOLD IN STREET NAME

Securities that are held in street name are registered in the name of the brokerage firm as the nominal owner of the securities, and the customer is the beneficial owner. Most securities are held in this manner to make transfer of ownership easier.

RECEIPT VS. PAYMENT (RVP)/ DELIVERY VS. PAYMENT (DVP)

These accounts are normally reserved for trusts and other institutional accounts that require that securities be delivered prior to releasing payment for the securities. These accounts are set up as cash-on-delivery (COD) accounts.

At the time the customer opens the account, the customer will also decide what to do with the distributions from the account. Investors may have the distributions sent directly to them or they may have them reinvested or swept into a money market account.

MAILING INSTRUCTIONS

All confirmations and statements will be sent to the customer's address of record. Statements and confirmations may be sent to an individual with power of attorney if the duplicates are requested in writing. A customer's mail may be held by a brokerage firm for up to two months if the customer is traveling within the United States and for up to three months if the customer is traveling outside the United States. Customers who are on active duty with the militarily and have no fixed address should be advised to open a military P.O. Box where statements may be sent.

TYPES OF ACCOUNTS

INDIVIDUAL ACCOUNT

An individual account is an account that is owned by one person. That person makes the determination as to what securities are purchased and sold. In addition, that person receives all of the distributions from the account.

JOINT ACCOUNT

A joint account is an account that is owned by two or more adults. Each party to the account may enter orders and request distributions. The registered representative does not need to confirm instructions with both parties. Joint accounts require the owners to sign a joint account agreement prior to the opening of the account. All parties must endorse all securities and all parties must be alive. Checks drawn from the account must be made out in the names of all of the parties.

JOINT TENANTS WITH RIGHTS OF SURVIVORSHIP (JTWROS)

In a joint account with rights of survivorship (JTWROS), all the assets are transferred into the name of the surviving party in the event of one tenant's death. The surviving party becomes the sole owner of all of the assets in the account. Both parties on the account have an equal and undivided interest in the assets in the account.

JOINT TENANTS IN COMMON (JTIC)

In a joint account that is established as tenants in common, if one party dies all the assets of the tenant who has died become the property of the decedent's estate. They do not become the property of the surviving tenant. An account registered as JTIC allows the assets in the account to be divided unequally. One party on the account could own 60% of the account's assets.

> ▶ **TAKENOTE!**
>
> Any securities registered in the names of two or more parties must be signed by all parties and all parties must be alive to be considered good delivery.

TRANSFER ON DEATH (TOD)

An account that has been registered as a transfer-on-death (TOD) account allows the account owner to stipulate to whom the account is to go to in the event of his or her death. Transfer on death accounts are sometimes referred to as pay on death or POD accounts. The party who will become the owner of the account in the event of the account holder's death is known as the beneficiary. The beneficiary may only enter orders for the account if he or she has power of attorney for the account. Unlike an account that is registered as JTWROS, the assets in the account will not be at risk should the beneficiary be the subject of a lawsuit, such as in a divorce proceeding.

DEATH OF A CUSTOMER

If an agent is notified of the death of a customer the agent must immediately cancel all open orders and mark the account deceased. The representative must await instructions from the executor or administrator of the estate. In order to sell or transfer the assets, the agent must receive:

- Letters testamentary
- Inheritance tax waivers
- Certified copy of the death certificate

The death of a customer with a discretionary account automatically terminates the discretionary authority.

CORPORATE ACCOUNTS

Corporations, like individuals, will purchase and sell securities. In order to open a corporate account, the registered representative must obtain a corporate resolution that states which individuals have the power to enter orders for the corporation. If a corporation wants to purchase securities on margin, then the registered representative must obtain a corporate charter and the bylaws that state that the corporation may purchase securities on margin. Finally, a certificate of incumbency must be obtained for the officers who are authorized to transact business for the corporation, within 60 days of the account opening.

TRUST ACCOUNTS

Trusts may be revocable or irrevocable. With a revocable trust, the individual who established the trust and contributes assets to the trust, known as the grantor or settlor, may, as the name suggests, revoke the trust and take the assets back. The income generated by a revocable trust is generally taxed as income to the grantor. If the trust is irrevocable, the grantor may not revoke the trust and take the assets back. With an irrevocable trust, the trust usually pays the taxes as its own entity or the beneficiaries of the trust are taxed on the income they receive. If the trust is established as a simple trust all income generated by the trust must be distributed to the beneficiaries in the year the income is earned. If the trust is established as a complex trust, the trust may retain some or all of the income earned and the trust will pay taxes on the income that is not distributed to the beneficiaries. The grantor of an irrevocable trust is generally not taxed on the income generated by the trust unless the assets in the trust are held for the benefit of the grantor, the grantor's spouse, or if the grantor has an interest in the income of the trust greater than 5 percent. A trust may also be established to hold or to distribute assets after a person's death under the terms of their Will. Trusts that are established under the terms of a Will are known as Testamentary trusts. All assets placed into a Testamentary trust are subject to both estate taxes and probate. A representative who opens a trust account must obtain documentation of the trustees investment powers over the trust's assets.

PARTNERSHIP ACCOUNTS

When a professional organization, such as a law partnership, opens an account, the registered representative must obtain a copy of the partnership agreement. The partnership agreement will state who may enter orders for the account of the partnership. If the partnership wishes to purchase securities on margin, it must not be prohibited by the partnership agreement. A family limited partnership is often used for estate planning. Parents may place significant assets into a family limited partnership as a way to transfer their ownership. Usually, the parents will act as the general partners and will transfer limited partnership interests to their children. As the interests are transferred to the children, the parents may become subject to gift taxes. However, the gift taxes usually will be lower than they would have suffered without the partnership.

TRADING AUTHORIZATION

From time to time, people other than the beneficial owner of the account may be authorized to enter orders for the account. All discretionary authority must be evidenced in writing for the following accounts:

- Discretionary account
- Custodial account
- Fiduciary account

OPERATING A DISCRETIONARY ACCOUNT

A discretionary account allows the registered representative to determine the following, without consulting the client first:

- The asset to be purchased or sold.
- The amount of the securities to be purchased or sold.
- The action to be taken in the account, whether to buy or sell.

The principal of the firm must accept the account and review it more frequently to ensure against abuses. The customer is required to sign a limited power of attorney that awards discretion to the registered representative. The limited power of attorney is good for up to three years; the customer is bound by the decisions of the representative, but may still enter orders. Once discretion is given to the representative, the representative may not, in turn, give discretion to another party. If the representative leaves the firm or stops managing the customer's account, the discretionary authority is automatically terminated. A standard power of attorney will also terminate upon the death or incapacitation of the account owner. A durable power of attorney will continue in full effect in the case of incapacitation and will only terminate upon the account owner's death. A full power of attorney allows an individual to deposit and withdraw cash and securities from the account. A full power of attorney is usually not given to a registered representative. A full power of attorney is more appropriate for fiduciaries such as a trustee, custodian, or a guardian. If a FINRA or MSRB broker dealer has a control relationship with an issuer of securities, the customer must be informed of the relationship and must give specific authorization for the purchase of the securities.

MANAGING DISCRETIONARY ACCOUNTS

All discretionary accounts must have the proper paperwork kept in the account file and must have:

- Every order entered marked discretionary, if discretion was exercised by the representative.
- Every order approved promptly by a principal.
- A designated principal to review the account.
- A record of all transactions.

Discretion may not be exercised by a representative until the discretionary papers have been received by the firm and approved by the principal.

THIRD-PARTY AND FIDUCIARY ACCOUNTS

A fiduciary account is one that is managed by a third party for the benefit of the account holder. The party managing the account has responsibility for making all of the investments and other decisions relating to the account. The individual with this responsibility must do as a prudent person would do for his or her self and may not speculate. This is known as the prudent man rule. Many states have an approved list of securities, known as the legal list, that may be purchased by fiduciaries. The authority to transact business for the account must be evidenced in writing by a power of attorney. The fiduciary may have full power of attorney, also known as full discretion, under which the fiduciary may purchase and sell securities, as well as withdraw cash and securities from the account. Under a limited power of attorney or limited discretion, the fiduciary may only buy and sell securities; assets may not be withdrawn. The fiduciary has been legally appointed to represent the account holder and may not use the assets in the account for his or her own benefit. The fiduciary may, however, be reimbursed for expenses incurred in connection with the management of the account. Examples of fiduciaries include:

- Administrators
- Custodians
- Receivers
- Trustees
- Conservators

- Executors
- Guardians
- Sheriffs/marshals

When opening a third party or fiduciary account, the registered representative is required to obtain documentation of the individual's appointment and authority to act on behalf of the account holder. Trust accounts require that the representative obtain a copy of the trust agreement. The trust agreement will state who has been appointed as the trustee and any limitations on the trust's operation. Most trusts may only open cash accounts and may not purchase securities on margin, unless specifically authorized to do so in the agreement. When opening an account for a guardian, the representative must obtain a copy of the court order appointing the guardian. The court order must be dated within 60 days of the opening of the account. If the court order is more than 60 days old, the representative may not open the account until a new court order is obtained. Guardians are usually appointed in cases of mentally incompetent adults and orphaned children.

UNIFORM GIFT TO MINORS ACCOUNT (UGMA)

Minors are not allowed to own securities in their own name because they are not old enough to enter into legally binding contracts. The decision to purchase or sell a security creates a legally binding contract between two parties. The Uniform Gift to Minors Act (UGMA) regulates how accounts are operated for the benefit of minors. All UMGA accounts must have:

- One custodian
- One minor
- UGMA and the state in the account title
- Assets registered to the child's name after he or she reaches the age of majority

All securities in a UGMA account will be registered in the custodian's name as the nominal owner for the benefit of the minor who is the beneficial owner of the account. For example, the account should be titled: Mr. Jones as custodian for Billy Jones under New Jersey Uniform Gift to Minors Act.

Only one custodian and one minor are allowed on each account. A husband and wife could not be joint custodians for their minor child. If there is more than one child, a separate account must be opened for each one. The same person may serve as custodian on several accounts for several minors, and the minor may have more than one account established by different custodians. The donor of the security does not have to be the custodian for the account. If the parents are not the custodians of the accounts, they have no authority over the accounts.

RESPONSIBILITIES OF THE CUSTODIAN

The custodian has a fiduciary duty to manage the account prudently for the benefit of the minor child within certain guidelines, such as:

- No margin accounts.
- No high-risk securities (i.e., penny stocks).
- The custodian may not borrow from the account.
- No commodities.
- No speculative option strategies.
- The custodian may not give discretion to a third party.
- All distributions must be reinvested within a reasonable time.
- The custodian may not let rights or warrants expire; they must be exercised or sold.
- The custodian must provide support for all withdrawals from the account.
- Withdrawals may only be made to reimburse the custodian for expenses incurred in connection with the operation of the account or for the benefit of the minor.

CONTRIBUTIONS OF A UGMA ACCOUNT

Gifts of cash and securities or other property may be given to the minor. There is no dollar limit as to the size of the gift that may be given. The limit on the size of the tax-free gift is $14,000 per year. An individual may give gifts valued at up to $14,000 to any number of people each year without incurring a tax liability. Once a gift has been given, it is irrevocable. Gifts to a UGMA account carry an indefeasible title and may not be taken back for any reason whatsoever. The custodian may, however, use the assets for the minor's welfare and educational needs.

 TAKENOTE!

A husband and wife may give up to $28,000 per year per person. The IRS considers half of the gift to be coming from each spouse. The annual gift limit is indexed for inflation since 1999.

UGMA TAXATION

The minor is responsible for the taxes on the account. However, any unearned income that exceeds $1,500 per year will be taxed at the parent's marginal tax rate if the child is younger than 14 years old. For gifts that exceed $14,000 per year, the tax liability is on the donor of the gift, not on the minor.

DEATH OF A MINOR OR CUSTODIAN

If the minor dies, the account becomes part of the child's estate. It does not automatically go to the parents. If the custodian dies, a court or the donor may appoint a new custodian.

UNIFORM TRANSFER TO MINORS ACT

Some states have adopted the Uniform Transfer to Minors Act rather than the Uniform Gifts to Minors Act. The main difference is that with a UTMA account the custodian may determine when the assets become the property of the child. The maximum age is 25 years old.

 **TAKENOTE!**

No evidence of custodial rights is required to open a UGMA or UTMA account.

ACCOUNTS FOR EMPLOYEES OF OTHER BROKER DEALERS

FINRA Rule 3210 regarding outside accounts will become effective on April 3, 2017. This rule requires that an employee of a broker dealer who wishes to open an account at another broker dealer to obtain the employer's written permission prior to opening the account. The employee must present written notification to the broker dealer opening the account that he/she is employed by a FINRA member firm at the time the account is opened. This rule is in effect for the employee or any of the employee's immediate family members. This rule will also require the employee to obtain the employer's written permission for accounts that were opened within 30 days of the start of employment. Excluded from this rule are accounts opened by the employee where no transactions may take place in individual securities such as accounts opened to purchase open end mutual funds, variable annuities and UITs. (Prior to the effective date of this rule only employer notification is required)

NUMBERED ACCOUNTS

A broker dealer, at the request of the customer, may open an account that is simply identified by a number or a symbol, so long as there is a statement signed by the customer attesting to the ownership of the account.

ACCOUNT TRANSFER

Clients from time to time will wish to have their accounts transferred from one brokerage firm to another. This is usually accomplished through an Automated Client Account Transfer (ACAT). The ACAT provides transfer and delivery instructions to the firm, which will be required to deliver the account to the client's new firm. The firm that receives the transfer instructions is required to validate the instructions and freeze the account or take exception to them within one business day. No new orders may be accepted and all open orders will be canceled. However, orders may be taken for options positions that expire in 7 days or less. Once the account and positions have been validated, the firm has three additional business days to complete the transfer. A firm may only take exception to the instructions for the following reasons:

- The customer's signature is missing or invalid.
- The account title does not match the carrying firm's account number.
- The social security number does not match.
- The account number is wrong.

From time to time certain investment positions will not be able to be transferred from the old firm to the new firm. A customer is required to give specific instructions as to what should be done with that investment. The customer may elect to:

- Leave the investment at the old firm.
- Have it liquidated.
- Have it shipped.

Any disputes between the two firms must be resolved within 5 business days. A registered rep who changes firms may utilize a bulk account transfer process for his clients' account so long as the clients have provided affirmative consent. FINRA does not allow customer accounts to be transferred or the broker of record to be changed through a negative consent letter.

OPTION ACCOUNTS

A customer wishing to trade options must be given a copy of the OCC's risk disclosure document and sign the firm's option agreement. The customer's account may be initially approved by a branch manager who is not a registered option and security futures principal (ROSFP), so long as the account is approved by a ROSFP within a reasonable amount of time. A branch manager with more than three representatives conducting options business is required to qualify as a registered option and security futures principal.

MARGIN ACCOUNTS

A margin account allows the investor to purchase securities without paying for the securities in full. The investor is required to deposit a portion of the securities' purchase price and may borrow the rest from the broker dealer. The portion of the securities' purchase price that an investor must deposit is called margin. The amount of the required deposit or margin is controlled by the Federal Reserve Board under Regulation T of the Securities Exchange Act of 1934. Regulation T gave the Federal Reserve Board the authority to regulate the extension of credit for securities purchases. The Federal Reserve Board controls:

- Which securities may be purchased on margin.
- The amount of the initial required deposit.
- Payment dates.

Unlike when opening a cash account, when a customer opens a margin account he or she will be required to sign certain account documents. The customer will be asked to sign the following:

- Credit agreement
- Hypothecation agreement
- Loan consent

THE CREDIT AGREEMENT

The credit agreement states the terms and conditions under which credit will be extended to the customer. It will include information about how interest is charged as well as information about the rates that will be charged. A margin loan does not amortize, meaning that the principal is not paid down on a regular schedule. The brokerage firm simply charges interest to the account.

THE HYPOTHECATION AGREEMENT

The hypothecation agreement pledges the customer's securities that were purchased on margin as collateral for the loan. It also allows the brokerage firm to take the same securities and repledge or rehypothecate them as collateral for a loan at a bank to obtain a loan for the customer.

LOAN CONSENT

By signing a loan consent agreement, the customer allows the brokerage firm to lend out the securities to customers who wish to sell the securities short. This is the only part of the margin agreement that the customer is not required to sign. The credit and hypothecation agreement must be signed prior to the account being approved to purchase securities on margin.

All securities purchased in a margin account will be held in street name, the name of the brokerage firm, so that the broker dealer may sell the securities to protect itself if the value of the securities falls significantly. Day trading is an investment strategy defined by the entering of round-trip orders, consisting of both a buy and sell order, on the same day for the same security. Firms that promote the use of day trading strategies to individual investors must adhere to special account opening requirements. A broker dealer will be considered to be promoting day trading strategies if it holds seminars, advertises, or uses another company to promote its services. If the firm promotes day trading, it must provide the customer with a risk disclosure document and approve the account for day trading. If the customer is not approved for day trading, the customer may still open an account so long as the firm obtains a written statement from the customer stating that he or she will not be engaging in day trading strategies. A firm will be considered to be promoting day trading if the registered representatives promote day trading strategies with the knowledge of the firm's principal.

COMMINGLING CUSTOMER'S PLEDGED SECURITIES

A broker dealer may not commingle a customer's pledged securities with another customer's pledged securities as joint collateral to obtain a loan from a bank without both customers' written authorization. This authorization is required by SEC Rule 15c2-1 and is part of most margin agreements. A customer's securities may never be commingled with the firm's securities.

WRAP ACCOUNTS

A wrap account is an account that charges the customer a set annual fee for both advice and execution costs. The fee is based on the assets in the account. Wrap account holders must be given Schedule H, which details how fees are to be charged, prior to opening the account. A firm that offers wrap accounts to its clients must be registered as investment advisers. Agents who service wrap accounts must have passed the Series 65 or Series 66 exams. Wrap accounts and other asset based fee accounts are usually not appropriate for clients who trade infrequently and use a buy and hold strategy. The practice of placing these types of accounts into fee based programs constitutes a violation known as reverse churning

REGULATION S-P

Regulation S-P requires that the firm maintain adequate procedures to protect the financial information of its customers. Firms must guard against unauthorized access to customer financial information and must employ policies to ensure its safety. Special concerns arise over the ability for a person to "hack" into a firm's customer data based by gaining unauthorized access. Firms must develop and maintain specific safeguards for its computer systems and WiFi access. Regulation S-P was derived from the privacy rules of the Gramm-Leach-Bliley Act. A firm must deliver:

- An initial privacy notice to customers, no later than when the account was opened.
- An annual privacy notice to all customers.

The annual privacy notice may be delivered electronically via the firm's website, so long as the customer has agreed to receive it in writing and it is clearly displayed. Regulation S-P also states that a firm may not disclose nonpublic personal information to nonaffiliated companies for clients who have opted out of the list.

The method by which a client may opt out may not be unreasonable. It is considered unreasonable to require a customer to write a letter to opt out. Reasonable methods are emails or a toll-free number. The rule also differentiates between who is a customer and who is a consumer. A customer is anyone who has an ongoing relationship with the firm (i.e., has an account). A consumer is someone who is providing information to the firm and is considering becoming a customer or who has purchased a product from the firms and has no other contact with the firm. The firm must give the privacy notice to consumers prior to sharing any nonpublic information with a non-affiliated company.

 TAKENOTE!

A client of a brokerage firm may not opt out of the sharing of information with an affiliated company.

Regulation S-AM prohibits broker dealers from soliciting business based on information received from affiliated third parties unless the potential marketing had been clearly disclosed to the potential customer, the potential customer was provided an opportunity to opt out, but did not opt out.

IDENTITY THEFT

The fraudulent practice of identity theft may be used by criminals in an attempt to obtain access to the assets or credit of another person. The Federal Trade Commission (FTC) requires banks and broker dealers to establish and maintain written identity theft prevention programs. A broker dealer's written supervisory procedures manual must reference its identity theft program. The program must be designed to detect red flags relating to the known suspicious activity employed during an attempt at identity theft. The identity theft prevention program should be designed to allow the firm to respond quickly to any attempted identity theft to mitigate any potential damage.

DAY TRADING ACCOUNTS

Day trading is an investment strategy defined by the entering of round-trip orders, consisting of both a buy and sell order, on the same day for the same security.

Firms that promote the use of day trading strategies to individual investors must adhere to special account opening requirements. A broker dealer will be considered to be promoting day trading strategies if it holds seminars, advertises, or uses another company to promote its services. If the firm promotes day trading, it must provide the customer with a risk disclosure document and approve the account for day trading. If the customer is not approved for day trading, the customer may still open an account so long as the firm obtains a written statement from the customer stating that he or she will not be engaging in day trading strategies. A firm will be considered to be promoting day trading if the registered representatives promote day trading strategies with the knowledge of the firm's principal. A pattern day trader is defined as anyone who enters 4 or more round trip orders in a 5 day period. The minimum equity for a day trading account is $25,000.

Pretest

CUSTOMER ACCOUNTS

1. A registered representative may accept orders for a client's account from which of the following?

    I. Client

    II. Client's spouse

    III. Client's attorney

    IV. Client's investment adviser

    a. I and II

    b. I, II, and III

    c. I only

    d. I, II, III, and IV

2. In which type of account does the nominal owner of the account enter all orders for the beneficial owner of the account?

    a. Custodial account

    b. Fiduciary account

    c. Authorized account

    d. Discretionary account

3. Which of the following is NOT allowed as a joint account?

    a. A registered representative and a customer

    b. A registered representative and a spouse

    c. A registered representative and a friend

    d. A registered representative and his 16-year-old child

4. A customer and his spouse have an account registered as joint tenants in common. If the customer dies, what would happen to the account?

   a. The decedent's assets will be distributed according to his will.

   b. The executor of the estate will determine how all of the assets are to be distributed.

   c. All of the assets in the account will be distributed according to the trustee.

   d. The spouse would get the assets in the account.

5. To open a guardian account, the firm must obtain:

   a. trust papers.

   b. power of attorney.

   c. declaration papers.

   d. affidavit of domicile.

6. In which type of account does a trustee enter all orders for the owners of the account?

   a. Custodial account

   b. Fiduciary account

   c. Authorized account

   d. Discretionary account

7. The maximum allowable gift to a minor under UGMA is:

   a. $14,000.

   b. $1,400.

   c. $30,000.

   d. There is no limit.

8. The nominal owner of a UGMA account is the:

   a. custodian.

   b. minor.

   c. trustee.

   d. parent.

9. A representative may borrow money from a client:

   a. if the client is the issuer of securities.

   b. if the client is a credit union.

   c. if the client is a wealthy individual who regularly makes private loans.

   d. under no circumstances.

10. Which of the following may be able to purchase shares of a hot issue?

    a. Registered representative

    b. Minor child of a firm employee

    c. Registered representative's spouse

    d. Registered representative's father-in-law

11. Which of the following is NOT required in the account title for a custodial account?

    a. The state

    b. The minor's social security number

    c. The name of the custodian

    d. UGMA

12. You have just opened up a new account for a customer. You are required to have all of the following, EXCEPT the:

    a. agent's signature.

    b. principal's signature.

    c. customer's signature.

    d. customer's social security number.

13. A customer calls in asking about how to put money aside for his children. He wants to open a custodial account for his two children, Bobby and Sue. What should you recommend?

    a. Open two accounts for both children, with him and his wife as custodian.

    b. Open two accounts for the two children, with him being the custodian on one and his wife being custodian on the other, as one parent may only be custodian for one child.

    c. Open one account immediately for both children.

    d. Open two accounts, one for each child with he or his wife as custodians for both or for either.

14. Which of the following is true?

    a. Representatives and broker dealers may not disclose any information regarding a client to a third party without the client's expressed consent or a court order.

    b. A representative may not obtain outside employment because of the potential conflict of interest.

    c. A client may not have a numbered account for his investment account.

    d. Broker dealers may not give gifts to the employees of other broker dealers.

15. A potential customer that you have been trying to get to open an account with you for some time has agreed to put some money in a mutual fund you have recommended. Which of the following customer information is NOT required on the new account form?

    a. Address

    b. Social security number

    c. Educational information

    d. Investment objective

16. Two brothers, both married with children, have opened an account with your firm as JTWROS. One brother has passed away. All of the following will happen with regard to the account, EXCEPT:

    a. all assets will become the property of the surviving party.

    b. the account will be retitled in the name of the surviving party.

    c. the portion of the assets belonging to the deceased will go to his estate.

    d. the original account will become an individual account.

17. Before opening a new account for any customer, a registered representative must:

    a. fill out and sign a new account form.

    b. send a declaration of investor intent (DII) to the IRS.

    c. fill out a new account form and present it to the investor for his signature.

    d. fill out and sign a full financial declaration.

18. A client died in testate. The client's assets will be liquidated by the:

    a. heirs.

    b. administrator.

    c. executor.

    d. spouse.

Margin Accounts

INTRODUCTION

Investors may borrow a portion of a security's purchase price directly from the broker dealer to establish a position. Investors who borrow money to purchase securities are said to be buying on margin. The term *margin* refers to the portion of the securities purchase price that must be deposited by the customer to establish the position. Series 7 candidates can expect to see several questions on margin accounts.

REGULATION OF CREDIT

One of the main reasons the stock market crashed in 1929 was the aggressive lending of money to investors who wanted to purchase securities on margin. In an effort to ward off future excessive lending practices, authority was given to the Federal Reserve Board to regulate the extension of credit for securities purchases. Regulation "T" of The Securities Exchange Act of 1934 allowed the Federal Reserve Board to regulate the extension of credit by broker dealers.

REGULATION T

Once a customer has established a margin account, Regulation T sets the minimum initial requirement that must be met by the customer to purchase securities on margin. Regulation T currently requires that the customer deposit 50% of the securities purchase price. However, the NYSE and FINRA require that a customer meet a minimum initial equity requirement of $2,000 before a firm may lend money to an investor. In order to establish a position in a new margin account, the investor must deposit the greater of $2,000 or 50% of the securities' purchase price. The broker dealer may pledge or rehypothecate the customer's securities to obtain a loan for the customer at a bank. The broker dealer may pledge the customer's securities with a value of 140% of the customer's debit balance to obtain the loan for the customer. All excess margin securities must be segregated.

EXAMPLE

Purchased	Minimum Equity	Reg. T at 50%	Required Deposit
1,000 ABC at 10	$2,000	$5,000	$5,000
1,000 XYZ at 5	$2,000	$2,500	$2,500
1,000 RTY at 3	$2,000	$1,500	$2,000
100 KLM at 15	$2,000	$750	$1,500

 TAKE**NOTE!**

A customer may never be required to deposit more than the purchase price of the securities.

Investors who purchase securities on margin are charged interest monthly on the amount of the loan. An investor in theory may hold the securities on margin indefinitely and will be required to repay the principal amount of the loan upon the sale of the securities. Investors purchasing securities on margin must hypothecate or pledge the securities they purchased as collateral for the loan. All securities purchased on margin will be held in the name of the broker dealer (street name). Holding the securities in the name of the broker dealer will allow the firm to liquidate the securities to protect its loan if the securities fall too far in value. Regulation T also establishes which securities may be purchased on margin. Marginable securities include:

- All exchange-listed stocks and bonds.
- All Nasdaq Global market stocks.
- All securities on the FRB's approved list.

Investors who purchase securities on margin must deposit the required amount within five business days. If the investor is unable to make the deposit by the fifth business day the broker dealer can apply for an extension on behalf of the customer. The broker dealer must request the extension by writing a letter to either the NYSE or FINRA by the expiration of the fifth business day. An investor may meet the margin requirement by meeting one of the following requirements:

- Depositing cash equal to the requirement.
- Depositing marginable securities with a loan value equal to the amount of the requirement.

 TAKENOTE!

Broker dealers may waive a call for $1,000 or less.

A marginable security's loan value is equal to the complement of Reg. T. When Reg. T is 50%, the security's loan value is 50%.

EXAMPLE

An investor purchasing $20,000 worth of securities in a margin account may meet the Reg. T requirement by:

- Depositing $10,000.
- Depositing $20,000 worth of fully paid for marginable securities.

  Nonmarginable securities include:

- Non-Nasdaq OTC securities
- Options
- IPOs and new issues for 30 days
- When issued, nonexempt securities

 TAKENOTE!

An investor may purchases a LEAP with an expiration exceeding nine months by depositing 75% of the option's premium.

Certain securities are exempt from the Reg. T margin requirements. Although an investor may still borrow money from the broker dealer to purchase these securities, the investor is not required to deposit 50% of the purchase price. Securities exempt from Reg. T include:

- U.S. government securities
- U.S. government agencies
- Municipal securities
- Nonconvertible corporate debt

The initial margin requirement for exempt securities is set by the NYSE or FINRA. The initial margin requirement for U.S. government securities is 1% to 7% of the par value. For municipal securities, it is the greater of 7% of par or 15% of the market value.

HOUSE RULES

A broker dealer may elect to increase the minimum amount of margin that must be deposited by the investor or it may elect not to extend credit to customers at all. A broker dealer may never lower the amount of the required deposit below Reg. T or below the requirements of the NYSE or FINRA.

ESTABLISHING A LONG POSITION IN A MARGIN ACCOUNT

A customer's long margin account will consist of the customer's equity and loan amount or debit balance. The customer's equity represents the portion of the securities that the customer has paid for in full. The customer's debit balance represents the portion of the securities purchase price that was loaned by the broker dealer. To determine the equity in the account, use the following formula:

equity = LMV − debit

EXAMPLE   A customer in a new margin account purchases 1,000 shares of XYZ at $40 per share and makes the required deposit when Reg. T is 50%. The investor's margin account will now look like this:

LMV	Debit
40,000	20,000

EQ 20,000

The long market value (LMV) of the stock is $40,000. The customer has a debit balance, or has borrowed $20,000 and has equity of $20,000.

In order to gain an understanding of the debit balance and equity components, one could compare a long margin account to home ownership. The homeowner's equity represents the portion of the home's market value that is fully paid for. The mortgage balance is the amount of money owed on the home. As the home's market value changes, so does the homeowner's equity. The mortgage balance, however, does not change as a result of a change in the market value of the home. A long margin account operates in much the same way. As the long market value of the account increases, so does the account holder's equity. Alternatively if the long market value of the account falls, the account holder's equity falls with it. The customer's debit balance or the amount that the customer has borrowed does not change as a result of a change in the market value of the securities. A broker dealer will closely monitor the relationship between the purchase price of the securities and the current market value of the securities through a process known as marking to the market.

AN INCREASE IN THE LONG MARKET VALUE

As the long market value in a margin account increases, the customer's equity will also increase. Let's look at our original example and see what happens to our customer's account if XYZ increases in value to $50 per share.

Original Position			XYZ at $50	
LMV	**Debit**		**LMV**	**Debit**
40,000	20,000		50,000	20,000

EQ 20,000   EQ 30,000

As the long market value increased by $10,000, the customer's equity also increased by $10,000. Notice that the debit balance or the amount of the customer's loan was not affected. As the long market value increases, the rise in value creates excess equity for the customer. Excess equity is the amount of the customer's equity that exceeds the initial Reg. T requirement at the current market value. Using our current example, the customer's excess equity is calculated as follows:

LMV	Debit
50,000	20,000

EQ 30,000
Reg. T 25,000
EE 5,000

The customer may do all of the following with the excess equity:

- Withdraw an amount equal to the excess equity.
- Use the excess equity to purchase two times the amount of marginable securities.
- Use the excess to purchase an equal amount of nonmarginable securities.

Customers may request that the brokerage firm send them a check in an amount equal to their excess equity. Withdrawing the excess equity will increase the customer's debit balance. If the customer in our example withdraws their excess equity, the account will look as follows:

LMV	Debit
50,000	25,000

EQ 25,000
Reg. T 25,000
EE   0

The customer's debit balance increased by the amount of the excess equity that was withdrawn. The customer may also use the excess equity to purchase marginable stock. To determine the customer's buying power, use the following formula:

buying power = excess equity/complement of Reg. T

Or, when Reg. T is 50%

buying power = excess equity × 2

If the customer uses the excess equity to purchase $10,000 worth of marginable stock, the account would appear as follows:

LMV	Debit
60,000	30,000

EQ 30,000
Reg. T 30,000
EE   0

The long market value and the debit have increased by the amount of the purchase.

SPECIAL MEMORANDUM ACCOUNT (SMA) LONG MARGIN ACCOUNT

When a customer's equity increases to over 50% of the long market value, it is credited to the special memorandum account, or SMA. The SMA is like a line of credit. Once the SMA has been created, it will remain in place until it is used by the customer. Customers may use an SMA to:

- Purchase additional securities.
- Have funds sent out to them by check.

A decline in the long market value in the account will not affect the customer's SMA. A customer may always use the SMA, unless doing so would cause the account to fall below the minimum equity requirement. An SMA will be created by any of the following:

- An increase in the long market value.
- A nonrequired cash deposit.
- Dividends and interest received.
- A nonrequired deposit of fully paid for marginable securities.
- A sale of securities 50% will be credited to SMA.

TAKENOTE!

A customer's SMA is the greater of the excess equity or the amount of the SMA already established by the account.

EXAMPLE   A customer's margin account is as follows:

LMV	Debit
60,000	40,000

EQ 20,000
Reg. T 30,000

EE   0
SMA   5,000

 TAKENOTE!

The margin account is restricted because the customer's equity is below the Reg. T requirement. If the customer in this case uses the SMA of $5,000 to purchase $10,000 worth of stock, the account will look as follows:

LMV	Debit
70,000	50,000

EQ 20,000
Reg. T 35,000

EE   0
SMA   0

The customer was able to use the SMA to purchase the stock because doing so did not cause the account to fall below the minimum equity requirement of 25%. An investor may never use an SMA to meet a margin call.

A DECREASE IN THE LONG MARKET VALUE

A decrease in the long market value of the securities in a margin account will cause the customer's equity to fall. Should the equity in the customer's account fall below 50% of the current market value, the account becomes restricted. A customer whose account is restricted may still:

- Buy additional marginable securities and deposit 50%.
- Sell securities and withdraw 50% of the proceeds.
- Withdraw securities by depositing 50% of their value in cash or by depositing securities with a loan value of 50%.

 TAKENOTE!

If a customer wants to withdraw cash from a restricted margin account, the customer must deposit marginable securities with a loan value equal to the amount of the cash withdrawn from the account.

MINIMUM EQUITY REQUIREMENT
LONG MARGIN ACCOUNTS

Once the Reg. T deposit has been made by the investor, the NYSE and FINRA set the minimum account equity that must be maintained by the investor. An investor is required to maintain a minimum equity equal to 25% of the long market value of the account. If the investor's equity falls below the minimum, the investor will receive a margin or maintenance call. A maintenance call can be met by:

- Depositing cash.
- Depositing marginable securities with a loan value equal to the call.
- Selling securities.

All margin calls must be met promptly. If the investor fails to meet the call, the firm will liquidate enough of the customer's securities to satisfy the call.

To determine the minimum equity at a given long market value, use the following formula:

minimum equity = LMV × 25%

EXAMPLE   A customer has a margin account with a long market value of $50,000. The customer's minimum equity would be found as follows:

$50,000 × .25 = $12,500

To determine how far a customer's account value can fall in order to be at the minimum equity requirement, use the following formula:

minimum equity = debit balance/.75

If a customer purchased $40,000 worth of securities and made the required deposit, the account would look as follows:

LMV	Debit
40,000	20,000

EQ 20,000

Using the above formula to determine how low the market value could fall for the account to be at the minimum equity, we get:

$20,000/.75 = $26,667

At the $26,667 level, the account is at the minimum equity of 25%. If the value falls any lower, the investor will receive a margin call.

ESTABLISHING A SHORT POSITION IN A MARGIN ACCOUNT

All short sales must be done in a margin account. Prior to establishing the short position, the customer must first borrow the stock that will be sold short. The customer is required to deposit 50% of the market value of the borrowed shares to ensure that enough resources are available to repurchase the shares if the stock price rises. The customer's deposit establishes the customer's equity in the account. The customer may meet the Reg. T requirement by depositing cash or fully paid for marginable securities with a loan value equal to the Reg. T requirement. In order to establish a short position in a new margin account, the investor must deposit the greater of $2,000 or 50% of the borrowed securities' market value. Special rules are in place for customers who want to sell low priced stocks short. If the stock sold short is less than $5 per share the required deposit is the greater of 100% of the market value or $2.50 per share.

EXAMPLE

Sold Short	Minimum Equity	Reg. T at 50%	Required Deposit
1,000 ABC at 50	$2,000	$25,000	$25,000
1,000 XYZ at 20	$2,000	$10,000	$10,000
100 RTY at 30	$2,000	$1,500	$2,000
100 KLM at 15	$2,000	$750	$2,000
1,000 FGTK at 3	$2,000	$1,500	$3,000

The credit balance in a short margin account remains constant while the short market value changes. To determine the equity in a short margin account, use the following formula:

equity = credit balance − SMV

Let's look at the account of a customer who sells 1,000 XYZ short at $40 per share. The account will look as follows:

Credit	SMV
60,000	40,000

EQ 20,000

 **TAKENOTE!**

The credit of $60,000 was created from the proceeds from the short sale of 1,000 XYZ at 40 and the investor's Reg. T deposit of $20,000.

A DECREASE IN THE SHORT MARKET VALUE

A customer who has sold stock short hopes that the value of the stock will fall and that it can then be bought back at a cheaper price. As a result, as the short market value (SMV) of the account falls, the investor's equity will increase. The credit balance in a short margin account remains constant

344   WILEY SERIES 7   Exam Review 2017

while the short market value changes. Let's look at what happens to the same account if XYZ falls to $30 per share:

Original Position			XYZ at $30	
Credit	**SMV**		**Credit**	**SMV**
60,000	40,000		60,000	30,000

EQ 20,000   EQ 30,000

Notice that as the short market value of the account fell from 40,000 to 30,000, the investor's equity increased from 20,000 to 30,000.

SPECIAL MEMORANDUM ACCOUNT (SMA) SHORT MARGIN ACCOUNT

When a customer's equity increases to over 50% of the short market value, it is credited to the special memorandum account, or SMA. Customers may use an SMA in a short margin account to:

- Sell short additional securities.
- Have funds sent out to them by check.

To determine if the customer has excess equity in a short margin account, use the following formula:

excess equity = customer's equity – Reg. T requirement of SMV

Let's look at the account again after XYZ has fallen to $30 per share:

Credit	SMV
60,000	30,000

EQ 30,000
Reg. T at 30 15,000
EE 15,000
SMA 15,000

As the short market value of the account has fallen, the investor's equity has increased. The customer's excess equity is credited to the SMA, just as in a long margin account. In this case, the customer may sell short an additional

$30,000 worth of securities based on the SMA. Let's look at the account if the investor sells short additional securities valued at $30,000:

Credit	SMV
90,000	60,000

EQ 30,000
Reg. T 30,000
_____
EE   0
SMA   0

The customer's account has exactly 50% equity, as required by Reg. T.

Let's look at the account if the customer withdraws the excess equity instead of selling additional securities short.

Credit	SMV
45,000	30,000

EQ 15,000
Reg. T at 30 15,000
_____
EE   0
SMA   0

AN INCREASE IN THE SHORT MARKET VALUE

An increase in the short market value in a short margin account will cause the investor's equity to fall. Should the equity in the customer's account fall below 50% of the current short market value, the account becomes restricted. A customer whose account is restricted may still:

- Sell short additional securities and deposit 50%.
- Cover the short securities and withdraw 50%.

An increase in the short market value of the account will not affect the customer's SMA. The customer's SMA will be the greater of:

- The excess equity, or
- The SMA already established

MINIMUM EQUITY REQUIREMENT
SHORT MARGIN ACCOUNTS

Once the Reg. T deposit has been made by the investor, the NYSE and FINRA set the minimum account equity that must be maintained by an investor who sells securities short. Because selling stock short involves unlimited risk, a higher level of minimum equity is required to be maintained. An investor is required to maintain a minimum equity equal to 30% of the short market value of the account. If the investor's equity falls below the minimum, the customer will receive a margin or maintenance call. A maintenance call can be met by:

- Depositing cash.
- Depositing marginable securities with a loan value equal to the call.
- Repurchasing securities.

All margin calls must be met promptly. If the investor fails to meet the call, the firm will repurchase enough of the customer's securities to satisfy the call.

To determine the minimum equity at a given short market value, use the following formula:

EXAMPLE	A customer has a margin account with an short market value of $50,000. The minimum equity would be found as follows:

$50,000 × .30 = $15,000

To determine how high the short market value can rise in order to be at the minimum equity requirement, use the following formula:

minimum equity = total credit balance/1.30

If a customer sold short $50,000 worth of securities and made the required deposit, the account would look as follows:

Credit	SMV
75,000	50,000

EQ 25,000

Using the above formula to determine how high the market value could rise for the account to be at the minimum equity we get:

$75,000/1.3 = $57,693

At the $57,693 level, the account is at the minimum equity of 30%. If the value rises any higher, the investor will receive a margin call.

COMBINED MARGIN ACCOUNTS

Investors may wish to purchase securities that they feel will rise and sell short other securities that they feel will fall. An investor establishing both long and short positions in a margin account is said to have a combined account. The investor will have to determine:

- The Reg. T requirement on the long side.
- The Reg. T requirement on the short side.
- The minimum equity on the long side.
- The minimum equity on the short side.

Let's look at a combined account that has the following:

LMV = $60,000

Debit = $25,000

SMV = $40,000

Credit = $62,000

To determine the customer's equity in a combined account, use the following formula:

(LMV – debit) + (credit – SMV)

Using the above example, we get:

(60,000 – 25,000) + (62,000 – 40,000) = $57,000

If you are asked to determine the minimum equity for a combined account, you must determine the minimum equity on the long side and the minimum equity on the short side and then add them together.

PORTFOLIO MARGIN ACCOUNTS

Broker dealers may offer sophisticated investors who properly hedge their position's portfolio-based margin. In contrast to strategy-based margin, which calculates the margin requirement for all positions in the account separately, portfolio-based margin calculates the potential losses in the account based on all of the positions and offsetting hedges to determine the investor's margin requirement. A institutional investor who is long a basket of S&P 500 stocks and short S&P 500 futures has dramatically lower risk than an investor who is outright long with no hedges. Broker dealers will use an SEC-approved risk-modeling system to determine both the risk to the portfolio and the amount of margin required to hold the positions. Portfolio-based margin calculations generally result in lower overall margin requirements and increased leverage. As a result, portfolio margin is only offered to the largest and most sophisticated investors, such as hedge funds, broker dealers, members of a futures exchange, and accounts with $5,000,000 in equity that have been approved for uncovered option writing. If an account approved for portfolio margin receives a margin call, it must be met in three business days.

SECURITIES BACKED LINES OF CREDIT

Some broker dealers allow customers to have a line of credit attached to their account which allow the investor to borrow funds based on the value of the fully paid for assets in the account. This is not a margin loan used to purchase securities. In some ways it functions like a home equity line of credit that allows the investor to borrow from the broker dealer to meet their cash needs or to pay for a large purchase such as a home renovation. Firms must have proper procedures in place to make sure the customers and the representatives understand the loan restrictions and features. Customers must understand how a fall in the market value of the securities in the account can impact their ability to borrow. Additionally, a significant fall in the value may also require additional collateral or a portion of the loan to be repaid.

MINIMUM MARGIN FOR LEVERAGED ETFs

To determine the minimum equity requirement for an exchange traded fund that employs leverage to return a multiple of the performance or inverse performance of an index, you must multiply the minimum equity requirement by the leverage factor. Therefore, buying an ETF that uses a leverage factor of 2:1 or 200% would have a minimum equity requirement of 50% (25% × 2). Buying an ETF that uses a leverage factor of 3:1 would have a minimum equity requirement of 75% (25% × 3). Investors who sell a leveraged ETF short would be subject to the 30% minimum requirement times the leveraged factor. Therefore selling an ETF short with a leverage factor of 3:1 or 300% would have a minimum equity requirement of 90% (30% × 3).

Pretest

MARGIN ACCOUNTS

1. Which of the following establishes the minimum maintenance amount on a new margin account?
   a. Federal Reserve Bank
   b. Regulation T
   c. NYSE/FINRA
   d. The brokerage firm

2. The initial minimum for a new margin account is:
   a. 50% of the purchase price.
   b. the greater of $2,000 or 50% of the purchase price.
   c. set by the Federal Reserve Board.
   d. set by the MSRB.

3. Margin customers must sign which of the following to pledge their securities as collateral for the loan?
   a. Loan consent
   b. Rehypothecation agreement
   c. Hypothecation agreement
   d. Collateral agreement

4. An investor has an open margin account with $48,000 in value and a debit balance of $10,000. What is his minimum equity at this level?

a. $24,000

b. $12,000

c. $13,333

d. $10,000

5. The initial margin requirement for municipal bonds is set by which of the following?

a. NYSE

b. Reg. T

c. MSRB

d. Federal Reserve Board

6. You have the following positions in your margin account:

Long 500 ABC at 27

Long 1500 XYZ at 42

Long 250 MCX at 80

You have a debit balance of $28,200. What is your minimum maintenance?

a. $24,125

b. $48,250

c. $22,500

d. $37,600

7. Your customer buys $100,000 principal amount of New York Bridge and Tunnel revenue bonds at 54 in her margin account. She must deposit:

a. $7,000.

b. $27,000.

c. $54,000.

d. $8,100.

8. An investor in a new margin account purchases 200 XYZ at 20 and deposits $2,000. XYZ falls to $18, and the investor's equity falls to $1,600. Which of the following is true?

   a. The investor will receive a margin call for $200.

   b. No action by the investor is required at this time.

   c. The investor must deposit $400 to maintain the $2,000 minimum equity requirement.

   d. The position could be liquidated if the investor doesn't meet the current margin call.

9. You have an open margin account with a long market value of $125,000 and a debit balance of $54,000. How low can the value of the securities drop before you get a margin call?

   a. $72,000

   b. $100,000

   c. $67,500

   d. $93,750

10. If a corporation wants to open a margin account, in addition to the usual paperwork, the representative must obtain which of the following?

   I. Corporate resolution

   II. Corporate charter

   III. Corporate bylaws

   IV. Authorization of the president

   a. I and IV

   b. II and IV

   c. I, II, and III

   d. I, II, III, and IV

11. Which of the following is true if a client uses an SMA to withdraw $2,500 from his margin account?

   a. The SMA is reduced and the debit balance is reduced.

   b. The SMA is increased and the debit balance is increased.

   c. The SMA is reduced and the debit balance is increased.

   d. The SMA is reduced and the debit balance is not affected.

Retirement Plans

INTRODUCTION

For most people, saving for retirement has become an important investment objective for at least part of their portfolio. Investors may participate in retirement plans that have been established by their employers, as well as those they have established for themselves. Both corporate and individual plans may be qualified or nonqualified, and it is important for an investor to understand the difference before deciding to participate. Series 7 candidates will see a fair number of questions on the exam dealing with retirement plans. The following table compares the key features of qualified and nonqualified plans.

Feature	Qualified	Nonqualified
Contributions	Pretax	After tax
Growth	Tax deferred	Tax deferred
Participation must be allowed	For everyone	The corporation may choose who gets to participate
IRS approval	Required	Not required
Withdrawals	100% taxed as ordinary income	Growth in excess of cost base is taxed as ordinary income

INDIVIDUAL PLANS

Individuals may set up a qualified retirement plan for themselves and allow contributions to the plan to be made with pre-tax dollars. Individuals may also purchase investment products such as annuities that allow their money to grow tax deferred. The money used to purchase an annuity has already been taxed, making an annuity a nonqualified product.

INDIVIDUAL RETIREMENT ACCOUNTS (IRAs)

All individuals with earned income may establish an Individual Retirement Account (IRA) for themselves. Contributions to traditional IRAs may or may not be tax deductible, depending on the individual's level of adjusted gross income and whether the individual is eligible to participate in an employer-sponsored plan. Individuals who do not qualify to participate in an employer-sponsored plan may deduct their IRA contributions regardless of their income level. The level of adjusted gross income that allows an investor to deduct their IRA contributions has been increasing since 1998. These tax law changes occur too frequently to make them a practical test question. Our review of IRAs will focus on the four main types, which are:

1. Traditional
2. Roth
3. SEP
4. Educational

TRADITIONAL IRAs

Currently, a traditional IRA allows an individual to contribute a maximum of 100% of earned income or $5,500 per year or up to $11,000 per couple. If only one spouse works, the working spouse may contribute $5,500 to an IRA for themselves and $5,500 to a separate IRA for their spouse, under the nonworking spousal option. Investors over 50 may contribute up to $6,500 of earned income to their IRA. Regardless of whether the IRA contribution was made with pre- or after-tax dollars, the money is allowed to grow tax deferred. All withdrawals from an IRA are taxed as ordinary income regardless of how the growth was generated in the account. Withdrawals from an IRA prior to age 59-1/2 are subject to a 10% penalty tax as well as ordinary income taxes. The 10% penalty will be waived for first-time homebuyers or educational expenses for the taxpayer's child, grandchildren, or spouse. The 10% penalty will also be waived if the payments are part of a series of substantially equal payments. Withdrawals from an IRA must begin by April 1st of the year following the year in which the taxpayer reaches 70-1/2. If an individual fails to make withdrawals that are sufficient in size and frequency, the individual will be subject to a 50% penalty on the insufficient amount. An individual who makes a contribution to an IRA that exceeds 100% of earned income or $5,500, whichever is less, will be subject to a penalty of 6% per year on the excess amount for as long as the excess contribution remains in the account.

ROTH IRAs

A Roth IRA is a nonqualified account. All contributions made to a Roth IRA, are made with after-tax dollars. The same contribution limits apply for Roth IRAs. An individual may contribute the lesser of 100% of earned income to a maximum of $5,500 per person or $11,000 per couple. Any contribution made to a Roth IRA reduces the amount that may be deposited into a traditional IRA, and vice versa. All contributions deposited in a Roth IRA are allowed to grow tax deferred, and all of the growth may be taken out of the account tax-free provided that the individual has reached age 59-1/2 and the assets have been in the account for at least five years. A 10% penalty tax will be charged on any withdrawal of earnings prior to age 59-1/2 unless the owner is purchasing a home, has become disabled, or has died. There are no requirements for an individual to take distributions from a Roth IRA by a certain age.

The following table details contribution limits that have in place for IRA contributions for the last several years:

Year	Age 49 and Below	Age 50 and Above
2015	$5,500	$6,500
2016	$5,500	$6,500
2017	$5,500	$6,500

 TAKENOTE!

Individuals and couples who are eligible to open a Roth IRA may convert their traditional IRA to a Roth IRA. The investor will have to pay income taxes on the amount converted, but it will not be subject to the 10% penalty.

SIMPLIFIED EMPLOYEE PENSION IRA (SEP IRA)

A SEP IRA is used by small corporations and self-employed individuals to plan for retirement. A SEP IRA is attractive to small employers because it allows them to set up a retirement plan for their employees rather quickly and inexpensively. The contribution limit for a SEP IRA far exceeds that of traditional IRAs. The contribution limit is the lesser of 25% of the employee's compensation or $54,000 per year. Employees may make their annual IRA contribution to their SEP IRA or they may make their standard contribution to a traditional or Roth IRA.

PARTICIPATION

All eligible employees must open an IRA to receive the employer's contribution to the SEP. If the employee does not open an IRA account, the employer must open one for the employee. The employee must be at least 21 years old and have worked during three of the last five years for the employer and have earned at least $550. All eligible employees must participate, as well as the employer.

EMPLOYER CONTRIBUTIONS

The employer may contribute between 0 and 25% of the employee's total compensation to a maximum of $54,000. Contributions to all SEP IRAs, including the employer's SEP IRA, must be made at the same rate. An employee who is over 70-1/2 must also participate and receive a contribution. All eligible employees are immediately vested in the employer's contributions to the plan.

SEP IRA TAXATION

The employer's contributions to a SEP IRA are immediately tax deductible by the employer. Contributions are not taxed at the employee's rate until the employee withdraws the funds. Employees may begin to withdraw money from the plan at age 59-1/2. All withdrawals are taxed as ordinary income, and withdrawals prior to age 59-1/2 are subject to a 10% penalty tax.

IRA CONTRIBUTIONS

All contributions to an IRA must be made by April 15th of the following calendar year, regardless of whether an extension has been filed by the taxpayer.

Contributions may be made between January 1 and April 15 for the previous year, the current year, or both. All IRA contributions must be made in cash.

IRA ACCOUNTS

All IRA accounts are held in the name of the custodian for the benefit of the account holder. Traditional custodians include banks, broker dealers, and mutual fund companies.

IRA INVESTMENTS

Individuals who establish IRAs have a wide variety of investments to choose from when deciding how to invest the funds. Investors should always choose investments that fit their investment objectives. The following is a comparison of allowable and nonallowable investments:

Allowable	Nonallowable
Stocks	Margin accounts
Bonds	Short sales
Mutual funds	Tangibles/collectibles/art
Annuities	Speculative option trading
UITs	Term life insurance
Limited partnerships	Rare coins
U.S. minted coins ETFs	Real estate

IT IS NOT WISE TO PUT A MUNICIPAL BOND IN AN IRA

Municipal bonds or municipal bond funds should never be placed in an IRA because the advantage of those investments is that the interest income is free from federal taxes. Because their interest is free from federal taxes, the interest rate that is offered will be less than the rates offered by other alternatives. The advantage of an IRA is that money is allowed to grow tax deferred, therefore an individual would be better off with a higher yielding taxable bond of the same quality.

ROLLOVER VS. TRANSFER

An individual may want or need to move an IRA from one custodian to another. There are two ways by which this can be accomplished. Individuals may rollover their IRA or they may transfer their IRA.

ROLLOVER

With an IRA rollover, the individual may take possession of the funds for a maximum of 60 calendar days prior to depositing the funds into another qualified account. Investors may only rollover their IRA once every 12 months. Investors have 60 days from the date of the distribution to deposit 100% of the funds into another qualified account or they must pay ordinary income taxes on the distribution and a 10% penalty tax, if the investor is under 59-1/2.

TRANSFER

An investor may transfer an IRA directly from one custodian to another by simply signing an account transfer form. The investor never takes possession of the assets in the account, and the investor may directly transfer an IRA as often as he or she would like.

DEATH OF AN IRA OWNER

Should the owner of an IRA die, the account will become the property of the beneficiary named on the account by the owner. If the beneficiary is the spouse of the owner, special rules apply. The spouse may elect to rollover the IRA into his or her own IRA or retirement plan, such as a 401K. If this is elected, there will be no tax presently due on the money. However, the spouse is still subject to the required minimum distribution rule at age 70-1/2. The surviving spouse may also elect to cash in the IRA. The distributions will be subject to income tax but will not be subject to the 10% penalty tax. If the beneficiary is not the spouse, the money may not be rolled into another IRA or retirement account. If the account owner died prior to age 70-1/2, when the required distributions need to be made, the money must all be distributed prior to the end of the fifth year, or the money may be distributed in equal installments based upon the beneficiary's life expectancy. If the account owner has died after the start of the required minimum distributions, the payment schedule of distributions will now be based on the life expectancy of the beneficiary.

EDUCATIONAL IRA/COVERDELL IRA

An educational IRA allows individuals to contribute up to $2,000 in after-tax dollars to an educational IRA for each student who is under age 18.

The money is allowed to grow tax deferred, and the growth may be withdrawn tax free, as long as the money is used for educational purposes. If all of the funds have not been used for educational purposes by the time the student reaches 30 years of age, the account must be rolled over to another family member who is under 30 years of age or distributed to the original student, at which point it is subject to a 10% penalty tax as well as ordinary income taxes.

529 PLANS

Qualified tuition plans more frequently referred to as 529 plans may be set up either as a prepaid tuition plan or as a college savings plan. With the prepaid tuition plan, the plan locks in a current tuition rate at a specific school.

The prepaid tuition plan can be set up as an installment plan or one where the contributor funds the plan with a lump sum deposit. Many states will guarantee the plans but may require that either the contributor or the beneficiary to be a state resident. The plan covers only tuition and mandatory fees. A room and board option is available for some plans. A college cost-savings account may be opened by any adult and the donor does not have to be related to the child. The assets in the college savings plan can be used to cover all costs of qualified higher education including tuition, room and board, books, computers, and mandatory fees. These plans generally have no age limit when assets must be used. College savings accounts are not guaranteed by the state and the value of the account may decline based on the investment results of the account. College savings accounts are not state specific and do not lock in a tuition rate. Contributions to a 529 plan are made with after-tax dollars and are allowed to grow tax deferred. The assets in the account remain under the control of the donor, even after the student reaches the age of majority. The funds may be used to meet the student's educational needs and the growth may be withdrawn federally tax-free. Most states also allow the assets to be withdrawn tax free. Any funds used for non-qualified education expenses will be subject to income tax and a 10% penalty tax. If funds remain or if the student does not attend or complete qualified higher education the funds may be rolled over to another family member within 60 days without incurring taxes and penalties.

There are no income limits for the donors and contribution limits vary from state to state. 529 plans have an impact on a student's ability to obtain need based financial aid. However, because the 529 plans are treated as parental assets and not as assets of the student, the plans are assessed at the expected family contribution (EFC) rate of 5.64%. This will have a significantly lower impact than plans and assets that are considered to be assets of the student. Student assets will be assessed at a 20% contribution rate.

LOCAL GOVERNMENT INVESTMENT POOLS (LGIPS)

Local government investment pools (LGIPs) allow states and local governments to manage their cash reserves and to receive money market rates on the funds. LGIPs may also be created to invest the proceeds of a bond offering if the proceeds of the offering are intended to be used to call in an existing bond issue. If the LGIP was created to prefund an existing issue, additional restrictions will apply as to the type of investments that may be purchased by the pool. LGIPs that are created to manage cash reserves must only invest in securities on the state's legal or approved list. The legal list usually includes investments such as:

- Commercial paper rated in the two highest categories.
- U.S. government and agency debt
- Bankers' acceptances
- Repurchase agreement
- Municipal debt issues within the state
- Investment company securities
- Certificates of deposit
- Savings accounts

Each state has an investment advisory board that works with the state treasury office to administer the pools. The main objective of these pools is safety of principal, with liquidity and interest income as secondary objectives. The pools require that the following be detailed in writing:

- Delegation of authority to make investments
- Annual investment activity reports
- Statement of safekeeping of securities

Municipal fund securities are not considered to be investment companies and are not required to register under the Investment Company Act of 1940. Additionally, prepaid tuition plans are not considered to be municipal fund securities. LGIP employees who market the plans directly to investors are exempt from MSRB rules; however, if the LGIP is marketed to investors by employees of a broker dealer, the broker dealer and all of its employees are subject to MSRB rules.

KEOGH PLANS (HR-10)

A Keogh is a qualified retirement plan set up by self-employed individuals, sole proprietors, and unincorporated businesses. If the business is set up as a corporation, a Keogh may not be used.

CONTRIBUTIONS

A Keogh may only be funded with earned income during a period when the business shows a gross profit. If the business realizes a loss, no Keogh contributions are allowed. A self-employed person may contribute the lesser of 25% of postcontribution income or $54,000. If the business has eligible employees, the employer must make a contribution for the employees at the same rate as his or her own contribution. Employee contributions are based on the employee's gross income and are limited to $54,000 per year. All money placed in a Keogh plan is allowed to grow tax deferred and is taxed as ordinary income when distributions are made to retiring employees and plan participants. From time to time, a self-employed person may make a nonqualified contribution to a Keogh plan; however, the total of the qualified and nonqualified contributions may not exceed the maximum contribution limit. Any excess contribution may be subject to a 10% penalty tax.

An eligible employee is defined as one that:

- Works full time (at least 1,000 hours per year).
- Is at least 21 years old.
- Has worked at least one year for the employer.

Employees who participate in a Keogh plan must be vested after five years. Withdrawals from a Keogh may begin when the participant reaches 59-1/2. Any premature withdrawals are subject to a 10% penalty tax. Keoghs, like IRAs, may be rolled over every 12 months. In the event of a participant's death, the assets will go to the individual's beneficiaries.

TAX-SHELTERED ANNUITIES (TSAs)/ TAX-DEFERRED ACCOUNTS (TDAs)

Tax-sheltered annuities (TSAs) and tax-deferred accounts (TDAs) are established as retirement plans for employees of nonprofit and public organizations such as:

- Public schools (403B)
- Nonprofit organizations (IRC 501C3)
- Religious organizations
- Nonprofit hospitals

TSAs/TDAs are qualified plans, and contributions are made with pretax dollars. The money in the plan is allowed to grow tax deferred until it is withdrawn. TSAs/TDAs offer a variety of investment vehicles for participants to choose from, such as:

- Stocks
- Bonds
- Mutual funds
- CDs

PUBLIC EDUCATIONAL INSTITUTIONS (403B)

In order for a school to be considered a public school and qualify to establish a TSA/TDA for its employees, the school must be supported by the state, the local government, or by a state agency. State-supported schools include:

- Elementary schools
- High schools
- State colleges and universities
- Medical schools

Any individual who works for a public school, regardless of the position held, may participate in the school's TSA or TDA.

NONPROFIT ORGANIZATIONS/ TAX-EXEMPT ORGANIZATIONS (501C3)

Organizations that qualify under Internal Revenue Code 501C3 as a nonprofit or tax-exempt entity may set up a TSA or TDA for their employees. Examples of nonprofit organizations are:

- Private hospitals
- Charitable organizations
- Trade schools
- Private colleges
- Parochial schools
- Museums
- Scientific foundations
- Zoos

All employees of organizations that qualify under Internal Revenue Code 501C3 or 403B are eligible to participate as long as they are at least 21 years old and have worked full time for at least one year.

CONTRIBUTIONS

In order to participate in a TSA or TDA, the employees must enter into a contract with their employer agreeing to make elective deferrals into the plan. The salary reduction agreement will state the amount and frequency of the elective deferral to be contributed to the TSA. The agreement is binding on both parties and covers only one year of contributions. Each year a new salary reduction agreement must be signed to set forth the contributions for the new year. The employee's elective deferral is limited to a maximum of $18,000 per year. Employer contributions are limited to the lesser of 25% of the employee's earnings or $54,000.

TAX TREATMENT OF DISTRIBUTIONS

All distributions for TSAs/TDAs are taxed as ordinary income in the year in which the distribution is made. Distributions from a TSA/TDA prior to age 59-1/2 are subject to a 10% penalty tax, as well as ordinary income taxes. Distributions from a TSA/TDA must begin by age 70-1/2 or be subject to an excess accumulation tax.

CORPORATE PLANS

Corporations may establish a variety of retirement plans for their employees. The type of plan that is established will be based on the type of entity and the employment of the participant. A corporate retirement plan can be qualified or nonqualified. We will first review the nonqualified plans.

NONQUALIFIED CORPORATE RETIREMENT PLANS

Nonqualified corporate plans are funded with after-tax dollars, and the money is allowed to grow tax deferred. If the corporation makes a contribution to the plan, it may not deduct the contribution from its corporate earnings until the plan participant receives the money. Distributions from a nonqualified plan that exceed the investor's cost base are taxed as ordinary income. All nonqualified plans must be in writing, and the employer may discriminate as to who may participate.

PAYROLL DEDUCTIONS

The employee may set up a payroll deduction plan by having the employer make systematic deductions from the employee's paycheck. The money that has been deducted from the employee's check may be invested in a variety of ways. Mutual funds, annuities, and savings bonds are all usually available for the employee to choose from. Contributions to a payroll deduction plan are made with after-tax dollars.

DEFERRED COMPENSATION PLANS

A deferred compensation plan is a contract between an employee and an employer. Under the contract, the employee agrees to defer the receipt of money owed to the employee from the employer until after the employee retires. After retirement, the employee will traditionally be in a lower tax bracket and will be able to keep a larger percentage of the money. Deferred compensation plans are traditionally unfunded and, if the corporation goes out of business, the employee becomes a creditor of the corporation and may lose all of the money due under the contract. The employee may only claim the assets if he or she retires or becomes disabled. In the case of death, the employee's beneficiaries may claim the money owed. Money due under a deferred compensation plan is paid out of the corporation's working funds when the employee or the employee's estate claims the assets. Should the employee leave the corporation and go to work for a competing company, the employee may lose the money owed under a noncompete clause. Money owed to the employee under a deferred compensation agreement is traditionally not invested for the benefit of the employee and, as a result, does not increase in value over time. The only product that traditionally is placed in a deferred compensation plan is a term life policy. In the case of the employee's death, the term life policy will pay the employee's estate the money owed under the contract.

QUALIFIED PLANS

All qualified corporate plans must be in writing and be established as a trust. A trustee or plan administrator will be appointed for the benefit of all plan holders.

TYPES OF PLANS

There are two main types of qualified corporate plans: defined benefit plans and defined contribution plans.

DEFINED BENEFIT PLANS

A defined benefit plan is designed to offer the participant a retirement benefit that is known or "defined." Most defined benefit plans are set up to provide employees with a fixed percentage of their salary during their retirement, such as 74% of their average earnings during their five highest paid years. Other defined benefit plans are structured to pay participants a fixed sum of money for life. Defined benefit plans require the services of an actuary to determine the employer's contribution to the plan based upon the participant's life expectancy and benefits promised.

DEFINED CONTRIBUTION PLAN

With a defined contribution plan, only the amount of money that is deposited into the account is known, such as 6% of the employee's salary. Both the employee and the employer may contribute a percentage of the employee's earnings into the plan. The money is allowed to grow tax deferred until the participant withdraws it at retirement. The ultimate benefit under a defined contribution plan is the result of the contributions into the plan, along with the investment results of the plan. The employee's maximum contribution to a defined contribution plan is $18,000 per year. Some types of defined contribution plans are:

- 401K
- Money purchase plan
- Profit sharing

- Thrift plans
- Stock bonus plans

All withdrawals from pension plans are taxed as ordinary income in the year in which the distribution is made.

PROFIT SHARING PLANS

Profit sharing plans let the employer reward the employees by letting them "share" in a percentage of the corporation's profits. Profit sharing plans are based on a preset formula, and the money may be paid directly to the employee or placed in a retirement account. In order for a profit sharing plan to be qualified, the corporation must have substantial and recurring profits. The maximum contribution to a profit sharing plan is the lesser of 25% of the employee's compensation or $54,000.

401K THRIFT PLANS

401K and thrift plans allow employees to contribute a fixed percentage of their salary to their retirement account and have the employer match some or all of their contributions.

ROLLING OVER A PENSION PLAN

An employee who leaves an employer may move his or her pension plan to another company's plan or to another qualified account. This may be accomplished by a direct transfer or by rolling over the plan. With a direct transfer, the assets in the plan go directly to another plan administrator, and the employee never has physical possession of the assets. When the employee rolls over a pension plan, the employee takes physical possession of the assets. The plan administrator is required to withhold 20% of the total amount to be distributed, and the employee has 60 calendar days to deposit 100% of the assets into another qualified plan. The employee must file with the federal government at tax time to receive a return of the 20% of the assets that were withheld by the plan administrator.

HEALTH SAVINGS ACCOUNTS

A tax advantaged health savings account may be established to help off-set the potential impact of medical expenses incurred by individuals who maintain a high deductible health insurance plan. Many individuals select a health insurance plan with a high deductible to lower the monthly premium expenses. A high deductible health plan is often used to insure against catastrophic illness. Individuals covered by these plans may elect to establish a health savings account. The individual, their employer, or both may make contributions to the health savings account. The contribution limit varies and is based on the person's age and the type of health insurance coverage. If a person is eligible on the first day of the last month of the year, the person may make a full contribution for that year. This is known as the "last month rule". Contributions to the health savings account may be made with pretax dollars. The money in the account grows tax free and can be used tax free for qualified medical expenses. The individual may use the money to pay the expense directly to the health care provider to reimburse themselves for payments they have made for qualified medical expenses incurred for themselves, their spouse or any dependent claimed on their tax return. Prescription drugs are considered to be qualified medical expenses. If the person requires a nonprescription drug to be covered the person still must get a prescription from their doctor. If money is used for non-qualified medical expenses the money will be subject to income taxes and could be subject to a 20% penalty tax. The money is allowed to accumulate over time and any unused amounts may be carried over to future years. If the owner of an HSA dies the account will pass to the owner's spouse and will be treated as the spouse's HSA. If the beneficiary is not the spouse the account will cease to be an HSA and the amount will be taxable to the beneficiary in the year in which the owner dies.

EMPLOYEE RETIREMENT INCOME SECURITY ACT OF 1974 (ERISA)

The Employee Retirement Income Security Act of 1974 (ERISA) is a federal law that establishes legal and operational guidelines for private pension and employee benefit plans. Not all decisions directly involving a plan, even when made by a fiduciary, are subject to ERISA's fiduciary rules. These decisions are business judgment type decisions and are commonly called "settlor" functions. This caveat is sometimes referred to as the "business decision" exception to ERISA's fiduciary rules. Under this concept, even though the employer is the plan sponsor and administrator, it will not be considered as acting in a fiduciary capacity when creating, amending or terminating a plan. Among the decisions which would be considered settlor functions are:

- Choosing the type of plan, or options in the plan.
- Amending a plan, including changing or eliminating plan options.

- Requiring employee contributions or changing the level of employee contributions.
- Terminating a plan, or part of a plan, including terminating or amending as part of a bankruptcy process.

ERISA also regulates all of the following:

- Pension plan participation
- Funding
- Vesting
- Communication
- Beneficiaries

PLAN PARTICIPATION

All plans governed by ERISA may not discriminate among who may participate in the plan. All employees must be allowed to participate if:

- They are at least 21 years old.
- They have worked at least one year full time (1,000 hours).

FUNDING

Plan funding requirements set forth guidelines on how the money is deposited into the plan and how the employer and employee may contribute to the plan.

VESTING

Vesting refers to the process of how the employer's contribution becomes the property of the employee. An employer may be as generous as it would like, but it may not be more restrictive than either one of the following vesting schedules:

- Three- to six-year gradual vesting schedule.
- Three-year cliff (the employee is not vested at all until three years, at which point the employee becomes 100% vested).

COMMUNICATION

All corporate plans must be in writing at inception, and the employee must be given annual updates.

BENEFICIARIES

All plan participants must be allowed to select a beneficiary who may claim the assets in case of the plan participant's death.

ERISA 404C SAFE HARBOR

All individuals and entities acting in a fiduciary capacity must act solely in the interest of the plan participants. Investment advisers, trustees and all individuals who exercise discretion over the plan including those who select the administrative personnel or committee are considered to be fiduciaries. ERISA Rule 404C provides an exemption from liability or a "safe harbor" for plan fiduciaries and protects them from liabilities that may arise from investment losses that result from the participant's own actions. This safe harbor is available so long as:

- The participant exercises control over the assets in their account.
- Participants have ample opportunity to enter orders for their account and to provide instructions regarding their account.
- A broad range of investment options is available for the participant to choose from and the options offer suitable investments for a variety or investment objectives and risk profiles.
- Information regarding the risks and objective of the investment options is readily available to plan participants.

DEPARTMENT OF LABOR FIDUCIARY RULES

The Department of Labor has enacted significant new legislation for financial professionals who service and maintain retirement accounts for clients. These new rules subject financial professionals to higher fiduciary standards. These standards require financial professionals to place the interest of the client ahead of the interest of the broker dealer or investment advisory firm. Professionals who service retirement accounts are still permitted to earn commissions and/or a fee based on the assets in the account and may still offer proprietary products to investors. However the rule requires that the client receive significant disclosures relating to the fees and costs associated with the servicing of the account. Simply charging the lowest fee will not ensure compliance with the fiduciary standard. Both the firm and the individual servicing the account must put the interests of the client ahead of their own. Broker dealers and advisory firms must establish written supervisory procedures and training programs designed to supervise and educate their personnel on the new requirements for retirement accounts. Many representatives will now be required to obtain the Series 65 or Series 66 license to comply with the new Department of Labor rules.

Pretest

RETIREMENT PLANS

1. Which of the following are features of a 401K plan?

   I. A 401K may be easily rolled over.

   II. Employees' contributions are excluded from their gross income.

   III. Employees are 100% vested in all contributions immediately.

   IV. The employer may match a certain percentage of the employee's contributions.

   a. I and II

   b. II and IV

   c. I, II, III, and IV

   d. I and III

2. Which of the following are funded with pre-tax dollars?

   I. Keogh

   II. Variable annuity

   III. Fixed annuity

   IV. TDA

   a. I and II

   b. I and IV

   c. II and IV

   d. II and III

3. You have been working for the local school system for 15 years and have been contributing to a payroll deduction plan for 9 years. You have deposited $11,000 during the period, and it has grown to $16,200. What is your tax liability upon a lump sum withdrawal, if you are in the 30% tax bracket when you retire?

   a. $4,840

   b. $0

   c. $3,300

   d. $1,560

4. The penalty for an excess contribution to a Keogh plan is:

   a. 8%.

   b. 6%.

   c. 20%.

   d. 10%.

5. A 45-year-old investor has rolled over $10,000 from an IRA to buy a home. How much time does he have to deposit the money into another qualified plan?

   a. 45 days

   b. 60 days

   c. 30 days

   d. 90 days

6. Which of the following is true of Keoghs?

   a. They are usually set up by individuals, sole proprietors, or unincorporated businesses.

   b. They are a type of qualified retirement plan.

   c. They may be funded only with earned income during a period when the business showed a gross profit.

   d. All of the above.

7. A qualified retirement plan differs from a nonqualified retirement plan in all of the following ways, EXCEPT:

    a. IRS approval is required for both plans.

    b. withdrawals from a qualified plan are 100% taxed as ordinary income, whereas growth in excess of the cost base is taxed as ordinary income in a nonqualified plan.

    c. contributions for the qualified plan are made pre-tax, whereas contributions for the nonqualified plan are made after tax.

    d. participation must be allowed for everyone in the qualified plan, whereas the corporation may choose who participates in the nonqualified plan.

8. An investor has deposited $100,000 into a qualified retirement account over a 10-year period. The value of the account has grown to $175,000, and the investor plans to retire and take a lump sum withdrawal. He will pay:

    a. ordinary income taxes on the $75,000 only.

    b. ordinary income taxes on the $100,000 and capital gains on the $75,000.

    c. ordinary income taxes on the whole $175,000.

    d. capital gains tax on $75,000 only.

9. Which of the following plans is nonfunded?

    a. Keogh

    b. TSA

    c. TDA

    d. Deferred compensation plan

Brokerage Office Procedure

INTRODUCTION

Guidelines for the practices that a brokerage firm uses to conduct the operation of its daily business are regulated by industry, state, and federal regulators. These guidelines are the foundation for the way that the firm does everything from hiring a new agent to executing a customer's order. All Series 7 candidates must have a full understanding of a brokerage firm's operations and procedures to successfully complete the exam.

EXECUTING AN ORDER

In Chapter 1, we outlined the important dates relating to a regular-way transaction for equities. An important part of executing a customer's order lies in the operational procedures that route the order to the markets and handle trade input functions for the order once it has been executed. The brokerage firm assigns specific departments to handle all of the important functions of trade execution and input. The departments are:

- Order room/wire room
- Purchase and sales department
- Margin department
- Cashiering department

ORDER ROOM/WIRE ROOM

Once a representative has received an order from a client, the representative must present the order for execution to the order room. The order room will promptly route the order to the appropriate market for execution. Once the order has been executed, the order room will forward a confirmation of the execution to the registered representative and to the purchase and sales department.

PURCHASE AND SALES DEPARTMENT

Once the order has been executed, the purchase and sales department inputs the transaction into the customer's account. The purchase and sales department, sometimes called "P&S," is also responsible for mailing confirmations to the customer and for all billing.

MARGIN DEPARTMENT

All transactions, regardless of the type of account, are sent through the margin department. The margin or credit department calculates the amount of money owed by the customer and the date when the money is due. The margin department will also calculate any amount due to a customer.

CASHIERING DEPARTMENT

The cashiering department handles all receipts and distributions of cash and securities. All securities and payments delivered to the firm from clients are processed by the cashiering department. The cashiering department will also issue checks to customers and, at the request of the margin department, will forward certificates to the transfer agent.

REORGANIZATION DEPARTMENT

A firm's reorganization department handles matters relating to mergers and acquisitions and other reclassification of an issuer's outstanding securities. Other matters handled by the reorganization department would include:

- Bond calls
- Preferred stock calls
- Tender offers
- Exchanges

CUSTOMER CONFIRMATIONS

All customers must be sent a confirmation at or before the completion of the transaction. Industry rules consider the completion of the transaction to be the settlement date. It is unlawful to settle a transaction without having sent a customer a confirmation of the transaction. If applicable, all customer confirmations must include:

- Customer's name and account number.
- Account executive number.
- Description of the transaction (i.e., buy or sell).
- Trade date and settlement date.
- Number of shares, bonds, or units.
- Price.
- Yield to the worst for bonds.
- CUSIP number.
- Amount due or owed.
- Type of account (i.e., cash or margin).
- Option specifics (open, closing, covered, uncovered).
- Location of securities sold.
- Price limits.
- Whether the firm acted as an agent or a principal.
- Whether the firm acted as an agent for the other side of the transaction (i.e., dual agency).
- Amount of commission or markup or markdown.
- Whether the firm makes a market in the security.
- Whether there is a control relationship between the firm and the issuer of the security.
- Information regarding where the transaction was executed.
- Whether the firm received payment for executing the order with another firm.
- The time of execution or a statement that the time will be furnished upon request.
- Settlement instructions.

CLEARLY ERRONEOUS REPORTS

If a registered representative reports the execution of a trade to a customer and that report is clearly an error, then that report is not binding on the agent or the firm. The customer must accept the trade as it actually occurred, not as it was erroneously reported, so long as the transaction was inline with the terms of the customer's order.

EXECUTION ERRORS

If a transaction is executed away from a customer's limit price or for too many shares of stock, the customer is not obligated to accept the transaction. A registered representative who is informed of an execution error should immediately inform the principal of the error.

CORPORATE AND MUNICIPAL SECURITIES SETTLEMENT OPTIONS

Regular-way transactions in corporate stocks and bonds and municipal bonds settle on the third business day, or T + 3. There are, however, times when either party to the transaction may request an alternative settlement. Other settlement options include:

- Cash
- Next day
- Seller's option
- Buyer's option
- RVP/DVP/COD

Cash: A transaction done on a cash basis settles the same day. A cash trade requires that the buyer have the funds available for payment and the seller have the securities available for delivery on the day the trade is executed. Cash trades executed prior to 2:00 p.m. settle by 2:30 p.m. Trades executed after 2:00 p.m. settle within 30 minutes.

Next day: A transaction executed for a next-day settlement requires that the buyer have the cash available for payment and the seller have the securities available for delivery on the next business day.

Seller's option: A seller who wishes to lock in a sale price for the securities but who, for some reason, is not able to deliver the securities may elect to specify a seller's option settlement. The seller may specify the date on which the securities will be delivered, but the securities may not be delivered any sooner than the fourth business day. If the seller wants to deliver the securities earlier than specified in the contract, the seller must give the buyer one-day written notice of the intention to settle the trade early.

Buyer's option: A buyer may specify the date when payment for the securities will be made and the securities will be delivered, much the same as a seller's option.

RVP/DVP/COD

Many trusts and other fiduciaries will not allow cash to be paid out until the securities they purchased are delivered. Alternatively, in the case of a sell, they will not allow the securities to be delivered until payment is received. A bona fide RVP/DVP account will allow the transaction to purchase to settle no sooner than regular way of T + 3 but no later than 35 calendar days. The account is given up to 35 days to settle the transaction. In the case of a purchase, the securities have to be registered in the buyer's name by the transfer agent and delivered. When an RYP/DVP account sells securities it has 3 business days to deliver the securities. The account owner must assure the brokerage firm that the bank will make payment for the securities at the time they are presented to the bank for payment.

WHEN-ISSUED SECURITIES

When a corporate issuer declares a stock split, the stock will trade in the marketplace on a when-issued basis prior to the distribution of the new shares. Sellers of the stock during this time may sell the stock on a when-issued basis or they may deliver the old securities with a due bill attached for the new shares. Corporate securities sold on a when-issued basis will normally settle three business days after the securities are issued. Municipal securities that are sold prior to the certificate being available for delivery are sold on a when-issued basis. The purchaser will receive a when-issued confirmation and a final confirmation three days prior to the certificate's delivery.

GOVERNMENT SECURITIES SETTLEMENT OPTIONS

Regular-way transactions in government securities settle on the next business day, or T + 1. There are, however, times when either party to the transaction may request an alternative settlement. Other settlement options include:

- Cash
- Next day
- Seller's option
- Buyer's option
- RVP/DVP/COD

The settlement options available to investors in government securities are similar to those for corporate and municipal securities. However, government securities that are traded on a when-issued basis settle the day after the securities are available for delivery.

ACCRUED INTEREST

Most bonds pay interest semiannually, based on their maturity date. An investor who wishes to sell a bond between the interest payment dates will be owed the interest that has become due or that has accrued during the holding period. Investors who purchase the bonds between interest payment dates will receive the full semiannual interest payment on the bond's next interest payment date. As a result, the purchaser of the bonds must pay the seller the portion of the interest payment that the seller earned, known as accrued interest. Most bonds trade with accrued interest, also known as "and interest."

There are only two dates during the month that a bond may pay interest; they are the 1st and the 15th of the month. Interest on a new issue of bonds begins to accrue on the dated date. It is not unusual for an investor who purchases a new issue of debt securities to owe accrued interest to the issuer for bonds that are delivered after the dated date.

Semiannual interest payments may be made on the 1st or 15th of the following months:

January and July
February and August
March and September
April and October
May and November
June and December

TAKENOTE!

Zero coupon bonds and bonds that are in default do not trade with accrued interest and are said to be trading "flat."

CALCULATING ACCRUED INTEREST

Interest on all bonds accrues from the last interest payment date up to, but not including, the settlement date. Accrued interest calculations for corporate and municipal securities use a 360-day year in which all months contain 30 days. To determine the amount of accrued interest due or owed, use the following formula:

principal × rate × time

(principal × interest rate) × (number of days/360) = accrued interest

EXAMPLE

An investor purchases 10M XYZ J & J 8% corporate bond on Monday April 1st for regular-way settlement. How much accrued interest will the investor owe?

(10,000 × 8%) × (93/360)

= 800 × .2583 = $206.67

To determine the number of days in the above calculation, we used the 30-day month as follows:

January	30 days
February	30 days
March	30 days
April	3 days
Total	**93 days**

Note: Interest accrues up to, but not including, the settlement date. The trade was done on Monday April 1st, so interest accrued up to Wednesday April 3rd. On Thursday April 4th the trade will settle and the buyer will begin earning the interest. If the trade had been executed on Friday April 1st, the calculation would look like this:

(10,000 × 8%) × (95/360)

= 800 × .2634 = $211.11

Interest continues to accrue on weekends even though weekends are not good settlement dates.

January	30 days
February	30 days
March	30 days
April	5 days
Total	**95 days**

ACCRUED INTEREST FOR GOVERNMENT NOTES AND BONDS

The calculation for accrued interest on U.S. government securities uses an actual calendar year, and each month contains the actual number of days. Keep in mind that interest accrues up to, but not including, the settlement date, and, because U.S. government securities settle on the next business day, interest accrues only up to the trade date.

EXAMPLE   An investor purchases 10M 8% U.S. Treasury bonds due January 1, 2030, on Monday April 1st for regular-way settlement. How much accrued interest will the investor owe?

$(10{,}000 \times 8\%) \times (91/365)$

$= 800 \times .2493 = \$199.44$

To determine the number of days in the above calculation, we used the actual calendar days in each month as follows:

January	31 days
February	28 days
March	31 days
April	1 day
Total	**91 days**

If the trade had been executed on Friday April 1st, the calculation would look like this:

$(10{,}000 \times 8\%) \times (93/365)$

$= 800 \times .2547 = \$203.83$

Interest continues to accrue on weekends even though weekends are not good settlement dates.

January	30 days
February	30 days
March	30 days
April	3 days
Total	**93 days**

RULES FOR GOOD DELIVERY

All securities delivered by a customer or another broker dealer must be in good condition and must:

- Be signed by all owners, and all owners must be alive.
- Be in the correct denominations (i.e., number of shares or par value of bonds).
- Have all attachments.
- Be accompanied by a uniform delivery ticket.

The owner of a security must endorse the certificate at the time of sale to ensure its negotiability or may sign a stock or bond power, also known as a power of substitution.

The stock power, when attached to the certificate, will make it negotiable and includes an irrevocable power of attorney. All signatures must be accepted by the transfer agent. To ensure that the transfer agent accepts the signatures on certificates delivered by NYSE member firms, the NYSE started the Medallion Signature Guarantee Program, which allows NYSE members to stamp the certificates with a medallion rather than sign them. This stamp ensures that the transfer agent will accept the certificates for transfer and provides indemnification insurance for fraud. The Medallion Program members pay a fee to participate in this program.

Examples of invalid signatures are:

- The signature of a minor
- The signature of a deceased person

- The signature of only one owner if jointly registered
- A forged signature

DELIVERY OF ROUND LOTS

Stock certificates must be delivered in denominations that are in round lots or in lots that easily add up to create round lots. Stock certificates for odd lots are cleared separately.

EXAMPLE	A customer sells 200 shares of XYZ. The following certificates are considered good delivery:

- One certificate for 200 shares
- Two certificates for 100 shares
- Two certificates for 60 shares and two certificates for 40 shares
- Twenty certificates for 10 shares

The following is not good delivery:

- Five certificates for 40 shares
- One certificate for 130 shares

Certificates that cannot be easily added up to 100 shares are not good delivery. If the selling broker dealer delivers a certificate for a portion of the trade and the remaining shares will add up to one round lot or multiples of round lots, then the buying broker dealer must accept the partial delivery.

DELIVERY OF BOND CERTIFICATES

Bond certificates delivered between broker dealers must be in par values of $1,000 or $5,000 and must be in bearer form unless clearly identified as otherwise at the time of the trade. Partially called bonds are not considered to be good delivery between broker dealers. However, bonds subject to a total call are good delivery. If a bond is delivered with a coupon missing, the buying broker dealer will deduct the value of the coupon payment from the amount delivered to the seller. Municipal bonds delivered without the legal opinion attached must be identified as being traded ex legal in order to be considered good delivery. In order for a bond in default to be considered to be good delivery all unpaid coupons must be attached including the coupons for the payments that were missed and are now past due.

REJECTION OF DELIVERY

The buying firm may reject the delivery of securities from the selling member if:

- The certificates are mutilated.
- The certificates are not in the proper denominations.
- All attachments are not present.
- The signatures are invalid.
- The signatures have not been guaranteed.
- The securities are delivered prior to settlement.

DON'T KNOW (DK) PROCEDURES

When one broker dealer confirms a trade with another broker dealer, the party receiving the confirmation must confirm the trade within four business days. After four business days have expired, the confirming party may demand a confirmation or that the receiving party don't know (DK) the trade. If the party does not know the trade, no settlement can occur, and the confirming party is not obligated to the terms of the transaction.

FAIL TO DELIVER/FAIL TO RECEIVE

A fail to deliver occurs when the sell-side broker dealer does not deliver the securities to the buying broker dealer on or before settlement. The broker dealer on the buy side has a fail to receive and may buy in the securities and charge the seller for any loss.

DUE BILLS

Should the wrong party receive a dividend or any other type of distribution, the buying broker dealer whose customer is owed the dividend will send a "due bill" to the selling broker for the amount of the dividend owed. In most cases, this would happen when the buyer purchased the stock just prior to the ex date and the security was delivered late to the buyer.

CUSTOMER ACCOUNT STATEMENTS

All customers must receive account statements at least quarterly when there has been no activity in the account. A customer must receive a statement every month that there is activity in the account. Examples of activity include:

- Purchases and sales
- Dividend and interest received
- Addition or withdraw of cash or securities
- Margin interest charged to the account

Customer account statements must show:

- All positions in the account
- All activity since the last statement
- All credit and debit balances

Brokerage firms that hold customer assets are required to disclose their financial condition to their clients by sending them a balance sheet every six months or upon the request of a customer with cash or securities on deposit with the firm. Special account statement requirements are in place for accounts of customers who hold unlisted penny stocks. These customers must receive a statement every month during the time the account contains penny stocks.

CARRYING OF CUSTOMER ACCOUNTS

Not all brokerage firms maintain the physical possession of the customers' cash and securities. A brokerage firm that maintains the account of its customers and holds their cash and securities is known as a carrying firm or as a self-clearing member. A broker dealer may find it easier to have another member provide the clearing and custodial functions for its customers' accounts. This type of broker dealer is known as an introducing broker dealer. The introducing member forwards all cash and securities to the carrying or clearing member for deposit into the customers' accounts. The clearing firm sends the customers' statements and confirmations to the introducing firm's customers. An introducing member may also choose to clear its trades through an omnibus account maintained at the clearing firm. In this case, all transactions are cleared though one account and the clearing member does not know for whom the trade was executed. The introducing member is required to send customer confirmations if they clear through an omnibus account. Omnibus accounts are not allowed to purchase securities on margin for customers. All securities must be paid for in full.

 TAKENOTE!

It is fair and reasonable for a brokerage firm to charge a fee for the collection of dividends and other services, as long as the fee is not excessive and is in line with the fees charged by similar firms.

PROXIES

Common stockholders have the right to vote on major corporate issues. Most stockholders, however, do not have the time to attend the meetings and must therefore vote using an absentee ballot, known as a proxy. The Securities Exchange Act of 1934 requires that all corporations that distribute proxies solicit votes from their shareholders. Proxies are sent out by the corporation to the shareholders of record. Stockholders, who have their securities held in street name, will have the proxies forwarded to them by the brokerage firm. The brokerage firm will then cast the beneficial shareholder's votes as indicated on the proxy as the shareholder of record. Proxies, which have been signed and returned without indicating how to vote, must be voted in accordance with the issuer's management's recommendation. If a shareholder fails to return the proxy to the member at least 10 days prior to the annual meeting, the member may vote the shares as it sees fit so long as the matter is not of major importance. If the vote concerns a major issue, such as a merger, the member may never cast the votes as it chooses. Member firms are required to forward proxies and other corporate communications, such as annual and quarterly reports, to the beneficial owner, and the issuer is required to reimburse the member for reasonable expenses.

Pretest

BROKERAGE OFFICE PROCEDURE

1. Which of the following is NOT required on an order ticket presented for execution?
   a. Commission
   b. Registered representative's number
   c. Customer's name
   d. Customer's account number

2. Which of the following is true regarding an investor who has failed to pay for a trade by the expiration of the fifth business day?
   a. He is responsible for any loss as a result of the sell out.
   b. The brokerage firm will sell out and freeze his account on the sixth business day after the trade date.
   c. They must deposit any money for stock purchases up front for the next 90 days as a result of the freeze.
   d. All of the above.

3. A firm's reorganization department would handle all of the following, EXCEPT:
   a. arbitrage.
   b. bond calls.
   c. redemption of preferred stock.
   d. tender offers.

4. Your customer has been unexpectedly called out of town prior to paying for his recent purchase. He will be gone for five days and needs more time to pay for the trade. An extension may be obtained:

    a. automatically, because he is acting in good faith.

    b. by requesting an extension from the firm's principal.

    c. by requesting an extension in writing from FINRA/NYSE.

    d. under no circumstances. The trade must be paid for by payment date as stipulated by Reg. T.

5. An investor who wishes to transfer 1,000 shares of common stock registered in his name may sign which of the following instead of the stock certificate?

    a. Title transfer

    b. Stock or bond power

    c. Letter of authorization

    d. Bill of sale

6. An investor has failed to pay for a security by the expiration of the fifth business day. Which of the following are true?

    I. She may keep any gain in the account as a result of the trade.

    II. She is responsible for any loss as a result of the trade.

    III. The account will not be allowed to transact business the regular way for 90 days.

    IV. She may write a letter to FINRA requesting an extension of time to pay.

    a. I and II

    b. III and IV

    c. I, II, and III

    d. I, II, III, and IV

7. A customer who purchased 1,000 shares of XYZ on margin two months ago and has not executed any order since:

    a. must receive a statement this month.

    b. need not receive a statement this month.

    c. must have received a statement for the last two months only.

    d. must have received a statement for the last two months and must receive one this month as well.

8. As it relates to securities held in street name, which of the following are true?

   I. The corporation will send proxies to the broker dealer.

   II. The corporation will not reimburse the broker dealer for forwarding the proxies.

   III. The broker dealer may vote blank proxies any way it wishes.

   IV. A shareholder who attends the annual meeting will have his proxies voided.

   a. I and III

   b. I and II

   c. I and IV

   d. II and IV

9. Your customer has a stock certificate registered in his name that is being held by your firm for safekeeping. He wishes to sell the stock but cannot make it to your office to sign the certificate. Which of the following may he do to transfer the ownership of the security?

   a. Send a letter of sale.

   b. Send a letter of authorization.

   c. Send a signed stock power.

   d. Send a letter of execution.

10. All of the following are reasons to reject delivery, EXCEPT:

    a. the signatures are not guaranteed.

    b. the customer has determined that the investment is unsuitable.

    c. the certificate is unclear.

    d. a bond is missing a coupon.

11. A customer who cannot deposit the Regulation T requirement by the fifth business day may:

    I. have a forced liquidation.

    II. apply for an extension.

    III. have a call for less than $1,000 waived.

    IV. be charged a fee for an extension.

    a. III and IV

    b. I and III

    c. I, II, and IV

    d. I, II, III, and IV

12. ABC declares a $.12 dividend to shareholders of record as of Tuesday January 15th. The stock will go ex dividend on:

    a. Sunday January 13th.

    b. Thursday January 10th.

    c. Friday January 11th.

    d. Saturday January 12th.

13. An investor buys 100M U.S. Treasury bonds on Tuesday April 10th. The investor will be an owner of record on:

    a. Friday April 13th.

    b. Wednesday April 11th.

    c. Thursday April 12th.

    d. Tuesday April 17th.

14. A brokerage firm may charge a fee for which of the following:

    I. The safekeeping of securities

    II. The collection of dividends

    III. Lack of activity in the account

    IV. The clipping of coupons

    a. III and IV

    b. I and IV

    c. I and II

    d. I, II, III, and IV

15. Which of the following may guarantee a customer's signature?

    I. Notary

    II. Court officer

    III. Exchange member

    IV. Bank officer

    a. II and III

    b. I and IV

    c. III and IV

    d. I and III

16. A security has been delivered late to the buying member after the record date for a dividend distribution. Which of the following are true?

    I. The seller will keep the dividend.

    II. The buyer will be owed the dividend.

    III. The buying member will send a due bill.

    IV. The selling member will receive the dividend.

    a. II and III

    b. II, III, and IV

    c. I only

    d. I and II

17. Which of the following sends out customer confirmations?

    a. Margin department

    b. Cashiering department

    c. Order department

    d. P&S department

18. Your customer is trying to obtain a distribution of stock being done by ABC. She calls you and asks that you buy 500 shares of ABC at the market on a cash basis. Which of the following is true?

    a. This would be an example of selling dividends and is a violation.

    b. Because this trade is being done for cash, the trade will settle the same day and the buyer must have the cash available in her account.

    c. The customer would have five business days to pay for the trade once the order is executed.

    d. This is not permitted; brokerage firms may not accept cash.

19. Which of the following is true?

    a. The representative's internal AE # need not appear on confirmations.

    b. The customer's confirmation only needs to display the settlement date.

    c. A broker dealer may charge an additional fee to customers who buy and sell odd lots.

    d. The CUSIP # need not appear on confirmations.

Fundamental and Technical Analysis

INTRODUCTION

Fundamental analysis and technical analysis are the two methods that an investor may use to analyze a potential equity investment. Fundamental analysis is concerned with the financial performance of the company. A fundamental analyst will investigate the company's financial picture to determine if an investment should be made. Technical analysis uses the past price performance of the stock to predict the stock's future price performance. A technical analyst is not concerned with the company's finances. The technical analysis is only concerned with the price patterns of the stock.

FUNDAMENTAL ANALYSIS

Fundamental analysts examine the company's financial statements and financial ratios to ascertain the company's overall financial performance. The fundamental analyst will use the following to determine a value for the company's stock:

- The balance sheet
- The income statement
- Financial ratios
- Liquidity ratios
- Valuation ratios

THE BALANCE SHEET

The balance sheet will show an investor everything that the corporation owns, or its assets, and everything that the corporation owes, or its liabilities, at the time the balance sheet was prepared. A balance sheet is a snapshot of the company's financial health on the day the balance sheet was created. The difference between the company's assets and its liabilities is its net worth. The corporation's net worth is the shareholders' equity. Remember that the shareholders own the corporation. The basic balance sheet equation is:

assets – liabilities = net worth

The balance sheet equation may also be presented as follows:

assets = liabilities + shareholder's equity

The two columns on the balance sheet contain the company's assets on the left and its liabilities and shareholder's equity on the right. The total dollar amount of both sides must be equal, that is, balance. The entries on a balance sheet look as follows:

Assets		Liabilities
Current assets		Current liabilities
Fixed assets		Long-term liabilities
Other assets		Equity/net worth
		Preferred stock par value
		Common stock par value
		Additional paid in surplus
		Treasury stock
		Retained earnings

The assets are listed in order of liquidity. Current assets include cash and assets that can be converted into cash within 12 months. Current assets include:

- Money market instruments
- Marketable securities
- Accounts receivable net of any delinquent accounts
- Inventory, including work in progress
- Prepaid expenses

Fixed assets are assets that have a long useful life and are used by the company in the operation of its business. Fixed assets include:

- Plant and equipment
- Property and real estate

Other assets are intangible assets that belong to the company. Other assets include:

- Goodwill
- Trademarks
- Patents
- Contract rights

The liabilities of the corporation are listed in the order in which they become due. Current liabilities are obligations that must be paid within 12 months. Current liabilities include:

- Wages payable, including salaries and commissions owed to employees.
- Accounts payable to vendors and suppliers.
- Current portion of long-term debt; that is, any portion of the company's long-term debt due within 12 months.
- Taxes due within 12 months.
- Short-term notes due within 12 months.

Long-term liabilities are debts that will become due after 12 months. Long-term liabilities include:

- Bonds
- Mortgages
- Notes

 TAKENOTE!

The corporation's debt that comes due in five years or more is known as funded debt.

Stockholders' equity is the net worth of the company. Stockholders' equity is broken up into the following categories:

- Capital stock at par: The aggregate par for both common and preferred stock.
- Additional paid in surplus: Any sum paid over par by investors when the shares were issued by the company.
- Retained earnings: Profits that have been kept by the corporation, sometimes called earned surplus.

	Balance Sheet ABC MILLS, Inc. As of December 31	
Assets		
Current Assets	Cash and Equivalents	$ 6,000,000
	Accounts Receivable	$ 12,000,000
	Inventory	$ 20,000,000
	Prepaid Expenses	$ 500,000
	Total Current Assets	**$ 38,500,000**
Fixed Assets	Buildings, Furniture & Fixtures (Including $5,000,000 Depreciation)	$ 50,000,000
	Land	$ 20,000,000
	Total Fixed Assets	**$ 70,000,000**
Other Assets (Goodwill, Intangibles)		$ 2,000,000
Total Assets		**$ 110,500,000**
Liabilities and Net Worth		
Current Liabilities	Accounts Payable	$ 3,000,000
	Accrued Wages Payable Current	$ 1,500,000
	Portion of Long-Term Debt	$ 1,500,000
	Total Current Liabilities	**$ 6,000,000**
Long-Term Liabilities	7% 30-Year Convertible Debentures	$ 40,000,000
Total Liabilities		**$ 46,000,000**
Net Worth	Preferred Stock $100 Par 7% Convertible noncumulative 250,000 shares issued	$ 25,000,000
	Common Stock $1 par 2,000,000 Shares Issued	$ 2,000,000
	Capital Paid in Excess of Par	$ 22,000,000
	Retained Earnings	$ 15,500,000
Total Net Worth		**$ 64,500,000**
Total Liabilities and Net Worth		**$ 110,500,000**

CAPITALIZATION

The term *capitalization* refers to the sources and makeup of the company's financial picture. The following are used to determine the company's capitalization:

- Long-term debt.
- Equity accounts, including par value of common and preferred and paid in and earned surplus.

A company that borrows a large portion of its capital through the issuance of bonds is said to be highly leveraged. Raising money through the sale of common stock is considered to be a more conservative method for a corporation to raise money because it does not require the corporation to pay the money back. When a company borrows funds, it is trying to use that borrowed capital to increase its return on equity.

CHANGES IN THE BALANCE SHEET

As a business conducts its operations, its daily transactions will affect the balance sheet. Every transaction requires an offsetting transaction to the appropriate account. This is known as double-entry bookkeeping. For example, if ABC Mills wrote a check to a large vendor for $1,000,000, the company's cash would be reduced by $1,000,000 and the company's accounts payable would be reduced by $1,000,000. Transactions that affect the balance sheet include:

- Purchasing equipment for cash
- Depreciation
- Issuing securities
- Declaring a dividend
- Conversion of convertible securities
- Bond redemption
- Stock splits

Purchasing equipment for cash: If the company purchases a piece of industrial equipment for cash, its long-term assets will increase and its cash and current assets will be decreased by the amount of the purchase.

Depreciation: Allows companies to amortize the cost of capital goods over their estimated useful life. As fixed assets wear out, their value declines. Companies may reduce the value of their assets through depreciation and may use the amount of the depreciation to offset taxes owed. Depreciation is a noncash charge that lowers a company's tax liability. Depending on the type of asset involved, depreciation may be taken as either straight line depreciation or as accelerated depreciation. Straight line deprecation is taken in equal amounts over the estimated useful life of the asset. A piece of heavy equipment costing $10,000,000 with a useful life of 10 years would be depreciated at $1,000,000 per year for 10 years. Accelerated depreciation depreciates most of the value of the asset in the first few years of useful life and by lesser amounts during the remaining years. Depreciation impacts both the income statement and balance sheet of a corporation. A company's taxable income is reduced by the amount of the depreciation taken in the current period and accumulated depreciation reduces the value of the asset on the company's balance sheet.

Issuing securities: If the company were to issue additional shares of $1 par common stock, the net worth of the company would increase by the amount of the par value sold, plus any paid in surplus. As a result of the issuance of the securities, the corporation's cash position would also be increased by the net proceeds of the offering.

Declaring a dividend: When a cash dividend is declared, the corporation's retained earnings are reduced by the amount of the dividend and the company's current liabilities are increased by the amount of the dividend payable. Once the dividend is paid, the company's cash and current assets are reduced by the amount of the dividend paid. The payment of the dividend also eliminates the current liability that resulted from the declaration of the dividend.

Conversion of convertible securities: If the holder of a convertible bond converts the bonds into common stock, the par value of the bonds will be eliminated as a long-term liability, and the par value will be credited to the equity account on the balance sheet.

Bond redemption: Bonds are redeemed at maturity. If the corporation uses cash to pay off the principal amount of the bonds, then the long-term liabilities and the cash and current assets of the corporation will be reduced by an equal amount.

Stock splits: A forward stock split will increase the number of shares outstanding and reduce the par value of the shares. A reverse stock split will reduce the number of outstanding shares and increase the par value. Shareholders' equity is not affected as a result of a stock split.

A fundamental analyst may look at the balance sheet to determine the following financial information:

- Net worth
- Working capital
- Current ratio
- Quick assets

- Acid-test ratio/quick ratio
- Cash assets ratio
- Debt-to-equity ratio
- Common stock ratio
- Preferred stock ratio
- Bond ratio

Measure	Formula	Purpose
Book value per share	assets – liabilities – intangibles – par value of preferred/# of outstanding common shares	To determine the value of the company's common stock
Working capital	current assets – current liabilities	To determine the company's liquidity
Current ratio	current assets/current liabilities	A relationship between current assets and liabilities
Quick assets	current assets – inventory	To determine highly liquid assets
Acid test/quick ratio	quick assets/current liabilities	To determine the company's liquidity
Cash assets ratio	cash & equivalents/current liabilities	The most stringent liquidity measure
Debt-to-equity ratio	total long-term debt/total shareholders' equity	To examine the company's capital structure
Common stock ratio	common shareholders' equity/total capitalization	To examine the company's capital structure
Preferred stock ratio	preferred stock/total capitalization	To examine the company's capital structure
Bond ratio	total long-term debt/total capitalization	To examine the company's capital structure

THE INCOME STATEMENT

The income statement details a corporation's revenue and expenses for the period for which it was produced. Income statements are usually prepared on a quarterly and an annual basis. A fundamental analyst will use the income statement to determine a corporation's profitability. The three levels of earnings listed on the income statement are:

1. Operating income
2. Net income after taxes
3. Earnings available to common

Operating income: The business's profit or loss from operations; also known as earnings before interest and taxes (EBIT).

Net income after taxes: The corporation's earnings after all federal and state taxes have been paid. Dividends to shareholders will be paid from net income after taxes.

Earnings available to common: What is left from the corporation's net income after taxes, after the corporation has paid preferred dividends. If the corporation wants to pay a dividend to common shareholders, the preferred dividends must have already been paid.

Income Statement
ABC Mills, Inc.
January 1–December 31

Net Sales		$ 100,000,000
	Cost of Goods Sold	$ 45,000,000
	General Operating Expenses (Including $5,000,000 Depreciation)	$ 32,000,000
		$ 77,000,000
Operating Income		$ 23,000,000
	Interest Expense	$ 2,800,000
Pretax Income		$ 20,200,000
	Taxes at 36%	$ 7,272,000
Net Income After Taxes		$ 12,928,000
	Preferred Dividends	$ 1,750,000
Earnings Available to Common		$ 11,178,000

By combining the information contained in the balance sheet and the income statement an analyst can determine:

- Earnings per share primary
- Earnings per share fully diluted
- Price-earnings ratio
- Dividend payout ratio
- Debt service ratio

Earnings per share primary: Tells the analyst how much of the company's earnings are credited to each common share.

Earnings per share fully diluted: Tells the analyst how much of the company's earnings are credited to each common share after all convertible securities and all rights and warrants have been exchanged for common stock.

Price-earnings ratio: Tells the analyst the relationship between the earnings per share and the common stock price.

Dividend payout ratio: Tells the analyst how much of the earnings per share were paid out to shareholders as dividends.

Debt service ratio: Tells the analyst the ability of the company to meet its debt service obligations.

Measure	Formula	Purpose
Earnings per share primary	earnings available to common/# of common shares	To determine the amount of the company's earnings for each share outstanding
Earnings per share fully diluted	earnings available to common/# of common shares	To determine the amount of the company's earnings for each share outstanding after all conversions
Price-earnings ratio	stock price/earnings per share	To determine a relationship between the stock price and the earnings per share
Dividend payout ratio	annual dividends per common share/earnings per share	To determine how much of the company's earnings per share are paid out in dividends
Debt service ratio	EBIT/annual interest and principal payments	To determine the company's ability to meet its debt service needs

 TAKENOTE!

Most balance sheets and income statements will include footnotes which give additional details regarding the items contained in the reports. These footnotes will detail the impact potential events may have on the financial information contained in the statements as well as any assumptions or calculations used to arrive at the information.

INDUSTRY FUNDAMENTALS

Fundamental economic factors affect different industries. Analysts must be able to determine how susceptible the company's earnings are to a change in the economy. There are three industry categories. They are:

1. Growth industries
2. Cyclical industries
3. Defensive industries

Growth industries: The earnings of companies in a growth industry will grow faster than the overall growth of the economy as whole. Growth industries include computers and technology.

Cyclical industries: The earnings of a company in a cyclical industry are highly susceptible to the condition of the overall economy. As the economy improves, the company will do well. If the economy does poorly, the company will perform poorly. Cyclical industries include manufacturing, raw materials, and automobiles.

Defensive industries: The earnings of a company in a defensive industry will be the least susceptible to the changes in the overall economy. Defensive industries include food and pharmaceuticals. These are things that people will buy no matter how the economy is performing. It is important to note that a manufacturer of military equipment is not considered to be in a defensive industry.

TOP DOWN AND BOTTOM UP ANALYSIS

Rather than simply zeroing in on the financial picture of a given company many analysts will include an evaluation of the industry or sector and the economy as a whole to further validate their research. An analyst who employs a top down approach would look at how the economy as a whole is performing and identify industries that will perform the best in the current and predicted economic climate. Once the industry is identified the analyst will try to identify the best performing company within that industry as a potential candidate for investment. Conversely an analyst who employs a bottom up approach would start their research with the company and expand it to the industry or sector and then finally to the economy as a whole to evaluate an investment opportunity.

TECHNICAL ANALYSIS

A technical analyst uses the patterns created by the past price performance of the stock to predict the direction of the stock price in the future. A technical analyst is not concerned with the fundamentals of the company or even what business the company is in. The technical analyst is only interpreting chart patterns and other technical factors relating to the price performance of the stock. Some of the chart patterns that a technical analyst will look to identify are:

- Support
- Resistance
- Trendlines
- Reversals
- Consolidations

Support: Support is created at the point to which the stock falls and attracts buyers. The new buyers that are brought into the market, because of the lower price, create demand for the stock and prevent it from falling any further.

Resistance: Resistance is created at the point to which the stock appreciates and attracts sellers. The new sellers that are brought into the market, because of the higher price, create supply for the stock and prevent it from rising any further.

Upward trendlines: An upward trendline is characterized by a series of higher highs and a series of higher lows. A chartist would draw a line connecting the series of higher lows to confirm the trend, and the trendline should provide some support to the stock price.

Downward trendlines: A downward trendline is characterized by a series of lower highs and a series of lower lows. A chartist would draw a line connecting the series of lower highs to confirm the downward trend, and the trendline should provide some resistance to the stock price.

Reversals: A reversal indicates a significant change in the price action of the stock. A bullish reversal indicates the end of a downward trend and the beginning of a new upward trend. A bearish reversal indicates the end of an upward trend and the beginning of a new downward trend. One of the most significant reversal patterns is the head-and-shoulders formation. A head-and-shoulders top is a bearish reversal of an uptrend, whereas a head-and-shoulders bottom is a bullish reversal of a downtrend.

Consolidation: A consolidation pattern is characterized by a horizontal movement in the stock price. Buyers and sellers are attracted to the market and are willing to trade the stock at almost the same prices.

The following illustrate the chart patterns outlined previously:

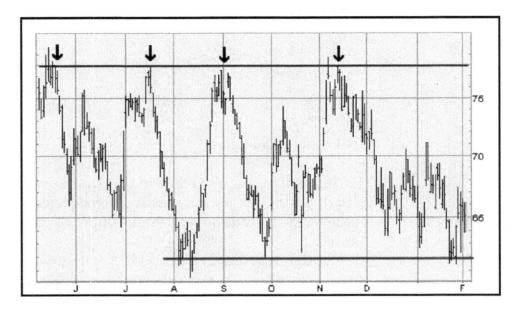

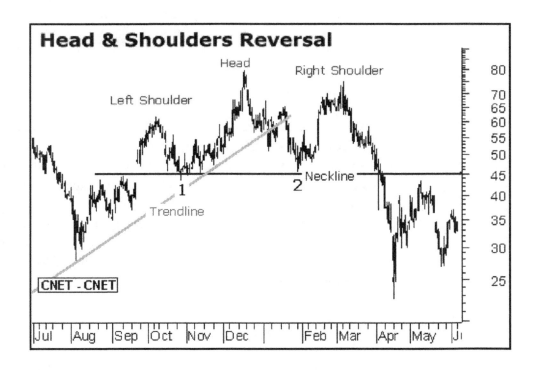

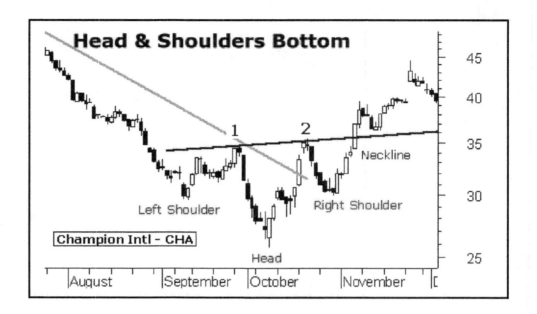

MARKET THEORIES AND INDICATORS

A technical analyst will look at various indicators to interpret the overall market's direction. These indicators include:

- Short interest
- Odd lot trading
- Advance decline line

Short interest: Investors who have sold stock short are betting that the stock price falls. In order to close out their position, they must repurchase the stock. All investors who have sold stock short must eventually repurchase the stock. Because all of the short sellers are potential buyers for the stock, a high short interest is considered a bullish indicator.

   Odd lot trading: The odd lot trading theory believes that smaller investors, who cannot afford to buy or sell one round lot of stock, will invariably buy and sell at the wrong time. A high level of odd lot purchases is indicative of a market top. A high level of odd lot sales is indicative of a market bottom.

 TAKENOTE!

Both the short interest theory and the odd lot trading theory are contrarian indicators.

Advance decline line: The advance decline line indicates the breadth of the market. The market's breadth is a good indicator of the overall health of the market and can be used to confirm or reject a trend. The advance decline line will tell an investor how many stocks are trading higher in price and how many are trading lower in price.

A technical analyst will always look for volume confirmation of any trend. A trend is confirmed by high levels of volume in the stock or in the market as a whole.

EFFICIENT MARKET THEORY

The efficient market theory believes that all of the available information is priced into the market at any given time and that it is impossible to beat the market by taking advantage of price or time inefficiencies. Proponents of the efficient market theory may follow the theory in the following ways:

Weak-form efficiency: States that the future price of a security cannot be predicted by studying the past price performance of the security. This form of the theory believes that technical analysis cannot produce excess returns.

Semistrong-form efficiency: States that the market price of a security adjusts too rapidly to newly available information to achieve an excess return by trading on that information.

Strong-form efficiency: States that the current price of a security reflects all information known and unknown to the public and that there is no opportunity to earn excess returns.

Pretest

FUNDAMENTAL AND TECHNICAL ANALYSIS

1. The financial officer of the XYZ must calculate the company's earnings per share. The company earned $2,000,000 after taxes and preferred dividends. The company has 3,000,000 shares issued stock, and 1,000,000 shares are treasury stock. What are XYZ's earnings per share?

   a. $1 per share

   b. 67 cents per share

   c. Unable to determine without more information

   d. 75 cents per share

2. What is the balance sheet equation?

   a. liabilities + assets = net worth

   b. liabilities − assets = net worth

   c. assets + liabilities = net worth

   d. assets − liabilities = net worth

3. XYZ has an EPS $2, a quarterly dividend of $.70, and is quoted in the marketplace at 20. What is XYZ's current yield?

   a. 10%

   b. 14%

   c. 3.5%

   d. 7%

4. Capitalization refers to:

    a. a corporation's assets.

    b. the company's net worth.

    c. the total amount of money invested in a company.

    d. the sources and makeup of the company's financial picture.

5. An investor who is taking a fundamental approach to investing would look all of the following, EXCEPT:

    a. the price-earnings ratio.

    b. support levels.

    c. EBIT.

    d. debt service.

6. A software company's stock has declined dramatically over the past year and has a high short interest. A technical analyst would consider this to be:

    a. bullish.

    b. bearish.

    c. an indication that the stock price will remain flat.

    d. of no value.

7. The risk that is inherent in any investment is called:

    a. credit risk.

    b. call risk.

    c. timing risk.

    d. systematic risk.

Direct Participation Programs

INTRODUCTION

Direct participation programs (DPPs) and limited partnerships (LPs) are entities that allow income, expenses, gains, losses, and tax benefits to be passed through to the investors. There is generally no active secondary market for these investments, so it's important that investors understand the risks and can afford the risks associated with DPPs and LPs. Series 7 candidates can expect to see several questions on this material on their exam.

LIMITED PARTNERSHIPS

A limited partnership is an entity that allows all of the economic events of the partnership to flow through to the partners. These economic events are:

- Income
- Gains
- Losses
- Tax credits
- Deductions

There are two types of partners in a limited partnership: limited partners and the general partners. The limited partners:

- Put up the investment capital.
- Losses are limited to their investment.
- Receive the benefits from the operation.
- May not exercise management over the operation.
- May vote to change the objective of the partnership.
- May vote to switch or remove the general partner.
- May sue the general partner, if the general partner does not act in the best interest of the partnership.

A limited partner may never exercise any management or control over the limited partnership. Doing so would jeopardize the partner's limited status such that he or she may be considered a general partner.

The general partner is the person or corporation that manages the business and has unlimited liability for the obligations of the partnership business. The general partner may also:

- Buy and sell property for the partnership.
- Receive compensation for managing the partnership.
- Enter into legally binding contracts for the partnership.

The general partner also must maintain a financial interest in the partnership of at least 1%. The general partner may not:

- Commingle funds of the general partner with the funds of the partnership.
- Compete against the partnership.
- Borrow from the partnership.

It is important to note that there are no tax consequences at the partnership level. In order to qualify for the preferential tax treatment, the DPP or LP must avoid at least two of the six characteristics of a corporation. These characteristics are:

- Continuity of life
- Profit motive

- Central management
- Limited liability
- Associates
- Freely transferable interest

Several of the characteristics cannot be avoided, such as associates and a profit motive. The hardest characteristic to avoid is centralized management in fact this cannot be avoided as someone must operate the partnership. The easiest two characteristics of a corporation to avoid are continuity of life and freely transferable interest. The LP can put a termination date on the partnership, and substitute limited partners may not be accepted or may only be accepted once the general partner has agreed.

STRUCTURING AND OFFERING LIMITED PARTNERSHIPS

The foundation of every limited partnership is the partnership agreement. All limited partners must be given a copy of the partnership agreement. The partnership agreement will spell out all of the terms and conditions, as well as the business purpose for the partnership. The powers and limitations of the general partner's authority will be one of the main points detailed in the partnership agreement. Prior to forming a limited partnership, the general partner will have to file a certificate of limited partnership in the state in which the partnership is formed. The certificate will include:

- Name and address of the partnership.
- A description of the partnership's business.
- The life of the partnership.
- Size of the limited partner's investments (if any).
- Conditions for assignment of interest by limited partners.
- Conditions for dissolving the partnership.
- Conditions for admitting new limited partners.
- The projected date for the return of capital, if one is set.

A material change to any of these conditions must be updated on the certificate within 30 days.

Most limited partnerships will be offered to investors through a private placement. All investors who purchase a limited partnership through a private placement must receive a private placement memorandum. Private placements, with very limited exceptions, may only be offered to accredited investors. However, a few limited partnerships will be offered to the public through a standard public offering. All investors who purchase a limited partnership though a public offering must receive a prospectus. If the partnership is sold through a syndicator, the syndicator is responsible for filing the partnership documents. The maximum fee that may be received by the syndicator is limited to 10% of the offering. If a secondary market develops for a partnership, the partnership will be known as a master limited partnership (MLP). All investors wishing to become a limited partner must complete the partnership's subscription agreement. The subscription agreement will include:

- A power of attorney appointing the general partner.
- A statement of the prospective limited partner's net worth.
- A statement regarding the prospective limited partner's income.
- A statement from the prospective limited partner that he or she understands and can afford the risks related to the partnership.

TYPES OF LIMITED PARTNERSHIPS

A limited partnership may be organized for any lawful purpose. Most commonly, limited partnerships are set up to:

- Invest in real estate.
- Invest in oil and gas wells.
- Engage in equipment leasing.

There are several types of real estate partnerships. They include:

- Existing property
- New construction
- Raw land
- Government-assisted housing
- Historic rehabilitation

Type of LP	Risk	Advantages	Disadvantages	Tax Benefits
Existing property (purchase income property)	Low	Immediate, predictable cash flow	Rental problems and repairs	Deductions for mortgage interest and depreciation
New construction (build units for appreciation or rental)	Higher	Potential capital gains, low maintenance	No deduction for current expenses and no promise of rental or sale	Deduction of expenses and depreciation only after completion
Raw land (purchase land for appreciation)	Highest	Only appreciation potential	No tax deductions or income	No tax benefits
Government-assisted housing (low-income housing)	Low	Government rent subsidies and tax credits	High maintenance costs and risk of a change in government programs	Tax credits and any losses on the property
Historic rehabilitation (restore sites for use)	Higher	Tax credits	Financing trouble; no rental history	Tax credits, deductions, and depreciation

There are several types of oil and gas partnerships that an investor may participate in. They are:

- Income programs
- Developmental programs
- Exploratory drilling or wildcatting

Intangible drilling costs are usually 100% deductible in the year they are incurred. Intangible drilling costs (IDC) include:

- Geological surveys
- Wages
- Supplies
- Insurance
- Well casings (Well heads have salvage value. Well casings may or may not have salvage value.)

Investors in oil and gas programs will be given a depletion allowance for the decreasing reserves.

Type of LP	Risk	Advantages	Disadvantages	Tax Benefits
Income (buys existing wells)	Low	Immediate, predictable cash flow	Reserves run out or prices fall	Depletion allowance
Developmental (drills near proven reserves)	Higher	Higher probability to find reserves than wildcatting	Not many fields ever produce	Immediate deductions for IDCs
Exploratory/wildcatting (drilling to find new reserves)	Highest	Huge payoff if significant reserves are found	Not many fields ever produce	Immediate deductions for a high level of IDCs

OIL AND GAS SHARING ARRANGEMENTS

Once the oil or gas partnership has been formed and has begun operating, the limited partners and the general partner will share in the income and tax benefits generated by the partnership according to the sharing arrangement laid out in the partnership agreement. There are several types of sharing arrangements. They are:

- Functional allocation
- Reversionary working interest
- Disproportionate working interest
- Net operation profits
- Carried interest
- Overriding royalty interest

Functional allocation: This is the most common sharing arrangement. The limited partners receive the deductions for the IDC and the general partner receives property write-offs. The revenue is shared between the limited and general partners.

Reversionary working interest: The limited partners bear all of the costs of the program. The general partner will receive no payments until the limited partners have gotten their investment back.

Disproportionate working interest: The general partner receives a large portion of the revenue but only bears a small portion of the costs.

Net operating profits: The limited partners bear all of the cost of the partnership. The general partner bears no costs but is entitled to a percentage of the net profits. This arrangement is only available for partnerships sold through a private placement.

Carried interest: The limited partners receive the IDC and the immediate write-offs. The general partner will share in the tangible drilling costs and will receive property depreciation benefits.

Overriding royalty interest: The holder of an overriding royalty interest has no partnership risks but receives a royalty from the partnership.

EQUIPMENT LEASING PROGRAMS

Equipment leasing programs are formed to purchase equipment with the intention of leasing it to a corporation. The program generates income from the lease payments received from the corporation. Investors will receive tax benefits from operating expenses, depreciation of equipment, and any interest expenses paid by the program.

TAX REPORTING FOR DIRECT PARTICIPATION PROGRAMS

Direct participation programs are organized as either limited partnerships or as subchapter S corporations. These entities allow for the flow-through of income and losses, and the DPP has no tax consequences. The DPP will only report the results of its operation to the IRS. The responsibility for paying any taxes due rests with the partners or shareholders. DPPs allow the losses to flow through to the investors. Losses from DPPs can only be used to offset the investor's passive income. Investors may not use the losses to shelter or offset the ordinary income. Investors should not purchase DPPs simply for the tax benefits; they should purchase them to earn a return. Any DPP that is found to have been formed simply to create tax benefits may subject the investors to strict penalties. Investors could owe back taxes, fines, or be prosecuted for fraud.

LIMITED PARTNERSHIP ANALYSIS

Before investing in a limited partnership, investors should analyze the key features of the partnership to ensure that the partnership's objectives meet their investment objectives. Investors should review:

- The program's economic viability.
- Tax considerations.
- Management's ability.
- Lack of liquidity.
- Time horizon.
- Whether it is a blind pool or a specified program.
- Internal rate of return (IRR) the IRR is used to measure the estimated present value of the future income and asset value. The IRR will allow the investor to measure DPP programs against each other.

A blind pool is a partnership where less than 75% of the assets that the partnership is going to acquire have been identified. In a specified program, more than 75% of the assets that the partnership is going to acquire have been identified.

A partnership's internal rate of return is the discounted present value of its projected future cash flow.

TAX DEDUCTIONS VS. TAX CREDITS

Tax deductions that are generated by partnerships are used to lower the investor's taxable income. A tax credit results in a dollar-for-dollar reduction in the amount of taxes due from the investor.

OTHER TAX CONSIDERATIONS

If a limited partnership has used up all of its deductions and has a gain on the sale of a depreciated asset, the sale above the asset's depreciated cost basis may subject the limited partners to a taxable recapture. This is known as the crossover point. The crossover point is also the time when the partnership begins to generate taxable income to its partners. There are two types of loans that a partnership may take out: nonrecourse loans and recourse loans. With a nonrecourse loan, if the partnership defaults the lender has no recourse to the limited partners. With a recourse loan, in the event of the partnership's default the lender can go after the limited partners for payment. A recourse loan can increase the investor's cost base. Partners must monitor their cost base and adjust it for:

- Cash or property contributions to the partnership.
- Recourse loans.
- Any cash or property received from the partnership.

Investors are responsible for any gain on the sale of their partnership interest in excess of their cost basis.

DISSOLVING A PARTNERSHIP

A partnership will terminate on the date set forth in a partnership agreement, unless earlier terminated. A partnership may dissolve if a majority of the limited partners vote for its dissolution. If the partnership terminates its activities, the general partner must cancel the certificate of limited partnership and liquidate the partnership assets. The priority of payment will be as follows:

- Secured lenders.
- General creditors.
- Limited partners' profits first, then return of investment.
- General partner for fees first, then profits, then return of capital.

Pretest

DIRECT PARTICIPATION PROGRAMS

1. A type of expense and profit sharing arrangement where the limited partners absorb all of the expenses and the general partner does not receive payment until the limited partners have recovered their costs is known as:

   a. disproportionate sharing.

   b. net operating profit interest.

   c. reversionary working interest.

   d. overriding royalty.

2. A customer seeking tax advantages from her investment in a DPP would most likely invest in:

   a. raw land real estate programs.

   b. developmental oil and gas programs.

   c. rental properties.

   d. historic rehabilitation programs.

3. While investing in a DPP, an asset is sold at a price above its depreciated basis and all tax credits have been used up. This is known as which of the following?

   a. Inversion

   b. Coaxial

   c. Crossover

   d. Conversion

4. A limited partner may do all of the following, EXCEPT:

    a. switch the general partner.

    b. vote to add a new general partner.

    c. advise the general partner.

    d. sue the general partner.

5. A participant in a limited partnership that has no partnership risk but receives payments is said to have a(n):

    a. reversionary interest.

    b. credit secured interest.

    c. overriding royalty interest.

    d. net income interest.

6. Which one of the following could result in additional payments being required by a limited partner?

    a. A recourse loan.

    b. A limited partnership may never require the limited partners to make additional payments.

    c. Additional cash requirements.

    d. A nonrecourse loan.

7. Your real estate limited partnership has taken out a recourse loan as an investor. Which of the following are true in this case?

    I. You can't be held liable.

    II. You can be held liable.

    III. It can't increase your cost basis.

    IV. It can increase your cost basis.

    a. I and III

    b. I only

    c. II and IV

    d. I and II

8. List the following in order from the least important to the most important factors when considering investing in a DPP.

    I. Tax considerations

    II. Profitability

    III. Liquidity

    IV. Safety

    a. III, II, I, IV

    b. III, IV, I, II

    c. II, I, IV, III

    d. IV, II, III, I

9. In a DPP, all of the following may be depreciated, EXCEPT:

    a. buildings.

    b. machinery.

    c. equipment.

    d. raw land.

10. When investing in a wildcat oil and gas program, most of the tax credits are generated by:

    a. depletion.

    b. depreciation.

    c. intangible drilling costs.

    d. management expenses.

Customer Recommendations, Professional Conduct, and Taxation

INTRODUCTION

All recommendations to customers must be suitable based on the customers' investment objectives, financial profile, and attitudes towards investing. Representatives usually make verbal recommendations to customers. The representative will review the customer's investment objective and offer facts to support the basis for his or her recommendations, as well as an explanation as to how the recommendations will help the customer meet the desired objective. Any predictions about the performance of an investment should be stated strictly as an opinion or belief, not as a fact. If the firm uses reports that cite past performance of the firm's previous recommendations, the report must contain:

- The prices and dates when the recommendations were made.
- General market conditions.
- The recommendations in all similar securities for 12 months.
- A statement disclosing that the firm is a market maker (if applicable).
- A statement regarding whether the firm or its officers or directors own any of the securities being recommended or options or warrants for the same security.
- If the firm managed or comanaged an underwriting of any of the issuer's securities in the last three years.

- A statement regarding the availability of supporting documentation for the recommendations.

  While making a recommendation, a representative may not:
- Guarantee or promise a profit or promise no loss.
- Make false, misleading, or fraudulent statements.
- Make unfair comparisons to dissimilar products.

PROFESSIONAL CONDUCT IN THE SECURITIES INDUSTRY

The securities industry is a highly regulated industry. All broker dealers are required to regulate their employees. A broker dealer must designate a principal to supervise all of the actions of the firm and its employees. The broker dealer and all of its employees are also regulated by a self-regulatory organization (SRO), such as FINRA or the NYSE. The SROs and all industry participants answer to the SEC. The SEC is the ultimate securities industry authority. Additionally, each state has adopted its own rules and regulations regarding securities transactions that occur within the state. Violations of industry regulations may lead to fines and expulsion from the industry. Violations of state and federal laws may result in fines, expulsion from the state or industry, or a jail term. Industry participants are expected to adhere to all of the industry's rules and regulations, as well as all state and federal laws.

FAIR DEALINGS WITH CUSTOMERS

All broker dealers are required to act in good faith in all of their dealings with customers and are required to uphold just and equitable trade practices. FINRA's rules of fair practice, also known as the rules of conduct, regulate how business is conducted with members of the general public. The rules of conduct prohibit all of the following:

- Churning.
- Manipulative and deceptive practices.
- Unauthorized trading.
- Fraudulent acts.
- Blanket recommendations.
- Misrepresentations.
- Omitting material facts.

- Making guarantees.
- Selling dividends.
- Recommending speculative securities without knowing the customer can afford the risk.
- Short-term trading in mutual funds.
- Switching fund families.

CHURNING

Most representatives are compensated when the customer makes a transaction based on their recommendation. Churning is a practice of making transactions that are excessive in size or frequency, with the intention to generate higher commissions for the representative. When determining if an account has been churned, regulators will look at the frequency of the transactions, the size of the transactions, and the amount of commission earned by the representative. Customer profitability is not an issue when determining if an account has been churned.

In addition to churning where the agent or firm executes too many transactions to increase revenue, a practice known as reverse churning is also a violation. Reverse churning is the practice of placing inactive accounts or accounts that do not trade frequently into fee based programs that charge an annual fee based on the assets in the account. This fee covers all advice and execution charges. Since these inactive accounts do not trade frequently it will cause the total fees charged to the account to increase and makes a fee based account unsuitable for inactive accounts and for accounts that simply buy and hold securities for a long period of time. These accounts will generally be charged an annual fee in the range of 1%–2% of the total value of the assets in lieu of commissions when orders are executed.

MANIPULATIVE AND DECEPTIVE DEVICES

It is a violation for a firm or representative to engage in or employ any artifice or scheme that is designed to gain an unfair advantage over another party. Some examples of manipulative or deceptive devices are:

- Capping
- Pegging
- Front running
- Trading ahead
- Painting the tape/matched purchases/matches sales

Capping: A manipulative act designed to keep a stock price from rising or to keep the price down.

Pegging: A manipulative act designed to keep a stock price up or to keep the price from falling.

Front running: The entering of an order for the account of an agent or firm prior to entering a large customer order. The firm or agent is using the customer's order to profit on the order it entered for its own account.

Trading ahead: The entering of an order for a security based on prior knowledge from a soon to be released research report.

Painting the tape: A manipulative act by two or more parties designed to create false activity in the security without any beneficial change in ownership. The increased activity is used to attract new buyers.

UNAUTHORIZED TRADING

An unauthorized transaction is one that is made for the benefit of a customer's account at a time when the customer has no knowledge of the trade and the representative does not have discretionary power over the account.

FRAUD

Fraud is defined as any act that is employed to obtain an unfair advantage over another party. Fraudulent acts include:

- False statements
- Deliberate omissions of material facts
- Concealment of material facts
- Manipulative and deceptive practices
- Forgery
- Material omission
- Lying

BLANKET RECOMMENDATIONS

It is inappropriate for a firm or a representative to make blanket recommendations in any security, especially low-priced speculative securities. No matter what type of investment is involved, a blanket recommendation to a large group of people will always be wrong for some investors. Different investors have different objectives, and the same recommendation will not be suitable for everyone.

EXAMPLE

Mr. Jones, an agent with XYZ brokers, has a large customer base that ranges from young investors who are just starting to save to institutions and retirees. Mr. Jones has been doing a significant amount of research on WSIA industries, a mining and materials company. Mr. Jones strongly believes that WSIA is significantly undervalued based on its assets and earning potential. Mr. Jones recommends WSIA to all his clients. In the next six months the share price of WSIA increases significantly as new production dramatically increases sales, just as Mr. Jones's research suggested. The clients then sell WSIA at Mr. Jones's suggestion and realize a significant profit.

ANALYSIS

Even though the clients who purchased WSIA based on Mr. Jones's recommendation made a significant profit, Mr. Jones has still committed a violation because he recommended it to all of his clients. Mr. Jones's clients have a wide variety of investment objectives, and the risk or income potential associated with an investment in WSIA would not be suitable for every client. Even if an investment is profitable for the client it does not mean it was suitable for the client. Blanket recommendations are never suitable.

SELLING DIVIDENDS

Selling dividends is a violation that occurs when a registered representative uses a pending dividend payment as the sole basis of a recommendation to purchase the stock or mutual fund. Additionally, using the pending dividend as a means to create urgency on the part of the investor to purchase the stock is a prime example of this type of violation. If the investor was to purchase the shares just prior to the ex dividend date simply to receive the dividend, the investor in many cases will end up worse off. The dividend in this case will actually be a return of the money that the investor used to purchase the stock, and then the investor will have a tax liability when the dividend is received.

MISREPRESENTATIONS

A representative or a firm may not knowingly make any misrepresentations regarding:

- A client's account status
- The representative
- The firm
- An investment
- Fees to be charged

OMITTING MATERIAL FACTS

A representative of a firm may not omit any material fact, either good or bad, when recommending a security. A material fact is one that an investor would need to know in order to make a well-informed investment decision. The representative may, however, omit an immaterial fact.

GUARANTEES

No representative, broker dealer, or investment adviser may make any guarantees of any kind. A profit may not be guaranteed, and a promise of no loss may not be made.

RECOMMENDATIONS TO AN INSTITUTIONAL CUSTOMER

FINRA recognizes an institutional customer as one that has at least $10,000,000 in assets. The agent's or member's suitability determination can be met if the customer:

- Can independently evaluate the investment risks and merits.
- Can independently make its own investment decisions.

If the customer meets the above criteria, the member or agent may recommend almost any investment to the customer and allow the customer to determine if it is suitable.

RECOMMENDING MUTUAL FUNDS

A representative recommending a mutual fund should ensure that the mutual fund's investment objective meets the customer's investment objective. If the mutual fund company or broker dealer distributes advertising or sales literature regarding the mutual fund, the following should be disclosed:

- The highest sales charge charged by the fund.
- The fund's current yield based on dividends only.
- Graph performance of the fund versus a broad-based index.
- The performance of the fund for 10 years or the life of the fund, whichever is less.
- Not imply that a mutual fund is safer than other investments.
- Source of graphs and charts.

PERIODIC PAYMENT PLANS

When recommending or advertising a periodic payment plan, the following must be disclosed:

- A statement that a profit is not guaranteed.
- A statement that investors are not protected from a loss.
- A statement that the plan involves continuous investments, regardless of market conditions.

MUTUAL FUND CURRENT YIELD

When advertising or recommending a mutual fund, any statement of claim regarding its current yield must be based solely on the annual dividends paid by the fund and may not include any capital gains distributions. Additionally, the public offering price, used to calculate the current yield, must contain the highest sales charge charged by the fund and may not be based on a breakpoint schedule or sales reduction charge.

EXAMPLE   ABC balanced fund has a POP of $10, has paid dividends totaling $1, and has distributed $.75 in capital gains distributions. What is the fund's current yield?

current yield = annual income/current price

$$\text{current yield} = \frac{\$1}{\$10} = 10\%$$

If the capital gains distributions were included, it would make the current yield look much higher than 10%. If the capital gains distribution of $.75 were included, the current yield would have been quoted at 17.5%.

INFORMATION OBTAINED FROM AN ISSUER

If a broker dealer obtains information during the performance of duties to an issuer of securities, it may not use that information to solicit business. A broker dealer may obtain information from an issuer while acting as:

- An underwriter
- Transfer agent
- Paying agent
- Investment banker

DISCLOSURE OF CLIENT INFORMATION

Registered representatives and broker dealers may not disclose any information regarding clients to a third party without the client's expressed consent or without a court order. If the client is an issuer of securities and the broker dealer is an underwriter, transfer agent, or paying agent for the issuer, then the broker dealer is precluded from using the information it obtains regarding the issuer's security holders for its own benefit.

BORROWING AND LENDING MONEY

Borrowing and lending of money between registered persons and customers is strictly regulated. If the member firm allows borrowing and lending between representatives and customers the firm must have policies in place that will allow for the loans to be made. Loans may be made between an agent and a customer if the customer is a bank or other lending institution, where there is a personal or outside business relationship and that relationship is the basis for the loan, or between two agents registered with the same firm. The firm must provide the agent with written preapproval for the loan unless the loan is being made between the agent and an immediate family member or a bank. The approval documentation must be maintained for three years from the date when the loan was repaid or three years from the rep's termination from the firm.

GIFT RULE

Broker dealers may not pay compensation to employees of other broker dealers. If a broker dealer wants to give a gift to an employee of another broker dealer, it must:

- Be valued at less than $100 per person per year.
- Be given directly to the employing member firm for distribution to the employee.
- Have the employing member's prior approval for the gift.

The employing member must obtain a record of the gift, including the name of the giver, the name of the recipient, and the nature of the gift. These rules have been established to ensure that broker dealers do not try to influence the employees of other broker dealers. An exception to this rule would be in cases where an employee of one broker dealer performs services for another broker dealer under an employment contract. Occasional meals, tickets to sporting events, and lucite plaques and prospectuses are all acceptable.

OUTSIDE EMPLOYMENT

If a registered representative wants to obtain employment outside of his or her position with a member firm, the registered representative must first notify the employing member prior engaging in the activity. Prior approval is not required but the employer has the right to refuse or limit the outside business activity. Exceptions to this rule are if the registered representative is a passive investor in a business or if the representative owns rental property. All other outside business activities must be disclosed to the member firm.

PRIVATE SECURITIES TRANSACTIONS

A registered representative may not engage in any private securities transactions without first obtaining the broker dealer's prior approval. The registered representative must provide the employing firm with all documentation regarding the investment and the proposed transaction. An example of a private securities transaction would be if a representative helped a startup business raise money through a private placement. If the representative is going to receive compensation, the employing member firm must supervise the transaction as if the firm itself executed the transaction. If a representative sells investment products that the employing member does not conduct business in without the member's knowledge, then the representative has committed a violation known as selling away.

CUSTOMER COMPLAINTS

All written complaints received from a customer or from an individual acting on behalf of the customer must be reported promptly to the principal of the firm. The firm is required to:

- Maintain a copy of the complaint in a supervising office of supervisory jurisdiction.
- Electronically report all complaints to FINRA within 15 days of the end of each calendar quarter.
- Report complaints within 10 days to FINRA if the complaint alleges misappropriation of funds or securities or forgery.

INVESTOR INFORMATION

All broker dealers that carry customer accounts must send their customers information detailing FINRA's BrokerCheck public disclosure program at least once per calendar year. The BrokerCheck program, accessible via the FINRA website, provides detailed registration and disciplinary history for firms and agents maintained at the central registration depository (CRD). The information must contain the program's 800 number, FINRA's website address, and a statement that an investor brochure includes the same information and is available.

NYSE/FINRA KNOW YOUR CUSTOMER

The NYSE and FINRA both require that any recommendation to a customer be suitable for the customer. The representative has an affirmative obligation to determine the suitability of the recommendations made to customers. The suitability obligation is triggered at the time the investment is discussed with the client not based on if the customer makes the investment. The rules require that the agent obtain enough information about the customer to ensure that all recommendations are suitable based on a review of the client's:

- Investment objectives
- Financial status
- Income
- Investment holdings
- Retirement needs
- College and other major expenses
- Tax bracket
- Attitude towards investing

The more you know about a customer's financial position, the better you will be able to help the customer meet his or her objectives. You should always ask questions like:

- How long have you been making these types of investments?
- Do you have any major expenses coming up?
- How long do you usually hold investments?
- How much risk do you normally take?

- What tax bracket are you in?
- How much money do you have invested in the market?
- Have you done any retirement planning?

Of course there are other questions that you should ask, but these are examples of the style of questions that all representatives should ask.

Other questions a representative should ask the customer include:

- How old are you?
- Are you married?
- Do you have any children?
- How long have you been employed at your current job?

Registered representatives must make sure that their recommendations meet their customers' objectives. Should a client have a primary and a secondary objective, a representative must make sure that the recommendation meets the investor's primary objective first and the secondary objective second.

INVESTMENT OBJECTIVES

All investors want to make or preserve money. However, these objectives can be met in different ways. Some of the different investment objectives are:

- Income
- Growth
- Preservation of capital
- Tax benefits
- Liquidity
- Speculation

INCOME

Many investors are looking to have their investments generate additional income to help meet their monthly expenses. Some investments that will help to meet this objective are:

- Corporate bonds
- Municipal bonds

- Government bonds
- Preferred stocks
- Money market funds
- Bond funds

GROWTH

Investors who seek capital appreciation over time want their money to grow in value and are not seeking any current income. The only investments that will achieve this goal are:

- Common stocks
- Common stock funds

PRESERVATION OF CAPITAL

Investors who have preservation of capital as an investment objective are very conservative and are more concerned with keeping the money they have saved. For these investors, high-quality debt will be an appropriate recommendation. The following are good investments for preserving capital:

- Money market funds
- Government bonds
- Municipal bonds
- High-grade corporate bonds

TAX BENEFITS

For investors seeking tax advantages, the only two possible recommendations are:

- Municipal bonds
- Municipal bond funds

LIQUIDITY

Investors who need immediate access to their money need to own liquid investments that will not fluctuate wildly in value in case they need to use the money. The following investments are listed from most liquid to least liquid:

- Money market funds
- Stocks/bonds/mutual funds

- Annuities
- Collateralized mortgage obligations (CMOs)
- Direct participation programs
- Real estate

SPECULATION

A customer investing in a speculative manner is willing to take a high degree of risk in order to earn a high rate of return. Some of the more speculative investments are:

- Penny stocks
- Small cap stocks
- Some growth stocks
- Junk bonds

RISK VS. REWARD

Risk is the reciprocal of reward. An investor must be offered a higher rate of return for each unit of additional risk the investor is willing to assume. There are many types of risk involved with investing money. They are as follows:

- Capital risk
- Market risk
- Nonsystematic risk
- Legislative risk
- Timing risk
- Credit risk
- Reinvestment risk
- Call risk
- Liquidity risk

CAPITAL RISK

Capital risk is the risk that an investor may lose all or part of the capital that has been invested.

MARKET RISK

Market risk is also known as a systematic risk, and it is the risk that is inherent in any investment in the markets. For example, you could own stock in the greatest company in the world and you could still lose money because the value of your stock is going down, simply because the market as a whole is going down.

NONSYSTEMATIC RISK

Nonsystematic risk is the risk that pertains to one company or industry. For example, the problems that the tobacco industry faced a few years ago would not have affected a computer company.

LEGISLATIVE RISK

Legislative risk is the risk that the government will do something that adversely affects an investment. For example, beer manufacturers probably did not fare too well when the government enacted prohibition.

TIMING RISK

Timing risk is simply the risk that an investor will buy and sell at the wrong time and will lose money as a result.

CREDIT RISK

Credit risk is the risk of default inherent in debt securities. An investor may lose all or part of an investment because the issuer has defaulted and cannot pay the interest or principal payments owed to the investor.

REINVESTMENT RISK

When interest rates decline and higher yielding bonds have been called or have matured, investors will not be able to receive the same return given the same amount of risk. This is reinvestment risk, and the investor is forced to either accept the lower rate or must take more risk to obtain the same rate.

CALL RISK

Call risk is the risk that, as interest rates decline, higher yielding bonds and preferred stocks will be called and investors will be forced to reinvest the proceeds at a lower rate of return or at a higher rate of risk to achieve the same return. Call risk only applies to preferred stocks and bonds with a call feature.

LIQUIDITY RISK

Liquidity risk is the risk that an investor will not be able to liquidate an investment when needed or will not be able to liquidate the investment without adversely affecting the price.

ALPHA

A stock's or portfolio's alpha is its projected independent rate of return, or the difference between an investment's expected (benchmark) return and its actual return. Portfolio managers whose portfolios have positive alphas are adding value through their asset selection. The outperformance as measured by alpha indicates that the portfolio manager is adding additional return for each unit of risk taken on in the portfolio.

BETA

A stock's beta is its projected rate of change relative to the market as a whole. If the market was up 10% for the year, a stock with a beta of 1.5 could reasonably be expected to be up 15%. A stock with a beta greater than one has a higher level of volatility than the market as a whole and is considered to be more risky than the overall market. A stock with a beta of less than one is less volatile than prices in the overall market and is considered to be less risky. An example of a low beta stock would be a utility stock. The price of utility stocks does not tend to move dramatically.

PRODUCTS MADE AVAILABLE THROUGH MEMBER FIRMS

All products offered through member firms must meet a reasonable basis suitability requirement. The reasonable basis suitability requirement has two parts. The member must understand the risks and performance characteristics of the investment and the agents offering the products for sale must understand the risks and performance characteristics of the investment. The member is required to educate agents about the risks and rewards of the products it allows agents to recommend to clients. If a member maintains a new product committee to review potential investments offered to clients the committee must believe that the products are suitable for at least some of the firm's clients. FINRA member firms should train representatives about the characteristics relating to specific products including product features, risks, and pricing. Members should also provide representatives with suitability guidance for recommending products and product related risk assessments and reviews. It is the responsibility of the representative to meet the client specific suitability requirement. The representative's principal will review the transaction promptly to ensure client specific suitability.

 TAKENOTE!

If the firm's product committee understands the risks and allows agents to offer the securities to clients, but the representative does not, neither the firm nor the representative has met their obligations under suitability standards.

Members must track ongoing changes that impact suitability such as changes in interest rates, and oil prices that can impact the suitability of an investment. Specifically members should discus, and disclose how changing interest rates may impact a portfolio of fixed income securities such as high yield bonds, CMOs, and other mortgaged-backed products.

RECOMMENDATIONS THROUGH SOCIAL MEDIA

The use of social media such as Linkedin, Facebook, and Twitter all need to be closely supervised by the member firm, specifically in cases where the communication posted by the firm or its agents could be deemed to be a recommendation. Being able to determine when communication reaches the level of a recommendation is a key element on the exam and for supervisors in general. When communication is deemed to be a recommendation it becomes subject to the suitability requirements of FINRA Rule 2111. Certain types of communications that are deemed to be recommendations are as follows:

- Targeted email distributions and tweets that advise the reader to buy or sell a security or securities within a sector
- Targeted pop up, redirect, and mouse-over messages displayed to website visitors that advise the visitor to buy or sell a security or securities within a sector.

If the firm maintains a website that allows access to a library of research containing pervious buy and sell recommendations the ability to access the library will not constitute a recommendation.

Due to the complex compliance issues social media present, member firms are within their rights to limit or restrict employees' use of social media. Should a member firm allow its representatives to communicate over social media the level of supervision required will depend on the type of social media used and the content of the communication. Member firms must properly train its employees on the use of social media and maintain written policies and procedures regarding its use and supervision. Static content that may be accessed by any visitor at any time requires prior approval from a principal before the static post is made. Static content includes Facebook walls, LinkedIn profiles, blogs, and Twitter posts. Aggressively tweeting positive or negative messages about an investment is a cause for concern and may result in sanctions being imposed on both the agent and the firm. Only agents who have the approval of their firm to tweet about investments should do so. Interactive blogs and chatroom conversations are deemed to be public appearances. These public appearances do not require prior principal approval but are subject to FINRA rules. Statements made must be factual and not exaggerated and no statements should be made about a security during a quiet period. It is important to note that most blogs are static and require prior approval for posts, merely updating a blog on a regular basis does not constitute an interactive blog. FINRA members must carefully supervise the use of social media by its agents and must have systems in place designed to detect potential violations. These systems should be designed to detect red flag words such as "guarantee" and "can't lose." Agents who have a history of questionable sales practices or who have been sanctioned should be prohibited from using social media for business purposes. A post on social media from a client of the firm or from an unrelated third party will not be deemed to have been made by the firm and is not subject to supervision unless the firm assisted in preparing such post or approved the content.

 TAKENOTE!

One way for a firm to keep close supervision for representatives who make recommendations using social media is to have a preapproved catalog of research available for the representatives to use.

TAX STRUCTURE

There are two types of taxes: progressive and regressive. A progressive tax levies a larger tax on higher income earners. Examples of progressive taxes are:

- Income taxes
- Estate taxes

Regressive taxes level the same tax rate on everyone, regardless of their income. As a result, a larger portion of the lower income earner's earnings will go toward the tax. Examples of regressive taxes are:

- Sales taxes
- Property taxes
- Gasoline taxes
- Excise taxes

INVESTMENT TAXATION

Investors must be aware of the impact that federal and state taxes will have on their investment results. A taxable event will occur in most cases when an investor:

- Sells a security at a profit.
- Sells a security at a loss.
- Receives interest or dividend income.

CALCULATING GAINS AND LOSSES

When investors sell their shares, in most cases they will have a capital gain or loss. In order to determine if there is a gain or loss, the investor must first calculate the cost basis, or cost base. An investor's cost base, in most cases, is equal to the price the investor paid for the shares plus any commissions or fees. Once an investor knows the cost base, calculating any gain or loss becomes easy. A capital gain is realized when the investor sells the shares at a price that is greater than the cost base. Any gain on an asset held more than one year is considered a long-term capital gain and is taxed at a maximum rate of 15%. Any gain on an asset held for less than one year is considered a short-term capital gain and is taxed at the investor's ordinary income tax rate. The investor's holding period begins the day after the purchase and ends on the sale date.

EXAMPLE	An investor who purchased a stock at $10 per share three years ago and receives $14 per share when he sells the shares has a $4 capital gain. This was found by subtracting the cost base from the sales proceeds: $14 − $10 = $4. If the investor had 1,000 shares, he would have a capital gain of $4,000.

An investor's cost base is always returned to the investor tax-free. A capital loss is realized when investors sell shares at a price that is less than their cost base. If the investor in the previous example were to have sold the shares at $8 instead of $14, the investor would have a $2 capital loss, or a total capital loss of $2,000 for the entire position.

Again this is found by subtracting the cost base from the sales proceeds: $8 − $10 = −$2. Capital gains, like dividends, are taxed at a 15% rate for ordinary income earners and at a 20% rate for high income earners.

COST BASE OF MULTIPLE PURCHASES

Investors who have been accumulating shares through multiple purchases must determine their cost base at the time of sale through one of the following methods:

- FIFO (first in, first out)
- Share identification
- Average cost

FIFO (FIRST IN, FIRST OUT)

If the investor does not identify which shares are being sold at the time of sale, the IRS will assume that the first shares that were purchased are the first shares that are sold under the FIFO method. In many cases, this will result in the largest capital gain, and, as a result, the investor will have the largest tax liability.

SHARE IDENTIFICATION

An investor may at the time of the sale specify which shares are being sold. By keeping a record of the purchase prices and the dates that the shares were purchased, the investor may elect to sell the shares that create the most favorable tax consequences.

AVERAGE COST

An investor may decide to sell shares based on their average cost. An investor must determine the shares' average cost by using the following formula:

$$\text{average cost} = \frac{\text{total dollars invested}}{\text{total \# of shares purchased}}$$

Once an investor has elected to use the average cost method to calculate gains and losses, another method may not be used without IRS approval.

DEDUCTING CAPITAL LOSSES

An investor may use capital losses to offset capital gains dollar for dollar in the year in which they are realized. A net capital loss may be used to reduce the investor's taxable ordinary income by up to $3,000 in the year in which it is realized. Any net capital losses that exceed $3,000 may be carried forward into future years and may be deducted at a rate of $3,000 from ordinary income every year until the loss is used up. If the investor has a capital gain in subsequent years, the investor may use the entire amount of the net capital loss remaining to offset the gain up to the amount of the gain.

WASH SALES

Investors may not sell a security at a loss and shortly after repurchase the security, or a security that is substantially the same, to reestablish the position if they intend to claim the loss for tax purposes and deduct the loss from their ordinary income. This is known as a wash sale, and the IRS will disallow the loss. In order to claim the loss, the investor has to have held the securities for 30 days and must wait at least 30 days before repurchasing the securities or securities that are substantially the same. The total number of days in the wash sale rule is 61.

- Holding period   30 days
- Sale date   1 day
- Waiting period   30 days
- Total   61 days

Securities that are substantially the same are call options, rights, warrants, and convertibles.

TAXATION OF INTEREST INCOME

Interest earned by investors may or may not be subject to taxes. The following table illustrates the tax consequences of various interest payment received by investors:

Resident	Investment	Taxation
New Jersey	Corporate bond	All taxes
New Jersey	CMO	All taxes
New Jersey	GNMA	All taxes
New Jersey	T-bond	Federal taxes only
New Jersey	New York muni bond	New Jersey taxes only
New Jersey	New Jersey muni bond	No taxes
New Jersey	Puerto Rico/Guam muni bond	No taxes

 TAKENOTE!

Investors may deduct margin interest only to the extent of their investment income. Investors may not deduct margin expenses from municipal bonds.

INHERITED SECURITIES

If an investor dies and leaves securities to another person, that person's cost base for those securities is the fair market value of the securities on the day the decedent died. The cost base of the original investor does not transfer to the person who inherited the securities.

 TAKENOTE!

If a person gives a gift of securities during his or her lifetime, that person's cost base is used for calculating the recipient's capital gain. If, however, there is a loss on the sale, the lower of the giver's cost base or the fair market value at the time of the gift is used to calculate the loss.

DONATING SECURITIES TO CHARITY

An investor who donates securities to a charity will receive a tax deduction equal to the value of the securities. If the investor has an unrealized gain and has held the securities for more than 12 months, the investor will not owe any taxes on the appreciation. If the securities were held less than 12 months, the investor will be responsible for taxes on the appreciation. The recipient's cost base will be equal to the value of the securities on the day the gift was received.

GIFT TAXES

When gifts are made to family members or others individuals, the donor does not receive any tax deduction. The donor's cost base will transfer to the recipient for tax purposes. Individuals may give gifts of up to $14,000 per person per year without incurring any tax liability. If a gift in excess of $14,000 is given to an individual, the donor owes the gift tax.

 TAKENOTE!

A husband and wife may give up to $28,000 per year per person. The IRS considers half of the gift to be coming from each spouse. The annual gift limit is indexed for inflation since 1999.

ESTATE TAXES

Individuals are allowed to leave an estate worth just over $5,000,000 without subjecting the beneficiaries to estate taxes. This rule is subject to continuous debate and change and the number is unlikely to be tested. This amount is increased periodically. There is an unlimited marital deduction or unified credit that allows surviving spouses to inherit the entire estate tax-free.

WITHHOLDING TAX

All broker dealers are required to withhold 31% of all sales proceeds if the investor has not provided a social security number or a tax identification number. In addition, 31% of all distributions from a mutual fund will also be withheld without a social security number or a tax identification number.

CORPORATE DIVIDEND EXCLUSION

Corporations that invest in the shares of other corporations will pay taxes only on 30% of the dividends it receives from those investments. In addition, 70% of the dividends are tax-free to the corporation.

 TAKENOTE!

Individuals who receive dividends from common stock and mutual funds will be subject to a 15% tax rate. High income earners are subjected to a 20% tax.

ALTERNATIVE MINIMUM TAX (AMT)

Certain items that receive beneficial tax treatment must be added back into the taxable income for some high-income earners. These items include:

- Interest on some industrial revenue bonds.
- Some stock options.
- Accelerated depreciation.
- Personal property tax on investments that do not generate income.
- Certain tax deductions passed through from DPPs.

TAXES ON FOREIGN SECURITIES

U.S. investors who own securities issued in a foreign country will owe federal taxes on any gains or income realized. In the event that the foreign country withholds taxes from the investor, the investor may file for a credit with the IRS at tax time. Most foreign governments that withhold taxes will withhold 15%.

Pretest

CUSTOMER RECOMMENDATIONS, PROFESSIONAL CONDUCT, AND TAXATION

1. Creating false activity in a security to attract new purchases is a fraudulent practice known as:
   a. trading ahead.
   b. painting the tape.
   c. active concealment.
   d. front running.

2. Which of the following could be subject to an investor's AMT?
   a. A limited partnership
   b. An open-end mutual fund
   c. A convertible preferred stock owned by a wealthy investor
   d. An industrial revenue bond

3. An investor has a conservative attitude towards investing and is seeking to invest $50,000 into an interest-bearing instrument that will provide current income and safety. You would most likely recommend which of the following?
   a. Treasury bill
   b. Ginnie Mae pass-through certificate
   c. Treasury STRIP
   d. Bankers' acceptance

4. A client has phoned in concerned about what will happen to his investment in a waste management company if the new EPA laws are enacted requiring disposal companies to reduce pollution. What type of risk is he concerned with?

   a. Call risk

   b. Environmental risk

   c. Investment risk

   d. Legislative risk

5. How would an investor who has held a long stock position for six months end her holding period?

   I. Sell an at the money call

   II. Sell a put

   III. Sell a deep in the money call

   IV. Purchase a put

   a. II and IV

   b. I and II

   c. III and IV

   d. I and III

6. A customer has a large position in GJH, a thinly traded stock whose share price has remained flat for some time. The customer contacts the agent and wants to sell his entire position. The customer is most subject to which of the following?

   a. Liquidity risk

   b. Credit risk

   c. Conversion risk

   d. Execution risk

7. An investor who is most concerned with changes in interest rates would least likely purchase which of the following?

   a. Long-term warrants

   b. Long-term corporate bonds

   c. Long-term equity

   d. Call options

8. An investor is looking for a risk-free investment. An agent should recommend which of the following to this investor?

   a. Series HH government savings bonds

   b. 90-day T-bill

   c. Convertible preferred stock

   d. Bankers' acceptances

9. Which of the following is true?

   a. If an investor buys shares just prior to the ex date, he will have his investment money returned.

   b. After an investor's money is returned, the investor is still liable for taxes on the dividend amount.

   c. A registered representative may not use the pending dividend payment as the sole basis for recommending stock purchase.

   d. All of the above.

10. A new investor is in the 15% tax bracket and is seeking some additional current income. Which of the following would you recommend?

    a. Growth fund

    b. Government bond fund

    c. Municipal bond fund

    d. Corporate bond fund

11. An investor gets advance notice of a research report being issued and enters an order to purchase the security that is the subject of the research report. This is known as:

    a. front running.

    b. trading ahead.

    c. insider trading.

    d. advance trading.

12. An investor has a conservative attitude towards investing and is seeking to invest $100,000 into an instrument that will provide current income and the most protection from interest rate risk. You would most likely recommend which of the following?

    a. Ginnie Mae pass-through certificate

    b. Bankers' acceptance

    c. Treasury STRIP

    d. A portfolio of T-bills

13. An investor who is seeking some current income would most likely invest in which of the following?

    a. Commercial paper

    b. Treasury bond

    c. Income bond

    d. Bankers' acceptance

14. You have recommended a CMO to a sophisticated investor. Which of the following would the investor be most concerned with?

    a. Default risk

    b. Foreclosure risk

    c. Interest rate risk

    d. Prepayment risk

15. Mr. and Mrs. Jones, a couple in their early forties, enjoy watching their son play baseball on the weekends. He is planning to go to college 11 years from September and they are looking to start saving for college expenses. Which of the following would you recommend?

    a. Educational IRA

    b. Growth fund

    c. Treasury STRIP

    d. Custodial account

16. Which of the following is not a violation of the rules of conduct?

    a. Recommending a security because of its future price appreciation

    b. Recommending a mutual fund based on a pending dividend to an investor seeking income

    c. Implying that FINRA has approved the firm

    d. Showing a client the past performance of a mutual fund for the last three years since its inception

17. An investor who may lose part or all of his investment is subject to which of the following?

   a. Capital risk

   b. Market risk

   c. Reinvestment risk

   d. Credit risk

18. A couple in their early thirties are seeking an investment for the $40,000 they have saved. They are planning on purchasing a new home in the next two years. You should most likely recommend which of the following?

   a. Preferred stock

   b. Common stock and common stock funds

   c. Money market funds

   d. Municipal bonds

Securities Industry Rules and Regulations

INTRODUCTION

Federal and state securities laws, as well as industry regulations, have been enacted to ensure that all industry participants adhere to a high standard of just and equitable trade practices. In this chapter, we will review the rules and regulations, as well as the registration requirements, for firms, agents, and securities.

THE SECURITIES EXCHANGE ACT OF 1934

The Securities Exchange Act of 1934 was the second major piece of legislation that resulted from the market crash of 1929. The Securities Exchange Act of 1934 regulates the secondary market that consists of investor-to-investor transactions. All transactions between two investors that are executed on any of the exchanges or in the over-the-counter (OTC) market are secondary market transactions. In a secondary market transaction, the selling security holder, not the issuing corporation, receives the money. The Securities Exchange Act of 1934 also regulates all individuals and firms that conduct business in the securities industry. The Securities Exchange Act of 1934:

- Created the Securities and Exchange Commission (SEC).
- Requires registration of broker dealers and agents.

- Regulates the exchanges and the NASD (now part of FINRA).
- Requires net capital for broker dealers.
- Regulates short sales.
- Regulates insider transactions.
- Requires public companies to solicit proxies.
- Requires segregation of customer and firm assets.
- Authorized the Federal Reserve Board to regulate the extension of credit for securities purchases under Regulation T.
- Regulates the handling of client accounts.

The Securities Exchange Act of 1934 also regulates the issuers of publicly owned securities and requires issuers of these securities to file annual reports (10-Ks) and quarterly reports (10-Qs). Issuers are also required to report material information to the public by filing form 8-K with the SEC. Issuers who file 10-K and 10-Qs are known as reporting issuers. All publicly traded corporations must solicit proxies from investors to vote on major issues relating to the corporation.

THE SECURITIES AND EXCHANGE COMMISSION (SEC)

One of the biggest components of the Securities Exchange Act of 1934 was the creation of the SEC. The SEC is the ultimate securities industry authority and is a direct government body. Five commissioners are appointed to five-year terms by the President of the United States, and each must be approved by the Senate. The SEC is not a self-regulatory organization (SRO) or a designated examining authority (DEA). An SRO is an entity that regulates its own members, such as the NYSE or the NASD (now part of FINRA). A DEA is an entity that inspects a broker dealer's books and records, and it can also be the NYSE or FINRA. All broker dealers, exchanges, agents, and securities must register with the SEC. All exchanges are required to file a registration statement with the SEC that includes the articles of incorporation, bylaws, and constitution. All new rules and regulations adopted by the exchanges must be disclosed to the SEC as soon as they are enacted. Issuers of securities with more than 500 shareholders and with assets exceeding $5,000,000 must register with the SEC, file quarterly and annual reports, and solicit proxies from stockholders. A broker dealer that conducts business with the public must register with the SEC and maintain a certain level of financial solvency known as net capital. All broker dealers are required to forward a financial statement to all customers of the firm. Additionally, all employees of the broker dealer who are involved in securities sales, have access to cash and securities, or who supervise employees must be fingerprinted.

EXTENSION OF CREDIT

The Securities Act of 1934 gave the authority to the Federal Reserve Board (FRB) to regulate the extension of credit by broker dealers for the purchase of securities by their customers. The following is a list of the regulations of the different lenders and the regulation that gave the FRB the authority to govern their activities:

- Regulation T: Broker dealers
- Regulation U: Banks
- Regulation G: All other financial institutions

THE NATIONAL ASSOCIATION OF SECURITIES DEALERS (NASD)

The Maloney Act of 1938 was an amendment to the Securities Exchange Act of 1934 that allowed for the creation of the NASD. The NASD was the SRO for OTC market, and its purpose was to regulate the broker dealers who conduct business in the OTC market. The NASD is now part of FINRA and has four major bylaws. They are:

1. The rules of fair practice
2. The uniform practice code
3. The code of procedure
4. The code of arbitration

THE RULES OF FAIR PRACTICE/ RULES OF CONDUCT

The rules of fair practice are designed to ensure just and equitable trade practices among members in their dealings with the public. In short, the rules of fair practice require members to deal fairly with the public. The rules of fair practice may also be called the conduct rules or the rules of conduct. Among other things, they govern:

- Commissions and markups
- Retail and institutional communication
- Customer recommendations
- Claims made by representatives

THE UNIFORM PRACTICE CODE

The uniform practice code sets forth guidelines for how FINRA members transact business with other members. The uniform practice code sets standards of business practices among its members and regulates:

- Settlement dates
- Ex dividend dates
- Rules of good delivery
- Confirmations
- Don't know (DK) procedures

THE CODE OF PROCEDURE

The code of procedure regulates how FINRA investigates complaints and violations. The code of procedure regulates the discovery phase of alleged violations of rules of fair practice. The code of procedure is not concerned with money; it is only concerned with rule violations.

THE CODE OF ARBITRATION

The code of arbitration provides a forum to resolve disputes. Arbitration provides a final and binding resolution to disputes involving a member and:

- Another member
- A registered agent
- A bank
- A customer

FINRA is divided into districts based on geography. Each district elects a committee to administer the association's rules. The committee is composed of up to 12 members who serve up to a three-year term. The committee appoints the Department of Enforcement to handle all trade practice complaints within the district and has the power to assess penalties against members who have violated one or more of the association's rules. FINRA's executive committee, which consists of the Board of Governors, oversees the national business of FINRA.

BECOMING A MEMBER OF FINRA

FINRA sets forth strict qualification standards that all prospective members must meet, prior to being granted membership with FINRA. Any firm that engages in interstate securities transactions with public customers is required to become a FINRA member. Additionally, any broker dealer that wishes to participate as a selling group member in the distribution of mutual fund shares must also be a FINRA member.

In order to become a FINRA member, a firm must:

- Meet net capital requirements (solvency).
- Have at least two principals to supervise the firm.
- Have an acceptable business plan detailing its proposed business activities.
- Attend a premembership interview.

Members must also agree to:

- Abide by all of the association's rules.
- Abide by all federal and state laws.
- Pay dues, fees, and membership assessments as required by the association.

FINRA members must pay the following fees:

- Basic membership fee
- Fee for each representative and principal
- Fee based on the gross income of the firm
- Fee for all branch offices

HIRING NEW EMPLOYEES

A registered principal of a firm will be the individual who interviews and screens potential new employees. The principal will be required to make a thorough investigation into the candidate's professional and personal backgrounds. With few exceptions, other than clerical personnel, all new employees will be required to become registered as an associated person with the firm. The new employee will begin the registration process by filling out and submitting a Uniform Application for Securities Industry Registration, also known as Form U4. Form U4 is used to collect the applicant's personal and professional history, including:

- 10-year employment history
- Five-year resident history
- Legal name and any aliases used
- Any legal or regulatory actions

The principal of the firm is required to verify the employment information for the last three years and must attest to the character of the applicant by signing Form U4 prior to its submission to FINRA. All U4 forms will be sent to the Central Registration Depository (CRD) along with a fingerprint card for processing and recording. Any applicant who has answered yes to any of the questions on the form regarding his or her background must give a detailed explanation in the DRP pages attached to the form. The applicant is not required to provide information regarding:

- Marital status
- Educational background
- Income or net worth

Information regarding the employee's finances is disclosed on Form U4 if the associated person has ever declared bankruptcy and if the employee has any unsatisfied judgments or liens. Any development that would cause an answer on the associated person's U4 to change requires that the member update the U4 within 30 days of when the member becomes informed of the event. In the case of an event that could cause the individual to become statutorily disqualified, such as a felony conviction or misdemeanor involving cash or securities, the member must update the associated person's U4 within 10 business days of learning of the event.

TAKENOTE!

Broker dealers are required to perform background checks on its employees every 5 years to ensure that no judgements, liens or disclosable events have gone unreported by the registered person. Registered persons who fail to disclose an unsatisfied judgements or liens are subject to significant regulatory action that could result in the person being barred from the industry in extreme cases.

DISCIPLINARY ACTIONS AGAINST A REGISTERED REPRESENTATIVE

If another industry regulator takes disciplinary action against a representative, the employing member firm must notify FINRA. Actions by any of the following should be immediately disclosed to the association:

- The SEC
- An exchange or association
- A state regulator
- A clearing firm
- A commodity regulatory body

Also immediately reportable to FINRA are any of the following:

- A customer compliant alleging theft, forgery, or misappropriation of customer assets
- Indictment, conviction, or plea of guilty or no contest to a criminal matter
- If the agent becomes a respondent or defendant in a matter in excess of $15,000 or if the firm becomes a respondent or defendant in a matter in excess of $25,000
- An agent is disciplined by the employing member firm or commissions are withheld from an agent or the agent is fined in either case in amounts in excess of $2,500.

FINRA defines immediate notification for the previously listed matters as being within 10 days. All disclosures must include the type of action brought as well as the name of the party bringing the actions and the name of the representative involved. The firm will make the disclosure on Form U4.

FINRA will submit disciplinary actions that are taken by FINRA on Form U6 and they will be recorded on the employee's record. All disciplinary actions, along with a record of the agent's registrations and employment history, are available through FINRA's BrokerCheck program. FINRA members are required to regulate the activities of its associated people and must disclose to the association any action that the member takes against a registered representative. Should a registered representative feel that the information disclosed through the BrokerCheck program is inaccurate the representative may request an amendment to the disclosure by filling out and submitting a BrokerCheck comment form.

RESIGNATION OF A REGISTERED REPRESENTATIVE

If a registered representative voluntarily terminates his or her association with a member firm, the member must fill out and submit a uniform termination notice known as a U-5 to FINRA within 30 days. An associated person's registration is nontransferable. A representative may not simply move the registration from one firm to another. The employing firm that the representative is leaving must fill out and submit a U-5 to FINRA, which terminates the representative's registration. The new employing firm must fill out and submit a new U-4 to begin a new registration for the associated person with the new employer. A representative who leaves the industry for more than 24 months is required to requalify by exam.

During a period of absence from the industry of two years or less, FINRA retains jurisdiction over the representative in cases involving customer complaints and violations. Agents who volunteer or who are called to active duty with the military have their registrations and continuing education requirements "tolled" and their registrations are placed in "special inactive" status. During this time, the 24-month requirement is not in effect and the agent may continue to receive compensation from transactions but may not contact customers during their time of active military duty. Once active duty ends the agent has 90 days to reenter the business. If the person is not associated with a member at that time the 24-month window will begin.

CONTINUING EDUCATION

Most registered agents and principals are required to participate in industry-mandated continuing education programs. The continuing education program consists of a firm element, which is administered by the broker dealer, and a regulatory element, which is administered by the regulators.

FIRM ELEMENT

Every FINRA member firm at least annually must identify the training needs of its covered employees and develop a written training plan based on their employees' needs. A covered employee is a registered person who engages in sales of securities to customers, trading, investment banking, and their immediate supervisors. The firm, at a minimum, should institute a plan that increases the covered employees' securities knowledge and should focus on the products offered by the firm. The plan should also highlight the risks and suitability requirements associated with the firm's investment products and strategies. The firm is not required to file its continuing education plan with FINRA unless it is specifically requested to do so. However, firms that fail to adequately document their continuing education program, including their covered agents' compliance with the program, may be subject to disciplinary action.

REGULATORY ELEMENT

All registered agents who were not registered on or before July 1, 1988, must participate in the regulatory element of the continuing education requirement. Agents subject to the requirement must complete the computer-based training at an approved facility on the second anniversary of their initial registration and every three years thereafter. The content of the exam is developed by The Securities Industry Regulatory Council on Continuing Education and is not the responsibility of the broker dealer. FINRA will notify the agent 30 days prior to their anniversary date. This notification provides the agent with a 120 day window to complete the regulatory continuing education requirement. An agent who fails to complete the requirement within that period will have their registration become inactive. Agents whose registrations have become inactive may not engage in any securities business that requires a license and may not receive commissions until their registration is reactivated. Registered representatives are subject to Series 101 of the regulatory element, while registered principals are subject to Series 201 of the requirement. Agents who were exempt from the regulatory element as a result of having been registered for 10 years or more with a clean disciplinary history on July 1, 1998, who become the subject of a significant disciplinary action, will now be required to participate in the regulatory element of the continuing education requirement. Additionally, if an agent who was exempt from the regulatory element subsequently becomes registered as a principal, they will become subject to the Series 201 requirement. The one-time exemption is only for the regulatory element; there is no exemption from the firm element of the continuing education program. An agent who leaves the industry for more than 24 months will have to requalify by exam and will have a regulatory education requirement based on the date of reassociation (the date they passed the exam for the second time). An agent who temporarily leaves the industry (less than 24 months) who is not required to requalify by exam will have a regulatory continuing education requirement based on the original sate of association.

TERMINATION FOR CAUSE

A member may terminate a registered representative for cause if the representative has:

- Violated firm policy.
- Violated the rules of the NYSE, FINRA, SEC, or any other industry regulator.
- Violated state or federal securities laws.

A firm may not terminate a representative who is the subject of investigation by any securities industry regulator until the investigation is completed.

RETIRING REPRESENTATIVES/ CONTINUING COMMISSIONS

Retiring representatives may continue to receive commissions from the business that they have built over their career provided that a contract is in place prior to the representative's retirement. A retiring representative may continue to receive commissions on old business only. The retiring representation may not receive commissions on any new business and may not receive finder's fees. If the retired representative dies, the representative's beneficiary may continue to receive the commissions that were due the representative.

STATE REGISTRATION

In addition to registering with FINRA, all broker dealers and agents must register in their home state as well as in any state in which they transact business.

REGISTRATION EXEMPTIONS

The following individuals are exempt from registration:

- Clerical
- Nonsupervising officers and managers not dealing with customers
- Non-U.S. citizens working abroad
- Floor personnel

PERSONS INELIGIBLE TO REGISTER

Individuals applying for registration must meet the association's requirements in the following areas:

- Training
- Competence
- Experience
- Character

Anyone who fails to meet the association's requirements in any of the above listed areas may not become registered. An individual may also be disqualified by statute or through rules for any of the following:

- Expulsion, suspension, or disciplinary actions by the SEC or any foreign or domestic SRO.
- The individual caused the expulsion or suspension of a broker dealer or principal.
- The individual made false or misleading statements on the application for registration on form U-4 or form B-D.
- Felony conviction or misdemeanor involving securities within the last 10 years.
- Court injunction or order barring the individual.

COMMUNICATIONS WITH THE PUBLIC

Member firms will seek to increase their business and exposure through the use of both retail and institutional communications. There are strict regulations in place in order to ensure all communications with the public adhere to industry guidelines. Some communications with the public are available to a general audience and include:

- Television/radio
- Publicly accessible websites
- Motion pictures
- Newspapers/magazines
- Telephone directory listings
- Signs/billboards
- Computer/internet postings
- Video tape displays
- Other public media
- Recorded telemarketing messages

Other types of communications are offered to a targeted audience. These communications include:

- Market reports
- Password-protected websites
- Telemarketing scripts
- Form letters or emails (sent to more than 25 people)
- Circulars
- Research reports
- Printed materials for seminars
- Option worksheets
- Performance reports
- Prepared scripts for TV or radio
- Reprints of ads

FINRA RULE 2210 COMMUNICATIONS WITH THE PUBLIC

FINRA Rule 2210 replaces the advertising and sales literature rules previously used to regulate member communications with the public. FINRA Rule

2210 streamlines member communication rules and reduces the number of communication categories from six to three. The three categories of member communication are:

1. Retail communication
2. Institutional communication
3. Correspondence

RETAIL COMMUNICATION

Retail communication is defined as any written communication distributed or made available to 25 or more retail investors in a 30-day period. The communication may be distributed in hard copy or in electronic formats. The definition of a retail investor is any investor who does not meet the definition of an institutional investor. Retail communications now contain all components of advertising and sales literature. All retail communications must be approved by a registered principal prior to first use. The publication of a post in a chat room or other online forum will not require the prior approval of a principal so long as such post does not promote the business of the member firm and does not provide investment advice. Additionally, generic advertising will also be exempt from the prior approval requirements. All retail communication must be maintained by the member for three years. If the member firm is a new member firm which has been in existence for less than 12 months based on the firm's approval date in the central registration depository or CRD the member must file all retail communications with FINRA 10 days prior to its first use unless the communication has been previously filed and contains no material changes or has been filed by another member such as investment company or ETF sponsor. Member firms who have been established for more than 12 months may file retail communications with FINRA 10 days after the communication is first used. Investment companies, ETF sponsors, and retail communications regarding variable annuities must be filed 10 days prior to first use. If the communication contains non-standardized performance rankings. Should FINRA determine that a member firm is making false or misleading statements in its retail communications with the public, FINRA may require the member to file all of its retail communication with the public with the association 10 days prior to its first use.

> ► **TAKENOTE!**
>
> Research reports concerning only securities listed on a national securities exchange are excluded from Rule 2210's filing requirements. Additionally, a free writing prospectus is exempt from filing with the SEC and not subject to Rule 2210's filing or content standards.

INSTITUTIONAL COMMUNICATIONS

Intuitional communication is defined as any written communication distributed or made available exclusively to institutional investors. The communication may be distributed in hard copy or in electronic formats. Institutional communications do not have to be approved by a principal prior to first use so long as the member has established policies and procedures regarding the use of institutional communications and has trained its employees on the proper use of institutional communication. Institutional communication is also exempt from FINRA's filing requirement but like retail communications it must be maintained by a member for three years. If the member believes that the institutional communication or any part thereof may be seen by even a single retail investor the communication must be handled as all other retail communication and is subject to the approval and filing requirements as if it was retail communication. An institutional investor is a person or firm that trades securities for his or her own account or for the account of others. Institutional investors are generally limited to large financial companies. Because of their size and sophistication, fewer protective laws cover institutional investors. It is important to note that there is no minimum size for an institutional account. Institutional investors include:

- Broker dealers
- Investment advisers
- Investment companies
- Insurance companies
- Banks
- Trusts
- Savings and loans

- Government agencies
- Employment benefit plans with more than 100 participants
- Any non-natural person with more than $50,000,000 in assets

CORRESPONDENCE

Correspondence consists of electronic and written communications between the member and up to 25 retail investors in a 30-calendar-day period. With the increase in acceptance of email as business communication, it would be impractical for a member to review all correspondence between the member and a customer. The member instead may set up procedures to review a sample of all correspondence, both electronic and hard copy. If the member reviews only a sample of the correspondence, the member must train their associated people on their firm's procedures relating to correspondence and must document the training and ensure the procedures are followed. Even though the member is not required to review all correspondence, the member must still retain all correspondence. The member should, where practical, review all incoming hard copy correspondence. Letters received by the firm could contain cash, checks, securities, or complaints.

BROKER DEALER WEBSITES

A broker dealer will not be deemed to have a place of business in a state where it does not maintain an office simply by virtue of the fact that the publicly available website established by the firm or one of its agents is accessible from that state so long as the following conditions are met:

- The website clearly states that the firm may only conduct business in states where it is properly registered to do so.
- The website only provides general information about the firm and does not provide specific investment advice.
- The firm or its agent may not respond to Internet inquiries with the intent to solicit business without first meeting the registration requirements in the state of the prospective customer.

The content of any website must be reviewed and approved by a principal prior to its first use and must be filed with FINRA within 10 days of use. If the firm or its agent updates the website and the update materially changes the information contained on the website, the updates must be reapproved by a principal and refiled with FINRA. The website may use the FINRA logo so long as the use is only to demonstrate that the firm is a FINRA member and a hyperlink to the FINRA website is included in close proximity to the logo. Member firms are not required to display the FINRA logo.

BLIND RECRUITING ADS

A blind recruiting ad is an ad placed by the member firm for the specific purpose of finding job applicants. Blind recruiting ads are the only form of advertising that does not require the member's name to appear in the ad. The ads may not distort the opportunities or salaries of the advertised position. All other ads are required to disclose the name of the member firm, as well as the relationship of the member to any other entities that appear in the ad.

GENERIC ADVERTISING

Generic advertising is generally designed to promote firm awareness and to advertise the products and services generally offered through the firm. Generic ads will generally include:

- Securities products offered (i.e., stocks, bonds, mutual funds)
- Contact name, number, and address
- Types of accounts offered (i.e., individual, IRA, 401K)

TOMBSTONE ADS

A tombstone ad is an announcement of a new security offering coming to market. Tombstone ads may be run while the securities are still in registration with the SEC and may only include:

- Description of securities.
- Description of business.
- Description of transaction.
- Required disclaimers.

- Time and place of any stockholders meetings regarding the sale of the securities.

All tombstone ads must include the following:

- A statement that the securities registration has not yet become effective.
- A statement that responding to the ad does not obligate the prospect.
- A statement as to where a prospectus may be obtained.
- A statement that the ad does not constitute an offer to sell the securities and that an offer may only be made by the prospectus.

All retail communication is required to be approved by a principal of the firm prior to its first use. A general security principal (Series 24) may approve most retail communication. Any retail communication relating to options must be approved by a registered option principal or the compliance registered options principal. Research reports must be approved by a supervisory analyst.

TESTIMONIALS

From time to time, firms will use testimonials made by people of national or local recognition in an effort to generate new business for the firm. If the individual giving the testimonial is quoting past performance relating to the firm's recommendations, it must be accompanied by a disclaimer that past performance is not indicative of future performance. If the individual giving the testimony was compensated in any way, the fact that the person received compensation must also be disclosed. Should the individual's testimony imply that the person making the testimony is an expert, a statement regarding the person's qualifications as an expert must also be contained in the ad or sales literature. Research prepared by outside parties must disclose the name of the preparer.

FREE SERVICES

If a member firm advertises free services to customers or to people who respond to an ad, the services must actually be free to everyone with no strings attached.

MISLEADING COMMUNICATION WITH THE PUBLIC

The following are some examples of misleading statements, which are not allowed to appear in communication with the public:

- Excessive hedge clauses.
- Implying an endorsement by FINRA, the NYSE, or the SEC.
- Printing the FINRA logo in type that is larger than the type of the member's name.
- Implying that the member has larger research facilities than it actually has.
- Implying that an individual has higher qualifications than he or she actually has.

SECURITIES INVESTOR PROTECTION CORPORATION ACT OF 1970

The Securities Investor Protection Corporation (SIPC) is a government-sponsored corporation that provides protection to customers in the event of a broker dealer's failure. All broker dealers that are registered with the SEC are required to be SIPC members. All broker dealers are required to pay annual dues to SIPC's insurance fund to cover losses due to broker dealer failure. If a broker dealer fails to pay its SIPC assessment, it may not transact business until the assessment is paid.

NET CAPITAL REQUIREMENT

All broker dealers are required to maintain a certain level of net capital in order to ensure that they are financially solvent. A broker dealer's capital requirement is contingent upon the type of business that it conducts. The larger and more complex the firm's business is, the greater the net capital requirement. Should a firm fall below its net capital requirement, it is deemed to be insolvent, and SIPC will petition in court to have a trustee appointed to liquidate the firm and protect the customers. The trustee must be a disinterested party and, once the trustee is appointed, the firm may not conduct business or try to conceal any assets.

CUSTOMER COVERAGE

SIPC protects customers of a brokerage firm in much the same way that the FDIC protects customers of banks. SIPC covers customer losses that result from broker dealer failure, not for market losses. SIPC covers customers for up to $500,000 per separate customer. Of the $500,000, up to $250,000 may be in cash. Most broker dealers carry additional private insurance to cover larger accounts, but SIPC is the industry-funded insurance and is required by all broker dealers. The following are examples of separate customers:

Customer	Securities Market Value	Cash	SIPC Coverage
Mr. Jones	$320,000	$75,000	All
Mr. & Mrs. Jones	$290,000	$90,000	All
Mrs. Jones	$397,000	$82,000	All

All of the accounts shown would be considered separate customers, and SIPC would cover the entire value of all of the accounts. If an account has in excess of $250,000 in cash, the individual would not be covered for any amount exceeding $250,000 in cash and would become a general creditor for the rest. SIPC does not consider a margin account and a cash account as separate customers and the customer would be covered for the maximum of $500,000. SIPC does not offer coverage for commodities contracts, and all member firms must display the SIPC sign in the lobby of the firm. Many firms purchase excess insurance for customers that go above and beyond SIPC coverage. If the firm reduces or eliminates this excess coverage it must inform customers 30 days prior to the effective date of the change.

FIDELITY BOND

All SIPC members are required to obtain a fidelity bond to protect customers in the event of employee dishonesty. Some things that a fidelity bond will insure against are check forgery and fraudulent trading. The minimum amount of the fidelity bond is $25,000; however, large firms are often required to carry a higher amount.

THE SECURITIES ACTS AMENDMENTS OF 1975

The Securities Acts Amendments of 1975 gave the authority to the MSRB to regulate the issuance and trading of municipal bonds. The MSRB has no enforcement division. Its rules are enforced by other regulators.

THE INSIDER TRADING & SECURITIES FRAUD ENFORCEMENT ACT OF 1988

The Insider Trading & Securities Fraud Enforcement Act of 1988 sets forth guidelines and controls for the use and dissemination of nonpublic material information. Nonpublic information is information that is not known by people outside of the company. Material information is information regarding a situation or development that will materially affect the company in the present or in the future. It is not only just for insiders to have this type of information, but it is required in order for them to do their jobs effectively. It is, however, unlawful for an insider to use this information to profit from a forthcoming move in the stock price. An insider is defined as any officer, director, 10% stockholder, or anyone who is in possession of nonpublic material information, as well as the spouse of any such person. Additionally, it is unlawful for the insider to divulge any of this information to any outside party. Trading on inside information has always been a violation of the Securities Exchange Act of 1934, and the Insider Trading Act prescribed penalties for violators, which include:

- A fine up to 300% of the amount of the gain or 300% of the amount of the loss avoided for the person who acts on the information.
- A civil or criminal fine for the person who divulges the information.
- Insider traders may be sued by the affected parties.
- Criminal prosecutions and a criminal fine of up to $1,000,000 and 20 years in prison.

Information becomes public information once it has been disseminated over public media. The SEC will pay a reward of up to 10% to informants who turn in individuals who trade on inside information. In addition to the insiders already listed, the following are also considered insiders:

- Accountants
- Attorneys
- Investment bankers

FIREWALL

Broker dealers who act as underwriters and investment bankers for corporate clients must have access to information regarding the company in order to advise the company properly. The broker dealer must ensure that no inside information is passed between its investment banking department and its retail trading departments. The broker dealer is required to physically separate these divisions by a firewall. The broker dealer must maintain written supervisory procedures to adequately guard against the wrongful use or dissemination of inside information.

TELEMARKETING RULES

FINRA Rule 3230 regulates how telemarketing calls are made by businesses. On your exam you may see the telemarketing rule tested under the telephone Consumer Protection Act of 1991, FINRA Rule 3230 or as telemarketing rules. Telemarketing calls that are designed to have consumers invest in or purchase goods, services, or property must adhere to the strict guidelines. All firms must:

- Call only between the hours of 8 a.m. and 9 p.m. in the customer's time zone.
- Maintain a do not call list. Individuals placed on the do not call list may not be contacted by anyone at the firm for 5 years.
- Solicitors must give the prospect the firm's name, address, and phone number. Caller ID must display firm name and phone number caller ID blocking may not be used.
- Must maintain adequate policies and procedures to maintain a firm specific do not call list.
- Maintain adequate policies and procedures to ensure numbers called do not appear on the national do not call list.
- Must train representatives on calling policies and use of the do not call list.
- Ensure that any fax solicitations have the firm's name, address, and phone number.

 TAKENOTE!

An interesting situation can arise when a customer of the firm who maintains an account with the firm is on the firm specific do not call list. In these cases, the representative may not contact the customer unless it is to verify account information such as the mailing address. The customer may not be contacted to discuss holdings in the account or to make a recommendation.

DO NOT CALL LIST EXEMPTIONS

The following are exempt from the prohibited calls listed above:

- Calls to existing customers who have executed a transaction or who have had an account containing cash or securities on deposit within the last 18 months or to a person who has contacted the member within the last 3 months.
- Calls to a person where the caller has a personal relationship with the recipient.
- Calls to a person who has given written permission to be contacted by the firm and the number where the person may be contacted.
- Inadvertent calls to a number that now appears on the national do not call list but were not included on the do not call list used by the member so long as that list was not more than 31 days old.

THE PENNY STOCK COLD CALL RULE

The penny stock cold call rule was enacted in order to ensure that investors do not purchase penny stocks without knowing the risks. A penny stock is an unlisted security that trades below $5 per share. Prior to purchasing a penny stock:

- The agent must make sure that the purchase is suitable.
- The customer must sign a suitability statement.
- The firm must supply a current quote.
- The firm must disclose the amount of commission earned by the firm and the agent.

 TAKENOTE!

Established customers are exempt from the penny stock cold call rule. An established customer is one that has made three transactions in three different penny stocks on three different days. An established customer is also one that has had cash or securities on deposit with the firm during the previous 12 months.

THE ROLE OF THE PRINCIPAL

Prior to any firm being admitted as a FINRA member, it must have at least two principals to supervise the firm's activities. All firms are required to have a written policy and procedures manual to ensure compliance with the firm's rules as well as the rules of the industry. The manual must be updated to reflect the adoption of new policies, a change in personnel, or new industry rules. It is the principal's responsibility to ensure that all rules in the policy and procedure manual are followed by all of the firm's employees. It is the responsibility of the principal to review and approve all of the following:

- New accounts
- Retail communication
- Transactions

VIOLATIONS AND COMPLAINTS

FINRA's code of procedure sets forth guidelines for the investigation of alleged violations and complaints against a member firm or a registered representative. The FINRA staff originates many complaints against member firms and associated persons during their routine examinations of member firms. Complaints and allegations of wrongdoing may also originate from a customer of the member firm or from another member. If a FINRA staff member has received the complaint that alleges a violation of securities regulations, it is up to FINRA to determine if the complaint is meritorious. FINRA will begin an investigation of the complaint by notifying the member and/or the associated person that a complaint has been received and will request the member or an associated person to respond in writing. All requests for information must be met within 25 days from the day that the request was made.

RESOLUTION OF ALLEGATIONS

Should FINRA find that the allegations are baseless, it may dismiss it without action. However, if FINRA finds that the allegation has merit, it may be resolved through summary complaint procedure or through a formal hearing process.

MINOR RULE VIOLATION

A minor rule violation letter is traditionally used in cases that involve only small violations. FINRA has outlined a number of rule violations that qualify to be resolved using a minor rule violation (MRV) procedure. It is offered to respondents in an effort to avoid a costly hearing. Under MRV procedure, the maximum penalty is a censure and a $2,500 fine. If the MRV procedure is offered, the member or associated person has 10 business days to accept it. By signing the MRV letter, the respondent does not admit or deny the allegations and gives up his or her right to appeal the decision. Should the offer of MRV procedure not be accepted, the Department of Enforcement will proceed with a formal hearing to determine if a violation has occurred. Possible penalties after having been found to have violated one or more of the association's rules include:

- Censure
- Suspension for up to one year
- Expulsion for up to 10 years
- Barred for life
- Fined any amount
- Any other penalty deemed appropriate, such as restitution

Decisions of the Department of Enforcement may be appealed within 15 days to the National Adjudicatory Counsel (NAC). If no action is taken, the decision of the Department of Enforcement becomes final in 45 days. Should the NAC determine that the appeal is meritorious, it must start a review within a 45-day period. The decision of the NAC may be appealed to the SEC and finally to the court system. Upon final determination, all fines, penalties, and costs must be paid promptly.

CODE OF ARBITRATION

FINRA's arbitration procedure provides parties with a forum to resolve disputes. Most claims submitted to arbitration are financial in nature, although other claims may be submitted. Sexual harassment and discrimination claims are not required to be resolved in arbitration unless both parties specifically agree to arbitrate. Class action claims are also not resolved in arbitration. Class action status is awarded by the court system. Arbitration provides a cost-effective alternative to dispute resolution, and many disputes will be resolved much sooner than they otherwise may have been in court. All industry members are required to settle all disputes through arbitration. A public customer, however, must agree in writing to settle any dispute through arbitration. When a customer opens an account with a broker dealer, the broker dealer will often have the customer sign a customer agreement, although not required by industry standards. The customer agreement usually contains a predispute arbitration cause where the customer agrees to settle any dispute that may arise in arbitration rather than in court. Should the customer request a copy of the predispute arbitration clause the member has 10 business days to provide it to the customer.

THE ARBITRATION PROCESS

Arbitration begins when an aggrieved party, known as the claimant, files a statement of claim, along with a submission agreement and payment for the arbitration fee, with FINRA. The party alleged to have caused the claimant harm (known as the respondent), must respond to the statement of claim within 45 calendar days. The response is sent to both the arbitration director and the claimant, and the claimant then has 10 calendar days to reply to both the arbitration director and respondent. Dispute resolution through arbitration is available for matters involving:

- Member vs. member
- Bank vs. member
- Member vs. bank
- Member vs. registered representative
- Registered representative vs. member
- Customer vs. member
- Member vs. customer

SIMPLIFIED ARBITRATION

Simplified arbitration is available for disputes involving amounts in dispute of $50,000 or less. Simplified arbitration provides no opportunity for a hearing. Parties submit their case in writing only. One arbitrator reviews the case and renders a decision. For amounts that exceed $50,000, a hearing must be held.

LARGER DISPUTES

Larger disputes will be submitted to a panel of up to three arbitrators to render a decision on the matter. A hearing will take place and evidence and testimony will be presented to the panel. The number of arbitrators must always be odd, so the panel will be made up of one or three arbitrators from both the public and the industry. An arbitrator will be deemed to be a nonpublic or industry arbitrator if the person is or was in the securities industry at any point in the last 5 years. Included in this definition are persons associated with hedge funds and accountants and attorneys whose practice is dedicated at least 20% of the time to industry clients within the last two years. An accountant or attorney will be deemed to be a public arbitrator if 10% or less of the business of such professional was dedicated to industry clients in the last two years and the revenue received was less than $50,000.

AWARDS UNDER ARBITRATION

Awards under arbitration are final and binding; there is no appeal. If a monetary payment has been awarded, the party required to pay has 30 days to comply with the decision. A member or a registered representative who fails to pay an award under arbitration is subject to suspension. All pending arbitrations, arbitrations settled prior to final judgement, and arbitrations settled in favor of the customer will be disclosed on BrokerCheck. If an arbitration is settled in favor of the firm or representative it will be removed from BrokerCheck. Any sanction by a regulator which carries a penalty of $15,000 or more will also be disclosed on BrokerCheck.

MEDIATION

Mediation is an informal attempt by two parties to try to resolve a dispute prior to entering into the formal arbitration process. During the mediation process the two parties meet to discuss the contested issue, and the dialog is monitored by a mediator. The mediator is a neutral person with industry knowledge suggested by FINRA who tries to help the parties reach an agreement. If the mediator is not acceptable, the parties may select another mediator from a list of approved mediators or provide their own independent mediator. Prior to entering into the mediation process, both parties must agree to try to resolve the issue in mediation and must split the mediator's fee. The mediation process begins with an initial joint meeting where both parties lay out their claims for the mediator and the other party. During the second phase of the process, each side meets with the mediator individually in meetings known as caucuses. The mediator is a neutral party and will not disclose information provided during the caucus sessions to the opposing side. The mediation process will continue until an agreement is reached, the mediator declares an impasse with no possible resolution, or one of the parties or the mediator withdraws from the process in writing. The mediation process may provide a resolution for all or some of the contested issues. Mediation may take place while the parties are moving forward with the arbitration process. Issues that are not resolved in mediation may be resolved through formal arbitration. The party who served as the mediator may not serve as an arbitrator for the same dispute.

CURRENCY TRANSACTIONS

The Bank Secrecy Act requires all member firms must guard against money laundering. Every member must report any currency receipt of $10,000 or more from any one customer on a single day. The firm must fill out and submit a currency transaction report, also known as Form 4789, to the IRS within 15 days of the receipt of the currency. Multiple deposits that total $10,000 or more will also require the firm to file a currency transaction report (CTR). Additionally, the firm is required to maintain a record of all international wire transfers of $3,000 or greater.

THE PATRIOT ACT

The Patriot Act, as part of the Bank Secrecy Act, requires broker dealers to have written policies and procedures designed to detect suspicious activity. The firm must designate a principal to ensure compliance with the firm's policies and to train firm personnel. The firm is required to file a Suspicious Activity Report (SAR) for any transaction of more than $5,000 that appears questionable. The firm must file the report within 30 days of identifying any suspicious activity. Anti-money-laundering rules require that all firms implement a customer identification program to ensure that the firm knows the true identity of its customers. All customers who open an account with the firm, as well as individuals with trading authority, are subject to this rule. The firm must ensure that its customers do not appear on any list of known or suspected terrorists. A firm's anti-money-laundering program must be approved by senior management. Should the approving member of management leave the firm the plan should be reapproved by the new member of senior management.

All records relating to the SAR filing, including a copy of the SAR report, must be maintained by the firm for 5 years. FINRA Rule 3310 requires member firms to identify to FINRA the name of the person in charge of the firm's AML program as well as the name and full contact details of the person(s) who are to oversee the day-to-day operation of the AML program. Any changes to AML persons identified to FINRA must be updated within 30 days. Members must also conduct an annual independent test of the program. The person conducting the test may not perform the daily AML duties at the firm or report to anyone in charge of the program. The person should have substantial knowledge of the Bank Secrecy Act and its related rules and regulations.

The money-laundering process begins with the placement of the funds. This is when the money is deposited in an account with the broker dealer. The second step of the laundering process is known as layering. The layering process consists of multiple deposits in amounts less than $10,000. The funds will often be drawn from different financial institutions; which is known as structuring. The launderers will then purchase and sell securities in the account. The integration of the proceeds back into the banking system completes the process. At this point, the launderers may use the money, which now appears to have come from legitimate sources, to purchase goods and services. Firms must also identify the customers who open the account and must make sure that they are not conducting business with anyone on the OFAC list. This list is maintained by the Treasury Department Office of Foreign Assets Control. It consists of known and suspected terrorists, criminals, and members of pariah nations. Individuals and entities who appear on this list are known as Specially Designated Nationals and Blocked Persons. Conducting business with anyone on this list is strictly prohibited. Registered representatives who aid in the laundering of money are subject to prosecution and face up to 20 years in prison and a $500,000 fine per transaction. The representative does not even have to be involved in the scheme or even know about it to be prosecuted.

FinCEN is a bureau of the U.S. Department of the Treasury. FinCEN's mission is to safeguard the financial system and guard against money laundering and promote national security. FinCEN collects, receives, and maintains financial transactions data; analyzes and disseminates that data for law enforcement purposes; and builds global cooperation with counterpart organizations in other countries and with international bodies. FinCEN will email a list of individuals and entities to a designated principal every few weeks. The principal is required to check the list against the firm's customer list. If a match is found the firm must notify FinCEN within 14 calendar days.

U.S. ACCOUNTS

Every member must obtain the following from U.S. customers:

- A social security number/documentation number
- Date of birth
- Address
- Place of business

FOREIGN ACCOUNTS

All non-U.S. customers must provide at least one of the following:

- A passport number and country of issuance.
- An alien ID number.
- A U.S. tax ID number.
- A number from another form of government-issued ID and the name of the issuing country.

ANNUAL COMPLIANCE REVIEW

At least once per year the member must conduct a compliance review of each OSJ, supervising branch office, and each registered representative. Nonsupervising branch offices should be directly reviewed every three years. When the member reviews the OSJ, the member is automatically inspecting the activities of the branch offices under the jurisdiction of the OSJ. Each member must designate a principal to test the firm's supervisory and compliance controls. This principal must file a report with senior management detailing the results of these tests. Controls must be in place to provide daily supervision of any producing managers.

BUSINESS CONTINUITY PLAN

One of the regulations developed as a result of the attack on 9/11 is the requirement for FINRA member firms to develop and maintain plans and backup facilities to ensure that the firm can meet its obligations to its customers and counterparties in the event that its main facilities are damaged, destroyed, or inaccessible. The plan must provide for alternative means of communication between the firm, its employees, customers, and regulators as well as a data backup. The plan must provide for data back up in both hard copy and electronic format. The plan must be approved and reviewed annually by a senior member of the firm's management team and provide plans to ensure that customers have access to their funds. The plan must be provided to FINRA upon request. The plan must identify two members of senior management as emergency contacts, one of whom must be a registered principal with the firm. Should one of the contact people change FINRA must be notified in 30 days. Customers of the firm must be advised of the business continuity plan at the time the account is open and in writing upon request. The plan must also be posted on the firms website. Small firms with one office should provide a contact number to the clearing firm.

SARBANES-OXLEY ACT

The Sarbanes-Oxley Act, also known as the Public Company Accounting Reform and Investor Protection Act of 2002, was enacted to help restore confidence in the financial reports and accounting standards of publicly traded companies. The act created the Public Company Accounting Oversight Board to oversee, regulate, and discipline accounting firms' activities when performing auditing functions for publicly traded companies. Section 302 of the Sarbanes-Oxley Act requires the management of publicly traded companies to affirm the accuracy of the company's financial reports and to accept responsibility for the content of the reports by signing all annual and quarterly reports filed under the Securities Exchange Act of 1934. The principal executive officer as well as the principal financial officer must:

- Sign an acknowledgment that they have read the report.
- Certify to their knowledge that the financial reports do not contain any untrue or misleading statements.
- Certify that to their knowledge the reports do not omit any material fact and accurately represent the company's financial condition for the period covered by the report.
- Establish internal controls to ensure the accurate reporting of all of the issuer's subsidiaries.

- Have evaluated the effectiveness of the internal controls within 90 days prior to the filing of the report and must file a report relating to the effectiveness of the internal controls.

- Disclose to the audit committee and the board of directors any deficiencies with internal controls or any act of fraud involving management or any employee significantly involved in the company's internal controls.

- Disclose any material changes to the internal controls or any weaknesses or corrective actions taken.

Section 401 of the Sarbanes-Oxley Act requires financial reports to contain detailed information regarding any off-balance-sheet transactions, obligations, and liabilities the company may have engaged in or have outstanding. The statement may not contain any false or misleading information.

Section 402 of the Sarbanes-Oxley Act enhanced conflict-of-interest rules regarding loans made by the company to any officer. Section 402 of the act made it unlawful for any company to extend or maintain personal loans either directly or indirectly through a subsidiary to or for any officer of the company.

Section 403 of the Sarbanes-Oxley Act requires that the company's management as well as any owner of 10% or more of the company's securities file reports regarding holdings and transactions in the company's securities. These reports must be filed within 10 days of the person becoming an officer or 10% holder. If any person subject to the reporting requirements of Section 403 purchases or sells the company's securities or enters into a security-based swap agreement, a report of the transaction must be filed within two business days. Such reports may be filed electronically.

Section 404 of the Sarbanes-Oxley Act requires that management file with the annual report a report detailing the company's internal controls over financial reporting. The company's independent auditor is required to certify management's report regarding its internal controls.

THE UNIFORM SECURITIES ACT

In the early half of the twentieth century, state securities regulators developed their state's rules and regulations for transacting securities business within their state. The result was a nation of states with regulations that varied widely from state to state. The Uniform Securities Act (USA) laid out model legislation for all states in an effort to make each state's rules and regulations more uniform and easier to address. The USA, also known as "The Act," sets minimum qualification standards for each state securities administrator. The state securities administrator is the top securities regulator within the state.

The state securities administrator may be the attorney general of that state or may be an individual appointed specifically to that post.

The USA also:

- Prohibits the state securities administrator from using the post for personal benefit or from disclosing information.
- Gives the state securities administrator authority to enforce the rules of the USA within that state.
- Gives the administrator the ability to set certain registration requirements for broker dealers, agents, and investment advisers.
- Administrators may set fee and testing requirements.
- Administrators may suspend or revoke the state registration of a broker dealer, agent, investment adviser, or a security or a security's exemption from registration.
- The USA also sets civil and criminal penalties for violators.

The state-based laws set forth by the USA are also known as blue-sky laws.

TENDER OFFERS

A tender offer is made by a person or firm who is seeking to purchase all or part of the outstanding securities of an issuer at a specific price. The SEC has issued strict guidelines that must be followed by both the person making the tender and investors who tender their securities. The guidelines to be followed by parties making a tender offer include:

- The offer must be open for 20 business days from the day it is announced.
- If any of the terms of the tender are changed, the tender must remain open for at least 10 business days from the day the change in the terms was announced.
- A party making a tender offer for stock may not buy the stock or the convertible securities of the issuer during the term of the tender. However, the party may purchase nonconvertible bonds.
- If the duration of the offer is extended, the announcement extending the offer must be released no later than the opening of the exchange on the business day following the original expiration date for exchange-listed

securities. The announcement must include the amount of securities tendered to date.

- If a tender offer is extended for securities that are not listed on an exchange, the announcement must be made no later than 9:00 a.m. EST the business day following the original expiration and must also include the amount of securities tendered to date.

- Shareholders must be notified of the tender offer not later than 10 business days after the tender is announced.

- Management of the company subject to the tender offer must advise shareholders as to management's opinion on the offer (i.e., accept, decline, or neutral).

- A party making a tender offer must pay the price offered for the securities to the extent the offer was made.

Investors may only tender securities that they actually own. An investor may not sell short into a tender, which is known as short tendering. Investors are considered long the security if they have possession of the security or have issued exercise or conversion instructions for an option, warrant, or convertible security. Additionally, investors may only tender their securities to the extent of their net long position. If an investor is short against the box or has written calls with a strike price lower than the tender price, then the investor's net long position will be reduced.

EXAMPLE   If an investor owns 1,000 XYZ and has written 5 XYZ June 40 calls when a tender offer is announced at $42 for XYZ, the investor could only tender 500 shares.

During a partial tender the exact amount of securities to be accepted from all tendering parities is not known. As a result, an investor who has a convertible security may tender an amount equal to the amount to be received upon conversion. If the investor is informed that its tender has been accepted, it must convert the securities and deliver the subject securities.

STOCKHOLDERS OWNING 5% OF AN ISSUER'S EQUITY SECURITIES

The Securities Exchange Act requires that individuals or entities who acquire 5% or more of an issuer's equity securities to file Form 13D with the SEC. Rule 13D requires that the SEC, the exchange where the securities are listed, and the issuer be informed of the size of the investor's holdings and the purpose for the investment. Rule 13D does not require that the stockholders be informed directly by the investor. An entity may acquire more than 5% of the issuer's securities for investment purposes, for control, or for acquisition.

Other entities must also disclose their large holdings in an issuer's securities. Investment companies who acquire 5% or more of an issuer will file a notice of their ownership on Form 13G. Investment advisers who have discretion over $100 million or more in assets must disclose their holding within 45 days of the end of each calendar quarter on Form 13F.

Pretest

SECURITIES INDUSTRY RULES AND REGULATIONS

1. You are the owner of a restaurant and you would like to have a guitarist play in the lounge on Saturday evenings. You have known your representative for 15 years and know her to be a great jazz guitarist. You think she would like to play and ask her if she is available to do so. She would have to notify from which of the following before accepting your offer?

   a. Her firm

   b. No one, because it is not securities related and is on her own time.

   c. FINRA

   d. NYSE

2. A firm has been taken to arbitration by a customer. The disputed amount is $47,400. Which of the following is true?

   a. There will be a hearing, and the decision may be appealed.

   b. There will not be a hearing, and the decision may not be appealed.

   c. There will be a hearing, and the arbitrator's decision is final.

   d. There will be a hearing with up to three arbitrators.

3. The Securities Exchange Act of 1934 regulates which of the following markets?

   a. Third

   b. Fourth

   c. Primary

   d. Secondary

4. Which of the following is an associated person of a member firm?

    I. Registered representative

    II. Trader

    III. Director

    IV. Manager

    a. I and III

    b. I and II

    c. I, II, and IV

    d. I, II, III, and IV

5. In the securities industry, which of the following is the ultimate industry authority regulating conduct?

    a. NYSE

    b. SRO

    c. SEC

    d. FINRA

6. A testimonial by a compensated expert, citing the results she realized following a member's recommendations, must include which of the following?

    I. A statement detailing the expert's credentials

    II. A statement that past performance is not a guarantee of future performance

    III. A statement that the individual is a compensated spokesperson

    IV. The name of the principal who approved the ad

    a. I, II, and III

    b. II and IV

    c. I and II

    d. I, II, III, and IV

7. FINRA's gift rule applies to all of the following, EXCEPT:

    a. noncash gifts.

    b. cash gratuities.

    c. entertainment.

    d. employment contracts to provide temporary services to another member.

8. At a member firm, which of the following must be registered?

   a. A corporate officer whose sole function is to act as liaison between the board of directors and management

   b. A part-time sales assistant who occasionally takes verbal orders from customers

   c. A back-office margin clerk who assists the head of the margin department

   d. A receptionist who takes messages from customers inquiring about their accounts

9. FINRA has taken disciplinary action against a member. The decision of the Department of Enforcement becomes final in:

   a. 30 days

   b. 45 days

   c. 60 days

   d. 90 days

10. A FINRA member has failed to receive a stock certificate in good form from the selling FINRA firm. Which FINRA bylaw defines good delivery?

   a. Rules of Fair Practice

   b. Code of Procedure

   c. Code of Arbitration

   d. Uniform Practice Code

11. Which act gave the NASD (now part of FINRA) the authority to regulate the OTC market?

   a. The NASD Act of 1929

   b. The Securities Act of 1933

   c. The Securities Act of 1934

   d. The Maloney Act of 1938

12. FINRA considers which of the following to be considered retail communication?

    I. Video displays

    II. Listings in phone directories

    III. Circulars

    IV. Telemarketing scripts

    a. II and III

    b. I and II

    c. I, II, III, and IV

    d. I and III

13. A principal must do all of the following, EXCEPT:

    a. report violations of professional conduct by broker dealers to the SEC.

    b. supervise all of the actions of a firm and its employees.

    c. report violations of state and federal laws to the proper authorities.

    d. approve all transactions before they are executed to ensure suitability and to prevent violations.

14. Your brokerage firm has placed an ad in the local newspaper, advertising its new line of services being offered to investors. The firm must maintain the ad for how long?

    a. 24 months

    b. 36 months

    c. 12 months

    d. 18 months

15. According to Rule 135, as it relates to generic advertising, which of the following is NOT true?

    a. The ad may contain information about the services a company offers.

    b. The ad may describe the nature of the investment company's business.

    c. The ad may contain information about exchange privileges.

    d. The ad may contain information about the performance of past recommendations.

16. Sanctions imposed by FINRA are effective within how many days of a written decision?

   a. 45 days

   b. 15 days

   c. 30 days

   d. 60 days

17. During registration of a new issue, false information is included in the prospectus to buyers. Which of the following may be held liable to investors?

   I. Officers of the issuer

   II. Accountants

   III. Syndicate members

   IV. People who signed the registration statement

   a. I and III

   b. I and II

   c. I, II, and III

   d. I, II, III, and IV

18. As it relates to a member firm conducting business with the public, all of the following are violations, EXCEPT:

   a. charging a customer a larger than normal commission for executing a specific order.

   b. failing to execute a customer's order for a speculative security.

   c. stating that a new issue has been approved for sale by the SEC.

   d. printing "FINRA" in large type on business cards.

19. A syndicate has published a tombstone ad prior to an issue becoming effective. Which of the following must appear in the tombstone?

   I. A statement that the registration has not yet become effective.

   II. A statement that the tombstone ad is not an offer to sell the securities.

   III. Contact information.

   IV. A no commitment statement.

   a. III and IV

   b. II and III

   c. I and II

   d. I, II, III, and IV

Answer Keys

CHAPTER 1: EQUITY SECURITIES

1. (D) Common stockholders have the right to receive a percentage of any residual assets.

2. (D) A company can pay a dividend in all of these ways.

3. (C) The yield on the stock will have gone up as the price has fallen because the dividend has remained constant.

4. (C) The transfer agent maintains a list of stockholders and locates lost stock certificates.

5. (D) All dividends received by ordinary income earners are taxed at a 15% rate for the year in which they were received.

6. (B) A stockholder does not get to vote directly for executive compensation.

7. (B) Each ADR represents between 1 and 10 shares. ADR holders do have the right to vote and receive dividends. Foreign governments put restrictions on the foreign ownership of stock from time to time.

8. (B) The current yield is found by using the following formula: annual income/current market price. Therefore, $10/$110 = 9.1%.

9. (C) First, determine the number of shares: par/conversion price = 100/20 = 5. They multiply this by the number of preferred shares: 5 × 100 = 500.

10. (B) An ADR may represent more than one share of the company's common stock and may be exchanged for the ordinary common shares. The dividend, however, is paid in the foreign currency and is received by the investor in U.S. dollars; as a result, the investor is subject to currency risk.

11. (D) The investor will receive $8 per share × 100 shares. Then, $800 plus $1 per share because it is participating, so $800 + $100 = $900.

12. (C) The investor who buys a 7% preferred stock is entitled to $7 per year, or $3.50 every six months.

13. (C) A holder of a cumulative preferred has all of the rights listed, except the right to convert the preferred into common stock.

14. (B) The shareholders may vote to approve an increase in the number of authorized shares.

15. (D) Common stockholders do not have voting power in the matter of bankruptcy.

16. (D) Dividend yield (or current yield) is found by dividing the annual income by the current market price.

17. (C) 800 shares × 5% = 40 shares.

18. (A) In addition to maintaining control, a company may want to increase its earnings per share, fund employee stock option plans, or use shares to pay for a merger or acquisition.

CHAPTER 2: DEBT SECURITIES

1. (A) If 1 bond point is worth $10, then 1.25 points is worth $12.50 × 10 bonds = $125.

2. (D) Bonds registered as to principal only will still require the investor to clip coupons.

3. (C) If the collateral in the portfolio of a private-label CMO is guaranteed by a U.S. government agency, that guarantee does not pass though to the investors in the CMOs. There is no guarantee that the issuer will receive the payments and pass them on to the investors in a timely manner.

4. (C) The yield to call will be the lowest for a bond purchased at a premium.

5. (D) Bearer bonds are issued without a name on them, meaning that whoever has possession of the bond may clip the coupons and claim the interest.

6. (C) All of the choices listed are reasons a corporation would attach warrants to its bonds, except to increase the number of shares outstanding.

7. (B) A mortgage bond is secured by real estate.

8. (D) Collateral trust certificates have pledged securities, which they own, issued by another company as collateral for the issue.

9. (C) An investor who has purchased an 8% corporate bond will receive the principal payment plus the last semiannual interest payment at maturity for a total of $1,040.

10. (B) The parity price of the stock is found by using the following formulas: # of shares = par/CVP, so 1,000/20 = 50. Then, parity price = CMV of bond/# of shares = 1,100/50 = 22.

11. (A) The yield to maturity for a bond purchased at a premium is found using the following formula: (annual income − annual premium)/(price paid + par), thus the answer of 5.45%.

12. (C) The parity price is found by determining the number of shares that can be received upon conversion par/conversion price = 1,000/25 = 40 shares, then the parity price equals the current market value of the convertible/# of shares, or 1,200/40 = $30.

13. (A) An investor would expect to realize the largest gain by purchasing bonds when rates are high. The bond with the longest time left to maturity will become worth the most as interest rates fall.

CHAPTER 3: GOVERNMENT SECURITIES

1. (D) The minimum dollar amount to purchase a Ginnie Mae pass-through certificate is $1,000.

2. (C) T-bonds are quoted as a percentage of par to 32nds of 1%. A quote of 103.16 = 103 16/32% × 1,000 = $1,035.

3. (A) The EE savings bonds are sold at a discount and at maturity are redeemed at face value, which includes the interest income.

4. (B) Interest earned by investors on Fannie Mae securities is taxable at all levels: federal, state, and local.

5. (C) The investor purchased the T-bond at 95.03: 95 3/32% of $1,000 = $950.9375.

CHAPTER 4: MUNICIPAL SECURITIES

1. (D) All of the answers are required on the confirmation except a legal opinion.

2. (A) To find the tax equivalent yield use the following: municipal rate/ (100% − tax bracket) = 6%/.7 = 8.57%.

3. (A) Trades between two MSRB members are reported to the NSCC.

4. (C) All MSRB member firms must have a copy of the MSRB Rule Book, and it must be made available to customers upon request.

5. (D) A new employee of an MSRB member firm must wait 90 days prior to dealing with the public.

6. (C) Many small municipal issues never get a legal opinion because the issue is too small to justify the cost.

7. (D) A round lot for municipal bonds is $100,000 of par value.

8. (B) A municipal bond will generally be more appropriate for an investor in a higher tax bracket. Investors in lower tax brackets may be better off with a higher yielding corporate issue.

9. (B) The bond counsel issues the legal opinion, stating it is a legal binding obligation of the issuer.

10. (C) The safest type of municipal bonds are PHA/NHA bonds, because the interest and principal is guaranteed by the federal government.

11. (B) An out firm quote means that the dealer quoting the prices is obligated to trade with another party at those prices.

12. (A) All capital gains on OID municipal bonds are considered ordinary income.

13. (B) An investor who purchases a municipal bond at a premium must amortize the premium over the number of years remaining until maturity.

14. (C) If an investor sells a municipal bond at a gain, the gain is taxed as ordinary income by the federal government.

15. (C) A syndicate member filling a customer's order will receive the total takedown.

16. (C) Most revenue bonds are awarded to syndicates through negotiation.

17. (A) To calculate the tax equivalent yield for this example, divide the tax exempt yield of the municipal bond (5%, or 0.05) by 1 minus the tax bracket of 30%, or (1 − 0.30, which equals 0.70). So, 0.05/0.70 = 0.0714, or 7.14%. This means that the taxable equivalent yield would need to be at least 7.14% if invested in a taxable vehicle.

18. (D) All of the issuers listed may issue municipal bonds.

19. (B) A firm may never use the information it obtains from an issuer to solicit sales or new business.

20. (B) The portion of a county's debt that a city is responsible for is known as overlapping debt.

CHAPTER 5: THE MONEY MARKET

1. (B) Treasury bills are government money market instruments, not corporate money market instruments.

2. (C) The short-term maturity and the fact that the issuers have solid credit ratings make money market instruments very safe.

3. (B) The money market is a place where issuers go solely for short-term financing, typically under a year.

4. (D) A high-quality debt instrument with less than one year to maturity, regardless of its original maturity, may trade in the money market.

5. (D) Only bankers' acceptances have an original maturity of less than a year.

6. (D) The maximum duration for a piece of commercial paper is nine months, or 270 days.

CHAPTER 6: ECONOMIC FUNDAMENTALS

1. (C) During an inflationary period, the price of a Treasury bond will fall the most. The fixed-income security with the longest maturity will change the most in price as interest rates change.

2. (D) Rising interest rates are bearish for the stock market.

3. (B) The main theory of economics is one of supply and demand; if the supply outpaces the demand, the price of the goods will fall.

4. (D) The discount rate is the rate that is actually controlled by the Federal Reserve Board. All of the other rates are adjusted in the marketplace by the lenders as a result of a change in the discount rate.

5. (C) Falling inventories is a sign of a pick up in the economy.

6. (A) A bank may borrow money from another bank to meet its reserve requirement and it will pay the other bank the federal funds rate.

7. (A) The two tools of the government are monetary policy, which is controlled by the Federal Reserve Board, because it controls the money supply, and fiscal policy, which is determined by the President and Congress, because it controls government spending and taxation.

8. (D) Fiscal policy is controlled by the President and Congress.

9. (C) The Federal Reserve sets all of these except government spending.

10. (A) A decline in the gross domestic product must last at least two quarters or six months to be considered a recession.

CHAPTER 7: OPTIONS

1. (B) Your maximum gain when you sell an option with no other positions in the account is always the premium received: 5.70 × 1,000 = $5,700

2. (C) The option is for $100,000 par value. The investor will receive accrued interest when the bond is delivered.

3. (D) When stock options are exercised, the underlying security will be delivered in three business days.

4. (C) With the opening sale of a naked option, the maximum gain is always the premium received.

5. (B) To gain some protection and take in premium income, you would sell 100 XYZ Oct 45 calls.

6. (D) Statement I is incorrect in that an option is a contract between two parties, which determines the time and price at which a security may be bought or sold.

7. (A) With a long straddle, the maximum gain is unlimited because the investor owns the calls.

8. (A) If you think that bond prices are going down, you would want to buy rate-based calls and/or price-based puts.

9. (B) A debit call spread and a credit put spread are both bullish. Straddles are neither bullish nor bearish.

10. (B) This is a credit spread; the investor wants the options to expire and the spread in the premiums to narrow.

11. (C) Call sellers and put buyers are both bearish. They want the value of the stock to fall.

12. (C) U.S. importers will always buy calls on the foreign currency to hedge themselves. The dollar-based answer is always wrong. There are no options trading on the U.S. dollar in the United States.

13. (B) Capped index options trade like spread and are automatically exercised if they go 30 points in the money.

14. (B) Option trades settle the next day.

15. (B) The Options Clearing Corporation (OCC) issues all standardized options.

16. (D) On a credit spread, your maximum gain is always the credit received.

17. (D) An investor selling stock short will gain the maximum protection by buying calls.

18. (A) An investor would be least likely to be approved to sell naked calls.

19. (D) The investor made $3,900. The options are worth $7,000 at expiration. The investor paid $3,100. Therefore, the profit is $3,900.

20. (A) The Options Clearing Corporation (OCC) issues all option contracts and guarantees their performance.

21. (A) A diagonal spread consists of a long and short option of the same type with different strike prices and expiration months.

22. (C) The maximum gain on a long straddle is unlimited because the investor is long the calls.

23. (B) It is not possible to write a rate-based covered call. Rate-based options are based on T-bills that have not been issued yet.

24. (C) A customer must return the signed option agreement within 15 days of the account's approval to trade options.

25. (A) The Options Clearing Corporation (OCC) is wholly owned by the exchanges.

CHAPTER 8: MUTUAL FUNDS

1. (A) A mutual fund encourages investors, be they individuals, corporations, trusts, or accounts for minors, to invest larger sums of money in the same mutual fund; this increased investment benefits everyone in the process.

2. (C) The letter of intent can be backdated up to 90 days to include the original purchase.

3. (B) An investment club may not qualify for breakpoint sales charge reductions.

4. (C) A registered investment company is prohibited from acting as a bank or a savings and loan.

5. (D) Only a no-load fund may sell its own shares to investors.

6. (B) The investment adviser is always a company, not a single person.

7. (B) An investment company must have at least 100 shareholders to start and to continue.

8. (C) A unit investment trust (UIT) is not actively managed. It does not have a board of directors or an investment adviser.

9. (C) A mutual fund may only send out capital gains distributions once per year.

10. (A) A diversified mutual fund may invest no more than 5% of its assets in any one company.

11. (D) The pricing formula for an open-end investment company is always NAV + SC = POP.

12. (B) To find out what price the investor will pay, take the POP and multiply it by the complement of the sales charge: .915(100% − SC%) = 20 × .915 = 18.30. This is the NAV of the fund. Then take the NAV and divide it by the complement of the sales charge percentage at the break point: (100% − SC%).94 = 18.30/.94 = 19.47. Then, take the total dollars invested ($70,000) and divide it by the POP at the breakpoint: $70,000/19.48 = $3,595.

13. (A) A mutual fund must send out 90% of its net investment income to shareholders in order to retain its tax advantages: net investment income = dividend income + interest income − expenses, or 22,450,000 + 21,670,000 − 5,250,000 = 38,870,000 × 90% = 34,983,000.

14. (B) The ex dividend date for an open-end mutual fund is set by the board of directors and is the day after the record date.

15. (A) A mutual fund prospectus must be updated every 13 months.

16. (D) In order for a mutual fund company to charge the maximum allowable sales charge of 8.5%, the mutual fund company must offer all of the features listed, except conversion privileges.

17. (C) An option income fund sells call options against its portfolio of common shares to increase the income into the portfolio. As the market price of the shares in the portfolio increase, the shares will be called away, and the upside appreciation will therefore be limited.

18. (C) The mutual fund prospectus must be presented to investors before or during the sales presentation.

19. (B) All of the choices listed are ways to accumulate mutual fund shares, except deferred investment.

CHAPTER 9: VARIABLE ANNUITIES

1. (C) The best payout option for this investor would be a life only payout option.

2. (C) An investor who owns a fixed annuity is subject to purchasing power risk.

3. (D) The AIR will affect the amount of the annuity payment the investor receives and the value of the annuity unit.

4. (D) An investor may never change the payout option once it has been selected.

5. (C) There is no such thing as a periodic payment immediate annuity.

6. (B) The investor will pay taxes on the entire $3,000. All random withdraws from a variable annuity will be done on a LIFO basis and will be made from the growth in the account.

7. (B) A fixed annuity cannot guarantee protection from inflation.

8. (B) If the separate account invests indirectly, it buys mutual funds. The separate account would have to be registered as a UIT.

9. (B) The number of annuity units is fixed and represents the proportion of the owner's shares in the separate accounts portfolio.

10. (B) Because the value of the account has fallen, there is no growth to be withdrawn. So, the entire amount is a return of principal and is not taxed.

CHAPTER 10: ISSUING CORPORATE SECURITIES

1. (D) All of the items listed must appear in the tombstone ad.

2. (D) All of the parties listed may be held liable to the purchasers of the new issue.

3. (B) A syndicate may only enter a stabilizing bid at or below the offering price.

4. (A) A corporation must issue common stock before it issues any preferred stock.

5. (C) The issuance of prior lien bonds requires the approval of shareholders.

6. (C) A greenshoe provision allows the syndicate to purchase up to an additional 15% of the offering from the issuer.

7. (A) All of the choices listed are types of offerings, except Rule 149.

8. (B) A business must first hire an underwriter to advise the issuer about the type of securities to issue.

9. (C) The number of nonaccredited investors is limited to 35 in any 12-month period.

10. (D) A company doing a preemptive rights offering will use a standby underwriting agreement where the underwriter will "standby" ready to purchase any shares not purchased by shareholders.

11. (B) Only one syndicate bid may be entered to the benefit of the syndicate.

12. (A) When existing stockholders are offered their "right," they may buy stock at the subscription price, which is generally below market value and to their benefit, also preserving their percentage holding in the company.

13. (C) When the SEC wants more information; it will most likely issue a deficiency letter.

14. (A) Primary commitment is not a type of underwriting commitment.

15. (B) Purchasers of stock that has just gone public must get a prospectus for 90 days.

16. (A) All of the answers listed will appear in the preliminary prospectus, except the offering price and the proceeds to the company.

17. (A) A selling group member has no liability to the syndicate if securities remain unsold.

CHAPTER 11: TRADING SECURITIES

1. (A) When acting as a market maker, the firm is trading for its own account and is acting as a dealer.

2. (D) In order to establish a short position, the investor must be able to borrow the security. Municipal bonds are not readily available to be borrowed.

3. (D) An allied member may not trade on the floor. It is only allowed to call itself a member and have electronic access to the exchange.

4. (C) Firms that act as market makers in Nasdaq securities are trying to make the spread, which is the difference between the bid and the ask.

5. (D) Mini maxi and best efforts are types of underwriting commitments, not types of orders.

6. (C) A technical analyst would want to buy the stock when it breaks through resistance.

7. (A) Selling stock short will expose an investor to unlimited risk because there is no limit to how high a stock price can go.

8. (A) The inside market is the highest bid and the lowest offer.

9. (A) Specialists on the NYSE work for themselves or for a specialist firm.

10. (D) Of the choices, preferred stock is most likely to trade in a round lot of 10 shares.

11. (D) 300 shares traded at 84.15; the s/s means that a round lot for the stock is 10 shares.

12. (C) An investor who is bullish would most likely enter a buy stop above the market.

13. (B) The order has been elected because the stock has traded though the stop price. The order has now become a limit order to sell the stock at 160.

CHAPTER 12: CUSTOMER ACCOUNTS

1. (C) A registered representative may only accept orders from the client.

2. (A) In a custodial account, the custodian is the nominal owner of the account and carries on all transactions for the minor, the real beneficial owner of the account.

3. (D) An adult may never have a joint account with a minor.

4. (A) The assets of the decedent will be distributed according to the decedent's will.

5. (C) An account set up by a guardian must be accompanied by declaration papers.

6. (B) In a fiduciary account, the trustee enters all orders for the owners of the account.

7. (D) There is no limit to the size of the gift that may be given to anyone, but $14,000 per year is the tax-free limit.

8. (A) The nominal owner of a UGMA account is the custodian.

9. (B) A representative may only borrow from a client if the client is in the business of making loans (i.e., a bank or credit union).

10. (D) The registered representative's father-in-law may be able to purchase a hot issue, provided strict conditions are met.

11. (B) Although the minor's social security number is listed on the account, it does not appear in the account title.

12. (C) The customer is not required to sign anything when opening a new account.

13. (D) The rule is one custodian and one minor for each UGMA account. There is not a rule regarding who must be custodian.

14. (A) A client may have a numbered account if his signature as owner is on file; broker dealers may give gifts to the employees of other broker dealers with certain restrictions. To obtain outside employment, a representative must first obtain approval from the member firm where he works.

15. (C) The customer's educational information is not required on the new account form.

16. (A) This is a joint account with rights of survivorship. All assets become the property of the surviving party.

17. (A) Before opening a new account for any new customer, a registered representative must fill out and sign a new account form, which does not require the signature of the new customer.

18. (B) If a client dies without a will, the client's assets will be distributed by the administrator.

CHAPTER 13: MARGIN ACCOUNTS

1. (C) The NYSE/FINRA set the minimum maintenance for a new margin account.

2. (B) The initial minimum for a new margin account is the greater of $2,000 or 50% of the purchase price.

3. (C) The customer must sign the hypothecation agreement.

4. (B) To find the minimum equity given a long market value, simply multiply the market value by .25.

5. (A) Municipal bonds are exempt from Regulation T; the margin requirement is set by the SROs.

6. (A) To find the minimum maintenance, multiply the long market value by .25 = 96,500 × .25 = $24,125.

7. (D) When buying a municipal bond in a margin account, investors must deposit the greater of 7% of par value or 15% of the market value. In this case 15% × $54,000 = $8,100.

8. (B) The $2,000 minimum equity requirement is only for the initial deposit.

9. (A) The market value could fall to $72,000. This is found by dividing the debit balance by .75, or $54,000/.75 = $72,000

10. (C) All of the answers listed are required, except the approval of the president.

11. (C) If an investor uses an SMA to withdraw cash, the SMA is reduced and the investor's debit balance is increased by an equal amount.

CHAPTER 14: RETIREMENT PLANS

1. (B) Of the choices listed, only II and IV are correct. A 401k may not be easily rolled over. Remember that a rollover allows the participant to take possession of the money. A plan participant is only vested immediately in his or her own contributions. The participant will become vested in the employer's contributions based on a vesting schedule.

2. (B) Only the Keogh plan and the TDA are funded with pre-tax dollars. The rest are funded with after-tax dollars.

3. (D) The money has been deposited into a nonqualified plan, and the $11,000 has therefore been placed into the plan with after-tax dollars. Only the growth in the account is taxable, or in this case: $5,200 \times 30\% = $1,560.

4. (D) The penalty for an excess Keogh contribution is 10%.

5. (B) An investor may roll over an IRA once per year and has 60 days to get the money into a qualified plan.

6. (D) A Keogh plan allows individuals, sole proprietors, and unincorporated small businesses to establish a retirement plan for themselves and their employees.

7. (A) IRS approval is required for participation in a qualified plan. IRS approval is not required for a nonqualified plan.

8. (C) The retirement account is qualified. Because the investors have deposited the money pre-tax, all of the money is taxed when it is withdrawn.

9. (D) A deferred compensation plan is nonfunded. There is no money set aside for the participant in the plan.

CHAPTER 15: BROKERAGE OFFICE PROCEDURE

1. (A) The amount of commission to be charged does not have to be on the ticket prior to execution.

2. (D) All of these are correct.

3. (A) Arbitrage is a type of trading or investing strategy and would not be handled by the reorganization department.

4. (C) The firm must request an extension in writing from the NYSE or FINRA, and it must be requested before the end of the fifth business day.

5. (B) The investor may transfer shares by signing a stock or bond power.

6. (C) An investor who fails to pay for a trade by the expiration of the fifth business may keep any gain and is responsible for any loss. The account will also be frozen for 90 days. The investor may not request an extension after the expiration of the fifth business day.

7. (D) A customer must receive a statement whenever there is activity in the account. The investor purchased the shares two months ago and must have received a statement that month. Because the shares were purchased on margin, interest is being charged on the loan. The debiting of interest to the customer's account is considered activity, and the customer must receive a statement for those months as well.

8. (C) A shareholder who attends the meeting will not be able to vote by proxy; the shareholder will vote at the meeting. Shareholders must return their proxies before 10 days prior to the annual meeting.

9. (C) A customer may sign a stock or bond power, which will make the certificate transferable.

10. (B) A customer who purchases a security and decides that it is unsuitable is not a reason to reject delivery.

11. (D) A customer who cannot deposit the funds to cover a purchase in the margin account by the fifth business day may experience all of the items listed.

12. (C) The ex dividend date for stock is two business days prior to the record date.

13. (B) Treasury securities settle on the next business day.

14. (D) A firm may charge a fee for all of the services listed.

15. (C) A signature may only be guaranteed by a bank officer or the principal of an exchange member firm.

16. (B) All of the choices listed are correct except that the seller will not get to keep the dividend.

17. (D) The purchase and sales department sends out customer confirmations.

18. (B) This trade requires the customer to have the money available in the account and the trade will settle the same day.

19. (C) A firm may charge an additional fee for the handling of odd lots. All of the other choices are false.

CHAPTER 16: FUNDAMENTAL AND TECHNICAL ANALYSIS

1. (A) The company's earnings per share are determined by dividing the earnings available to common shareholders by the number of outstanding shares: $2,000,000/2,000,000 = $1.

2. (D) Everything that a company owns (assets) minus everything that a company owes (liabilities) results in the corporation's net worth and the stockholders' equity.

3. (B) The current yield is found by multiplying the quarterly dividend by four—$.70 × 4 = $2.80—and then dividing it by the market price: $2.80/20 = 14%.

4. (D) Capitalization refers to the overall picture of a company's financial situation, including its assets, liabilities, net worth, and stockholders' equity, as shown on its balance sheet.

5. (B) A fundamental investment approach would not look at support for a stock price.

6. (A) A high short interest is considered bullish.

7. (D) Systematic risk is inherent in any investment in the market. An investment may decline in value simply because prices in the overall market are falling.

CHAPTER 17: DIRECT PARTICIPATION PROGRAMS

1. (C) This type of sharing arrangement is known as a reversionary working interest.

2. (D) Historic rehabilitation programs generate the most tax advantages.

3. (C) This is known as the crossover point, and it is bad for investors.

4. (C) A limited partner may not advise the general partner. If a limited partner advises the general partner, it risks losing its limited partner status and could be considered a general partner.

5. (C) The holder of an overriding royalty interest has no partnership risks but receives a royalty from the partnership.

6. (A) A recourse loan could require the limited partners to make additional payments.

7. (C) A recourse loan means that the lender has recourse to the limited partners. They can be held liable for the debt service, and it can increase their cost base.

8. (B) DPPs are generally very illiquid and fairly speculative. The main concern is profitability and tax considerations.

9. (D) Raw land may never be depreciated.

10. (C) Intangible drilling costs, such as geological surveys, will generate the largest tax credits.

CHAPTER 18: CUSTOMER RECOMMENDATIONS, PROFESSIONAL CONDUCT, AND TAXATION

1. (B) This is known as painting the tape matched purchases or matched sales.

2. (D) An industrial revenue bond may subject some wealthy investors to the alternative minimum tax.

3. (B) Of all the investments listed, only the Ginnie Mae pass-through certificate will provide income. Ginnie Mae pass-through certificates pay monthly interest and principal payments.

4. (D) This client is concerned about legislative risk, which is the risk that the government will do something that adversely affects an investment.

5. (C) The holding period would end if the investor sells a deep in the money call or if the investor purchases a put.

6. (A) The investor has a large position in a thinly traded stock; as a result, the investor is subject to a large amount of liquidity risk.

7. (B) An investor who is concerned with the changes in interest rates would be least likely to purchase long-term bonds. As interest rates change, the price of the long-term bonds will fluctuate the most.

8. (B) Bankers' acceptances are money market instruments and are short term; series HH government bonds can only be exchanged for mature series EE; and convertible preferred stock is a security with risk. A 90-day T-bill is considered a risk-free investment.

9. (D) Using the pending dividend to create an urgency on the part of the investor to purchase this stock is a perfect example of this violation, and the results are listed in answers A, B, and C.

10. (D) An investor in a low tax bracket seeking current income would be best suited for a corporate bond fund.

11. (B) This is a violation known as trading ahead.

12. (D) An investor seeking protection from interest rate risk will most likely be best suited for a portfolio of Treasury bills. As the bills mature, the investor can roll over the position into the newly issued bills with new interest rates.

13. (B) An investor seeking some current income would least likely invest in an income bond. An income bond, also known as an adjustment bond, will only pay interest if the company has enough income to do so.

14. (D) The greatest risk when purchasing a CMO is the risk of early refinancing or prepayment risk.

15. (C) Treasury STRIPS are government-issued zero-coupon bonds. They are issued at a discount and mature at par, or $1,000. For the exam, they are the best answer for college expense planning if the question is asking for an investment recommendation, not the type of account that it is deposited into.

16. (D) Showing a client the past performance for a mutual fund that has only been around for three years is in line with the regulations. All of the other choices are violations.

17. (A) If an investor may lose part or all of his capital, it is called capital risk.

18. (C) A money market fund is the best recommendation for investors who will need access to their funds in the next few years.

CHAPTER 19: SECURITIES INDUSTRY RULES AND REGULATIONS

1. (A) The representative would have to notify from her employer before working outside the office in any capacity.

2. (B) There will be no hearing, and the decision of the arbitrator is final and binding. Claims under $50,000 will be resolved in simplified arbitration.

3. (D) The Securities Exchange Act of 1934 regulates the secondary market.

4. (D) All of the choices listed are associated people.

5. (C) The SEC is the ultimate industry authority in regulating conduct.

6. (A) All of the choices listed must be included, except for the name of the principal who approved the ad for use.

7. (D) The FINRA rule regarding gifts or payments to employees of another member covers all of those things listed, except contract employees of another member firm who are exempt from the gift rule.

8. (B) The part-time sales assistant who takes orders from customers must be registered because she is taking orders.

9. (B) The decision of the DOE becomes final in 45 days if not appealed.

10. (D) The Uniform Practice Code regulates the way that members conduct business with other members.

11. (D) The Maloney Act of 1938 was an amendment to the Securities Exchange Act of 1934 and established the NASD (now part of FINRA) as the self-regulatory organization for the over-the-counter market.

12. (C) All of the choices listed would be considered to be retail communication if any part of the communications listed could be seen by an individual investor.

13. (D) A principal is designated to supervise all of the actions of a firm and its employees; a principal must prevent any violation of industry, state, or federal laws or regulations. However, the principal need not approve all transactions prior to their execution.

14. (B) Brokerage firms must maintain their advertising for at least three years.

15. (D) Generic advertising may not contain information about past recommendations.

16. (C) The decisions are final after 30 days.

17. (D) All of the parties listed may be held liable to the purchasers of the new issue.

18. (A) A member firm may charge a customer a larger than ordinary commission for the execution of a specific order so long as it is disclosed to the customer. A member firm must always execute a customer's order.

19. (D) All of the items listed must appear in the tombstone ad.

Glossary of Exam Terms

A

AAA/Aaa
The highest investment-grade rating for bond issuers awarded by Standard & Poor's and Moody's ratings agencies.

acceptance waiver and consent (AWAC)
A process used when a respondent does not contest an allegation made by FINRA. The respondent accepts the findings without admitting any wrongdoing and agrees to accept any penalty for the violation.

account executive (AE)
An individual who is duly licensed to represent a broker dealer in securities transactions or investment banking business. Also known as a registered representative.

accredited investor
Any individual or institution that meets one or more of the following: (1) a net worth exceeding $1 million, excluding the primary residence, or (2) is single and has an annual income of $200,000 or more or $300,000 jointly with a spouse.

accretion
An accounting method used to step up an investor's cost base for a bond purchased at a discount.

accrued interest
The portion of a debt securities future interest payment that has been earned by the seller of the security. The purchaser must pay this amount of accrued interest to the seller at the time of the transaction's settlement. Interest accrues from the date of the last interest payment date up to, but not including, the transaction's settlement date.

accumulation stage
The period during which an annuitant is making contributions to an annuity contract.

accumulation unit
A measure used to determine the annuitant's proportional ownership interest in the insurance company's separate account during the accumulation

stage. During the accumulation stage, the number of accumulation units owned by the annuitant changes and their value varies.

acid-test ratio
A measure of corporate liquidity found by subtracting inventory from current assets and dividing the result by the current liabilities.

ACT
See Automated Comparison Transaction (ACT) service.

ad valorem tax
A tax based on the value of the subject property.

adjusted basis
The value assigned to an asset after all deductions or additions for improvements have been taken into consideration.

adjusted gross income (AGI)
An accounting measure employed by the IRS to help determine tax liability. AGI = earned income + investment income (portfolio income) + capital gains + net passive income.

administrator
(1) An individual authorized to oversee the liquidation of an intestate decedent's estate. (2) An individual or agency that administers securities' laws within a state.

ADR/ADS
See American depositary receipt (ADR).

advance/decline line
Measures the health of the overall market by calculating advancing issues and subtracting the number of declining issues.

advance refunding
The early refinancing of municipal securities. A new issue of bonds is sold to retire the old issue at its first available call date or maturity.

advertisement
Any material that is distributed by a broker dealer or issuer for the purpose of increasing business or public awareness for the firm or issuer. The broker dealer or issuer must distribute advertisements to an audience that is not controlled. Advertisements are distributed through any of the following: newspapers/magazines, radio, TV, billboards, telephone.

affiliate
An individual who owns 10% or more of the company's voting stock. In the case of a direct participation program (DPP), this is anyone who controls the partnership or is controlled by the partnership.

agency issue
A debt security issued by any authorized entity of the U.S. government. The debt security is an obligation of the issuing entity, not an obligation of the U.S. government (with the exception of Ginnie Mae and the Federal Import Export Bank issues).

agency transaction
A transaction made by a firm for the benefit of a customer. The firm merely executes a customer's order and charges a fee for the service, which is known as a commission.

agent
A firm or an individual who executes securities transactions for customers and charges a service fee known as a commission. Also known as a broker.

aggregate indebtedness	The total amount of the firm's customer-related debts.
allied member	An owner-director or 5% owner of an NYSE member firm. Allied members may not trade on the floor.
all-or-none (AON) order	A non-time-sensitive order that stipulates that the customer wants to buy or sell all of the securities in the order.
all-or-none underwriting	A type of underwriting that states that the issuer wants to sell all of the securities being offered or none of the securities being offered. The proceeds from the issue will be held in escrow until all securities are sold.
alpha	A measure of the projected change in the security's price as a result of fundamental factors relating only to that company.
alternative minimum tax (AMT)	A method used to calculate the tax liability for some high-income earners that adds back the deductions taken for certain tax preference items.
AMBAC Indemnity Corporation	Insures the interest and principal payments for municipal bonds.
American depositary receipt (ADR)/ American depositary security (ADS)	A receipt representing the beneficial ownership of foreign securities being held in trust overseas by a foreign branch of a U.S. bank. ADRs/ADSs facilitate the trading and ownership of foreign securities and trade in the United States on an exchange or in the over-the-counter markets.
American Stock Exchange (AMEX)	An exchange located in New York using the dual-auction method and specialist system to facilitate trading in stocks, options, exchange-traded funds, and portfolios. AMEX was acquired by the NYSE Euronext and is now part of NYSE Alternext.
amortization	An accounting method that reduces the value of an asset over its projected useful life. Also the way that loan principal is systematically paid off over the life of a loan.
annual compliance review	All firms must hold at least one compliance meeting per year with all of its agents.
annuitant	An individual who receives scheduled payments from an annuity contract.
annuitize	A process by which an individual converts from the accumulation stage to the payout stage of an annuity contract. This is accomplished by exchanging accumulation units for annuity units. Once a payout option is selected, it cannot be changed.
annuity	A contract between an individual and an insurance company that is designed to provide the annuitant with lifetime income in exchange for either a lump sum or periodic deposits into the contract.

annuity unit
An accounting measure used to determine an individual's proportionate ownership of the separate account during the payout stage of the contract. The number of annuity units owned by an individual remains constant, and their value, which may vary, is used to determine the amount of the individual's annuity payment.

appreciation
An asset's increase in value over time.

arbitrage
An investment strategy used to profit from market inefficiencies.

arbitration
A forum provided by both the NYSE and FINRA to resolve disputes between two parties. Only a public customer may not be forced to settle a dispute through arbitration. The public customer must agree to arbitration in writing. All industry participants must settle disputes through arbitration.

ask
See offer.

assessed value
A base value assigned to property for the purpose of determining tax liability.

assessment
An additional amount of taxes due as a result of a municipal project that the homeowner benefits from. Also an additional call for capital by a direct participation program.

asset
Anything of value owned by an individual or a corporation.

asset allocation fund
A mutual fund that spreads its investments among different asset classes (i.e., stocks, bonds, and other investments) based on a predetermined formula.

assignee
A person to whom the ownership of an asset is being transferred.

assignment
(1) The transfer of ownership or rights through a signature. (2) The notification given to investors who are short an option that the option holder has exercised its right and they must now meet their obligations as detailed in the option contract.

associated person
Any individual under the control of a broker dealer, issuer, or bank, including employees, officers, and directors, as well as those individuals who control or have common control of a broker dealer, issuer, or bank.

assumed interest rate (AIR)
(1) A benchmark used to determine the minimum rate of return that must be realized by a variable annuity's separate account during the payout phase in order to keep the annuitant's payments consistent. (2) In the case of a variable life insurance policy, the minimum rate of return that must be achieved in order to maintain the policy's variable death benefit.

at-the-close order
An order that stipulates that the security is to be bought or sold only at the close of the market, or as close to the close as is reasonable, or not at all.

at the money
A term used to describe an option when the underlying security price is equal to the exercise price of the option.

at-the-opening order	An order that stipulates that the security is to be bought or sold only at the opening of the market, or as close to the opening as is reasonable, or not at all.
auction market	The method of trading employed by stock exchanges that allows buyers and sellers to compete with one another in a centralized location.
authorized stock	The maximum number of shares that a corporation can sell in an effort to raise capital. The number of authorized shares may only be changed by a vote of the shareholders.
Automated Comparison Transaction (ACT) service	ACT is the service that clears and locks Nasdaq trades.
average cost	A method used to determine the cost of an investment for an investor who has made multiple purchases of the same security at different times and prices. An investor's average cost may be used to determine a cost base for tax purposes or to evaluate the profitability of an investment program, such as dollar-cost averaging. Average cost is determined by dividing the total dollars invested by the number of shares purchased.
average price	A method used to determine the average price paid by an investor for a security that has been purchased at different times and prices, such as through dollar-cost averaging. An investor's average price is determined by dividing the total of the purchase prices by the number of purchases.

B

BBB/Baa	The lowest ratings assigned by Standard & Poor's and Moody's for debt in the investment-grade category.
backing away	The failure of an over-the-counter market maker to honor firm quotes. It is a violation of FINRA rules.
back-end load	A mutual fund sales charge that is assessed upon the redemption of the shares. The amount of the sales charge to be assessed upon redemption decreases the longer the shares are held. Also known as a contingent deferred sales charge.
balanced fund	A mutual fund whose investment policy requires that the portfolio's holdings are diversified among asset classes and invested in common and preferred stock, bonds, and other debt instruments. The exact asset distribution among the asset classes will be predetermined by a set formula that is designed to balance out the investment return of the fund.
balance of payments	The net balance of all international transactions for a country in a given time.

balance of trade	The net flow of goods into or out of a country for a given period. Net exports result in a surplus or credit; net exports result in a deficit or net debit.
balance sheet	A corporate report that shows a company's financial condition at the time the balance sheet was created.
balance sheet equation	Assets = liabilities + shareholders equity.
balloon maturity	A bond maturity schedule that requires the largest portion of the principal to be repaid on the last maturity date.
bankers' acceptance (BA)	A letter of credit that facilitates foreign trade. BAs are traded in the money market and have a maximum maturity of 270 days.
basis	The cost that is assigned to an asset.
basis book	A table used to calculate bond prices for bonds quoted on a yield basis and to calculate yields for bonds quoted on a price basis.
basis point	Measures a bond's yield; 1 basis point is equal to 1/100 of 1%.
basis quote	A bond quote based on the bond's yield.
bearish	An investor's belief that prices will decline.
bearer bond	A bond that is issued without the owner's name being registered on the bond certificate or the books of the issuer. Whoever has possession of (bears) the certificate is deemed to be the rightful owner.
bear market	A market condition that is characterized by continuing falling prices and a series of lower lows in overall prices.
best efforts underwriting	A type of underwriting that does not guarantee the issuer that any of its securities will be sold.
beta	A measure of a security's or portfolio's volatility relative to the market as a whole. A security or portfolio whose beta is greater than 1 will experience a greater change in price than overall market prices. A security or portfolio with a beta of less than 1 will experience a price change that is less than the price changes realized by the market as a whole.
bid	A price that an investor or broker dealer is willing to pay for a security. It is also a price at which an investor may sell a security immediately and the price at which a market maker will buy a security.
blind pool	A type of direct participation program where less than 75% of the assets to be acquired have been identified.
block trade	A trade involving 10,000 shares or market value of over $200,000.
blotter	A daily record of broker dealer transactions.
blue chip stock	Stock of a company whose earnings and dividends are stable regardless of the economy.

Blue List	A daily publication of municipal bond offerings and secondary market interest.
blue sky	A term used to describe the state registration process for a security offering.
blue-sky laws	Term used to describe the state-based laws enacted under the Uniform Securities Act.
board broker	*See* order book official.
board of directors	A group of directors elected by the stockholders of a corporation to appoint and oversee corporate management.
Board of Governors	The governing body of FINRA. The board is made up of 27 members elected by FINRA's membership and the board itself.
bona fide quote	*See* firm quote.
bond	The legal obligation of a corporation or government to repay the principal amount of debt along with interest at a predetermined schedule.
bond anticipation note	Short-term municipal financing sold in anticipation of long-term financing.
bond buyer indexes	A group of yield-based municipal bond indexes published daily in the *Daily Bond Buyer*.
bond counsel	An attorney for the issuer of municipal securities who renders the legal opinion.
bond fund	A fund whose portfolio is made up of debt instruments issued by corporations, governments, and/or their agencies. The fund's investment objective is usually current income.
bond interest coverage ratio	A measure of the issuer's liquidity. It demonstrates how many times the issuer's earnings will cover its bond interest expense.
bond quotes	Corporate and government bond quotes are based on a percentage of par. Municipal bonds are usually quoted on a yield-to-maturity basis.
bond rating	A rating that assesses the financial soundness of issuers and their ability to make interest and principal payments in a timely manner. Standard & Poor's and Moody's are the two largest ratings agencies. Issuers must request and pay for the service to rate their bonds.
bond ratio	A measure used to determine how much of the corporation's capitalization was obtained through the issuance of bonds.
bond swap	The sale and purchase of two different bonds to allow the investor to claim a loss on the bond being sold without violating wash sale rules.
book entry	Securities that are issued in book entry form do not offer any physical certificates as evidence of ownership. The owner's name is registered on the books of the issuer, and the only evidence of ownership is the trade confirmation.

book value	A corporation's book value is the theoretical liquidation value of the company. Book value is in theory what someone would be willing to pay for the entire company.
book value per bond	A measure used to determine the amount of the corporation's tangible value for each bond issued.
book value per share	Used to determine the tangible value of each common share. It is found by subtracting intangible assets and the par value of preferred stock from the corporation's total net worth and dividing that figure by the number of common shares outstanding.
branch office	A branch office of a member firm is required to display the name of the member firm and is any office in which the member conducts securities business outside of its main office.
breadth	A measure of the broad market's health. It measures how many stocks are increasing and how many are declining.
breakdown	A technical term used to describe the price action of a security when it falls below support to a lower level and into a new trading range.
breakeven point	The point at which the value of a security or portfolio is exactly equal to the investor's cost for that security or portfolio.
breakout	A technical term used to describe the price action of a security when it increases past resistance to a higher level and into a new trading range.
breakpoint sale	The practice of selling mutual fund shares in dollar amounts that are just below the point where an investor would be entitled to a sales charge reduction. A breakpoint sale is designed for the purpose of trying to earn a larger commission. This is a violation of the Rules of Fair Practice and should never be done.
breakpoint schedule	A breakpoint schedule offers mutual fund investors reduced sales charges for larger dollar investments.
broad-based index	An index that represents a large cross-section of the market as a whole. The price movement of the index reflects the price movement of a large portion of the market, such as the S&P 500 or the Wilshire 5000.
broker	*See* agent.
broker dealer	A person or firm who buys and sells securities for its own account and for the accounts of others. When acting as a broker or agent for a customer, the broker dealer is merely executing the customer's orders and charging the customer a fee known as a commission. When acting as a dealer or principal, the broker dealer is trading for its own account and participating in the customer's transaction by taking the other side of the trade and charging the customer

a markup or markdown. A firm also is acting as a principal or dealer when it is trading for its own account and making markets in OTC securities.

broker's broker	(1) A municipal bond dealer who specializes in executing orders for other dealers who are not active in the municipal bond market. (2) A specialist on the exchange executing orders for other members or an OTC market.
bullish	An investor who believes that the price of a security or prices as a whole will rise is said to be bullish.
bull market	A market condition that is characterized by rising prices and a series of higher highs.
business cycle	The normal economic pattern that is characterized by four stages: expansion, peak, contraction, and trough. The business cycle constantly repeats itself and the economy is always in flux.
business day	The business day in the securities industry is defined as the time when the financial markets are open for trading.
buyer's option	A settlement option that allows the buyer to determine when the transaction will settle.
buy in	An order executed in the event of a customer's or firm's failure to deliver the securities it sold. The buyer repurchases the securities in the open market and charges the seller for any loss.
buying power	The amount of money available to buy securities.
buy stop order	A buy stop order is used to protect against a loss or to protect a profit on a short sale of stock.

C

call	(1) A type of option that gives the holder the right to purchase a specified amount of the underlying security at a stated price for a specified period of time. (2) The act of exercising a call option.
callable bond	A bond that may be called in or retired by the issuer prior to its maturity date.
callable preferred	A preferred share issued with a feature allowing the issuing corporation to retire it under certain conditions.
call date	A specific date after which the securities in question become callable by the issuer.
call feature	A condition attached to some bonds and preferred stocks that allows the issuer to call in or redeem the securities prior to their maturity date and according to certain conditions.

call price	The price that will be paid by the issuer to retire the callable securities in question. The call price is usually set at a price above the par value of the bond or preferred stock, which is the subject of the call.
call protection	A period of time, usually right after the securities' issuance, when the securities may not be called by the issuer. Call protection usually ranges from 5 to 10 years.
call provision	*See* call feature.
call risk	The risk borne by the owner of callable securities that may require that the investor accept a lower rate of return once the securities have been called. Callable bonds and preferred stock are more likely to be called when interest rates are low or are falling.
call spread	An option position consisting of one long and one short call on the same underlying security with different strike prices, expirations, or both.
call writer	An investor who has sold a call.
capital	Money and assets available to use in an attempt to earn more money or to accumulate more assets.
capital appreciation	An increase in an asset's value over time.
capital assets	Tangible assets, including securities, real estate, equipment, and other assets, owned for the long term.
capital gain	A profit realized on the sale of an asset at a price that exceeds its cost.
capitalization	The composition of a company's financial structure. It is the sum of paid-in capital + paid-in surplus + long-term debt + retained earnings.
capital loss	A loss realized on the sale of an asset at a price that is lower than its cost.
capital market	The securities markets that deal in equity and debt securities with more than 1 year to maturity.
capital risk	The risk that the value of an asset will decline and cause an investor to lose all or part of the invested capital.
capital stock	The sum of the par value of all of a corporation's outstanding common and preferred stock.
capital structure	*See* capitalization.
capital surplus	The amount of money received by an issuer in excess of the par value of the stock at the time of its initial sale to the public.
capped index option	An index option that trades like a spread and is automatically exercised if it goes 30 points in the money.
capping	A manipulative practice of selling stock to depress the price.

carried interest	A sharing arrangement for an oil and gas direct participation program where the general partner shares in the tangible drilling costs with the limited partners.
cash account	An account in which the investor must deposit the full purchase price of the securities by the fifth business day after the trade date. The investor is not required by industry regulations to sign anything to open a cash account.
cash assets ratio	The most liquid measure of a company's solvency. The cash asset ratio is found by dividing cash and equivalents by current liabilities.
cash dividend	The distribution of corporate profits to shareholders of record. Cash dividends must be declared by the company's board of directors.
cash equivalent	Short-term liquid securities that can quickly be converted into cash. Money market instruments and funds are the most common examples.
cash flow	A company's cash flow equals net income plus depreciation.
cashiering department	The department in a brokerage firm that is responsible for the receipt and delivery of cash and securities.
cash management bill	Short-term federal financing issued in minimum denominations of $10 million.
cash settlement	A transaction that settles for cash requires the delivery of the securities from the seller as well as the delivery of cash from the buyer on the same day of the trade. A trade done for cash settles the same day.
catastrophe call	The redemption of a bond by an issuer due to the destruction of the facility that was financed by the issue. Issuers will carry insurance to cover such events and to pay off the bondholders.
certificate of deposit (CD)	An unsecured promissory note issued as evidence of ownership of a time deposit that has been guaranteed by the issuing bank.
certificates of accrual on Treasury securities	Zero-coupon bonds issued by brokerage firms and collateralized by Treasury securities.
change	The difference between the current price and the previous day's closing price.
Chicago Board of Trade (CBOT)	A commodity exchange that provides a marketplace for agricultural and financial futures.
Chicago Board Options Exchange (CBOE)	The premier option exchange in the United States for listed options.
Chinese wall	The physical separation that is required between investment banking and trading and retail divisions of a brokerage firm. Now known as a firewall.

churning	Executing transactions that are excessive in their frequency or size in light of the resources of the account for the purpose of generating commissions. Churning is a violation of the Rules of Fair Practice.
class A share	A mutual fund share that charges a front-end load.
class B share	A mutual fund share that charges a back-end load.
class C share	A mutual fund share that charges a level load.
class D share	A mutual fund share that charges a level load and a back-end load.
classical economics	A theory stating that the economy will do the best when the government does not interfere.
clearing firm	A firm that carries its customers' cash and securities and/or provides the service to customers of other firms.
clearinghouse	An agency that guarantees and settles futures and option transactions.
close	The last price at which a security traded for the day.
closed-end indenture	A bond indenture that will not allow additional bonds to be issued with the same claim on the issuer's assets.
closed-end investment company	A management company that issues a fixed number of shares to investors in a managed portfolio and whose shares are traded in the secondary market.
closing date	The date when sales of interest in a direct participation plan will cease.
closing purchase	An order executed to close out a short option position.
Code of Arbitration Procedure	The FINRA bylaw that provides for a forum for dispute resolution relating to industry matters. All industry participants must arbitrate in public and the customer must agree to arbitration in writing.
Code of Procedure	The FINRA bylaw that sets guidelines for the investigation of trade practice complaints and alleged rule violations.
coincident indicator	An economic indicator that moves simultaneously with the movement of the underlying economy.
collateral	Assets pledged to a lender. If the borrower defaults, the lender will take possession of the collateral.
collateral trust certificate	A bond backed by the pledge of securities the issuer owns in another entity.
collateralized mortgage obligation (CMO)	A corporate debt security that is secured by an underlying pool of mortgages.
collection ratio	A measure of a municipality's ability to collect the taxes it has assessed.
collect on delivery (COD)	A method of trade settlement that requires the physical delivery of the securities to receive payment.

combination	An option position with a call and put on the same underlying security with different strike prices and expiration months on both.
combination fund	A mutual fund that tries to achieve growth and current income by combining portfolios of common stock with portfolios of high-yielding equities.
combination preferred stock	A preferred share with multiple features, such as cumulative and participating.
combination privileges	A feature offered by a mutual fund family that allows an investor to combine two simultaneous purchases of different portfolios in order to receive a reduced sales charge on the total amount invested.
combined account	A margin account that contains both long and short positions.
commercial paper	Short-term unsecured promissory notes issued by large financially stable corporations to obtain short-term financing. Commercial paper does not pay interest and is issued at a discount from its face value. All commercial paper matures in 270 days or less and matures at its face value.
commingling	A FINRA violation resulting from the mixing of customer and firm assets in the same account.
commission	A fee charged by a broker or agent for executing a securities transaction.
commission house broker	A floor broker who executes orders for the firm's account and for the accounts of the firm's customers on an exchange.
common stock	A security that represents the ownership of a corporation. Common stockholders vote to elect the board of directors and to institute major corporate policies.
common stock ratio	A measure of how much of a company's capitalization was obtained through the sale of common stock. The ratio is found by summing the par value of the common stock, excess paid in capital, and retained earnings, and then dividing that number by the total capitalization.
competitive bid underwriting	A method of underwriter selection that solicits bids from multiple underwriters. The underwriter submitting the best terms will be awarded the issue.
compliance department	The department of a broker dealer that ensures that the firm adheres to industry rules and regulations.
concession	The amount of an underwriting discount that is allocated to a syndicate member or a selling group member for selling new securities.
conduct rules	The Rules of Fair Practice.
conduit theory	The IRS classification that allows a regulated investment company to avoid paying taxes on investment income it distributes to its shareholders.

confirmation	The receipt for a securities transaction that must be sent to all customers either on or before the completion of a transaction. The confirmation must show the trade date, settlement date, and total amount due to or from the customer. A transaction is considered to be complete on settlement date.
consolidated tape	The consolidated tape A displays transactions for NYSE securities that take place on the NYSE, all regional exchanges, and the third markets. The consolidated tape B reports transactions for AMEX stocks that take place on the American Stock Exchange, all regional exchanges, and in the third market.
consolidation	A chart pattern that results from a narrowing of a security's trading range.
constant dollar plan	An investment plan designed to keep a specific amount of money invested in the market regardless of the market's condition. An investor will sell when the value of the account rises and buy when the value of the account falls.
constant ratio plan	An investment plan designed to keep the investor's portfolio invested at a constant ratio of equity and debt securities.
construction loan note	A short-term municipal note designed to provide financing for construction projects.
constructive receipt	The time when the IRS determines that the taxpayer has effectively received payment.
consumer price index (CPI)	A price-based index made up of a basket of goods and services that are used by consumers in their daily lives. An increase in the CPI indicates a rise in overall prices, while a decline in the index represents a fall in overall prices.
consumption	A term used to describe the purchase of newly produced household goods.
contemporaneous trader	A trader who enters an order on the other side of the market at the same time as a trader with inside information enters an order. Contemporaneous traders can sue traders who act on inside information to recover losses.
contingent deferred sales charge	*See* back-end load.
contraction	A period of declining economic output. Also known as a recession.
contractual plan	A mutual fund accumulation plan under which the investor agrees to contribute a fixed sum of money over time. If the investor does not complete or terminates the contract early, the investor may be subject to penalties.
control	The ability to influence the actions of an organization or individual.
control person	A director or officer of an issuer or broker dealer or a 10% stockholder of a corporation.
control stock	Stock that is acquired or owned by an officer, director, or person owning 10% or more of the outstanding stock of a company.

conversion price	The set price at which a convertible security may be exchanged for another security.
conversion privilege	The right offered to a mutual fund investor that allows the investor to move money between different portfolios offered by the same mutual fund family without paying another sales charge.
conversion ratio	The number of shares that can be received by the holder of a convertible security if it were converted into the underlying common stock.
convertible bond	A bond that may be converted or exchanged for common shares of the corporation at a predetermined price.
convertible preferred stock	A preferred stock that may be converted or exchanged for common shares of the corporation at a predetermined price.
cooling-off period	The period of time between the filing of a registration statement and its effective date. During this time, the SEC is reviewing the registration statement and no sales may take place. The cooling-off period is at least 20 days.
coordination	A method of securities registration during which a new issue is registered simultaneously at both the federal and state levels.
corporate account	An investment account for the benefit of a company that requires a corporate resolution listing the names of individuals who may transact business in the company's name.
corporate bond	A legally binding obligation of a corporation to repay a principal amount of debt along with interest at a predetermined rate and schedule.
corporation	A perpetual entity that survives after the death of its officers, directors, and stockholders. It is the most common form of business entity.
correspondent broker dealer	A broker dealer who introduces customer accounts to a clearing broker dealer.
cost basis	The cost of an asset, including any acquisition costs. It is used to determine capital gains and losses.
cost depletion	A method used to determine the tax deductions for investors in oil and gas programs.
cost of carry	All costs incurred by an investor for maintaining a position in a security, including margin interest and opportunity costs.
coterminous	Municipalities that share the same borders and have overlapping debt.
coupon bond	*See* bearer bond.
coupon yield	*See* nominal yield.
covenant	A promise made by an issuer of debt that describes the issuer's obligations and the bondholders' rights.

covered call	The sale of a call against a long position in the underlying security.
covered put	The sale of a put against a short position in the underlying security or against cash that will allow the person to purchase the security if the put is exercised.
CPI	*See* consumer price index (CPI).
credit agreement	The portion of the margin agreement that describes the terms and conditions under which credit will be extended to the customer.
credit balance	The cash balance in a customer's account.
credit department	*See* margin department.
credit risk	The risk that the issuer of debt securities will default on its obligation to pay interest or principal on a timely basis.
credit spread	An option position that results in a net premium or credit received by the investor from the simultaneous purchase and sale of two calls or two puts on the same security.
crossed market	A market condition that results when a broker enters a bid for a stock that exceeds the offering price for that stock. Also a condition that may result when a broker enters an offer that is lower than the bid price for that stock.
crossing stock	The pairing off of two offsetting customer orders by the same floor broker. The floor broker executing the cross must first show the order to the crowd for possible price improvement before crossing the orders.
crossover point	The point at which all tax credits have been used up by a limited partnership; results in a tax liability for the partners.
cum rights	A stock that is the subject of a rights offering and is trading with the rights attached to the common stock.
cumulative preferred stock	A preferred stock that entitles the holder to receive unpaid dividends prior to the payment of any dividends to common stockholders. Dividends that accumulate in arrears on cumulative issues are always the first dividends to be paid by a corporation.
cumulative voting	A method of voting that allows stockholders to cast all of their votes for one director or to distribute them among the candidates they wish to vote for. Cumulative voting favors smaller investors by allowing them to have a larger say in the election of the board of directors.
current assets	Cash, securities, accounts receivable, and other assets that can be converted into cash within 12 months.
current liabilities	Corporate obligations, including accounts payable, that must be paid within 12 months.

current market value (CMV)/current market price (CMP)	The present value of a marketable security or of a portfolio of marketable securities.
current ratio	A measure of a corporation's short-term liquidity found by dividing its current assets by its current liabilities.
current yield	A relationship between a securities annual income relative to its current market price. Determined by dividing annual income by the current market price.
CUSIP (Committee on Uniform Securities Identification Procedures)	A committee that assigns identification numbers to securities to help identify them.
custodial account	An account operated by a custodian for the benefit of a minor.
custodian	A party responsible for managing an account for another party. In acting as a custodian, the individual or corporation must adhere to the prudent man rule and only take such actions as a prudent person would do for him- or herself.
customer	Any individual or entity that maintains an account with a broker dealer.
customer agreement	An agreement signed by a customer at the time the account is opened, detailing the conditions of the customer's relationship with the firm. The customer agreement usually contains a predispute arbitration clause.
customer ledger	A ledger that lists all customer cash and margin accounts.
customer protection rule	Rule 15C3-3 requires that customer assets be kept segregated from the firm assets.
cyclical industry	An industry whose prospects fluctuate with the business cycle.

D

Daily Bond Buyer	A daily publication for the municipal securities industry that publishes information related to the municipal bond market and official notices of sales.
dated date	The day when interest starts to accrue for bonds.
dealer	(1) A person or firm who transacts securities business for its own account. (2) A brokerage firm acting as a principal when executing a customer's transaction or making markets over the counter.
dealer paper	Commercial paper sold to the public by a dealer, rather than placed with investors directly by the issuer.
debenture	An unsecured promissory note issued by a corporation backed only by the issuer's credit and promise to pay.

debit balance	The amount of money a customer owes a broker dealer.
debit spread	An option position that results in a net premium paid by the investor from the simultaneous purchase and sale of two calls or two puts on the same security.
debt securities	A security that represents a loan to the issuer. The owner of a debt security is a creditor of the issuing entity, be it a corporation or a government.
debt service	The scheduled interest payments and repayment of principal for debt securities.
debt service account	An account set up by a municipal issuer to pay the debt service of municipal revenue bonds.
debt service ratio	Indicates the issuer's ability to pay its interest and principal payments.
debt-to-equity ratio	A ratio that shows how highly leveraged the company is. It is found by dividing total long-term debt by total shareholder equity.
declaration date	The day chosen by the board of directors of a corporation to pay a dividend to shareholders.
deduction	An adjustment taken from gross income to reduce tax liability.
default	The failure of an issuer of debt securities to make interest and principal payments when they are due.
default risk	*See* credit risk.
defeasance	Results in the elimination of the issuer's debt obligations by issuing a new debt instrument to pay off the outstanding issue. The old issue is removed from the issuer's balance sheet and the proceeds of the new issue are placed in an escrow account to pay off the now-defeased issue.
defensive industry	A term used to describe a business whose economic prospects are independent from the business cycle. Pharmaceutical companies, utilities, and food producers are examples of defensive industries.
deferred annuity	A contract between an individual and an insurance company that delays payments to the annuitant until some future date.
deferred compensation plan	A contractual agreement between an employer and an employee under which the employee elects to defer receiving money owed until after retirement. Deferred compensation plans are typically unfunded, and the employee could lose all the money due under the agreement if the company goes out of business.
deficiency letter	A letter sent to a corporate issuer by the SEC, requesting additional information regarding the issuer's registration statement.
defined benefit plan	A qualified retirement plan established to provide a specific amount of retirement income for the plan participants. Unlike a defined contribution plan, the individual's retirement benefits are known prior to reaching retirement.

defined contribution plan	A qualified retirement plan that details the amount of money that the employer will contribute to the plan for the benefit of the employee. This amount is usually expressed as a percentage of the employee's gross annual income. The actual retirement benefits are not known until the employee reaches retirement, and the amount of the retirement benefit is a result of the contributions to the plan, along with the investment experience of the plan.
deflation	The economic condition that is characterized by a persistent decline in overall prices.
delivery	As used in the settlement process, results in the change of ownership of cash or securities.
delivery vs. payment	A type of settlement option that requires that the securities be physically received at the time payment is made.
delta	A measure of an option's price change in relation to a price change in the underlying security.
demand deposit	A deposit that a customer has with a bank or other financial institution that will allow the customer to withdraw the money at any time or on demand.
Department of Enforcement	The FINRA committee that has original jurisdiction over complaints and violations.
depletion	A tax deduction taken for the reduction in the amount of natural resources (e.g., gas, gold, oil) available to a business or partnership.
depreciation	A tax deduction taken for the reduction of value in a capital asset.
depreciation expense	A noncash expense that results in a reduction in taxable income.
depression	An economic condition that is characterized by a protracted decline in economic output and a rising level of unemployment.
derivative	A security that derives its value in whole or in part based on the price of another security. Options and futures are examples of derivative securities.
designated order	An order entered by an institution for a new issue of municipal bonds that states what firm and what agent is going to get the sales credit for the order.
devaluation	A significant fall in the value of a country's currency relative to other currencies. Devaluation could be the result of poor economic prospects in the home country. In extreme circumstances, it can be the result of government intervention.
developmental drilling program	An oil or gas program that drills for wells in areas of proven reserves.
developmental fee	A fee paid to organizers of a direct participation plan for the development of plans, obtaining financing or zoning authorizations, and other services.

diagonal spread	A spread that is created through the simultaneous purchase and sale of two calls or two puts on the same underlying security that differ in both strike price and expiration months.
dilution	A reduction in a stockholder's proportional ownership of a corporation as a result of the issuance of more shares. Earnings per share may also be diluted as a result of the issuance of additional shares.
direct debt	The total amount of a municipality's debt that has been issued by the municipality for its own benefit and for which the municipality is responsible to repay.
direct paper	Commercial paper sold to investors directly from the issuer without the use of a dealer.
direct participation program (DPP)	An entity that allows all taxable events to be passed through to investors, including limited partnerships and subchapter S corporations.
discount	The amount by which the price of a security is lower than its par value.
discount bond	A bond that is selling for a price that is lower than its par value.
discount rate	The rate that is charged to Federal Reserve member banks on loans directly from the Federal Reserve. This rate is largely symbolic, and member banks only borrow directly from the Federal Reserve as a last resort.
discretion	Authorization given to a firm or a representative to determine which securities are to be purchased and sold for the benefit of the customer without the customer's prior knowledge or approval.
discretionary account	An account where the owner has given the firm or the representative authority to transact business without the customer's prior knowledge or approval. All discretionary accounts must be approved and monitored closely by a principal of the firm.
disintermediation	The flow of money from traditional bank accounts to alternative higher yielding investments. This is more likely to occur as the Federal Reserve tightens monetary policy and interest rates rise.
disposable income	The sum of money an individual has left after paying taxes and required expenditures.
disproportional allocation	A method used by FINRA to determine if a free-riding violation has occurred with respect to a hot issuer. A firm is only allowed to sell up to 10% of a new issue to conditionally approved purchasers.
disproportionate sharing	An oil and gas sharing arrangement where the general partner pays a portion of the cost but receives a larger portion of the program's revenues.
distribution	Cash or property sent to shareholders or partners.

distribution stage	The period of time during which an annuitant is receiving payments from an annuity contract.
diversification	The distribution of investment capital among different investment choices. By purchasing several different investments, investors may be able to reduce their overall risk by minimizing the impact of any one security's adverse performance.
diversified fund/ diversified management company	A mutual fund that distributes its investment capital among a wide variety of investments. In order for a mutual fund to market itself as a diversified mutual fund it must meet the 75-5-10 rule: 75% of the fund's assets must be invested in securities issued by other entities, no more than 5% of the fund's assets may be invested in any one issuer, and the fund may own no more than 10% of any one company's outstanding securities.
dividend	A distribution of corporate assets to shareholders. A dividend may be paid in cash, stock, or property or product.
dividend department	The department in a brokerage firm that is responsible for the collecting of dividends and crediting them to customer accounts.
dividend disbursement agent	An agent of the issuer who pays out the dividends to shareholders of record.
dividend payout ratio	The amount of a company's earnings that were paid out to shareholders relative to the total earnings that were available to be paid out to shareholders. It can be calculated by dividing dividends per share by earnings per share.
dividend yield	Also known as a stock's current yield. It is a relationship between the annual dividends paid to shareholders relative to the stock's current market price. To determine a stock's dividend yield, divide annual dividends by the current market price.
DJIA	*See* Dow Jones Industrial Average.
doctrine of mutual reciprocity	An agreement that the federal government would not tax interest income received by investors in municipal bonds and that reciprocally the states would not tax interest income received by investors in federal debt obligations.
dollar bonds	A term issue of municipal bonds that are quoted as a percentage of par rather than on a yield basis.
dollar-cost averaging	A strategy of investing a fixed sum of money on a regular basis into a fluctuating market price. Over time an investor should be able to achieve an average cost per share that is below the average price per share. Dollar-cost averaging is a popular investment strategy with mutual fund investors.
donor	A person who gives a gift of cash or securities to another person. Once the gift has been made, the donor no longer has any rights or claim to the security. All gifts to a minor are irrevocable.

do not reduce (DNR)	An order qualifier for an order placed under the market that stipulates that the price of the order is not to be reduced for the distribution of ordinary dividends.
don't know (DK)	A term used to describe a dealer's response to a confirmation for a trade they "don't know" doing.
Dow Jones Composite Average	An index composed of 65 stocks that is used as an indicator of market performance.
Dow Jones Industrial Average (DJIA)	An index composed of 30 industrial companies. The Dow Jones is the most widely quoted market index.
Dow Jones Transportation Average	An index composed of 20 transportation stocks.
Dow Jones Utility Average	An index composed of 15 utility stocks.
Dow theory	A theory that believes that the health both of the market and of the economy may be predicted by the performance of the Dow Jones Industrial Average.
dry hole	A term used to describe a nonproducing well.
dual-purpose fund	A mutual fund that offers two classes of shares to investors. One class is sold to investors seeking income and the other class is sold to investors seeking capital appreciation.

E

early withdrawal penalty	A penalty tax charged to an investor for withdrawing money from a qualified retirement plan prior to age 59-1/2, usually 10% on top of ordinary income taxes.
earned income	Money received by an individual in return for performing services.
earnings per share	The net amount of a corporation's earnings available to common shareholders divided by the number of common shares outstanding.
earnings per share fully diluted	The net amount of a corporation's earnings available to common shareholders after taking into consideration the potential conversion of all convertible securities.
eastern account	A type of syndicate account that requires all members to be responsible for their own allocation as well as for their proportional share of any member's unsold securities.
economic risk	The risk of loss of principal associated with the purchase of securities.
EE savings bonds	Nonmarketable U.S. government zero-coupon bonds that must be purchased from the government and redeemed to the government.

effective date	The day when a new issue's registration with the SEC becomes effective. Once the issue's registration statement has become effective, the securities may then be sold to investors.
efficient market theory	A theory that states that the market operates and processes information efficiently and prices in all information as soon as it becomes known.
Employee Retirement Income Security Act of 1974 (ERISA)	The legislation that governs the operation of private-sector pension plans. Corporate pension plans organized under ERISA guidelines qualify for beneficial tax treatment by the IRS.
endorsement	The signature on the back of a security that allows its ownership to be transferred.
EPS	*See* earnings per share.
equipment leasing limited partnership	A limited partnership that is organized to purchase equipment and lease it to corporations to earn lease income and to shelter passive income for investors.
equipment trust certificate	A bond backed by a pledge of large equipment, such as airplanes, railroad cars, and ships.
equity	A security that represents the ownership in a corporation. Both preferred and common equity holders have an ownership interest in the corporation.
equity financing	The sale of common or preferred equity by a corporation in an effort to raise capital.
equity option	An option to purchase or sell common stock.
ERISA	*See* Employee Retirement Income Security Act of 1974.
erroneous report	A report of an execution given in error to a client. The report is not binding on the firm or on the agent.
escrow agreement	Evidence of ownership of a security provided to a broker dealer as proof of ownership of the underlying security for covered call writers.
Eurobond	A bond issued in domestic currency of the issuer but sold outside of the issuer's country.
Eurodollar	A deposit held outside of the United States denominated in U.S. dollars.
Eurodollar bonds	A bond issued by a foreign issuer denominated in U.S. dollars.
Euroyen bonds	Bonds issued outside of Japan but denominated in yen.
excess equity (EE)	The value of an account's equity in excess of Regulation T.
exchange	A market, whether physical or electronic, that provides a forum for trading securities through a dual-auction process.
exchange distribution	A distribution of a large block of stock on the floor of the exchange that is crossed with offsetting orders.

exchange privilege	The right offered by many mutual funds that allows an investor to transfer or move money between different portfolios offered through the same fund company. An investor may redeem shares of the fund, which is being sold at the NAV, and purchase shares of the new portfolio at the NAV without paying another sales charge.
ex date/ex-dividend date	The first day when purchasers of a security will no longer be entitled to receive a previously declared dividend.
executor/executrix	An individual with the authority to manage the affairs of a decedent's estate.
exempt security	A security that is exempt from the registration requirements of the Securities Act of 1933.
exempt transaction	A transaction that is not subject to state registration.
exercise	An investor's election to take advantage of the rights offered through the terms of an option, a right, or a warrant.
exercise price	The price at which an option investor may purchase or sell a security. Also the price at which an investor may purchase a security through a warrant or right.
existing property program	A type of real estate direct participation program that purchases existing property for the established rental income.
expansion	A period marked by a general increase in business activity and an increase in gross domestic product.
expansionary policy	A monetary policy enacted through the Federal Reserve Board that increases money supply and reduces interest rates in an effort to stimulate the economy.
expense ratio	The amount of a mutual fund's expenses relative to its assets. The higher the expense ratio, the lower the investor's return. A mutual fund's expense ratio tells an investor how efficiently a mutual fund operates, not how profitable the mutual fund is.
expiration cycle	A 4-month cycle for option expiration: January, April, July, and October; February, May, August, and November; or March, June, September, and December.
expiration date	The date on which an option ceases to exist.
exploratory drilling program	A direct participation program that engages in the drilling for oil or gas in new areas seeking to find new wells.
exploratory well	Also known as wildcatting. The drilling for oil or gas in new areas in an effort to find new wells.
ex rights	The common stock subject to a rights offering trade without the rights attached.

ex rights date	The first day when the common stock is subject to a rights offering trade without the rights attached.
ex warrants	Common trading without the warrants attached.

F

face-amount certificate company (FAC)	A type of investment company that requires an investor to make fixed payments over time or to deposit a lump sum, and that will return to the investor a stated sum known as the face amount on a specific date.
face amount/face value	*See* par.
fail to deliver	An event where the broker on the sell side of the transaction fails to deliver the security.
fail to receive	An event where the broker on the buy side of the transaction fails to receive the security from the broker on the sell side.
Fannie Mae	*See* Federal National Mortgage Association.
Farm Credit Administrator	The agency that oversees all of the activities of the banks in the Federal Farm Credit System.
Federal Deposit Insurance Corporation (FDIC)	The government insurance agency that provides insurance for bank depositors in case of bank failure.
Federal Farm Credit System	An organization of banks that is designed to provide financing to farmers for mortgages, feed and grain, and equipment.
federal funds rate	The rate banks charge each other on overnight loans.
Federal Home Loan Mortgage Corporation (FHLMC; Freddie Mac)	A publicly traded for-profit corporation that provides liquidity to the secondary mortgage market by purchasing pools of mortgages from lenders and, in turn, issues mortgage-backed securities.
Federal Intermediate Credit Bank	Provides short-term financing to farmers for equipment.
Federal National Mortgage Association (FNMA; Fannie Mae)	A publicly traded for-profit corporation that provides liquidity to the secondary mortgage market by purchasing pools of mortgages and issuing mortgage-backed securities.
Federal Open Market Committee (FOMC)	The committee of the Federal Reserve Board that makes policy decisions relating to the nation's money supply.

Federal Reserve Board	A seven-member board that directs the policies of the Federal Reserve System. The members are appointed by the President and approved by Congress.
Federal Reserve System	The nation's central banking system, the purpose of which is to regulate money supply and the extension of credit. The Federal Reserve System is composed of 12 central banks and 24 regional banks, along with hundreds of national and state chartered banks.
fictitious quote	A quote that is not representative of an actual bid or offer for a security.
fidelity bond	A bond that must be posted by all broker dealers to ensure the public against employee dishonesty.
fill or kill (FK)	A type of order that requires that all of the securities in the order be purchased or sold immediately or not at all.
final prospectus	The official offering document for a security that contains the security's final offering price along with all information required by law for an investor to make an informed decision.
firm commitment underwriting	Guarantees the issuer all of the money right away. The underwriters purchase all of the securities from the issuer regardless of whether they can sell the securities to their customers.
firm quote	A quote displayed at which the dealer is obligated to buy or sell at least one round lot at the quoted price.
fiscal policy	Government policy designed to influence the economy through government tax and spending programs. The President and Congress control fiscal policy.
5% markup policy	FINRA's guideline that requires all prices paid by customers to be reasonably related to a security's market price. The 5% policy is a guideline, not a rule, and it does not apply to securities sold through a prospectus.
fixed annuity	An insurance contract where the insurance company guarantees fixed payments to the annuitant, usually until the annuitant's death.
fixed assets	Assets used by a corporation to conduct its business, such as plant and equipment.
flat	A term used to describe a bond that trades without accrued interest, such as a zero-coupon bond or a bond that is in default.
floor broker	An individual member of an exchange who may execute orders on the floor.
floor trader	Members of the exchange who trade for their own accounts. Members of the NYSE may not trade from the floor for their own accounts.
flow of funds	A schedule of expenses and interested parties that prioritizes how payments will be made from the revenue generated by a facility financed by a municipal revenue bond.

forced conversion	The calling in of convertible bonds at a price that is less than the market value of the underlying common stock into which the bonds may be converted.
foreign currency	Currency of another country.
foreign currency option	An option to purchase or sell a specified amount of another country's currency.
Form 10-K	An annual report filed by a corporation detailing its financial performance for the year.
Form 10-Q	A quarterly report filed by a corporation detailing its financial performance for the quarter.
form letter	A letter sent out by a brokerage firm or a registered representative to more than 25 people in a 90-day period. Form letters are subject to approval and recordkeeping requirements.
forward pricing	The way in which open-end mutual funds are valued for investors who wish to purchase or redeem shares of the fund. Mutual funds usually price their shares at the end of the business day. The price to be paid or received by the investor will be the price that is next calculated after the fund receives the order.
401K	A qualified retirement plan offered by an employer.
403B	A qualified retirement plan offered to teachers and employees of nonprofit organizations.
fourth market	A transaction between two large institutions without the use of a broker dealer.
fractional share	A portion of a whole share that represents ownership of an open-end mutual fund.
fraud	Any attempt to gain an unfair advantage over another party through the use of deception, concealment, or misrepresentation.
free credit balance	Cash reserves in a customer's account that have not been invested. Customers must be notified of their free credit balances at least quarterly.
free look	A privilege offered to purchasers of contractual plans and insurance policies that will allow the individual to cancel the contract within the free-look period, usually 45 days.
freeriding	The purchase and sale of a security without depositing the money required to cover the purchase price as required by Regulation T.
freeriding and withholding	The withholding of new issue securities offered by a broker dealer for the benefit of the brokerage firm or an employee.
front-end load	(1) A sales charge paid by investors in open-end mutual funds that is paid at the time of purchase. (2) A contractual plan that seeks to assess sales

charges in the first years of the plan and may charge up to 50% of the first year's payments as sales charges.

frozen account
An account where the owner is required to deposit cash or securities up front, prior to any purchase or sale taking place. An account is usually frozen as a result of a customer's failure to pay or deliver securities.

full power of attorney
A type of discretionary authority that allows a third party to purchase and sell securities as well as to withdraw cash and securities without the owner's prior consent or knowledge. This type of authority is usually reserved to trustees and attorneys.

fully registered bonds
A type of bond issuance where the issuer has a complete record of the owners of the bonds and who is entitled to receive interest and principal payments. The owners of fully registered bonds are not required to clip coupons.

functional allocation
An arrangement for oil and gas programs where the general partner pays the tangible drilling costs and the limited partner absorbs the intangible drilling costs.

fundamental analyst
A method of valuing the company that takes into consideration the financial performance of the corporation, the value of its assets, and the quality of its management.

funded debt
Long-term debt obligations of corporations or municipalities.

fungible
Easily exchangeable items with the same conditions.

G

general account
An insurance company's account that holds the money and investments for fixed contracts and traditional life insurance policies.

general obligation bond
A municipal bond that is backed by the taxing power of the state or municipality.

general partner
The partner in a general partnership who manages the business and is responsible for any debt of the program.

general securities principal
An individual who has passed the Series 24 exam and may supervise the activities of the firm and its agents.

generic advertising
Advertising designed to promote name recognition for a firm and securities as investments, but does not recommend specific securities.

good 'til cancel (GTC)
An order that remains on the books until it is executed or canceled.

goodwill
An intangible asset of a corporation, such as its name recognition and reputation, that adds to its value.

Government National Mortgage Association (GNMA; Ginnie Mae)	A government corporation that provides liquidity to the mortgage markets by purchasing pools of mortgages that have been insured by the Federal Housing Administration and the Veterans Administration. Ginnie Mae issues pass-through certificates to investors backed by the pools of mortgages.
government security	A security that is an obligation of the U.S. government and that is backed by the full faith and credit of the U.S. government, such as Treasury bills, notes, and bonds.
grant anticipation note (GAN)	Short-term municipal financing issued in anticipation of receiving a grant from the federal government or one of its agencies.
greenshoe option	An option given to an underwriter of common stock that will allow it to purchase up to an additional 15% of the offering from the issuer at the original offering price to cover over-allotments for securities that are in high demand.
gross domestic product (GDP)	The value of all goods and services produced by a country within a period of time. GDP includes government purchases, investments, and exports minus imports.
gross income	All income received by a taxpayer before deductions for taxes.
gross revenue pledge	A flow-of-funds pledge for a municipal revenue bond that states that debt service will be paid first.
growth fund	A fund whose objective is capital appreciation. Growth funds invest in common stocks to achieve their objective.
growth stock	The stock of a company whose earnings grow at a rate that is faster than the growth rate of the economy as a whole. Growth stocks are characterized by increased opportunities for appreciation and little or no dividends.
guardian	An individual who has a fiduciary responsibility for another, usually a minor.

H

HH bond	A nonmarketable government security that pays semiannual interest. Series HH bonds are issued with a $500 minimum value and may only be purchased by trading matured series EE bonds; they may not be purchased with cash.
halt	A temporary stop in the trading of a security. If a common stock is halted, all derivatives and convertibles will be halted as well.
head and shoulders	A chart pattern that indicates a reversal of a trend. A head-and-shoulders top indicates a reversal of an uptrend and is considered bearish. A head-and-shoulders bottom is the reversal of a downtrend and is considered bullish.

hedge	A position taken in a security to offset or reduce the risk associated with the risk of another security.
high	The highest price paid for a security during a trading session or during a 52-week period.
holder	An individual or corporation that owns a security. The holder of a security is also known as being long the security.
holding period	The length of time during which an investor owns a security. The holding period is important for calculating tax liability.
hold in street name	The registration of customer securities in the name of the broker dealer. Most customers register securities in the name of the broker dealer to make the transfer of ownership easier.
horizontal spread	Also known as a calendar spread. The simultaneous purchase and sale of two calls or two puts on the same underlying security with the same exercise price but with different expiration months.
hot issue	A new issue of securities that trades at an immediate premium to its offering price in the secondary market.
HR 10 plan	*See* Keogh plan.
hypothecation	The customer's pledge of securities as collateral for a margin loan.

I

immediate annuity	An annuity contract purchased with a single payment that entitles the holder to receive immediate payments from the contract. The annuitant purchases annuity units and usually begins receiving payments within 60 days.
immediate family	An individual's immediate family includes parents, parents-in-law, children, spouse, and any relative financially dependent upon the individual.
immediate or cancel (IOC)	An order that is to be executed as fully as possible immediately and whatever is not executed will be canceled.
income bond	A highly speculative bond that is issued at a discount from par and only pays interest if the issuer has enough income to do so. The issuer of the income bond only promises to pay principal at maturity. Income bonds trade flat without accrued interest.
income fund	A mutual fund whose investment objective is to achieve current income for its shareholders by investing in bonds and preferred stocks.
income program	A type of oil and gas program that purchases producing wells to receive the income received from the sale of the proven reserves.

income statement	A financial statement that shows a corporation's revenue and expenses for the time period in question.
indefeasible title	A record of ownership that cannot be challenged.
index	A representation of the price action of a given group of securities. Indexes are used to measure the condition of the market as a whole, such as with the S&P 500, or can be used to measure the condition of an industry group, such as with the Biotech index.
index option	An option on an underlying financial index. Index options settle in cash.
indication of interest	An investor's expression of a willingness to purchase a new issue of securities after receiving a preliminary prospectus. The investor's indication of interest is not binding on either the investor or the firm.
Individual Retirement Account (IRA)	A self-directed retirement account that allows individuals with earned income to contribute the lesser of 100% of earned income or the annual maximum per year. The contributions may be made with pre- or after-tax dollars, depending on the individual's level of income and whether he or she is eligible to participate in an employer's sponsored plan.
industrial development bond	A private-purpose municipal bond whose proceeds are used to build a facility that is leased to a corporation. The debt service on the bonds is supported by the lease payments.
inflation	The persistent upward pressure on the price of goods and services over time.
initial margin requirement	The initial amount of equity that a customer must deposit to establish a position. The initial margin requirement is set by the Federal Reserve Board under Regulation T.
initial public offering (IPO)	The first offering of common stock to the general investing public.
in part call	A partial call of a bond issue for redemption.
inside information	Information that is not known to people outside of the corporation. Information becomes public only after it is released by the corporation through a recognized media source. Inside information may be both material and immaterial. It is only illegal to trade on inside material information.
inside market	The highest bid and the lowest offer for a security.
insider	A company's officers, directors, large stockholders of 10% or more of the company, and anyone who is in possession of nonpublic material information, along with the immediate family members of the same.

Insider Trading and Securities Fraud Enforcement Act of 1988	Federal legislation that made the penalties for people trading on material nonpublic information more severe. Penalties for insider traders are up to the greater of 300% of the amount of money made or the loss avoided or $1 million and up to 5 years in prison. People who disseminate inside information may be imprisoned and fined up to $1 million.
INSTINET	A computer network that facilitates trading of large blocks of stocks between institutions without the use of a broker dealer.
institutional account	An account in the name of an institution but operated for the benefit of others (i.e., banks and mutual funds). There is no minimum size for an institutional account.
institutional communication	Any communication that is distributed exclusively to institutional investors. Institutional communication does not require the preapproval of a principal but must be maintained for 3 years by the firm.
institutional investor	An investor who trades for its own account or for the accounts of others in large quantities and is covered by fewer protective laws.
insurance covenant	The promise of an issuer of revenue bonds to maintain insurance on the financed project.
intangible asset	Nonphysical property of a corporation, such as trademarks and copyrights.
intangible drilling cost (IDC)	Costs for an oil and gas program that are expensed in the year in which they are incurred for such things as wages, surveys, and well casings.
interbank market	An international currency market.
interest	The cost for borrowing money, usually charged at an annual percentage rate.
interest rate option	An option based on U.S. government securities. The options are either rate-based or priced-based options.
interest rate risk	The risk borne by investors in interest-bearing securities, which subjects the holder to a loss of principal should interest rates rise.
interlocking directorate	Corporate boards that share one or more directors.
Intermarket Trading System/ Computer-Assisted Execution System (ITS/CAES)	A computer system that links the third market for securities with the exchanges.
Internal Revenue Code (IRC)	The codes that define tax liabilities for U.S. taxpayers.

interpositioning	The placing of another broker dealer in between the customer and the best market. Interpositioning is prohibited unless it can be demonstrated that the customer received a better price because of it.
interstate offering	A multistate offering of securities that requires that the issuer register with the SEC as well as with the states in which the securities will be sold.
in the money	A relationship between the strike price of an option and the underlying security's price. A call is in the money when the strike price is lower than the security's price. A put is in the money when the strike price is higher than the security's price.
intrastate offering	*See* Rule 147.
intrinsic value	The amount by which an option is in the money.
introducing broker	*See* correspondent broker dealer.
inverted yield curve	A yield curve where the cost of short-term financing exceeds the cost of long-term financing.
investment adviser	Anyone who charges a fee for investment advice or who holds himself out to the public as being in the business of giving investment advice for a fee.
Investment Advisers Act of 1940	The federal legislation that sets forth guidelines for business requirements and activities of investment advisers.
investment banker	A financial institution that is in the business of raising capital for companies and municipalities by underwriting securities.
investment company	A company that sells undivided interests in a pool of securities and manages the portfolio for the benefit of the investors. Investment companies include management companies, unit investment trusts, and face-amount companies.
Investment Company Act of 1940	Federal legislation that regulates the operation and registration of investment companies.
investment-grade security	A security that has been assigned a rating in the highest rating tier by a recognized ratings agency.
investment objective	An investor's set of goals as to how he or she is seeking to make money, such as capital appreciation or current income.
investor	The purchaser of a security who seeks to realize a profit.
IRA rollover	The temporary distribution of assets from an IRA and the subsequent reinvestment of the assets into another IRA within 60 days. An IRA may be rolled over only once per year and is subject to a 10% penalty and ordinary income taxes if the investor is under 59-1/2 and if the assets are not deposited in another qualified account within 60 days.

IRA transfer	The movement of assets from one qualified account to another without the account holder taking possession of the assets. Investors may transfer an IRA as often as they like.
issued stock	Stock that has actually been sold to the investing public.
issuer	Any entity that issues or proposes to issue securities.

J

joint account	An account that is owned by two or more parties. Joint accounts allow either party to enter transactions for the account. Both parties must sign a joint account agreement. All joint accounts must be designated as joint tenants in common or with rights of survivorship.
joint tenants in common (JTIC)	A joint account where the assets of a party who has died transfer to the decedent's estate, not the other tenant.
joint tenants with rights of survivorship (JTWROS)	A joint account where the assets of a party who has died transfer to the surviving party, not the decedent's estate.
joint venture	An interest in an operation shared by two or more parties. The parties have no other relationship beyond the joint venture.
junk bond	A bond with a high degree of default risk that has been assigned a speculative rating by the ratings agencies.
junk bond fund	A speculative bond fund that invests in high-yield bonds in order to achieve a high degree of current income.

K

Keogh plan	A qualified retirement account for self-employed individuals. Contributions are limited to the lesser of 20% of their gross income or $51,000.
Keynesian economics	An economic theory that states that government intervention in the marketplace helps sustain economic growth.
know-your-customer rule	Industry regulation that requires a registered representative to be familiar with the customer's financial objectives and needs prior to making a recommendation; also known as Rule 405.

L

lagging indicator	A measurement of economic activity that changes after a change has taken place in economic activity. Lagging indicators are useful confirmation tools when determining the strength of an economic trend. Lagging indicators include corporate profits, average duration of unemployment, and labor costs.
last in, first out (LIFO)	An accounting method used that states that the last item that was produced is the first item sold.
leading indicator	A measurement of economic activity that changes prior to a change in economic activity. Leading economic indicators are useful in predicting a coming trend in economic activity. Leading economic indicators include housing permits, new orders for durable goods, and the S&P 500.
LEAPS (long-term equity anticipation securities)	A long-term option on a security that has an expiration of up to 39 months.
lease rental bonds	A municipal bond that is issued to finance the building of a facility that will be rented out. The lease payments on the facility will support the bond's debt service.
legal list	A list of securities that have been approved by certain state securities regulators for purchase by fiduciaries.
legal opinion	An opinion issued by a bond attorney stating that the issue is a legally binding obligation of the state or municipality. The legal opinion also contains a statement regarding the tax status of the interest payments received by investors.
legislative risk	The risk that the government may do something that adversely affects an investment.
letter of intent (LOI)	A letter signed by the purchaser of mutual fund shares that states the investor's intention to invest a certain amount of money over a 13-month period. By agreeing to invest this sum, the investor is entitled to receive a lower sales charge on all purchases covered by the letter of intent. The letter of intent may be backdated up to 90 days from an initial purchase. Should the investor fail to invest the stated sum, a sales charge adjustment will be charged.
level load	A mutual fund share that charges a flat annual fee, such as a 12B-1 fee.
level one	A Nasdaq workstation service that allows the agent to see the inside market only.
level two	A Nasdaq workstation service that allows the order-entry firm to see the inside market, to view the quotes entered by all market makers, and to execute orders.

level three	A Nasdaq workstation service that allows market-making firms to see the inside market, to view the quotes entered by all market makers, to execute orders, and to enter their own quotes for the security. This is the highest level of Nasdaq service.
leverage	The use of borrowed funds to try to obtain a rate of return that exceeds the cost of the funds.
liability	A legal obligation to pay a debt either incurred through borrowing or through the normal course of business.
life annuity/straight life	An annuity payout option that provides payments over the life of the annuitant.
life annuity with period certain	An annuity payout option that provides payments to the annuitant for life or to the annuitant's estate for the period certain, whichever is longer.
life contingency	An annuity payout option that provides a death benefit in case the annuitant dies during the accumulation stage.
limit order	An order that sets a maximum price that the investor will pay in the case of a buy order or the minimum price the investor will accept in the case of a sell order.
limited liability	A protection afforded to investors in securities that limits their liability to the amount of money invested in the securities.
limited partner	A passive investor in a direct participation program who has no role in the project's management.
limited partnership (LP)	An association of two or more partners with at least one partner being the general partner who is responsible for the management of the partnership.
limited partnership agreement	The foundation of all limited partnerships. The agreement is the contract between all partners, and it spells out the authority of the general partner and the rights of all limited partners.
limited power of attorney/limited trading authorization	Legal authorization for a representative or a firm to effect purchases and sales for a customer's account without the customer's prior knowledge. The authorization is limited to buying and selling securities and may not be given to another party.
limited principal	An individual who has passed the Series 26 exam and may supervise Series 6 limited representatives.
limited representative	An individual who has passed the Series 6 exam and may represent a broker dealer in the sale of mutual fund shares and variable contracts.
limited tax bond	A type of general obligation bond that is issued by a municipality that may not increase its tax rate to pay the debt service of the issue.

liquidity	The ability of an investment to be readily converted into cash.
liquidity risk	The risk that an investor may not be able to sell a security when needed or that selling a security when needed will adversely affect the price.
listed option	A standardized option contract that is traded on an exchange.
listed security	A security that trades on one of the exchanges. Only securities that trade on an exchange are known as listed securities.
loan consent agreement	A portion of the margin agreement that allows the broker dealer to loan out the customer's securities to another customer who wishes to borrow them to sell the security short.
locked market	A market condition that results when the bid and the offer for a security are equal.
LOI	*See* letter of intent.
London Interbank Offered Rate (LIBOR)	The interbank rates for dollar-denominated deposits in England.
long	A term used to describe an investor who owns a security.
long market value	The total long market value of a customer's account.
long-term gain	A profit realized through the sale of a security at a price that is higher than its purchase price after a being held for more than 12 months.
long-term loss	A loss realized through the sale of a security at a price that is lower than its purchase price after being held for more than 12 months.
loss carry forward	A capital loss realized on the sale of an asset in 1 year that is carried forward in whole or part to subsequent tax years.
low	The lowest price at which a security has traded in any given period, usually measured during a trading day or for 52 weeks.

M

M1	The most liquid measure of the money supply. It includes all currency and demand and NOW deposits (checking accounts).
M2	A measure of the money supply that includes M1 plus all time deposits, savings accounts, and noninstitutional money market accounts.
M3	A measure of the money supply that includes M2 and large time deposits, institutional money market funds, short-term repurchase agreements, and other large liquid assets.

maintenance call	A demand for additional cash or collateral made by a broker dealer when a margin customer's account equity has fallen below the minimum requirement of the NYSE or that is set by the broker dealer.
maintenance covenant	A promise made by an issuer of a municipal revenue bond to maintain the facility in good repair.
Major Market Index (XMI)	An index created by the Amex to AMEX 15 of the 30 largest stocks in the Dow Jones Industrial Average.
Maloney Act of 1938	An amendment to the Securities Exchange Act of 1934 that gave the NASD (now part of FINRA) the authority to regulate the over-the-counter market.
managed underwriting	An underwriting conducted by a syndicate led by the managing underwriter.
management company	A type of investment company that actively manages a portfolio of securities in order to meet a stated investment objective. Management companies are also known as mutual funds.
management fee	(1) The fee received by the lead or managing underwriter of a syndicate. (2) The fee received by a sponsor of a direct participation program.
managing partner	The general partner in a direct participation program.
managing underwriter	The lead underwriter in a syndicate who is responsible for negotiating with the issuer, forming the syndicate, and settling the syndicate account.
margin	The amount of customer equity that is required to hold a position in a security.
margin account	An account that allows the customer to borrow money from the brokerage firm to buy securities.
margin call	A demand for cash or collateral mandated by the Federal Reserve Board under Regulation T.
margin department	The department in a broker dealer that calculates money owed by the customer or money due the customer.
margin maintenance call	*See* maintenance call.
markdown	The profit earned by a dealer on a transaction when purchasing securities for its own account from a customer.
mark to the market	The monitoring of a the current value of a position relative to the price at which the trade was executed for securities purchased on margin or on a when-issued basis.
marketability	The ability of an investment to be exchanged between two investors. A security with an active secondary market has a higher level of marketability than one whose market is not as active.

market arbitrage	A type of arbitrage that consists of purchasing a security in one marketplace and selling it in another to take advantage of price inefficiencies.
market letter	A regular publication, usually issued by an investment adviser, that offers information and/or advice regarding a security, market conditions, or the economy as a whole.
market maker	A Nasdaq firm that is required to quote a continuous two-sided market for the securities in which it trades.
market not held	A type of order that gives the floor broker discretion over the time and price of execution.
market on close	An order that will be executed at whatever price the market is at, either on the closing print or just prior to the closing print.
market on open	An order that will be executed at whatever price the market is at, either on the opening print or just after the opening print.
market order	A type of order that will be executed immediately at the best available price once it is presented to the market.
market-out clause	A clause in an underwriting agreement that gives the syndicate the ability to cancel the underwriting if it finds a material problem with the information or condition of the issuer.
market risk/ systematic risk	The risk inherent in any investment in the market that states an investor may lose money simply because the market is going down.
market value	The value of a security that is determined in the marketplace by the investors who enter bids and offers for a security.
markup	The compensation paid to a securities dealer for selling a security to a customer from its inventory.
markup policy	FINRA's guideline that states that the price that is paid or received by an investor must be reasonably related to the market price for that security. FINRA offers 5% as a guideline for what is reasonable to charge investors when they purchase or sell securities.
material information	Information that would affect a company's current or future prospects or an investor's decision to invest in the company.
maturity date	The date on which a bond's principal amount becomes payable to its holders.
member	A member of FINRA or one of the 1,366 members of the NYSE.
member firm	A firm that is a member of the NYSE, FINRA, or another self-regulatory organization.
member order	A retail order entered by a member of a municipal bond syndicate for which the member will receive all of the sales credit.

mini maxi underwriting	A type of best efforts underwriting that states that the offering will not become effective until a minimum amount is sold and sets a maximum amount that may be sold.
minimum death benefit	The minimum guaranteed death benefit that will be paid to the beneficiaries if the holder of a variable life insurance policy dies.
minus tick	A trade in an exchange-listed security that is at a price that is lower than the previous trade.
modern portfolio theory	An investing approach that looks at the overall return and risk of a portfolio as a whole, not as a collection of single investments.
modified accelerated cost recovery system (MACRS)	An accounting method that allows the owner to recover a larger portion of the asset's value in the early years of its life.
monetary policy	Economic policy that is controlled by the Federal Reserve Board and controls the amount of money in circulation and the level of interest rates.
monetarist theory	A theory that states that the money supply is the driving force in the economy and that a well-managed money supply will benefit the economy.
money market	The secondary market where short-term highly liquid securities are traded. Securities traded in the money market include T-bills, negotiable CDs, bankers' acceptances, commercial paper, and other short-term securities with less than 12 months to maturity.
money market mutual fund	A mutual fund that invests in money market instruments to generate monthly interest for its shareholders. Money market mutual funds have a stable NAV that is equal to $1, but it is not guaranteed.
money supply	The total amount of currency, loans, and credit in the economy. The money supply is measured by M1, M2, M3, and L.
moral obligation bond	A type of municipal revenue bond that will allow the state or municipality to vote to cover a shortfall in the debt service.
multiplier effect	The ability of the money supply to grow simply through the normal course of banking. When banks and other financial institutions accept deposits and subsequently loan out those deposits to earn interest, the amount of money in the system grows.
municipal bond	A bond issued by a state or political subdivision of a state in an effort to finance its operations. Interest earned by investors in municipal bonds is almost always free from federal income taxes.
municipal bond fund	A mutual fund that invests in a portfolio of municipal debt in an effort to produce income that is free from federal income taxes for its investors.

Municipal Bond Investors Assurance Corp. (MBIA)	An independent insurance company that will, for a fee received from the issuer, insure the interest and principal payments on a municipal bond.
municipal note	A short-term municipal issue sold to manage the issuer's cash flow, usually in anticipation of the offering of long-term financing.
Munifacts	A service that provides real-time secondary market quotes. Munifacts is now known as Thomson Muni Market Monitor.
Municipal Securities Rulemaking Board (MSRB)	The self-regulatory organization that oversees the issuance and trading of municipal bonds. The MSRB's rules are enforced by other industry SROs.
mutual fund	An investment company that invests in and manages a portfolio of securities for its shareholders. Open-end mutual funds sell their shares to investors on a continuous basis and must stand ready to redeem their shares upon the shareholder's request.
mutual fund custodian	A qualified financial institution that maintains physical custody of a mutual fund's cash and securities. Custodians are usually banks, trust companies, or exchange member firms.

N

naked	The sale of a call option without owning the underlying security or the sale of a put option without being short the stock or having cash on deposit that is sufficient to purchase the underlying security.
narrow-based index	An index that is based on a market sector or a limited number of securities.
NASD (National Association of Securities Dealers)	The industry self-regulatory agency that was authorized by the Maloney Act of 1938 and empowered to regulate the over-the-counter market. The NASD is now part of FINRA.
NASD bylaws	The rules that define the operation of the NASD and how it regulates the over-the-counter market. The four major bylaws are the Rules of Fair Practice, the Uniform Practice Code, the Code of Procedure, and the Code of Arbitration. Now known as FINRA bylaws.
NASD Manual	An NASD publication that outlines the rules and regulations of NASD membership. Now known as the FINRA Manual.
National Securities Clearing Corporation (NSCC)	The clearing intermediary through which clearing member firms reconcile their securities accounts.

NAV (net asset value)	The net value of a mutual fund after deducting all its liabilities. A mutual fund must calculate its NAV at least once per business day. To determine NAV per share, simply divide the mutual fund's NAV by the total number of shares outstanding.
negotiability	The ability of an investment to be freely exchanged between noninterested parties.
negotiable certificate of deposit	A certificate issued by a bank for a time deposit in excess of $100,000 that can be exchanged between parties prior to its maturity date. FDIC insurance only covers the first $250,000 of the principal amount should the bank fail.
NOW (negotiable order of withdrawal) Account	A type of demand deposit that allows the holder to write checks against an interest-bearing account.
net change	The difference between the previous day's closing price and the price of the most recently reported trade for a security.
net current assets per share	A calculation of the value per share that excludes fixed assets and intangibles.
net debt per capita	A measure of a municipal issuer's ability to meet its obligations. It measures the debt level of the issuer in relation to the population.
net debt to assessed valuation	A measure of the issuer's ability to meet its obligations and to raise additional revenue through property taxes.
net direct debt	The total amount of general obligation debt, including notes and short-term financing, issued by a municipality or state.
net interest cost (NIC)	A calculation that measures the interest cost of a municipal issue over the life of all bonds. Most competitive underwritings for municipal securities are awarded to the syndicate that submits the bid with the lowest NIC.
net investment income	The total sum of investment income derived from dividend and interest income after subtracting expenses.
net revenue pledge	A pledge from a revenue bond that pays maintenance and operation expenses first, then debt service.
net total debt	The total of a municipality's direct debt plus its overlapping debt.
net worth	The value of a corporation after subtracting all of its liabilities. A corporation's net worth is also equal to shareholder's equity.
new account form	Paperwork that must be filled out and signed by the representative and a principal of the firm prior to the opening of any account being opened for a customer.

new construction program	A real estate program that seeks to achieve capital appreciation by building new properties.
new housing authority (NHA)	A municipal bond issued to build low-income housing. NHA bonds are guaranteed by the U.S. government and are considered the safest type of municipal bonds. NHA bonds are not considered to be double-barreled bonds.
new issue	*See* initial public offering (IPO).
New York Stock Exchange (NYSE)	A membership organization that provides a marketplace for securities to be exchanged in one centralized location through a dual-auction process.
no-load fund	A fund that does not charge the investor a sales charge to invest in the fund. Shares of no-load mutual funds are sold directly from the fund company to the investor.
nominal owner	An individual or entity registered as the owner of record of securities for the benefit of another party.
nominal quote	A quote given for informational purposes only. A trader who identifies a quote as being nominal cannot be held to trading at the prices that were clearly identified as being nominal.
nominal yield	The yield that is stated or named on the security. The nominal yield, once it has been set, never changes, regardless of the market price of the security.
noncompetitive bid	A bid submitted for Treasury bills where the purchaser agrees to accept the average of all yields accepted at the auction. Noncompetitive tenders are always the first orders filled at the auction.
noncumulative preferred	A type of preferred stock whose dividends do not accumulate in arrears if the issuer misses the payment.
nondiscrimination	A clause that states that all eligible individuals must be allowed to participate in a qualified retirement plan.
nondiversification	An investment strategy that concentrates its investments among a small group of securities or issuers.
nondiversified management company	An investment company that concentrates its investments among a few issuers or securities and does not meet the diversification requirements of the Investment Company Act of 1940.
nonfixed UIT	A type of UIT that allows changes in the portfolio and traditionally invests in mutual fund shares.
nonqualified retirement plan	A retirement plan that does not allow contributions to be made with pre-tax dollars; that is, the retirement plan does not qualify for beneficial tax treatment from the IRS for its contributions.
nonsystematic risk	A risk that is specific to an issuer or an industry.

note	An intermediate-term interest-bearing security that represents an obligation of its issuer.
not-held (NH) order	An order that gives the floor broker discretion as to the time and price of execution.
numbered account	An account that has been designated a number for identification purposes in order to maintain anonymity for its owner. The owner must sign a statement acknowledging ownership.

O

odd lot	A transaction that is for less than 100 shares of stock or for less than 5 bonds.
odd lot differential	An additional fee that may be charged to an investor for the handling of odd lot transactions (usually waived).
odd lot theory	A contrarian theory that states that small investors will invariably buy and sell at the wrong time.
offer	A price published at which an investor or broker dealer is willing to sell a security.
offering circular	The offering document that is prepared by a corporation selling securities under a Regulation A offering.
office of supervisory jurisdiction (OSJ)	An office identified by the broker dealer as having supervisory responsibilities for agents. It has final approval of new accounts, makes markets, and structures offerings.
Office of the Comptroller of the Currency	An office of the U.S. Treasury that is responsible for regulating the practices of national banks.
official notice of sale	The notice of sale published in the *Daily Bond Buyer* by a municipal issuer that is used to obtain an underwriter for municipal bonds.
official statement	The offering document for a municipal issuer that must be provided to every purchaser if the issuer prepares one.
oil and gas direct participation program	A type of direct participation program designed to invest in oil and gas production or exploration.
oil depletion allowance	An accounting method used to reduce the amount of reserves available from a producing well.
omnibus account	An account used by an introducing member to execute and clear all of its customers' trades.
open-end covenant	A type of bond indenture that allows for the issuance of additional bonds with the same claim on the collateral as the original issue.

open-end investment company	*See* mutual fund.
option	A contract between two investors to purchase or sell a security at a given price for a certain period of time.
option agreement	A form that must be signed and returned by an option investor within 15 days of the account's approval to trade options.
Options Clearing Corporation (OCC)	The organization that issues and guarantees the performance of standardized options.
option disclosure document	A document that must be furnished to all option investors at the time the account is approved for options trading. It is published by the Options Clearing Corporation (OCC), and it details the risks and features of standardized options.
order book official (OBO)	Employees of the CBOE who are responsible for maintaining a fair and orderly market in the options assigned to them and for executing orders that have been left with them.
order department	The department of a broker dealer that is responsible for routing orders to the markets for execution.
order memorandum/ order ticket	The written document filled out by a registered representative that identifies, among other things, the security, the amount, the customer, and the account number for which the order is being entered.
original issue discount (OID)	A bond that has been issued to the public at a discount to its par value. The OID on a corporate bond is taxed as if it was earned annually. The OID on a municipal bond is exempt from taxation.
OTC market	*See* over-the-counter (OTC) market.
out of the money	The relationship of an option's strike price to the underlying security's price when exercising the option would not make economic sense. A call is out of the money when the security's price is below the option's strike price. A put is out of the money when the security's price is above the option's strike price.
outstanding stock	The total amount of a security that has been sold to the investing public and that remains in the hands of the investing public.
overlapping debt	The portion of another taxing authority's debt that a municipality is responsible for.
overriding royalty interest	A type of sharing arrangement that offers an individual with no risk a portion of the revenue in exchange for something of value, such as the right to drill on the owner's land.
over-the-counter (OTC) market	An interdealer market that consists of a computer and phone network through which broker dealers trade securities.

P

par	The stated principal amount of a security. Par value is of great importance for fixed-income securities such as bonds or preferred stock. Par value for bonds is traditionally $1,000, whereas par for a preferred stock is normally $100. Par value is of little importance when looking at common stock.
parity	A condition that results when the value of an underlying common stock to be received upon conversion equals the value of the convertible security.
partial call	A call of a portion of an issuer's callable securities.
participation	The code set forth in the Employee Retirement Income Security Act of 1974 that states who is eligible to participate in an employer sponsored retirement plan.
pass-through certificate	A security that passes through income and principal payments made to an underlying portfolio of mortgages. Ginnie Mae is one of the biggest issuers of this type of security.
passive income	Income received by an individual for which no work was performed, such as rental income received from a rental property.
passive loss	A loss realized on an investment in a limited partnership or rental property that can be used to offset passive income.
payment date	The day when a dividend will actually be sent to investors. The payment date is set by the corporation's board of directors at the time when they initially declare the dividend.
payout stage	The period during which an annuitant receives payments from an annuity contract.
payroll deduction plan	A nonqualified retirement plan where employees authorize the employer to take regular deductions from their paychecks to invest in a retirement account.
pension plan	A contractual retirement plan between an employee and an employer that is designed to provide regular income for the employee after retirement.
percentage depletion	An accounting method that allows for a tax deduction for the reduction of reserves.
periodic payment plan	A contract to purchase mutual fund shares over an extended period of time, usually in exchange for the fund company waiving its minimum investment requirement.
person	Any individual or entity that can enter into a legally binding contract for the purchase and sale of securities.

personal income	Income earned by an individual from providing services and through investments.
phantom income	(1) A term used to describe the taxable appreciation on a zero-coupon bond. (2) The term used to describe taxable income generated by a limited partnership that is not producing positive cash flow.
Philadelphia Automated Communication Execution System (PACE)	The computerized order-routing system for the Philadelphia Stock Exchange.
pink sheets	An electronic quote service containing quotes for unlisted securities that is published by the National Quotation Bureau; operated as the PINK over-the-counter market.
placement ratio	A ratio that details the percentage of municipal bonds sold, relative to the number of bonds offered in the last week, published by the *Daily Bond Buyer*.
plus tick	A transaction in an exchange-listed security that is higher than the previous transaction.
point	An increment of change in the price of a security: 1 bond point equals 1% of par or 1% of $1,000, or $10.
POP	*See* public offering price (POP).
portfolio income	Interest and dividends earned through investing in securities.
portfolio manager	An entity that is hired to manage the investment portfolios of a mutual fund. The portfolio manager is paid a fee that is based on the net assets of the fund.
position	The amount of a security in which an investor has an interest by either being long (owning) or short (owing) the security.
power of substitution	*See* stock power.
preemptive right	The right of a common stockholder to maintain proportional ownership interest in a security. A corporation may not issue additional shares of common stock without first offering those shares to existing stockholders.
preferred stock	An equity security issued with a stated dividend rate. Preferred stockholders have a higher claim on a corporation's dividends and assets than common holders.
preferred stock ratio	A ratio detailing the amount of an issuer's total capitalization that is made up of preferred stock. The ratio is found by dividing the total par value of preferred stock by the issuer's total capitalization.

preliminary prospectus/red herring	A document used to solicit indications of interest during the cooling-off period for a new issue of securities. All of the information in the preliminary prospectus is subject to revision and change. The cover of a preliminary prospectus must have a statement saying that the securities have not yet become registered and that they may not be sold until the registration becomes effective. This statement is written in red ink, and this is where the term *red herring* comes from.
price-earnings ratio (PE)	A measure of value used by analysts. It is calculated by dividing the issuer's stock price by its earnings per share.
price spread	A term used to describe an option spread where the long and short options differ only in their exercise prices.
primary earnings per share	The amount of earnings available per common share prior to the conversion of any outstanding convertible securities.
prime rate	The interest rate that banks charge their best corporate customers on loans.
principal	(1) The face amount of a bond. (2) A broker dealer trading for its own account. (3) An individual who has successfully completed a principal exam and may supervise representatives.
principal transaction	A transaction where a broker dealer participates in a trade by buying or selling securities for its own account.
priority	The acceptance of bids and offers for exchange-listed securities on a first-come, first-served (FCFS) basis.
private placement	The private sale of securities to a limited number of investors. Also known as a Regulation D offering.
profit sharing plan	A plan that allows the employer to distribute a percentage of its profits to its employees at a predetermined rate. The money may be paid directly to the employee or deposited into a retirement account.
progressive tax	A tax structure where the tax rate increases as the income level of the individual or entity increases.
project note	A municipal bond issued as interim financing in anticipation of the issuance of new housing authority bonds.
prospectus	*See* final prospectus.
proxy	A limited authority given by stockholders to another party to vote their shares in a corporate election. The stockholder may specify how the votes are cast or may give the party discretion.
proxy department	The department in a brokerage firm that is responsible for forwarding proxies and financial information to investors whose stock is held in street name.

prudent man rule	A rule that governs investments made by fiduciaries for the benefit of a third party. The rule states that the investments must be similar to those that a prudent person would make for him- or herself.
public offering	The sale of securities by an issuer to public investors.
public offering price (POP)	The price paid by an investor to purchase open-end mutual fund shares. Also the price set for a security the first time it is sold to the investing public.
put	An option contract that allows the buyer to sell a security at a set price for a specific period of time. The seller of a put is obligated to purchase the security at a set price for a specific period of time, should the buyer exercise the option.
put buyer	A bearish investor who pays a premium for the right to sell a security at a set price for a certain period of time.
put spread	An option position created by the simultaneous purchase and sale of two put options on the same underlying security that differ in strike prices, expiration months, or both.
put writer	A bullish investor who sells a put option in order to receive the option premium. The writer is obligated to purchase the security if the buyer exercises the option.

Q

qualified legal opinion	A legal opinion containing conditions or reservations relating to the issue. A legal opinion is issued by a bond counsel for a municipal issuer.
quick assets	A measure of liquidity that subtracts the value of a corporation's unsold inventory from its current assets.
quick ratio	*See* acid-test ratio.
qualified retirement plan	A retirement plan that qualifies for favorable tax treatment by the IRS for contributions made into the plan.
quote	A bid and offer broadcast from the exchange or through the Nasdaq system that displays the prices at which a security may be purchased and sold and in what quantities.

R

| range | The price difference between the high and low for a security. |

rate covenant	A promise in the trust indenture of a municipal revenue bond to keep the user fees high enough to support the debt service.
rating	A judgment of an issuer's ability to meet its credit obligations. The higher the credit quality of the issuer is, the higher the credit rating. The lower the credit quality is, the lower the credit rating, and the higher the risk associated with the securities.
rating service	Major financial organizations that evaluate the credit quality of issuers. Issuers have to request and pay for the service. Standard and Poor's, Moody's, and Fitch are the most widely followed rating services.
raw land program	A type of real estate limited partnership that invests in land for capital appreciation.
real estate investment trust (REIT)	An entity that is organized to invest in or manage real estate. REITs offer investors certain tax advantages that are beyond the scope of the exam.
real estate limited partnership	A type of direct participation program that invests in real estate projects to produce income or capital appreciation.
real estate mortgage investment conduit (REMIC)	An organization that pools investors' capital to purchase portfolios of mortgages.
realized gain	A profit earned on the sale of a security at a price that exceeds its purchase price.
realized loss	A loss recognized by an investor by selling a security at a price that is less than its purchase price.
reallowance	A sales concession available to dealers who sell securities subject to an offering who are not syndicate or selling group members.
recapture	An event that causes a tax liability on a previously taken deduction, such as selling an asset above its depreciated cost base.
recession	A decline in GDP that lasts for at least 6 months but not longer than 18 months.
reclamation	The right of a seller to demand or claim any loss from the buying party due to the buyer's failure to settle the transaction.
record date	A date set by a corporation's board of directors that determines which shareholders will be entitled to receive a declared dividend. Shareholders must be owners of record on this date in order to collect the dividend.
recourse loan	A loan taken out by a limited partnership that allows the lender to seek payment from the limited partners in the case of the partnership's failure to pay.
redeemable security	A security that can be redeemed by the issuer at the investor's request. Open-end mutual funds are an example of redeemable securities.

redemption	The return of an investor's capital by an issuer. Open-end mutual funds must redeem their securities within 7 days of an investor's request.
red herring	*See* preliminary prospectus.
registered	A term that describes the level of owner information that is recorded by the security's issuer.
registered as to principal only	A type of bond registration that requires the investor to clip coupons to receive the bond's interest payments. The issuer will automatically send the investor the bond's principal amount at maturity.
registered options principal (ROP)	An individual who has passed the Series 4 exam.
registered principal	A supervisor of a member firm who has passed the principal examination.
registered representative	An individual who has successfully completed a qualified examination to represent a broker dealer or issuer in securities transactions.
registrar	An independent organization that accounts for all outstanding stock and bonds of an issuer.
registration statement	The full disclosure statement that nonexempt issuers must file with the SEC prior to offering securities for sale to the public. The Securities Act of 1933 requires that a registration statement be filed.
regressive tax	A tax that is levied on all parties at the same rate, regardless of their income. An example of a regressive tax is a sales tax. A larger percentage of a low-income earner's income is taken away by the tax.
regular-way settlement	The standard number of business days in which a securities transaction is completed and paid for. Corporate securities and municipal bonds settle the, regular way on the third business day after the trade date with payment due on the fifth business day. Government securities settle the next business day.
regulated investment company	An investment company that qualifies as a conduit for net investment income under Internal Revenue Code subchapter M, so long as it distributes at least 90% of its net investment income to shareholders.
Regulation A	A small company offering that allows a company to raise up to $5 million in any 12-month period, without filing a full registration.
Regulation D	A private placement or sale of securities that allows for an exemption from registration under the Securities Act of 1933. A private placement may be sold to an unlimited number of accredited investors but may only be sold to 35 nonaccredited investors in any 12-month period.
Regulation G	Regulates the extension of credit for securities purchases by other commercial lenders.

Regulation T	Regulates the extension of credit by broker dealers for securities purchases.
Regulation U	Regulates the extension of credit by banks for securities purchases.
Regulation X	Regulates the extension of credit by overseas lenders for securities purchases.
Rehypothecation	The act of a broker dealer repledging a customer's securities as collateral at a bank to obtain a loan for the customer.
REIT	*See* real estate investment trust (REIT).
rejection	The act of a buyer of a security refusing delivery.
reorganization department	The department in a brokerage firm that handles changes in securities that result from a merger or acquisition or calls.
repurchase agreement (REPO)	A fully collateralized loan that results in a sale of securities to the lender, with the borrower agreeing to repurchase them at a higher price in the future. The higher price represents the lender's interest.
reserve maintenance fund	An account set up to provide additional funds to maintain a revenue-producing facility financed by a revenue bond.
reserve requirement	A deposit required to be placed on account with the Federal Reserve Board by banks. The requirement is a percentage of the bank's customers' deposits.
resistance	A price level to which a security appreciates and attracts sellers. The new sellers keep the security's price from rising any higher.
restricted account	(1) A long margin account that has less than 50% equity but more than 25%. (2) A customer account that has been subject to a sellout.
restricted stock	A nonexempt unregistered security that has been obtained by means other than a public offering.
retained earnings	The amount of a corporation's net income that has not been paid out to shareholders as dividends.
retail communication	Any communication that may be seen in whole or in part by an individual investor. Retail communication must be approved by a principal prior to first use and maintained by the firm for 3 years.
retention	The amount of a new issue that an underwriter allocates to its own clients.
retention requirement	The amount of equity that must be left in a restricted margin account when withdrawing securities.
return on equity	A measure of performance found by dividing after-tax income by common stockholders' equity.
return on investment (ROI)	The profit or loss realized by an investor from holding a security expressed as a percentage of the invested capital.
revenue anticipation note	A short-term municipal issue that is sold to manage an issuer's cash flow in anticipation of other revenue in the future.

reverse repurchase agreement	A fully collateralized loan that results in the purchase of securities with the intention of reselling them to the borrower at a higher price. The higher price represents the buyer's/lender's interest.
reverse split	A stock split that results in fewer shares outstanding, with each share being worth proportionally more.
reversionary working interest	A revenue-sharing arrangement where the general partner shares none of the cost and receives none of the revenue until the limited partners have received their payments back, plus any predetermined amount of return.
right	A short-term security issued in conjunction with a shareholder's preemptive right. The maximum length of a right is 45 days, and it is issued with a subscription price, which allows the holder to purchase the underlying security at a discount from its market price.
rights of accumulation	A right offered to mutual fund investors that allows them to calculate all past contributions and growth to reach a breakpoint to receive a sales charge discount on future purchases.
rights agent	An independent entity responsible for maintaining the records for rights holders.
rights offering	The offering of new shares by a corporation that is preceded by the offering of the new shares to existing shareholders.
riskless simultaneous transaction	The purchase of a security on a principal basis by a brokerage firm for the sole purpose of filling a customer's order that the firm has already received. The markup on riskless principal transactions has to be based on the firm's actual cost for the security.
rollover	The distribution of assets from a qualified account to an investor for the purpose of depositing the assets in another qualified account within 60 days. An investor may only roll over an IRA once every 12 months.
round lot	A standard trading unit for securities. For common and preferred stock, a round lot is 100 shares. For bonds, it is 5 bonds.
Rule 144	SEC rule that regulates the sale of restricted and control securities requiring the seller to file Form 144 at the time the order is entered to sell. Rule 144 also regulates the number of securities that may be sold.
Rule 145	SEC rule that requires a corporation to provide stockholders with full disclosure relating to reorganizations and to solicit proxies.
Rule 147	An intrastate offering that provides an exemption from SEC registration.
Rule 405	The NYSE rule that requires that all customer recommendations must be suitable and that the representative must "know" the customer.

S

sale	*See* sell.
sales charge	*See* commission.
sales literature	Written material distributed by a firm to a controlled audience for the purpose of increasing business. Sales literature includes market letters, research reports, and form letters sent to more than 25 customers.
sales load	The amount of commission charged to investors in open-end mutual funds. The amount of the sales load is added to the net asset value of the fund to determine the public offering price of the fund.
satellite office	An office not identified to the public as an office of the member, such as an agent's home office.
savings bond	A nonnegotiable U.S. government bond that must be purchased from the government and redeemed to the government. These bonds are generally known as series EE and HH bonds.
scale	A list of maturities and yields for a new serial bond issue.
Schedule 13D	A form that must be filed with the SEC by any individual or group of individuals acquiring 5% or more of a corporation's nonexempt equity securities. Form 13D must be filed within 10 days of the acquisition.
scheduled premium policy	A variable life insurance policy with fixed premium payments.
SEC	*See* Securities and Exchange Commission (SEC).
secondary distribution	A distribution of a large number of securities by a large shareholder or group of large shareholders. The distribution may or may not be done under a prospectus.
secondary offering	An underwriting of a large block of stock being sold by large shareholders. The proceeds of the issue are received by the selling shareholders, not the corporation.
secondary market	A marketplace where securities are exchanged between investors. All transactions that take place on an exchange or on the Nasdaq are secondary market transactions.
sector fund	A mutual fund that invests in companies within a specific business area in an effort to maximize gains. Sector funds have larger risk-reward ratios because of the concentration of investments.
Securities Act of 1933	The first major piece of securities industry legislation. It regulates the primary market and requires that nonexempt issuers file a registration statement

with the SEC. The act also requires that investors in new issues be given a prospectus.

Securities Act Amendments of 1975	Created the Municipal Securities Rulemaking Board (MSRB).
Securities Exchange Act of 1934	Regulates the secondary market and all broker dealers and industry participants. It created the Securities and Exchange Commission, the industry's ultimate authority. The act gave the authority to the Federal Reserve Board to regulate the extension of credit for securities purchases through Regulation T.
Securities and Exchange Commission	The ultimate securities industry authority. The SEC is a direct government body, not a self-regulatory organization. The commissioners are appointed by the U.S. President and must be approved by Congress.
Securities Investor Protection Corporation (SIPC)	The industry's nonprofit insurance company that provides protection for investors in case of broker dealer failure. All member firms must pay dues to SIPC based upon their revenue. SIPC provides coverage for each separate customer for up to $500,000, of which a maximum of $250,000 may be cash. The Securities Investor Protection Act of 1970 created SIPC.
security	Any investment that can be exchanged for value between two parties that contains risk. Securities include stocks, bonds, mutual funds, notes, rights, warrants, and options, among others.
segregation	The physical separation of customer and firm assets.
self-regulatory organization (SRO)	An industry authority that regulates its own members. FINRA, the NYSE, and the CBOE are all self-regulatory organizations that regulate their own members.
sell	The act of conveying the ownership of a security for value to another party. A sale includes any security that is attached to another security, as well as any security which the security may be converted or exchanged into.
seller's option	A type of settlement option that allows the seller to determine when delivery of the securities and final settlement of the trade will occur.
selling away	Any recommendation to a customer that involves an investment product that is not offered through the employing firm without the firm's knowledge and consent. This is a violation of industry regulations and may result in action being taken against the representative.
selling concession	*See* concession.
selling dividends	The act of using a pending dividend to create urgency for the customer to purchase a security. This is a violation and could result in action being taken against the representative.

selling group	A group of broker dealers who may sell a new issue of securities but who are not members of the syndicate and who have no liability to the issuer.
sell out	A transaction executed by a broker dealer when a customer fails to pay for the securities.
sell-stop order	An order placed beneath the current market for a security to protect a profit, to guard against a loss, or to establish a short position.
separate account	The account established by an insurance company to invest the pooled funds of variable contract holders in the securities markets. The separate account must register as either an open-end investment company or as a unit investment trust.
separate trading of registered interest and principal securities (STRIPS)	A zero-coupon bond issued by the U.S. government. The principal payment due in the future is sold to investors at a discount and appreciates to par at maturity. The interest payment component is sold to other investors who want some current income.
serial bonds	A bond issue that has an increasing amount of principal maturing in successive years.
series EE bond	A nonmarketable U.S. government zero-coupon bond that is issued at a discount and matures at its face value. Investors must purchase the bonds from the U.S. government and redeem them to the government at maturity.
series HH bond	A nonmarketable U.S. government interest-bearing bond that can only be purchased by trading in matured series EE bonds. Series HH bonds may not be purchased with cash and are issued with a $500 minimum denomination.
settlement	The completion of a securities transaction. A transaction settles and is completed when the security is delivered to the buyer and the cash is delivered to the seller.
settlement date	The date when a securities ownership changes. Settlement dates are set by FINRA's Uniform Practice Code.
75-5-10 diversification	The diversification test that must be met by mutual funds under the Investment Company Act of 1940 in order to market themselves as a diversified mutual fund: 75% of the fund's assets must be invested in other issuer's securities, no more than 5% of the fund's assets may be invested in any one company, and the fund may own no more than 10% of an issuer's outstanding securities.
shareholder's equity	*See* net worth.
share identification	The process of identifying which shares are being sold at the time the sale order is entered in order to minimize an investor's tax liability.

shelf offering	A type of securities registration that allows the issuer to sell the securities over a 2-year period.
short	A position established by a bearish investor that is created by borrowing the security and selling in the hopes that the price of the security will fall. The investor hopes to be able to repurchase the security at a lower price, thus replacing it cheaply. If the security's price rises, the investor will suffer a loss.
short against the box	A short position established against an equal long position in the security to roll tax liabilities forward. Most of the benefits of establishing a short against the box position have been eliminated.
short straddle	The simultaneous sale of a call and a put on the same underlying security with the same strike price and expiration. A short straddle would be established by an investor who believes that the security price will move sideways.
simplified arbitration	A method of resolving disputes of $50,000 or less. There is no hearing; one arbitrator reads the submissions and renders a final decision.
Simplified Employee Pension (SEP)	A qualified retirement plan created for small employers with 25 or fewer employees that allows the employees' money to grow tax-deferred until retirement.
single account	An account operated for one individual. The individual has control of the account, and the assets go to the individual's estate in the case of his or her death.
sinking fund	An account established by an issuer of debt to place money for the exclusive purpose of paying bond principal.
special assessment bond	A municipal bond backed by assessments from the property that benefits from the improvements.
specialist	Member of an exchange responsible for maintaining a fair and orderly market in the securities that he or she specializes in and for executing orders left with him or her.
specialist book	A book of limit orders left with the specialist for execution.
special situation fund	A fund that seeks to take advantage of unusual corporate developments, such as take mergers and restructuring.
special tax bond	A type of municipal revenue bond that is supported only by revenue from certain taxes.
speculation	An investment objective where the investor is willing to accept a high degree of risk in exchange for the opportunity to realize a high return.
split offering	An offering where a portion of the proceeds from the underwriting goes to the issuer and a portion goes to the selling shareholders.

spousal account	An IRA opened for a nonworking spouse that allows a full contribution to be made for the nonworking spouse.
spread	(1) The difference between the bid and ask for a security. (2) The simultaneous purchase and sale of two calls or two puts on the same underlying security.
spread load plan	A contractual plan that seeks to spread the sales charge over a longer period of time, as detailed in the Spread Load Plan Act of 1970. The maximum sales charge over the life of the plan is 9%, while the maximum sales charge in any one year is 20%.
stabilizing	The only form of price manipulation allowed by the SEC. The managing underwriter enters a bid at or below the offering price to ensure even distribution of shares.
standby underwriting	An underwriting used in connection with a preemptive rights offering. The standby underwriter must purchase any shares not subscribed to by existing shareholders.
statutory disqualification	A set of rules that prohibit an individual who has been barred or suspended or convicted of a securities-related crime from becoming registered.
statutory voting	A method of voting that requires investors to cast their votes evenly for the directors they wish to elect.
stock ahead	A condition that causes an investor's order not to be executed, even though the stock is trading at a price that would satisfy the customer's limit order, because other limit orders have been entered prior to the customer's order.
stock certificate	Evidence of equity ownership.
stock or bond power	A form that, when signed by the owner and attached to a security, makes the security negotiable.
stock split	A change in the number of outstanding shares, the par value, and the number of authorized shares that has been approved through a vote of the shareholders. Forward-stock splits increase the number of shares outstanding and reduce the stock price in order to make the security more attractive to individual investors.
stop limit order	An order that becomes a limit order to buy or sell the stock when the stock trades at or through the stop price.
stop order	An order that becomes a market order to buy or sell the stock when the stock trades at or through the stop price.
stopping stock	A courtesy offered by a specialist to public customers, whereby the specialist guarantees a price but tries to obtain a better price for the customer.
straddle	The simultaneous purchase or sale of a call and a put on the same security with the same strike price and expiration.

straight line depreciation	An accounting method that allows an owner to take equal tax deductions over the useful life of the asset.
strangle	The purchase or sale of a call and a put on either side of the current market price. The options have the same expiration months but different strike prices.
stripped bond	A bond that has had its coupons removed by a broker dealer and that is selling at a deep discount to its principal payment in the future.
stripper well	An oil well that is in operation just to recover a very limited amount of reserves.
subchapter S corporation	A business organization that allows the tax consequences of the organization to flow through to the owners.
subscription agreement	An application signed by the purchaser of an interest in a direct participation plan. An investor in a limited partnership does not become an investor until the general partner signs the subscription agreement.
subscription right	*See* right.
suitability	A determination that the characteristics of a security are in line with an investor's objectives, financial profile, and attitudes.
Super Display Book System (SDBK)	The electronic order-routing system used by the NYSE to route orders directly to the trading post.
supervise	The actions of a principal that ensure that the actions of a firm and its representatives are in compliance with industry regulations.
support	The price to which a security will fall and attract new buyers. As the new buyers enter the market, it keeps the price from falling any lower.
surplus fund	An account set up for funds generated by a project financed by a municipal revenue bond to pay a variety of expenses.
syndicate	A group of underwriters responsible for underwriting a new issue.
systematic risk	A risk inherent in any investment in the market. An investor may lose money simply because the market is going down.

T

takedown	The price at which a syndicate purchases a new issue of securities from the issuer.
tax anticipation note (TAN)	A short-term note sold by a municipal issuer as interim financing in anticipation of tax revenue.

tax and revenue anticipation note	A short-term note sold by a municipal issuer as interim financing in anticipation of tax and other revenue.
tax-deferred annuity	A nonqualified retirement account that allows an investor's money to grow tax deferred. A tax-deferred annuity is a contract between an insurance company and an investor.
tax equivalent yield	The interest rate that must be offered by a taxable bond of similar quality in order to be equal to the rate that is offered by a municipal bond.
tax-exempt bond fund	A bond fund that seeks to produce investment income that is free from federal tax by investing in a portfolio of municipal bonds.
tax liability	The amount of money that is owed by an investor after realizing a gain on the sale of an investment or after receiving investment income.
tax preference item	An item that receives preferential tax treatment and must be added back into income when calculating an investor's alternative minimum tax.
tax-sheltered annuity (TSA)	A qualified retirement plan offered to employees of governments, school systems, or nonprofit organizations. Contributions to TSAs are made with pre-tax dollars.
technical analysis	A method of security analysis that uses past price performance to predict the future performance of a security.
Telephone Consumer Protection Act of 1991	Legislation that regulates how potential customers are contacted by phone at home.
tenants in common	*See* joint tenants in common.
tender offer	An offer to buy all or part of a company's outstanding securities for cash or cash and securities.
term bond	A bond issue that has its entire principal due on one date.
term maturity	A type of bond maturity that has all principal due on one date.
testimonial	The use of a recognized expert or leader to endorse the services of a firm.
third market	A transaction in an exchange-listed security executed over the Nasdaq workstation.
third-party account	An account that is managed for the benefit of a customer by another party, such as an investment adviser, a trustee, or an attorney.
30-day visible supply	The total par value of all new issue municipal bonds coming to market in the next 30 days.
time deposit	An account that is established by a bank customer where the customer agrees to leave the funds on deposit for an agreed upon amount of time.

time value	The value of an option that exceeds its intrinsic value or its in-the-money amount.
tombstone ad	An announcement published in financial papers advertising the offering of securities by a group of underwriters. Only basic information may be contained in the tombstone ad, and all offers must be made through the prospectus only.
top heavy rule	The rule that states the maximum salary for which a Keogh contribution may be based. This is in effect to limit the disparity between high- and low-salary employees.
trade confirmation	The printed notification of a securities transaction. A confirmation must be sent to a customer on or before the completion of a transaction. The completion of a transaction is considered to be the settlement date.
trade date	The day when an investor's order is executed.
tranche	A class of collateralized mortgage obligation (CMO) that has a predicted maturity and interest rate.
transfer agent	An independent entity that handles name changes, records the names of security holders of record, and ensures that all certificates are properly endorsed.
transfer and hold in safekeeping	A request by customers for the brokerage firm to transfer their securities into the firm's name and to hold them in safekeeping at the firm. A brokerage may charge a fee for holding a customer's securities that have been registered in its name.
transfer and ship	A request by customers for the brokerage firm to transfer their securities into their name and to ship them to their address of record.
Treasury bill	A U.S. government security that is issued at a discount and matures at par in 4, 13, 26, and 52 weeks.
Treasury bond	A long-term U.S. government security that pays semiannual interest and matures in 10 to 30 years.
Treasury note	An intermediate-term U.S. government security that pays semiannual interest and matures in 1 to 10 years.
Treasury receipt	A zero-coupon bond created by a brokerage firm that is backed by U.S. government securities. It is issued at a discount and matures at par.
treasury stock	Stock that has been issued by a corporation and that has subsequently been repurchased by the corporation. Treasury stock does not vote or receive dividends. It is not used in the calculation of earnings per share.
trendline	A line used to predict the future price movement for a security. Drawing a line under the successive lows or successive highs creates a trendline.

trough	The bottoming out of the business cycle just prior to an new upward movement in activity.
true interest cost (TIC)	A calculation for the cost of a municipal issuer's interest expense that includes the time value of money.
Trust Indenture Act of 1940	Regulates the issuance of corporate debt in excess of $5 million and with a term exceeding 1 year. It requires an indenture between the issuer and the trustee.
trustee	A person who legally acts for the benefit of another party.
12B-1 fee	An asset-based distribution fee that is assessed annually and paid out quarterly to cover advertising and distribution costs. All 12B-1 fees must be reasonable.
two-dollar broker	An independent exchange member who executes orders for commission house brokers and other customers for a fee.
type	A classification method for an option as either a call or a put.

U

uncovered	*See* naked.
underlying security	A security for which an investor has an option to buy or sell.
underwriting	The process of marketing a new issue of securities to the investing public. A broker dealer forwards the proceeds of the sale to the issuer minus its fee for selling the securities.
unearned income	Any income received by an individual from an investment, such as dividends and interest income.
uniform delivery ticket	A document that must be attached to every security delivered by the seller, making the security "good delivery."
Uniform Gifts to Minors Act (UGMA)	Sets forth guidelines for the gifting of cash and securities to minors and for the operation of accounts managed for the benefit of minors. Once a gift is given to a minor, it is irrevocable.
Uniform Practice Code	The FINRA bylaw that sets guidelines for how industry members transact business with other members. The Uniform Practice Code establishes such things as settlement dates, rules of good delivery, and ex-dividend dates.
Uniform Securities Act (USA)	The framework for state-based securities legislation. The act is a model that can be adapted to each state's particular needs.

Uniform Transfer to Minors Act (UTMA)	Legislation that has been adopted in certain states, in lieu of the Uniform Gifts to Minors Act. UTMA allows the custodian to determine the age at which the assets become the property of the minor. The maximum age for transfer of ownership is 25.
unit investment trust (UIT)	A type of investment company organized as a trust to invest in a portfolio of securities. The UIT sells redeemable securities to investors in the form of shares or units of beneficial interest.
unit of beneficial interest	The redeemable share issued to investors in a unit investment trust.
unit refund annuity	An annuity payout option that will make payments to the annuitant for life. If the annuitant dies prior to receiving an amount that is equal to his or her account value, the balance of the account will be paid to the annuitant's beneficiaries.
unqualified legal opinion	A legal opinion issued by a bond attorney for the issue where there are no reservations relating to the issue.
unrealized	A paper profit or loss on a security that is still owned.

V

variable annuity	A contract issued by an insurance company that is both a security and an insurance product. The annuitant's contributions are invested through the separate account into a portfolio of securities. The annuitant's payments depend largely on the investment results of the separate account.
variable death benefit	The amount of a death benefit paid to a beneficiary that is based on the investment results of the insurance company's separate account. This amount is over the contract's minimum guaranteed death benefit.
variable life insurance	A life insurance policy that provides for a minimum guaranteed death benefit, as well as an additional death benefit, based on the investment results of the separate account.
variable rate municipal security	Interim municipal financing issued with a variable rate.
vertical spread	The simultaneous purchase and sale of two calls or two puts on the same underlying security that differ only in strike price.
vesting	The process by which an employer's contributions to an employee's retirement account become the property of the employee.
visible supply	*See* 30-day visible supply.

voluntary accumulation plan	A method, such as dollar-cost averaging, by which an investor regularly makes contributions to acquire mutual fund shares.
voting right	The right of a corporation's stockholders to cast their votes for the election of the corporation's board of directors as well as for certain major corporate issues.

W

warrant	A long-term security that gives the holder the right to purchase the common shares of a corporation for up to 10 years. The warrant's subscription price is always higher than the price of the underlying common shares when the warrant is initially issued.
wash sale	The sale of a security at a loss and the subsequent repurchase of that security or of a security that is substantially the same within 30 days of the sale. The repurchase disallows the claim of the loss for tax purposes.
western account	A type of municipal security syndicate account where only the member with unsold bonds is responsible for the unsold bonds.
when-issued security	A security that has been sold prior to the certificates being available for delivery.
wildcatting	An exploratory oil- and gas-drilling program.
wire room	*See* order department.
withdrawal plan	The systematic removal of funds from a mutual fund account over time. Withdrawal plans vary in type and availability among fund companies.
workable indication	An indication of the prices and yields that a municipal securities dealer may be willing to buy or sell bonds.
working capital	A measure of a corporation's liquidity that is found by subtracting current liabilities from current assets.
working interest	An interest that requires the holder to bear the proportional expenses and allows the holder to share in the revenue produced by an oil or gas project in relation to the interest.
workout quote	A nonfirm quote that requires handling and settlement conditions to be worked out between the parties prior to the trade.
writer	An investor who sells an option to receive the premium income.
writing the scale	The procedure of assigning prospective yields to a new issuer of serial municipal bonds.

Y

Yellow Sheets	A daily publication published by the national quotation bureau providing quotes for corporate bonds.
yield	The annual amount of income generated by a security relative to its price; expressed as a percentage.
yield-based option	An interest rate option that allows the holder to receive the in-the-money amount in cash upon exercise or expiration.
yield curve	The rate at which interest rates vary among investments of similar quality with different maturities. Longer-term securities generally offer higher yields.
yield to call	An investor's overall return for owning a bond should it be called in prior to maturity by the issuer.
yield to maturity	An investor's overall return for owning a bond if the bond is held until maturity.

Z

zero-coupon bond	A bond that is issued at a discount from its par value and makes no regular interest payments. An investor's interest is reflected by the security's appreciation toward par at maturity. The appreciation is taxable each year even though it is not actually received by the investor (phantom income).
zero-minus tick	A trade in an exchange-listed security that occurs at the same price as the previous transaction, but at a price that is lower than the last transaction that was different.
zero-plus tick	A trade in an exchange-listed security that occurs at the same price as the previous transaction, but at a price that is higher than the last transaction that was different.

Index

Get Your Securities License Now with Wiley Expertise

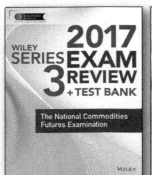 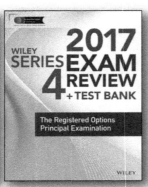 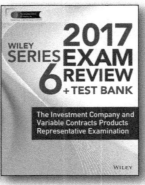 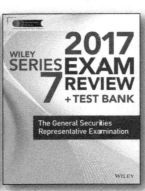 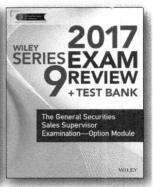

978-1-119-37976-8   978-1-119-37980-5   978-1-119-37979-9   978-1-119-37975-1   978-1-119-37977-5

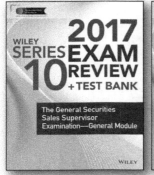 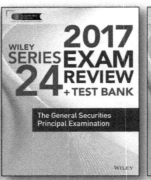 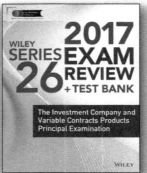 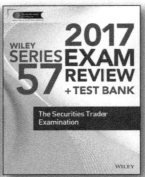 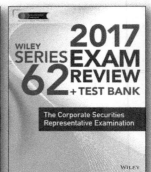

978-1-119-37986-7   978-1-119-37978-2   978-1-119-37985-0   978-1-119-37981-2   978-1-119-37989-8

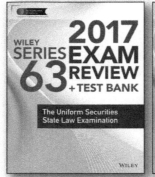 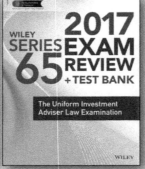 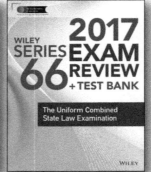 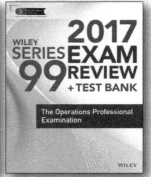

978-1-119-37984-3   978-1-119-37974-4   978-1-119-37991-1   978-1-119-37987-4

 **Available in print and e-book formats.**

For more information visit www.efficientlearning.com/finra

WILEY